GIANT BOOK
OF THE
CAT

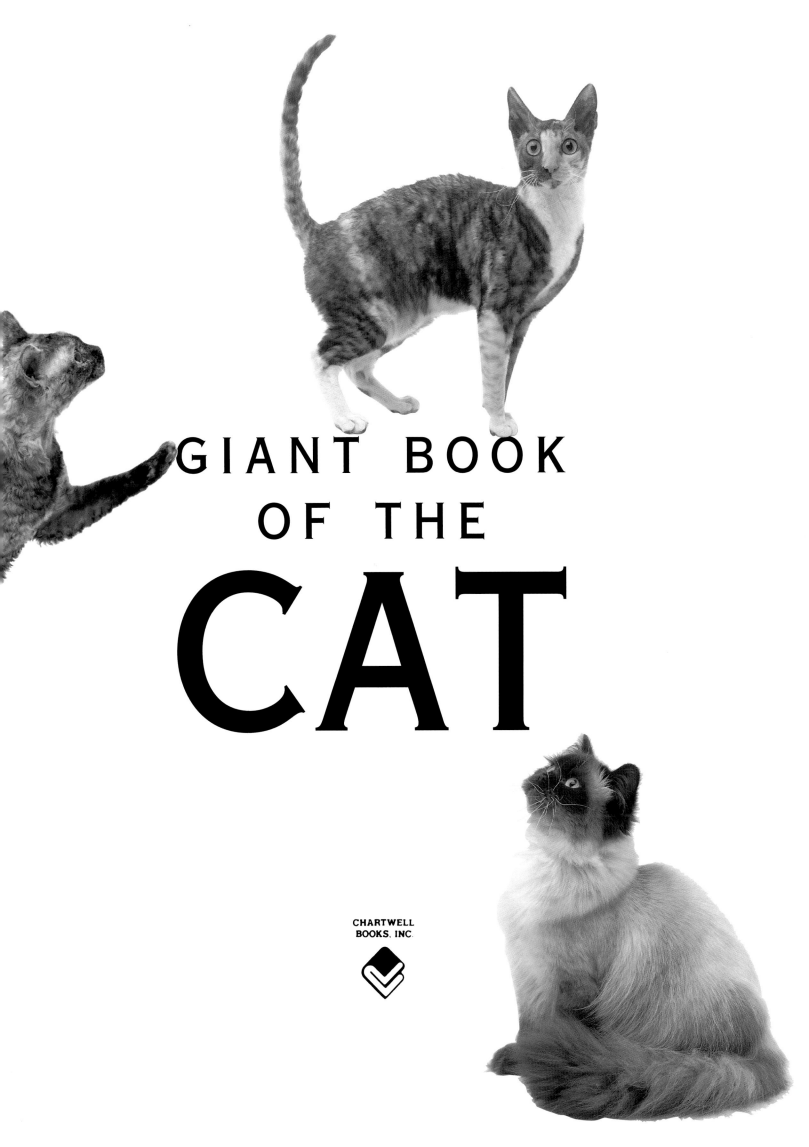

GIANT BOOK
OF THE
CAT

CHARTWELL
BOOKS, INC.

A QUARTO BOOK

Published by Chartwell books
A Division of Book Sales, Inc.
114, North Avenue
Edison, New Jersey 08837

This edition produced for sale in the U.S.A.,
its territories and dependencies only.

ISBN 0-7858-0946-5

This book was designed and produced by
Quarto Publishing plc
6 Blundell Street
London N7 9BH

Editor: Lin Esposito

Designer: Louise Morley

Art Director: Moira Clinch

Manufactured in Hong Kong by Regent Publishing
Printed in China by Leefung-Asco Printers Ltd

The material in this book previously appeared in the
following titles: The illustrated Eucyclopedia of Cat Breeds
by Angela Rixon; The Cat by David Alderton;
The Cat Care Manual by Bradely Viner; The Cat Owner's Handbook
by Marcus Schneck and Jill Caravan; The Natural Health
Care Cat Manual by Don Harper; Understanding Your Cat
by Frank Manolson

CONTENTS

INTRODUCTION

FOREWORD

The domestic cat enjoys a special niche in human society. There are anthologies of poems and prose, encyclopedias of breeds, manuals on care, breeding and showing. Cats appear on greeting cards, stationary and fabrics; glass and china ornaments abound – whether in natural or cartoon form, the cat is the most enduringly popular animal portrayed throughout the world.

CATS HAVE BEEN valued and protected and their history recorded since the days of the ancient Egyptians, and although their fortunes have fluctuated from time to time, they have managed to remain virtually unchanged in overall size and basic character. Today's domestic cat tolerates its relationship with humans and takes advantage of the comforts of a good home environment while retaining its independent nature.

The innate behavior patterns of the cat's wild ancestors still exist, even in a highly bred pedigree cat whose coat and conformation bear little resemblance to them. Even the most pampered of today's pet cats reacts to the thrill of hunting and retains all the physical skills and abilities of its ancestors.

Having a pet cat in the home can be therapeutic, as well as rewarding. No other pet is as clean and fastidious in its habits, or as easy to care for. Every cat is beautiful in its own way, but the very wide range of breeds, colors, and varieties of pedigree cats existing today means every cat lover can indulge his or her particular preference.

The cat is probably the most common domestic animal in most parts of the world. Wherever there are concentrated populations of people, there are groups of cats, either living as free-ranging feral animals or kept as pets to keep down rodents, insects, or snakes. Yet despite its familiarity with humans, the domestic cat manages to retain its air of mysterious independence.

A paradoxical animal, the cat can be both loving and bold. It combines caution with courage, and alternates periods of total relaxation with those of remarkable agility. It is often easy to imagine, in watching one's pet cat, its successful little mammalian ancestor *miacis*, which first evolved during the age of the dinosaurs. Small in build, the cat has always had to rely on skill and speed to escape from predators and to catch its own prey. Its specialized dentition and retractile claws helped to guarantee its survival as a

A resting ginger adorns the lid of a small tin (top left), a nursery rhyme feline family make a simple jigsaw puzzle (top), while a trio of stylized nesting cats make an unusual keepsake (left).

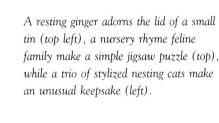

Even the most sophisticated of today's pedigree cats, like this Abyssinian (right), retains all of its natural hunting instincts.

THE EVOLUTION OF THE CAT

Dinictis About 50 million years ago, this carnivorous cat-like mammal, ancestor of the cats, inhabited the earth.

Pseudaelurus Until about 25 million years ago, this relatively long-legged mammal had evolved with more cat-like features.

Felis lunensis Among several species of wild cat that evolved and lived until about 12 million years ago was Martelli's wildcat.

Felidae Today's cats, large and small. Highly developed and efficient carnivores, designed for hunting and killing.

SELECTIVE BREEDING
Over the years, cats have been selectively bred to conform to standards of points laid down by various cat associations. Here we see the extremes in type between the svelte, long-headed Oriental (left) and the heavy, round-headed Persian (below).

carnivore during its evolution, and these qualities stand the cat in good stead.

Today, the genetic make-up of the domestic cat has been so manipulated by selective breeding that some felines bear very little resemblance to those of ancient Egypt's homes and granaries. The noses of Persian cats have been reduced in size, those of the Orientals have been lengthened. Breeders have selected for heavy bone in some breeds, for light bone in others. Despite all the efforts to thwart nature, however, the basic structure of the domestic cat has been undefiled by human intervention, and the biology of the animal is the same whether it is a champion Chinchilla or a stray tabby. The great cat goddess Bast continues to watch over *Felis domesticus*, making sure that all cats remain virtually the same in size and character; affectionate, fastidious felines who are willing companions, but who will never be subordinate or subservient to humans.

The aim of this book is to show the diverse and interesting range of domestic felines throughout the world, exploring conformation, coat types, and patterns. It also examines the breeds' varying care requirements and their special characteristics, and acts as an introduction to the world of showing.

ORIGINS

A weasel-like creature called Miacis lived on Earth in the Eocene period of 50 million years ago. From this fierce, successful creature evolved countless generations of carnivores. We can recognize in those early creatures the ancestors of our domestic cats, and identify the same survival skills.

ANCIENT EGYPT
The cat was deified in ancient Egypt and, also used for the protection of the granaries and for wildfowling.

AS ANY PAIR of domestic cats, from anywhere in the world, will readily interbreed, it means that they are of a single species, descended from a common ancestor.

Domestication of the cat probably first took place in the Middle East, and the cats encouraged to approach people were almost certainly *Felis lybica*, the African wild cat. This is a lithe animal, very similar to a domestic tabby in color. Many of the skulls from ancient Egyptian cat cemeteries resemble *Felis lybica*, while a small proportion are of cats resembling the jungle cat, *Felis chaus*. It would appear that the ancient Egyptians tamed both types, but the African wild cat was easily the more popular, and probably more amenable to domestication.

Egypt was the greatest grain-growing area of the ancient world, and huge granaries were constructed to store the grain from good harvests for use in leaner years. As rodent controllers, cats must have been vital to the economy of those times. The ancient Egyptians also appreciated the natural link between the cat and the lion, and worshipped the goddess Bast, also called Pasht or Oubasted, who first appeared with the head of a lion, and later with the head of a cat. Bast was seen as a goddess of love, and of the moon. The cat was connected with her as love-goddess because of the animal's natural fecundity, and as moon-goddess because of the varying shape of the pupils of the cat's eyes, which were thought to enlarge and contract with

BAST, PASHT, or OUBASTED
The Cat-goddess Bast, with a sistrum, used as a sacred rattle to frighten evil gods, and a small, lion-headed aegis or shield. Both objects serve to protect the litter of kittens sitting at her feet.

DESCENT OF THE MODERN CAT

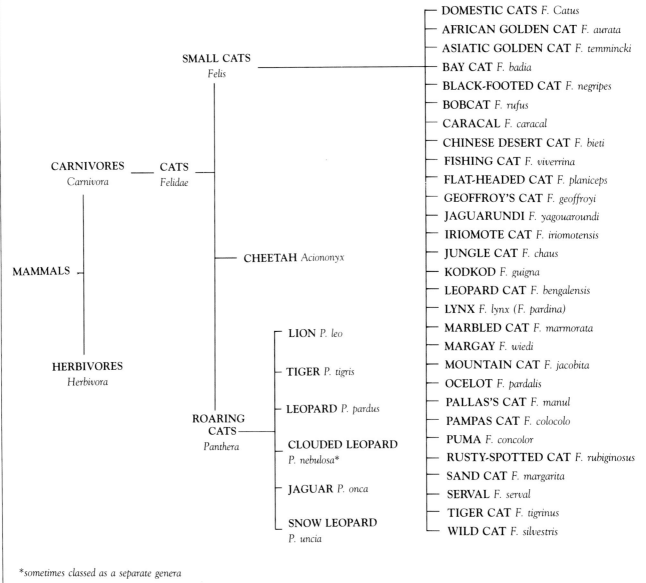

SMALL CATS
Felis

CARNIVORES ___ **CATS** ___
Carnivora   *Felidae*

MAMMALS –

HERBIVORES
Herbivora

CHEETAH *Aciononyx*

**ROARING
CATS**
Panthera

┌ **LION** *P. leo*

├ **TIGER** *P. tigris*

├ **LEOPARD** *P. pardus*

├ **CLOUDED LEOPARD**
│ *P. nebulosa**

├ **JAGUAR** *P. onca*

└ **SNOW LEOPARD**
   P. uncia

┌ **DOMESTIC CATS** *F. Catus*
├ **AFRICAN GOLDEN CAT** *F. aurata*
├ **ASIATIC GOLDEN CAT** *F. temmincki*
├ **BAY CAT** *F. badia*
├ **BLACK-FOOTED CAT** *F. negripes*
├ **BOBCAT** *F. rufus*
├ **CARACAL** *F. caracal*
├ **CHINESE DESERT CAT** *F. bieti*
├ **FISHING CAT** *F. viverrina*
├ **FLAT-HEADED CAT** *F. planiceps*
├ **GEOFFROY'S CAT** *F. geoffroyi*
├ **JAGUARUNDI** *F. yagouaroundi*
├ **IRIOMOTE CAT** *F. iriomotensis*
├ **JUNGLE CAT** *F. chaus*
├ **KODKOD** *F. guigna*
├ **LEOPARD CAT** *F. bengalensis*
├ **LYNX** *F. lynx (F. pardina)*
├ **MARBLED CAT** *F. marmorata*
├ **MARGAY** *F. wiedi*
├ **MOUNTAIN CAT** *F. jacobita*
├ **OCELOT** *F. pardalis*
├ **PALLAS'S CAT** *F. manul*
├ **PAMPAS CAT** *F. colocolo*
├ **PUMA** *F. concolor*
├ **RUSTY-SPOTTED CAT** *F. rubiginosus*
├ **SAND CAT** *F. margarita*
├ **SERVAL** *F. serval*
├ **TIGER CAT** *F. tigrinus*
└ **WILD CAT** *F. silvestris*

*sometimes classed as a separate genera

A Roman mosaic found in the ruins of Pompeii, dating from the first century B.C., depicts a bright-eyed cat pouncing on its prey.

the waxing and waning of the moon. Egyptian statues of Bast show her connection with fertility and pleasure. In several statues, she stands upright, an alert cat's head surmounting a figure holding a sistrum in one hand and a rattle in the other. The rattle symbolized both phallus and womb, and the symbolic fertility of the goddess was further reinforced by several kittens, usually five, sitting at her feet. Women of the period often wore fertility amulets depicting Bast and her feline family.

The original Egyptian name of the cat was *mau*, perhaps from its call of "meow," which also meant "to see." The Egyptians considered that the cat's unblinking gaze gave it powers to seek out truth and to see into the afterlife. Bast was sometimes called the Lady of Truth, and was used in mummification ceremonies to ensure life after death.

Cats played such a complex and important part in the lives of the ancient Egyptians that the living animals were pampered and in some cases worshipped. After the death of a cat, whole families would go into mourning, and the cat's body was embalmed and placed in a sacred vault. Thousands of mummified cats have been discovered in Egypt, some so well-preserved that they have added to our store of knowledge of the earliest domesticated cats.

The custom of keeping cats spread slowly throughout the Middle Eastern countries. A Sanskrit document of 1000 B.C. mentions a pet cat, and the Indian epics *Ramayana* and *Mahabharata*, of about 500 B.C., both contain stories about cats. The Indians at that time worshipped a feline goddess of maternity called Sasti, and for decades Hindus were obliged to take responsibility for feeding at least one cat. Cats reached China around A.D. 400, and in A.D. 595 an empress was recorded as having been bewitched by a cat spirit. By the twelfth century A.D. rich Chinese families kept yellow and white cats known as "lion-cats," which

were highly valued as pets. Vermin control was undertaken by longhaired cats, and cats were traded in street markets. Pet cats were introduced into Japan from China in the reign of Emperor Ichi-Jo, who lived from A.D. 986 to 1011. It is recorded that on the tenth day of the fifth moon, the emperor's white cat gave birth to five white kittens, and a nurse was appointed to see that they were brought up as carefully as royal princes. Many legends and stories of cats survive in Japanese literature, the most enduring image being that of the *Maneki-neko*, the listening or beckoning cat, which can still be found in ornaments and amulets today.

The beckoning cat provides an example of the dual role of charms and amulets to attract good fortune and to ward off evil.

Throughout the world, prior to the witch hunts of the Middle Ages, cats were treated with affection and respect. Their greatest attribute was their efficiency in controlling vermin.

Gods of one religion may become the demons of its successor, and in the case of the cat, its nocturnal habits, independence, sense of self-preservation, and often erotic behavior accelerated the process during the sixteenth and seventeenth centuries. Witch hunting then reached its climax, and cats figured prominently in most witch trials throughout Europe. Even as late as the nineteenth century, Basque farmers claimed that witches appeared as black cats, which made such animals greatly feared.

Eventually the cat's fortunes turned once more. They became prized possessions, and those with unusual colors and markings were favored as pets. They were carried between the world's continents as precious gifts, and gave rise to the many breeds and varieties that we know today.

In the Middle Ages, the art of witchcraft was rife. A witch would often have as her "familiar" a black cat. The witch was said to be able to transform herself into her familiar's form.

North America

The fact that domestic cats have been systematically bred for only about one hundred years makes it difficult to ascertain the origins of certain key factors in their makeup. The stocky body type found in the Persians and the various Shorthairs points to the possible influence of the European wild cat in their ancestry, whereas the lightboned and slender "foreign" cats, such as the Abyssinian, have bodies similar to that exhibited by the African wild cat. In Asia, lightboned cats have been known for centuries, and isolated gene pools aided the standardization of specific colors and coat patterns. Very few mutations affecting the original wild type conformation, coat length, color and pattern have been necessary to provide the ingredients from which all of today, cats have been bred.

REX
The first Cornish Rex, its curled coat caused by the action of a mutant gene, was discovered in a litter of kittens in 1950.

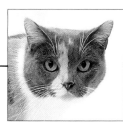

MANX
The Isle of Man, midway between England and Ireland, is generally agreed to be the homeland and birthplace of the Manx.

MAPS

The country of origin of the cat is given for each breed. This is shown on the small map at the top of the entry in every case.

SPREAD OF THE DOMESTIC CAT

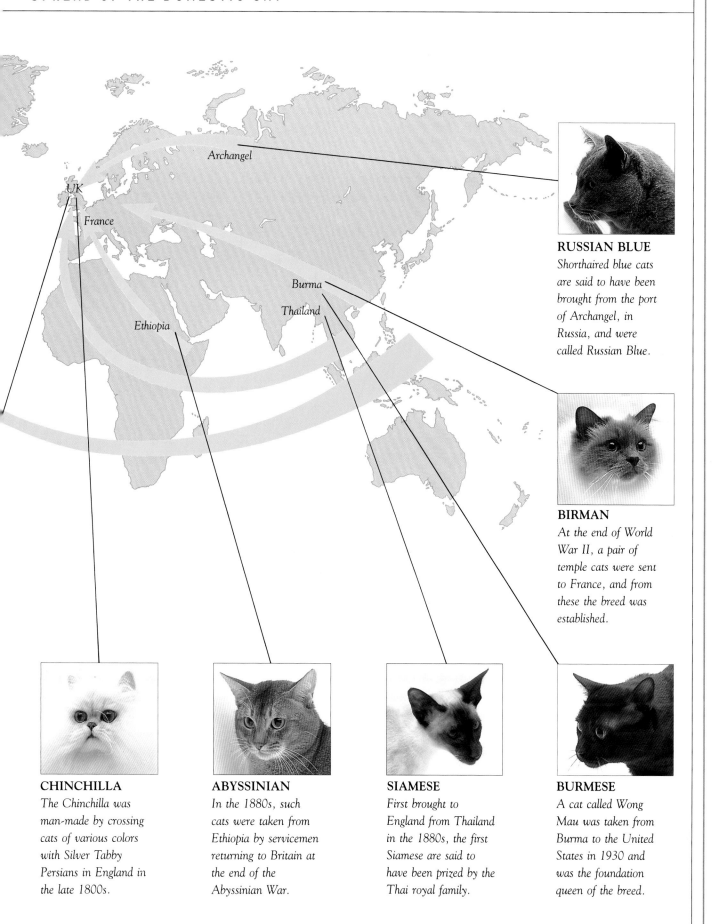

Archangel

UK

France

Burma

Thailand

Ethiopia

RUSSIAN BLUE
*Shorthaired blue cats
are said to have been
brought from the port
of Archangel, in
Russia, and were
called Russian Blue.*

BIRMAN
*At the end of World
War II, a pair of
temple cats were sent
to France, and from
these the breed was
established.*

CHINCHILLA
*The Chinchilla was
man-made by crossing
cats of various colors
with Silver Tabby
Persians in England in
the late 1800s.*

ABYSSINIAN
*In the 1880s, such
cats were taken from
Ethiopia by servicemen
returning to Britain at
the end of the
Abyssinian War.*

SIAMESE
*First brought to
England from Thailand
in the 1880s, the first
Siamese are said to
have been prized by the
Thai royal family.*

BURMESE
*A cat called Wong
Mau was taken from
Burma to the United
States in 1930 and
was the foundation
queen of the breed.*

BREEDS OF THE WORLD

A ginger kitten leaping from the arm of a chair.

HEADS AND EYES

Most cat breeds with heavy conformation, such as the Persian and the Shorthair, have large round heads, with large round eyes set wide apart above a short snub nose on a broad face. The ears are small but have a wide base, and are placed far apart on the head, complementing the rounded appearance of the skull.

Cats of light conformation, such as the Oriental and Foreign Shorthairs, have longer heads of various shapes, and the eye shape varies for each specific breed. Long-coated cats with light conformation have various head and eye shapes, according to the standards laid down by their breed associations.

The head of the Longhair or Persian is typically round, with round eyes and full cheeks. The tiny ears set wide apart.

The head of the Shorthair is similar in shape to that of the Persian when viewed from the front only.

Foreign and oriental cats have long, narrow heads and large ears. Head shape varies in the individual breeds.

In profile, the Persian's head is rather flat. The short snub nose shows a definite "break" at eye level.

The profile of a typical Shorthair breed is less flat than that of the Persian with its short, broad nose.

Oriental cats have long, almost Roman noses with no "break" at eye level and a flat forehead.

EYES

ROUND

Longhaired or Persian cats as well as most of the Shorthairs have large, round, lustrous eyes.

OVAL/ALMOND

Some breed standards call for oval or almond-shaped eyes, often tilted at the outer edge toward the ears.

ORIENTAL

Siamese and similar related breeds have eyes of Oriental shape, set slanting toward the outer edge of the ear.

COAT TYPES

Pedigree cats have diverse variations of coat types, ranging from the full and profuse pelt of the Persian to the very fine sleek and close-lying coats of the Siamese and Orientals. Between the two extremes are the long, soft and silky coats of the longhaired foreign breeds and the thick, dense coats of some of the shorthaired varieties. Some breeds should have "double" coats, with a thick wooly undercoat and a longer, sleeker top coat. The Cornish Rex has a coat devoid of guard hairs, and naturally curled awn and down hairs. The Devon Rex has modified guard, awn, and down hairs, which produce a waxy effect. The Sphynx or Canadian Hairless cat is at the extreme end of the coat-type range, being covered in some parts merely with a fine down.

PERSIAN

Long, soft coat with profuse down hairs nearly as long as the guard hairs, producing a typically long and full coat.

MAINE COON

Long silky coat, heavier and less uniform than that of the Persian due to less uniform and denser down hairs.

SHORTHAIR

Shorthair coats are very variable, ranging from the British and American breeds to the foreigns.

SPHYNX

Apparently hairless, the Sphynx does have a light covering of down hairs on some areas of the body.

CORNISH REX

The tightly curled coat of the Cornish Rex is caused by the absence of guard hairs and short awn hairs.

DEVON REX

Genetically modified guard and awn hairs in this breed closely resemble down hairs.

AMERICAN WIREHAIR

Quite different to the two rex coats, the wirehair has crimped awn hairs and waved guard hairs.

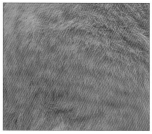

ORIENTAL

In the Siamese and Oriental cats, the coat is short, fine, and close-lying, quite different from other cats.

TYPES OF TIPPING

In the unusually colored tipped, shaded, and smoke breeds, each effect is produced by a proportion of each hair having a colored tip while the rest of the hair is of a paler color.

1 *Tipped cats such as the British Tipped or Chinchilla have tipping at the very ends of the hairs, producing a sparkling effect.*
2 *Tipping extending further down the hair shaft produces the more strongly colored shaded varieties.*
3 *Variable bands of color in different areas of the coat give rise to tabby effects.*
4 *Tipping extending almost to the white hair roots produces the smoke coat in many breeds.*
5 *In golden varieties, the white base coat of the silver varieties is replaced by a tawny yellow color.*

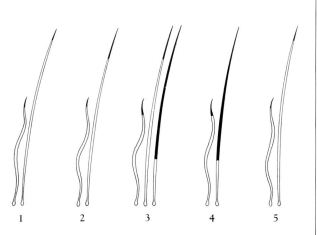

COAT COLORS AND PATTERNS

The natural color of the domestic cat is tabby, which may be one of four basic patterns. The wild type is ticked tabby or agouti, and the other tabby patterns are mackerel (striped), spotted, and classic (marbled or blotched). The pigment melanin produces black hairs, and most of the self-colored coats seen in cats are produced by modification of this pigment, or by the way in which it is distributed in the individual hair fibers.

Solids
Cats of self- or solid-colored breeds must be of a single, solid color throughout with no pattern, shading, ticking, or other variation in color. These are the most common solid colors.

BLACK

BLUE

CHOCOLATE

LILAC

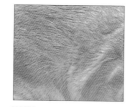
RED

CREAM

CINNAMON

WHITE

Tabby Markings
There are four varieties of tabby patterns, each of which can be found in any of the tabby colors.

TICKED

MACKEREL

SPOTTED

CLASSIC

Tabby Colors
Tabbies are found in a wide variety of colors. Here we show a selection.

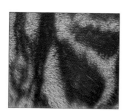
BROWN

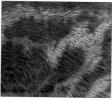
BLUE

CHOCOLATE

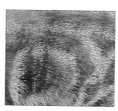
BROWN PATCHED

BLUE PATCHED

RED

Abyssinian
Abyssinian cats have coats which are gently shaded, because each hair is lighter at the root and darker at the tip.

USUAL

BLUE

SORREL

FAWN

Colored Tips
Coats of this sort, with the hairs darkening in varying degrees toward the roots, are found in a number of colors, some of which are shown here.

BLACK SMOKE

BLUE SMOKE

CHOCOLATE SMOKE

LILAC SMOKE

CHINCHILLA SILVER

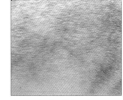

CHINCHILLA GOLDEN

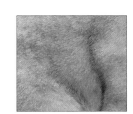

BLACK TIPPED SILVER

BLUE TIPPED SILVER

Himalayan
Cats with the Himalayan coat pattern, such as the Siamese, have pale coats with the main color restricted to the head and extremeties.

SEAL POINT

BLUE POINT

RED POINT

CREAM POINT

LILAC POINT

CHOCOLATE POINT

SEAL TABBY

RED TABBY POINT

26

Tonkinese

Tonkinese cats, which are light-phase Burmese cats, show a modified "pointed" effect. The coats are darker than those of cats with true Himalayan coloring, so the "points" are not so dramatic.

BROWN

LILAC

CHOCOLATE

RED

CREAM

LILAC TORTIE

BLUE TORTIE

TABBY

Multiple Colors

As every cat lover knows, cats come in coats of many colors in addition to those already described, most of which are recognized for show purposes in one breed or another. The tortoiseshells are the most common, but there are endless varieties, including the unusual Mi-ke pattern of the Japanese Bobtail.

TORTOISESHELL

CHOCOLATE TORTOISESHELL

LILAC TORTOISESHELL

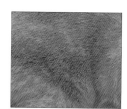

BLUE TORTOISESHELL

MI-KE

TORTOISESHELL AND WHITE

BLUE TORTOISESHELL AND WHITE

LONGHAIRED BREEDS

LONGHAIR

ALTHOUGH THEY HAVE been officially classified by the GCCF in Britain as Longhairs, these cats are popularly referred to as Persians, and are officially classified as such in the United States.

The typical Persian is a substantial, strong cat, with a full and flowing coat of long, dense fur concealing a sturdy body and thick legs. The head is large and round with tiny ears and large, round eyes. The fur around the neck is extra long, forming the typical ruff or frill, and the long hair on the tail makes it resemble a fox's tail or brush.

Persian cats first arrived in Europe in the sixteenth century and became more popular than the imported Angoras. Charles H. Ross reported, in a book published in 1868: "The Persian is a variety with hair very long and silky; perhaps more so than that of the Angora; it is however differently coloured, being of a fine uniform grey on the upper part with the texture of the fur as soft as silk and the lustre glossy; the color fades off on the lower parts of the sides and fades, or nearly does so, on the belly." This preceded the first cat shows.

Over the years, selective breeding standardized the type of the Persian breed so that all the varieties would closely conform to one basic standard. However, various cat associations designated different points awards for

BREAKDOWN OF 100 SHOW POINTS

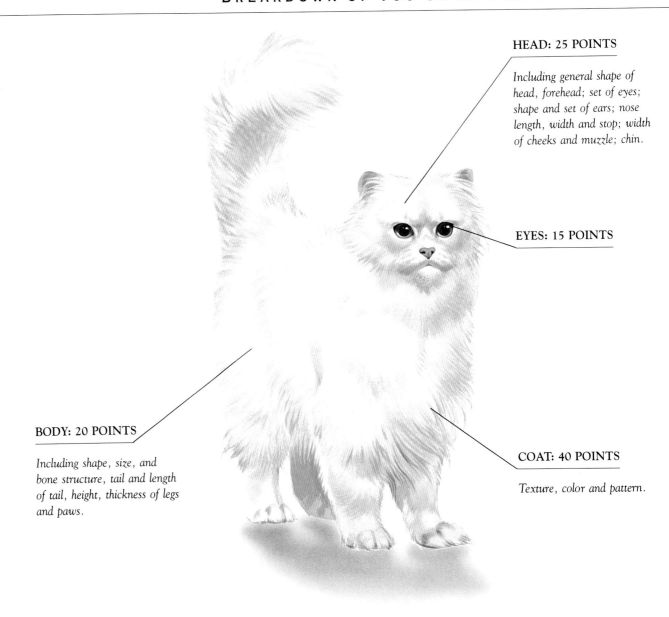

HEAD: 25 POINTS

Including general shape of head, forehead; set of eyes; shape and set of ears; nose length, width and stop; width of cheeks and muzzle; chin.

EYES: 15 POINTS

BODY: 20 POINTS

Including shape, size, and bone structure, tail and length of tail, height, thickness of legs and paws.

COAT: 40 POINTS

Texture, color and pattern.

different features as incentives for breeders to work toward refinement of those features.

Character and Care

Persian cats are generally placid and gentle by nature, and as kittens are playful and mischievous. They make very affectionate and loving pets, and are generally quiet and restful to have in the home. The females make excellent mothers, and the kittens rarely give problems during lactation and weaning.

The long, dense coat must be brushed and combed daily to prevent tangles and matting, and kittens must be accustomed to being groomed all over, including their underparts, from a very early age. In adults, particular attention must be paid to the frill or ruff, under the belly, and the flowing hair of the tail.

PENALTIES

The Persian is penalized for having a kinked or abnormal tail; a locket or button; any apparent weakness in the hindquarters; any apparent deformity of the spine; asymmetrical appearance of the head, and incorrect eye color.

KEY CHARACTERISTICS

- **CATEGORY** Longhair.

- **OVERALL BUILD** Medium to large, with massive shoulders and back, muscular.

- **COAT** Long and dense, standing off from the body, fine and silky texture, with a full ruff (frill) over shoulders and chest.

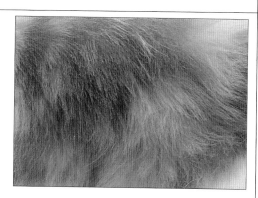

- **HEAD** Round and massive with a broad skull, round forehead, full cheeks, and powerful jaws.

- **NOSE** Short and broad with a definite stop.

- **CHIN** Strong and well-developed.

- **EYES** Large, round and full, set wide apart.

- **EARS** Small, round-tipped, set wide apart and rather low on the head.

- **BODY** Of cobby type, low on the legs, with a broad chest, massive shoulders, and well-muscled back.

- **LEGS** Short, thick, and strong.

- **PAWS** Large, round, and firm. Toe tufts preferred.

- **TAIL** Short, but in proportion to the length of the body, carried without a curve.

- **COLORS** White with blue, orange or copper, odd eyes; black, red, cream, blue, chocolate, lilac; smoke: black, blue, red, torbie, blue-cream; cameo: shell, shaded, shell tortoiseshell, shaded tortoiseshell; bicolor: black, blue, red, cream, and Van patterns; tabby (Classic and Mackeral patterns): silver, brown, red (*UK and US*), blue, cream, cameo, silver patched, brown patched, blue patched (*US only*).

WHITE

ODD-EYED WHITE

In this variety of Persian, one eye should be orange or copper, and the other deep blue, and both eyes should be of equal color intensity.

THIS VARIETY HAS been popular for more than a hundred years, and is the result of matings between the earliest imported Angora and Persian cats. The original white longhairs had blue eyes. Because of a genetic anomaly connected to blue eye color in cats, many of them were deaf. Eventually, efforts were made to improve the overall type and conformation of the whites, and cross-matings were made with Blue Persian and Black Persian show winners. Not only did the resulting offspring have more solid bone and better body and head type, some cats had orange or copper eye color, and in some cases, were odd-eyed, having one blue eye and one of orange or copper. An added bonus was that these cats had good hearing,

although some of the odd-eyed whites were found to be deaf in the ear adjacent to the blue eye. Today's White Persians are judged as three separate varieties, according to eye color, in Britain.

Special care is needed in grooming these white varieties, as they can easily become soiled with yellow staining around the eyes, nostrils, lips, and under the tail. If neglected, the stains may prove impossible to remove, spoiling the beauty of the coat. Fanciers generally use a white grooming powder to clean and enhance their pets' white coats, and this helps to prevent staining.

Coloring
The coat should be pure, glistening white, without markings or shadings of any kind. Nose leather and paw pads are pink. In the blue-eyed White, eye color is deep blue. In the copper-eyed (USA) or orange-eyed (UK) White, eye color is brilliant copper (USA) or orange or copper (UK). The odd-eyed White has one eye of deep blue, the other of copper or orange.

BLUE-EYED WHITE

These cats are sometimes found to be deaf, due to a genetic factor.

ORANGE-EYED WHITE

Cats with this copper or orange eye color are not affected by problems with their hearing and often appear more responsive than their blue-eyed cousins.

BLACK

ONE OF THE oldest of the pedigree breeds, the Black Persian is one of the most difficult to produce in top show condition. It is a massive, handsome cat, and the glossy, raven-black coat is complemented by the large glowing eyes. The black hair is prone to developing rusty tinges, thought to be caused by strong sunlight or damp conditions, and periods of molting cause brownish bars to appear in the flowing coat. Young black kittens are often quite disappointing, with lots of shading in the undercoat and rustiness in the top coat, but these defects usually disappear with maturity.

Coloring
The coat should be dense coal black from roots to tips of hair, free from any tinge or markings or shadings of any kind, and with no white hair. The nose leather is black, and the paw pads black or brown. Eye color is brilliant copper (USA) or copper or deep orange (UK), with no green rim.

BLACK PERSIAN
The eyes of the Black Persian should be brilliant copper or deep orange, setting off the jet-black coat to perfection.

33

RED

RED PERSIAN
*Comparatively rare at
cat shows, a good Red
Persian has a rich red
coat, free from ghost
tabby markings.*

ALTHOUGH THIS HAS been a favorite show breed for over a hundred years, in the days of the first cat shows there was some confusion in contemporary writings as to the true description of the variety's color. Until 1894, shows at London's Crystal Palace offered classes for Brown or Red Tabby Persians, but in 1895 a class for Orange and Cream was added. The Orange, Cream, Fawn and Tortoiseshell Society revised the standard for the Orange Persian, requiring "the colour to be as bright as possible, and either self or markings to be as distinct as can be got." Judges obviously selected their winners irrespective of markings. Over the years breeders selected for either self-colored or tabby in the reds, and by 1912 they had separate classes, still being described as Orange Self or Orange Tabby. The deeper color was selected, and although World War II decimated the variety's numbers, the past fifty years have seen wonderful improvements in Red Persians in the world's show rings.

Coloring
The coat should be deep, rich, clear, brilliant red without markings or shadings or ticking. Lips and chin are the same color as the coat. Nose leather and paw pads are brick red and eye color is brilliant copper (USA) or deep copper (UK).

CREAM

IN THE EARLY DAYS, cream cats were often called "fawns" and were often discarded by keen exhibitors in favor of cats with stronger coat colors. Some of the first Angoras were probably cream, for Charles H. Ross, writing in 1868, describes the Angora as "a very beautiful variety, with silvery hair of fine silken texture . . . some are yellowish, and others olive, approaching the colour of a lion . . ."

In 1903, Frances Simpson wrote that creams were becoming fashionable, but the first cats of this variety had been considered "freaks or flukes" and were given away. Cream cats were eventually imported into the United States from Britain and soon established themselves as successful show winners. Today's exhibition Cream Persian is a refined and sophisticated breed, exemplifying all the best features of the typical Longhair.

Coloring

The requirements for coat color differ between the United States, the United Kingdom, and Europe in general. The CFA standard requires one level shade of buff cream, sound to the roots, without markings, and with lighter shades preferred. Britain's GCCF calls for pure and sound pale to medium color, without shadings or markings. The FIFe standard requires pale, pure, pastel cream with no warm tone or any lighter shadings or markings, the color to be sound and even from roots to tips. Nose leather and paw pads are pink; eye color is brilliant copper (USA) [deep copper (UK)].

CREAM PERSIAN
This Cream Persian is of very good type and has the desired pale cream coat color, free from lighter shading, and ghost marks.

BLUE

THE BLUE COLOR in cats is caused by the action of the dilution factor on black, and some of the earliest Persian imports had this attractive coat color. In the first cat shows, lots of blue cats were exhibited, but they did not closely resemble the cats seen in the show rings today. By the turn of the century, early show faults such as white lockets and tabby markings had been largely eliminated, and in 1901 the Blue Persian Society was founded to promote the breeding and exhibiting of cats of this variety. Members of society, including Queen Victoria, owned Blue Persian cats, and this added to their general status and popularity, which remains to this day.

Coloring
The blue coat should be of one level tone from nose to tail tip, and sound from roots to tips of hair. Any shade of blue is allowed, but in the USA the lighter shades are preferred. The coat must be free from all markings, shadings, or white hairs. The nose leather and paw pads are blue; the eye color is brilliant copper (USA); deep orange or copper without any trace of green (UK).

BLUE PERSIAN
Most popular of all the Persian varieties is the Blue. Any shade of blue coat color is allowed, but the lighter shades are preferred for showing.

BLUE-CREAM

**BLUE-CREAM
PERSIAN**

*In American shows,
this variety is required
to have cream patches
on its blue coat, while
the GCCF expects an
intermingled coat.*

CONSIDERED TO BE a fairly new variety, the Blue-cream Persian was not recognized in Britain until 1930, although reports of kittens with blue and cream markings appeared at the turn of the century. Blue-cream coloring is the dilute equivalent of tortoiseshell. Just as a tortoiseshell has patches of black and red, so the blue-cream cat has corresponding dilute patches of blue (from black) and cream (from red). Although early cat fanciers understood little of feline genetics, some, by careful observation, were able to deduce some of the results to be expected by cross-matings between cats of various colors. The biggest problem to beset the early cat breeders was that they did not recognize the fact that the "marked blue cats," or blue-creams, were all female, and that the color was sex-linked. Breeders waited hopefully for similar male kittens to be born so that like-to-like matings could take place, to produce a "true" breed.

Coloring

The requirements for coat color and pattern differ between the United States, the United Kingdom, and Europe in general. In North America, the coat is required to be blue with clearly defined patches of solid cream, well broken on both body and extremities. Britain's GCCF requires the coat to consist of pastel shades of blue and cream, softly intermingled. In Europe, FIFe refers to Blue-cream as Blue Tortie, and the coat requirement is for light blue-gray and pale cream, patched and/or mingled, both colors to be evenly distributed over the body and extremities. Although breeders and show judges like the Blue-cream to have a facial blaze, USA and UK standards do not stipulate this, though it is featured as desirable by FIFe.

The eye color is brilliant copper (*USA*) or deep copper or orange (*UK*).

SMOKE

FIRST GIVEN A breed class at a British cat show in 1893, a contemporary author wrote of the Smoke Persian, "The Smoke is a cat of great beauty, but unfortunately is very rare." Sadly, this remains as true today, though there was a time in the early 1900s when the variety enjoyed more popularity. One of the early successful breeders and exhibitors was Mrs. H.V. James, who wrote about her beloved breed in 1903 and later supplied information for a cat book published in 1948, showing clearly her dedication to Smoke Persians. Mrs. James bought a Blue Persian kitten which died, and the replacement she received from the breeder proved most disappointing, developing into a cat of "a deep cinder colour," nothing like a

Blue Persian. Mrs. James thought he looked rather smoky in color and so entered him as a Smoke Persian in a show, where, to her surprise, he was placed first in all his classes.

The National Cat Club's stud book, published in Britain for the years 1900 to 1905, listed thirty Smoke Persians, but when the newly established GCCF published its first stud book in 1912, only eighteen such cats were

CREAM SMOKE PERSIAN

The cream variety is a dilute version of the Red Smoke. The cream coloring shades to white on the side and flanks.

BLACK SMOKE PERSIAN

The Smoke Persian's typical white undercoat shows only when the animal is in motion.

BLUE SMOKE PERSIAN

An excellent example of this variety with a full pale frill or ruff and ear tufts as required in the show standard.

LILAC SMOKE PERSIAN

Both Chocolate and Lilac Smoke Persians are accepted by several feline bodies and apart from color, should conform in every other way to the basic standard of points.

listed. By the end of World War II, the Smoke Persian, like so many other minority breeds, had become practically non-existent.

Today's Smoke Persian is known as "the cat of contrasts" and though rare, is generally of excellent longhair type. The breed has always been popular in the United States, and in recent years has been bred in colors other than the original black.

BLACK SMOKE The undercoat is pure white, deeply tipped with black. In repose the cat appears black, but in motion the white undercoat is clearly apparent. The mask and points are black with a narrow band of white at the base of the hairs next to the skin, seen only when the hair is parted. The frill (ruff) and ear tufts are light silver. Nose leather and paw pads are black; eye color is brilliant copper (USA) or orange or copper (UK).

BLUE SMOKE The white undercoat is deeply tipped with blue so that in repose the cat appears blue, but in motion the white undercoat is clearly apparent. Mask and points are blue with a narrow band of white next to the skin which is seen only when the hair is parted. The frill (ruff) and ear tufts are all white; the nose leather and paw pads are blue; the eyes are a brilliant copper or orange or copper.

RED SMOKE The undercoat is white, deeply tipped with red. In repose the cat appears red, but in motion the white undercoat is clearly apparent. Mask and points are red with a narrow band of white next to the skin, seen only when the hair is parted. The frill (ruff) and ear tufts are white, the eye rims, nose leather and paw pads rose; eye color is brilliant copper.

39

SMOKE TORTOISESHELL The white under-coat is deeply tipped with black, with clearly defined, unbrindled patches of red and light red hairs in the pattern of a Tortoiseshell. In repose the cat appears to be tortoiseshell, but in motion the white undercoat is clearly apparent. The face and ears are tortoiseshell patterned with a narrow band of white next to the skin, seen only when the hair is parted. A blaze of red or light red tipping on the face is desirable. The frill (ruff) and ear tufts are white and the eyes a brilliant copper.

BLUE-CREAM SMOKE The white undercoat is deeply tipped with blue, with clearly defined, unbrindled patches of cream in the pattern of a Blue-cream. In repose the cat appears to be blue-cream, but in motion the white undercoat is clearly apparent. Face and ears are blue-cream patterned with a narrow band of white next to the skin, seen only when the hair is parted. A blaze of cream tipping on the face is desirable. The frill (ruff) and ear tufts are white, and the eye color a brilliant copper.

CHOCOLATE SMOKE PERSIAN
Although only accepted as a provisional variety, this young cat has very good type and excellent eyes for both color and shape.

LILAC TORTIE SMOKE
The dilute version of the Blue-Cream Smoke, just beginning to develop the desired pale frill or ruff.

RED SMOKE PERSIAN
An excellent example of a variety that is difficult to breed without tabby markings. This fine cat has a superb coat and has been perfectly groomed.

CAMEO

CAMEO PERSIAN
In kittens of the Cameo series, the full color effect takes some time to develop. This youngster has very good type.

FIRST BRED IN the United States in 1954, Cameo Persians were the result of matings between Smoke and Tortoiseshell cats of outstanding type. Cameo kittens are born almost white and develop their subtle color as they grow. There are three intensities of coloring within the Cameo group: Shell is very pale, Shaded somewhat darker, and Smoke is darker.

Cameo cats are naturally affectionate, and their unusual coloring soon gained popularity for the new varieties in countries outside the United States.

SHELL CAMEO (RED CHINCHILLA) The white undercoat must be sufficiently tipped with red on the head, back, flanks, and tail to give the characteristic sparkling appearance of the variety. The face and legs may be lightly shaded with tipping. The chin, ear tufts, stomach, and chest are white. Eye rims, nose leather, and paw pads are all rose, and the eye color a brilliant copper.

SHADED CAMEO (RED SHADED) A white undercoat has a mantle of red tipping shading the face, the sides, and the tail. The color ranges from dark on the ridge to white on the chest, stomach, under the tail, and on the chin. The legs are the same tone as the face. The general effect is much more red than the Shell Cameo. Eye rims are rose; eye color is a brilliant copper.

RED SHELL The white undercoat, delicately tipped with black, has well-defined patches of red and light red tipped hairs, in the tortoiseshell pattern, on the head, back, flanks, and tail. The face and legs may be slightly shaded with tipping. The chin, ear tufts, stomach, and chest are white. A blaze of red or light red tipping on the face is desirable. The eyes are brilliant copper.

RED SHADED The white undercoat has a mantle of black tipping and clearly defined patches of red and light red tipped hairs in the tortoiseshell pattern. This covers the face, down the sides and the tail, the color ranging from dark on the ridge to white on the chest, stomach, under the tail, and on the chin. The general effect is much darker than the Shell Tortoiseshell. Eye color is a brilliant copper.

BLUE-CREAM CAMEO
The softly intermingled blue and cream tipping of this variety may be of any intensity, overlaying the white undercoat.

41

BICOLOR

THE EARLIEST RECORDS of fancy cats give several examples of two-colored cats. Mainly Shorthairs, they include several colors, each with white. At the first cat shows, black and white cats were known as Magpies and were expected to have very precise and even markings. Such precise markings proved very difficult to achieve, and few breeders were prepared to persevere in order to produce the perfect Bicolor. Eventually, new standards were formulated by cat associations around the world.

The Bicolor may be of any solid color with white: black and white, blue and white, red and white, cream and white. In the United States, the cats are required to have white legs and paws, white on the chest, the underbody, and the muzzle, and an inverted "V" of white on the face is desirable. White is also allowed under the tail and as a marking resembling a collar around the neck.

The British standard is less precise in the requirements for the distribution of color and white. The patches of color should be clear and evenly distributed, with not more than two-thirds of the coat being colored, and not more than one half of the coat being white. The face must be patched with color and white. Faults in the bicolor include tabby markings, a long tail, or incorrect eye color.

RED AND WHITE BICOLOR
Red and Cream Bi-colored cats should be free from any shading in the colored areas of their coats.

BLACK AND WHITE BICOLOR
This massive cat has very good markings, particularly the desired white "collar."

BLUE AND WHITE BICOLOR

The inverted "V" on the face of this fine Persian is one of the features required for exhibition of this variety in the USA.

CREAM AND WHITE BICOLOR

In the Bicolor, the face is required to show both colored and white areas.

PERSIAN VAN BICOLOR

THIS SUB-VARIETY may be shown in black and white, blue and white, red and white, or cream and white. The color distribution is quite different from that of the Persian Bicolor. The Van Bicolor is basically a white cat with the colour confined to the extremities – head, legs, and tail. Only one or two small colored patches on the body are allowed.

VAN BICOLOR

The distribution of color is unusual; .the coat is basically white, with colored areas confined to the head, ears, and tail.

TABBY

PEDIGREE TABBY CATS have always caused controversy over their standards of points throughout the cat world. In the early days of the development of breeds, there were arguments about pattern and clarity of markings, and even more disagreement about the correct eye color. Tabby Persians are quite rare in the show rings of the world, possibly because it is difficult to reach the high standard demanded.

In Britain, the Tabby Persian is shown in three color varieties – Silver, Brown, and Red, whereas American show rings exhibit a wider variety of colors.

Coat Patterns

The Classic Tabby pattern, sometimes referred to as the "marbled" or "blotched," calls for precise dense markings, clearly defined and broad. The legs must be evenly barred, with bracelets extending as far as the body markings. The tail should be evenly ringed. Several

unbroken necklaces ring the neck and upper chest, frown marks form a letter "M" on the forehead, and unbroken lines run back from the outer corner of each eye. Swirls on the cheeks and vertical lines over the back of the head extend to the shoulder markings, which are in the shape of a butterfly with both upper and lower wings distinctly outlined, and marked with dots inside the outline. Three parallel lines run down the spine from the butterfly to the tail, well separated by stripes of the coat's ground color. A large, solid blotch on each side is encircled by one or more unbroken rings. There should be a double vertical row of "buttons" on the chest and stomach.

In the Mackerel Tabby pattern, dense and clearly defined narrow penciling marks the coat. The legs are evenly barred, with narrow bracelets extending as far as the body markings. The tail is barred, and distinct chain-like necklaces encircle the neck. The head is barred, with a distinct "M" on the forehead. Unbroken lines run back from the eyes, and lines run back from the head to meet the shoulders. The spine lines form a narrow saddle, and pencilings run around the body.

SILVER TABBY A ground color of pure pale silver includes the lips and chin; the markings are dense black. Nose leather is brick red, paw pads black, and eye color green or hazel.

SILVER TABBY
The dense black markings of the longhaired Silver Tabby show up clearly on the pale silver base coat.

TORBIE
The Tortie Tabby Persian is a cat in which the tabby pattern in the main coat color, is overlaid with shading of red, while still allowing both tabby and tortie areas to remain clearly visible.

BROWN TABBY
A very good example of a variety rarely seen on the show benches of today.

RED TABBY
A deep red coat with even deeper red markings is required by the show standards for the Red Tabby Persian.

RED TABBY The ground color is red, including the lips and chin; the markings deep rich red. Nose leather is brick red, paw pads black or brown, and eyes brilliant copper.

BROWN TABBY The ground color is a brilliant coppery brown; the markings dense black. The lips and chin are the same color as the rings around the eyes. The backs of the legs should be black from the paw to the heel. Nose leather is brick red, paw pads black or brown, and the eyes copper or hazel (UK).

BLUE TABBY The ground color of pale bluish ivory includes the lips and chin; the markings are very deep blue, affording good contrast with the ground color. A warm fawn patina covers the whole of the cat. Nose leather is old rose, paw pads rose, and eye color copper.

CREAM TABBY The ground color is a very pale cream, and includes the lips and chin. The markings of buff or cream are sufficiently darker than the ground color to afford good contrast. Nose leather and paw pads are all pink; eye color is brilliant copper.

CAMEO TABBY The ground color is off-white, including the lips and chin. The markings are red. Nose leather and paw pads are rose and eye color is brilliant copper.

SILVER TORBIE TABBY A pale silver ground color includes the lips and chin. Classic or mackerel markings of black and patches of red and/or light red are clearly defined on the body and extremities. A blaze of red or light red on the face is desirable. Eye color is a brilliant copper or hazel.

BROWN TORBIE TABBY The ground color is a brilliant coppery brown with the lips and chin the same shade as the rings around the eyes; with classic or mackerel markings of dense black and patches of red and/or light red clearly defined on both body and extremities. Eye color is brilliant copper.

BLUE TORBIE TABBY A pale bluish ivory ground color includes the lips and chin. Classic or mackerel markings of very deep blue afford good contrast with the ground color. There are clearly defined patches of cream on the body and extremities, and a warm fawn overtone or patina over the whole of the cat. A blaze of cream on the face is desirable. Eye color is brilliant copper.

LILAC TABBY

In the dilute range of Tabby longhairs, the markings are less distinct.

CHOCOLATE TORBIE

Warm markings on a bronze agouti base coat give this cat its glowing coat pattern.

BLUE TABBY

The Blue Tabby's strong blue markings are set on an unusual gray base coat with a slight fawn color cast, called "blue biscuit."

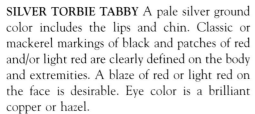

TORTOISESHELL AND WHITE

THE FIRST RECORDED tortoiseshell cats were short-coated, but around the early 1900s, long-coated tortoiseshells were seen at cat shows; they have always been popular as pets. Breeders are intriguted by the female-only variety, and enjoy the variety of colors a tortoiseshell queen can produce, depending on the recessive color genes she carries, and the color and genotype of the male to which she is mated. A similar situation exists with tortoiseshell-and-white cats, once known as Chintz cats in Britain, and referred to as Calico cats in the United States. In the Dilute Calico, the effect of the dilute gene replaces the black color with blue, and the red patches with cream, giving a blue, cream, and white cat. A dilute tortoiseshell (without white) is a blue-cream, which has been described on page 65. As there are no males in these varieties (very occasionally a male is born, but invariably proves to be sterile at maturity), solid-colored cats are generally used for stud purposes.

CALICO (USA) The body color is white with unbrindled patches of black and red; white is predominant on the underparts. The eye color is brilliant copper.

DILUTE CALICO (USA) The body color is white with unbrindled patches of blue and cream; white is predominant on the underparts. The eye color is brilliant copper.

TORTOISESHELL The body color is black with unbrindled and clearly defined patches of red and light red on both the body and extremities. A blaze of red or light red on the face is desirable. The eye color is brilliant copper.

TORTOISESHELL and WHITE (UK) The body color is black, red, and light red or their dilutions, (blue, cream and light cream), with the colors well distributed and interspersed with white. The eye color is deep orange or copper.

TORTOISESHELL
Popular since the pioneer days of cat breeding, the Tortoiseshell Persian always attracts public interest at shows by its striking coat of black patched with areas of red.

TORTOISESHELL AND WHITE
In America, this variety is known as a Calico Cat.

CHOCOLATE TORTIE
The black and red areas of the Tortie are replaced with warm chocolate and light red.

BLUE TORTIE AND WHITE
The patches of color are required to be distinct and free from scattered white hairs.

SILVER AND GOLDEN

PERHAPS THE MOST glamorous of the Persians, the Chinchilla has a characteristic sparkling, silvery appearance. It has a long history, being first recorded by John Jennings in 1893, who described it as "a peculiar but beautiful variety; the fur at the roots is silver and shades to the tips to a decided slate hue, giving it a most pleasing and attractive appearance." Exhibitors at London's first Crystal Palace cat shows described their cats variously as "Silver Grey," "Blue or Silver Striped," "Chinchilla Tabby," or "Silver Chinchilla."

The first Chinchilla cats were born by accident when silver tabbies were mated with cats of other colors. Early Chinchillas were much darker than those seen today, having heavier tipping, tabby markings on the face, and heavy barring on the legs. As the breed developed, the lighter cats came to be known as Chinchilla, and the darker ones, when successfully bred to a different standard, were designated the Shaded Silver. The question of

eye color proved difficult to resolve, the early specimens having a range of color from yellow, to amber and bright green. Chinchilla cats were imported into the United States from Britain from the early 1900s, and soon became well-established and popular on both sides of the Atlantic.

In recent years American breeders have found it possible to add the chinchilla and shaded silver appearance to other colors, and Chinchilla Golden and Shaded Golden cats have begun to appear at shows.

CHINCHILLA SILVER The cat has a pure white undercoat, sufficiently tipped with black on the head, back, flanks, and tail to give the characteristic sparkling silver appearance of this variety. The legs may be slightly shaded with tipping. The chin, ear tufts, chest, and stomach are pure white, and the rims of the eyes, lips, and nose are outlined with black. The nose leather is brick red; the paw pads are black; the eye color is green or blue-green.

SHADED SILVER/PEWTER The cat has a white undercoat with a mantle of black tipping shading down the face, sides and tail, from dark

CHINCHILLA
Often thought rather too dainty and fairylike to be a Persian breed, the Chinchilla is perhaps the most glamorous of all the longhaired varieties.

With the same silvery-white undercoat as its Chinchilla cousin, the Shaded Silver has heavier tipping giving it its typical shaded appearance.

on the ridge to white on the chin, chest, stomach, and under the tail. The legs are the same tone as the face, and the general effect is darker than the Chinchilla. The rims of the eyes, lips and nose are outlined with black. The nose leather is brick red; the paw pads are black; the eye color is green or blue-green. Note that the Pewter Longhair (UK) eye color is orange or copper with black rims.

CHINCHILLA GOLDEN The cat has a rich, warm cream undercoat, sufficiently tipped with seal brown on the head, back, flanks, and tail to give a golden appearance. The legs may be slightly shaded with tipping, and the rims of the eyes, lips, and nose are outlined with seal brown. The nose leather is deep rose; the paw pads are seal brown; the eye color is green or blue-green.

SHADED GOLDEN The cat has a rich, warm cream undercoat and a mantle of seal brown

tipping shading down the face, sides and tail, from dark on the ridge to cream on the chin, chest, stomach, and under the tail. The legs are the same tone as the face, and the general effect is darker than the Chinchilla. The rims of the eyes, lips, and nose are outlined with seal brown. The nose leather is deep rose; the paw pads are seal brown; the eye color is green or blue-green.

GOLDEN PERSIAN

Seal brown tipping on a base coat of golden apricot produces this unusual variety. As with the Chinchilla, this cat should have eyes of green or blue-green.

COLORPOINT

THIS BREED IS a cat of true Persian type with the markings first known in Siamese cats, where the true coat color is restricted to the cooler areas of the cat's body, known as the "points." These include the face, or mask, the ears, the legs and paws, and the tail. This coloring is produced by a recessive gene, often referred to as the Himalayan factor, hence the name used by American fanciers for Persian cats of this pattern.

The first crosses between Siamese and Persian cats were made in Sweden as long ago as 1922. Further experimental matings were made in the United States during the 1920s and 1930s, but it was not until the 1950s that breeders on both sides of the Atlantic, working with carefully planned breeding programs, produced cats with the desired type and coat pattern. In 1955, Britain's GCCF issued a breed number and approved a standard of points for the Himalayan-patterned Persians, but designated them as Colourpoint Longhairs. In the United States recognition of the Himalayan was approved by the CFA in 1957, and by the 1960s all other American associations had accepted the variety. The Himalayan, or Colorpoint Longhair, in all its color subvarieties, soon became well established as one of the most popular of all the longhaired cats in the world's show rings.

Character and Care

The character of the Colorpoint combines the best traits of the cats used in its creation – the Siamese and the Persian. It is generally a little livelier and more entertaining than its solid-colored Persian cousins, but less vocal and boisterous than the typical Siamese. The precocious breeding tendencies of its Siamese ancestry have been passed on, with Colorpoint females coming into season and "calling" as early as eight months of age, though the males often do not reach maturity until they are 18 months old.

Regular grooming is essential to keep the long full coat in good condition, paying particular attention to the underparts, between the hind and fore legs, under the tail and around the neck, thoroughly brushing out the frill or ruff.

BREAKDOWN OF 100 SHOW POINTS

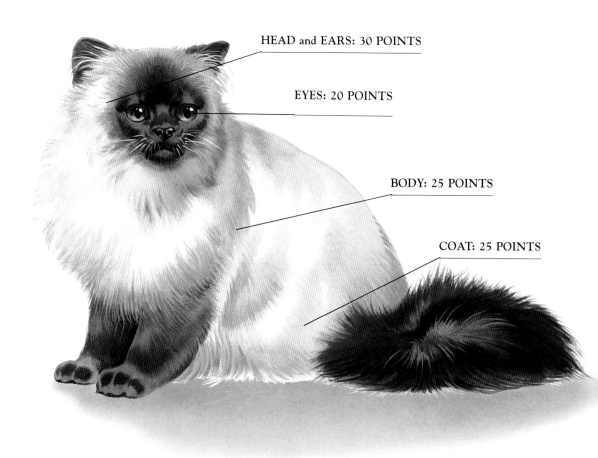

HEAD and EARS: 30 POINTS

EYES: 20 POINTS

BODY: 25 POINTS

COAT: 25 POINTS

KEY CHARACTERISTICS

- **CATEGORY** Longhair.

- **OVERALL BUILD** Medium or large, stocky.

- **COAT** Long and thick over the entire body, of fine texture and glossy; immense ruff (frill) around the neck and extending between the forelegs. Long tufts on the ears and between the toes.

- **HEAD** Round and massive, with very broad skull, round face, and set on a short, thick neck. Full cheeks.

- **NOSE** Short, broad nose with stop.

- **CHIN** Full, well-developed.

- **EYES** Large, full, round, and set far apart.

- **EARS** Small, round-tipped, tilted slightly forward and set far apart on the head.

- **BODY** Of stocky type, low on the legs, with a deep chest, and equally massive across the shoulders and rump.

- **LEGS** Short, thick, and heavy; straight forelegs.

- **PAWS** Large, round, and firm; toes not splayed.

- **TAIL** Short, but in proportion to body length; hair forms a "brush."

- **COLORS** Seal point, blue point, chocolate point, lilac point, red point, cream point, seal tortie point, chocolate tortie point, blue-cream point, seal tabby point, blue tabby point, chocolate tabby point, lilac tabby point, lilac-cream point; red tabby point, cream tabby point, seal tortie tabby point, blue-cream tabby point, chocolate tortie tabby point, lilac-cream tabby point.

PENALTIES

The Himalayan is penalized for lack of pigmentation in paw pads and/or nose leather; a locket or button; any abnormality of the tail; a squint; white toes; eye color other than blue; deformity of the skull and/or the mouth; any apparent weakness in the hindquarters.

SOLID POINTS

IN THE COLORPOINTS with solid points color, the standard requires that the coloring on all of the points should match in tone and be free from shadow markings or any patchiness.

SEAL POINT The body color is an even, pale fawn or cream, warm in tone, which shades gradually into lighter color on the chest and stomach. The points are deep seal brown. The nose leather and the paw pads are the same color as the points; the eye color is a deep, vivid blue.

BLUE POINT The body color is bluish-white, cold in tone, which shades gradually to white on the chest and stomach. The points are blue. The nose leather and paw pads are slate gray; the eye color is deep, vivid blue.

CHOCOLATE POINT The body color is ivory, with no shading. The points are milk chocolate, warm in tone. The nose leather and paw pads are cinnamon pink; the eye color is deep, vivid blue.

LILAC POINT The body color is glacial white, with no shading. The points are frosty gray with a pinkish tone. The nose leather and paw

SEAL POINT COLORPOINT

In Colorpoint kittens the facial markings or mask is not complete, leaving a typically pale forehead.

BLUE POINT COLORPOINT

This cat has tiny and very well-set ears, and the desired broad head.

CREAM POINT

A very pale variety of Colorpoint with the cream points only slightly darker than the body.

RED POINT COLORPOINT

The Red Point has a body of apricot-toned white and points of a deeper apricot-red. As in all Colorpoints, the eyes are ideally deep blue.

pads are lavender-pink; the eye color is deep, vivid blue.

RED POINT The body color is creamy white. The points color varied from deep orange flame to deep red. The nose leather and paw pads are flesh or coral pink; the eye color is deep, vivid blue.

CREAM POINT The body color is creamy white with no shading. The points are buff cream and should have no apricot tinges. The nose leather and paw pads are flesh pink or salmon coral; eye color is deep, vivid blue.

TORTIE POINT The body color is creamy white or pale fawn; the points are seal brown, with unbrindled patches of red and light red. A blaze of red or light red on the face is desirable. The nose leather and paw pads are seal brown with flesh and/or coral pink mottling to conform with the points' color; the eye color is deep, vivid blue.

BLUE-CREAM POINT The body color is bluish-white or creamy white, which shades gradually to white on the chest and stomach. The points are blue with patches of cream. The nose leather and paw pads are slate-grey or pink, or a combination of slate gray and pink mottling; the eye color is deep, vivid blue.

TABBY POINTS

THE TABBY-POINTED varieties should have a clear "M" marking on the forehead, spotted whisker pads and typical "glasses" marks around the eyes. Tips of the ears and tail should match.

SEAL TABBY POINT The body color is pale cream to fawn, and warm in tone. The mask is clearly lined with dark stripes: vertical lines on the forehead form the classic "M" shape; horizontal lines bar the cheeks; dark spots appear on the whisker pads. The inner ear is light, and there is a "thumb-print" on the back of the outer ear. The legs are evenly barred with bracelets, and the tail is barred. All markings should be broad, dense, and clearly defined. No striping or mottling is allowed on the body, but consideration is given to shading in older cats.

The points are beige brown ticked with darker brown tabby markings. The nose leather is seal or brick red; the paw pads are seal brown; the eyes deep blue.

BLUE TABBY POINT The body color is bluish-white, and cold in tone. The mask is clearly lined with dark stripes: vertical lines on the forehead form the classic "M" shape; horizontal lines bar the cheeks; dark spots appear on the whisker pads. The inner ear is light, and there is a "thumb-print" on the back of the outer ear. The legs are evenly barred with bracelets, and the tail is barred. All markings should be broad, dense, and clearly defined. No striping or mottling is allowed on the body, but consideration is given to shading in older cats. The points are light silvery blue, ticked with darker

SEAL TABBY POINT

This variety is known as the Seal Lynxpoint in the United States, and this cat's head type conforms to the American standards.

RED TABBY POINT

In the red series, some slight shading similar to that of the Points' color may be seen on the pale body.

COLORPOINT KITTEN

Colorpoint kittens are very inquisitive, friendly, and playful. The markings develop slowly, showing their true color a few weeks after birth.

blue tabby markings. The nose leather is blue or brick red; the paw pads are blue; the eye color is deep, vivid blue.

CHOCOLATE TABBY POINT The body color is ivory. The mask is clearly lined with dark stripes: vertical lines on the forehead form the classic "M" shape; horizontal lines bar the cheeks; dark spots appear on the whisker pads. The inner ear is light, and there is a "thumb-print" on the back of the outer ear. The legs are evenly barred with bracelets, and the tail is barred. All markings should be broad, dense, and clearly defined. No striping or mottling is allowed on the body, but consideration is given to shading in older cats. The points are warm fawn, ticked with milk-chocolate markings. The nose leather and paw pads are cinnamon pink; the eye color is deep, vivid blue.

LILAC TABBY POINT The body color is glacial white. The mask is clearly lined with dark

stripes: vertical lines on the forehead form the classic "M" shape; horizontal lines bar the cheeks; dark spots appear on the whisker pads. The inner ear is light, and there is a "thumb-print" on the back of the outer ear. The legs are evenly barred with bracelets, and the tail is barred. All markings should be broad, dense, and clearly defined. No striping or mottling is allowed on the body, but consideration is given to shading in older cats. The points are frosty gray ticked with darker frosty gray tabby markings. The nose leather and paw pads are lavender pink; the eye color is deep, vivid blue.

BLUE-CREAM POINT

Softly intermingled blue and cream pattern the points of this Colorpoint. It has a wonderfully full and well-groomed coat.

CHOCOLATE TORTIE COLORPOINT

This cute kitten shows the warm chocolate and light red markings on its points that identify the chocolate tortoiseshell coloration. As with all Colorpoint kittens, the markings take some time to develop fully.

CHOCOLATE AND LILAC

DURING THE BREEDING and development of the Himalayan or Colorpoint Longhairs, breeders realized it might also be possible to produce self-colored chocolate and lilac longhaired cats. This proved quite simple to put into practice, and cats with the desired coat color were bred quite easily, but their body type and coat quality were extremely poor when judged against Persian standards. The pioneer breeders of these varieties also had to contend with the natural fading and bleaching effect on the coat color caused by the chocolate gene, and some of the early chocolate and lilac cats were very disappointing. Never to be outdone, the breeders determined to select for the characteristics they most desired in their dreamed-of color varieties, and eventually they succeeded in establishing chocolate and lilac longhaired cats of equal quality to their Himalayan cousins. Some North American associations decided to group the self-colored chocolate and lilac longhairs under the breed name of Kashmir; others grouped them with the Himalayans. Britain's GCCF preferred to call them the Chocolate Longhair and the Lilac Longhair.

CHOCOLATE LONGHAIR The color is a rich, warm, chocolate brown, sound from the roots to the tips of the hair, and free from markings, shading, or white hairs. The nose leather and paw pads are brown; the eye color is deep orange or copper (UK), or brilliant copper (USA).

LILAC LONGHAIR The color is a rich, warm, lavender with a pinkish tone, sound from the roots to the tips of the hair, and free from markings, shading, or white hairs. The nose leather and paw pads are pink; the eye color is pale orange in the UK, brilliant copper in the USA.

CHOCOLATE PERSIAN
Known as the Kashmir in some associations, the self-colored chocolate Persian is one of the most difficult cats to breed to the exacting standard of points.

LILAC-CREAM

*This variety was
created when the red
or orange genetic
factor was added to
some breeding
programs. Lilac and
light cream hairs are
patched or intermingled.*

LILAC PERSIAN

*Often called the Lilac
Kashmir, this cat has
true Persian type and a
full, flowing coat.*

SEMI LONGHAIRED BREEDS

BIRMAN

ALSO KNOWN AS THE Sacred Cat of Burma, the Birman is quite unrelated to the Burmese, despite the similarity in names. It is a unique breed, for although it bears a superficial resemblance to the Himalayan, or Colorpoint Longhair, it has stark white paws on all four feet. Its coat is silky, more like that of the Turkish Angora than the Himalayan, and its body type differs from that of the Persian, being longer and less cobby.

Legends about explaining the origins of this beautiful breed, and one in particular attempts to explain the Birman's coloring. Before the time of Buddha, the Khmer people built temples in honor of their gods. One such temple was raised to Tsun-Kyan-Kse, where a golden statue of the goddess so named was worshipped.

In the early 1900s the temple was raided, but it was saved by Major Gordon Russell and Monsieur Auguste Pavie. As a gesture of thanks, a pair of temple cats were sent to the two men, now living in France. The male cat died en route, but the female arrived safely and gave birth to kittens which founded the Birman breed in Europe.

Whatever the true origins of the breed, it survived in Europe and was imported into Britain and accepted for championship status by 1966. Separate breeding lines were established in the United States, with the first championship showing at the Madison Square Garden Cat Show, having been given official status by the CFA in 1967.

Character and Care
The Birman is quieter and more placid than a Siamese, but also less staid than a Persian. It is an inquisitive and affectionate cat, with a rather aloof appearance, giving the impression

BREAKDOWN OF 100 SHOW POINTS

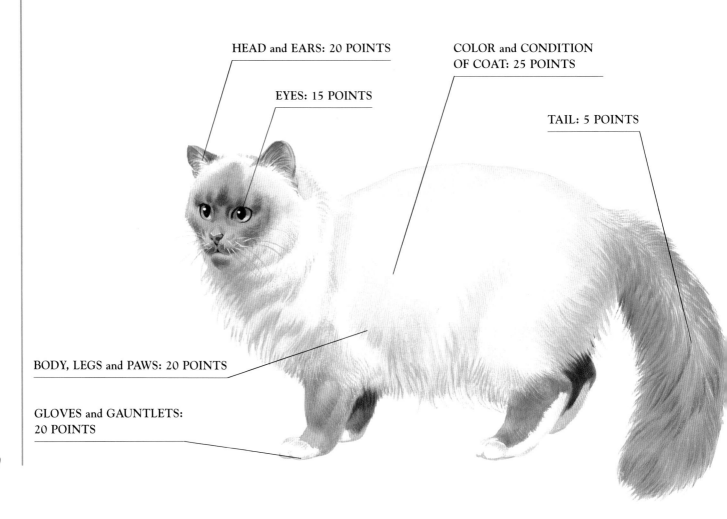

HEAD and EARS: 20 POINTS

EYES: 15 POINTS

COLOR and CONDITION OF COAT: 25 POINTS

TAIL: 5 POINTS

BODY, LEGS and PAWS: 20 POINTS

GLOVES and GAUNTLETS: 20 POINTS

that it is fully aware of its mystical origins. Unlike many other longhaired breeds, the Birman matures early, and the females often start to "call" as early as seven months of age. The queens make excellent caring mothers, and males kept at stud are often renowned for their extra-loving temperament.

The Birman coat is silkier and less dense than that of the Persian. It is comparitively easy to keep well groomed with regular brushing and combing. The white gloves and gauntlets must be kept free from staining by regular washing, careful drying, and the application of white grooming powder which is rubbed in, then completely brushed out, leaving the white areas spotlessly clean.

PENALTIES

The Birman is penalized for having white areas that do not run across the front paws in an even line; lack of white gloves on any paw; white shading on the stomach and chest; areas of pure white in the points (except the paws); a Siamese head type; and crossed eyes.

KEY CHARACTERISTICS

- **CATEGORY** Longhair.

- **OVERALL BUILD** Medium sized, long but stocky.

- **COAT** Long, silky texture; heavy ruff (frill) around the neck; long on the back and flanks, may curl slightly on the stomach; little undercoat; rarely becomes matted.

- **HEAD** Strong, broad, rounded skull with full cheeks.

- **NOSE** Medium length, roman in shape.

- **CHIN** Firm, with the lower lip forming a perpendicular line with the upper lip.

- **EYES** Almost round in shape.

- **EARS** Medium sized with rounded tips, set slightly tipped forward, not upright on the skull and with good width between.

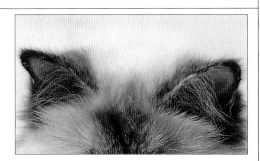

- **BODY** Fairly long but not stocky, males more massive than females.

- **LEGS** Short to medium in length, and heavy.

- **PAWS** Large and rounded.

- **TAIL** Medium length, forming a plume.

- **COLORS** Seal point, blue point, chocolate point, lilac point, red point, cream point, seal tortie point, blue tortie point, chocolate tortie point, lilac tortie point solid points, tortie points, tabby points and tortie tabby all in the following colors: seal, blue, chocolate, lilac, red, cream.

61

SOLID POINTS

SEAL POINT BIRMAN

The characteristic white forepaws of this breed are called "gloves" and should end in a symmetrical line on or below the angle formed by the paw and leg.

A LITTER OF BIRMANS normally consists of three, four, or five kittens which are born almost white all over. Within a few days, the points color starts to develop at the edges of the ears and on the tail. The eyes, when they open at seven to ten days, are a cloudy baby-blue which changes to the true blue color as the kittens grow.

SEAL POINT The body is even fawn to pale cream, warm in tone shading to lighter color on the stomach and chest. The points are deep seal brown apart from the gloves, which are pure white. The nose leather should match the points. The paw pads are pink, and eye color is blue, the deeper and more violet the better.

BLUE POINT The body is bluish-white, cold in tone, shading gradually to almost white on the stomach and chest. The points are deep blue except for the gloves, which are pure white. The nose leather is slate and the paw pads pink. Eye color should be blue, the deeper and more violet the better.

CHOCOLATE POINT The body is ivory with no shading. Points are milk-chocolate of warm tone except for the gloves, which are pure white. The nose leather is cinnamon pink and the paw pads pink. Eye color should be blue, the deeper and more violet the better.

BLUE POINT BIRMAN

The gloves on the hind paws are called "gauntlets." They cover the entire paw and taper up the back of the leg to a point just below the hock.

CREAM POINT BIRMAN

A slightly golden-hued white body and pale cream points are the hallmarks of the Cream Point Birman.

CHOCOLATE POINT BIRMAN

Warm toned milk-chocolate points identify this recently accepted color variety in the Birman.

LILAC POINT BIRMAN

Apart from its four white paws, the Birman has normal Himalayan or Siamese coloring on the extremities of the body, known as the points.

LILAC POINT The body has a cold glacial tone verging on white with no shading. The points are frosty gray with a pinkish tinge, with pure white gloves. The nose leather is lavender pink, the paw pads pink, and the eye color blue, the deeper and more violet the better.

RED POINT The body is creamy white. The points, except for the gloves, are bright warm orange; the gloves are white. The nose leather and paw pads are pink; eye color is blue.

CREAM POINT The body is creamy white. The points, except for the gloves, are pastel cream; the gloves are white. The nose leather and paw pads are pink; the eye colour is blue.

63

TABBY AND TORTOISESHELL POINTS

ALTHOUGH PURISTS CLAIM that only Seal Point and Blue Point Birman cats should be considered as the true Sacred Cats of Burma, the CFA in the United States also recognizes the Chocolate Point and Lilac Point varieties, and FIFe in Europe has produced standards of points for both the tabby and red series, including tortoiseshell, and tortoiseshell–tabbies in the four basic color combinations.

SEAL TABBY POINT The body is beige, with dark seal tabby points, except for gloves which are white. The nose leather is brick red, pink, or seal brown, and the paw pads are pink.

BLUE TABBY POINT The body is bluish-white, with blue-gray tabby points, except for the gloves which are white. The nose leather is old rose or blue-gray.

CHOCOLATE TABBY POINT The body is ivory. The points, except for the gloves, are milk-chocolate tabby; the gloves are white. The nose leather is pale red, pink, or milk-chocolate.

LILAC TABBY POINT The body is glacial white (magnolia) with lilac tabby (frosty gray with a slight pinkish tinge) points, except the gloves, which are white. The nose leather is pink or lavender-pink.

RED TABBY POINT The body is off-white with a slight red tinge. The points, except for the gloves, are warm orange tabby; the gloves are white. The nose leather is pink or brick-red.

CREAM TABBY POINT The body is off-white. The points, except for the gloves, are cream tabby; the gloves are white.

SEAL TORTIE POINT The body is beige, shading to fawn. The points, except for the gloves, are seal brown patched or mingled with red and/or light red. The gloves are white. The nose leather is pink and/or seal.

SEAL TORTIE TABBY POINT The body is beige. The points, except for the gloves, have tabby markings in seal brown patched or mingled with red and/or light red. The gloves are white and the nose leather seal, brick red or pink, or seal mottled with brick red or pink.

BLUE TABBY POINT BIRMAN

The Birman is alert and interested in everything that is going on. It makes an excellent pet, and its long coat is easier to care for than that of the cats of the Persian group.

SEAL TORTIE POINT BIRMAN

Seal brown overlaid and intermingled with red and light red produce the tortoiseshell coloring.

SEAL TABBY POINT BIRMAN
Tabby pointed Birman cats are now accepted with provisional status in Britain by GCCF.

BLUE TORTIE POINT The body is bluish white. The points, except for the gloves, are blue-gray patched or mottled with pastel cream. The gloves are white. The nose leather is blue-gray and/or pink.

BLUE TORBIE TABBY POINT The body is glacial white with a slight bluish tinge. The points, except for the gloves, have tabby markings in blue-gray patched or mingled with pastel cream. The gloves are white and the nose leather blue-gray, old rose or pink, or blue-gray mottled with old rose and/or pink.

CHOCOLATE TORTIE POINT The body is ivory. The points, except for the gloves, are milk-chocolate patched or mingled with red and/or light red; the gloves are white. The nose leather is milk-chocolate and/or pink.

CHOCOLATE TORTIE TABBY POINT The body is ivory. The points, except for the gloves, have tabby markings in milk-chocolate patched or mingled with red and/or light red; the gloves are white. The nose leather is milk-chocolate, light red or pink, or milk-chocolate mottled with light red and/or pink.

LILAC TORTIE POINT The body is glacial white (magnolia). The points, except for the gloves, are lilac (frosty gray with a slight pinkish tinge) patched or mingled with pale cream; the gloves are white. The nose leather is lavender pink and/or pink.

LILAC TORBIE TABBY POINT The body is glacial white (magnolia). The points, except for the gloves, have tabby markings in lilac (frosty gray with a slight pinkish tinge) patched or mingled with pale cream; the gloves are white. The nose leather is lavender pink or pale pink, or lavender pink mottled with pale pink.

RED TABBY POINT BIRMAN
The slight golden shaded effect on the coat of this color variety is known as a "halo."

65

MAINE COON

ONE OF THE OLDEST NATURAL BREEDS of North America, the Maine Coon, or Maine Cat, has been known as a true variety for more than a hundred years. As its name implies, it originated in the state of Maine. At one time it was thought that the cat was the product of matings between semi-wild domestic cats and raccoons, hence the name "coon," though this is now known to be a biological impossibility. Another legend tells how Marie Antoinette, in planning her escape from the horrors of the French Revolution, sent her pet cats to be cared for in Maine until she could find herself, and them, a new home. Today's more enlightened felinophiles believe that long-coated cats such as the Angora were introduced to coastal towns as trade goods by visting seamen, and these cats bred with the local domestic cats, resulting eventually in the large and handsome American longhaired breed we know today.

A tabby Maine Coon is recorded as having won the Best in Show at the Madison Square Garden Cat Show in 1895, but with the introduction of more striking breeds from Europe at the turn of the century, the popularity of the Maine Coon declined. Though the breed flourished as a popular and hardy pet for some years, it was not until 1953 that the Central Maine Coon Cat Club was formed to promote the breed. By 1967 a show standard was accepted by some American cat associa-

BREAKDOWN OF 100 SHOW POINTS

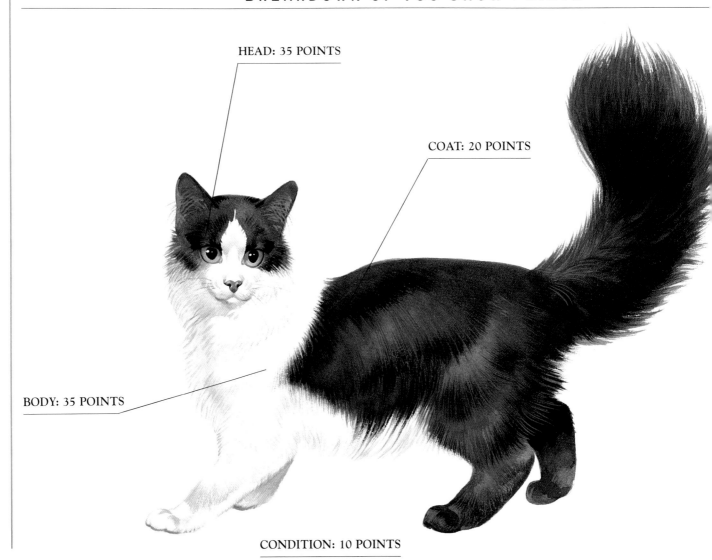

HEAD: 35 POINTS

COAT: 20 POINTS

BODY: 35 POINTS

CONDITION: 10 POINTS

tions. In 1976 the International Society for the Preservation of the Maine Coon was formed, and the Cat Fanciers' Association accepted the breed with full championship status.

Character and Care

Considered by their fans to be perfect domestic pets, typical Maine Coons have extrovert personalities and are very playful and amusing, often teaching themselves tricks. They may take three or four years to develop their full size and stature, being very slow to mature.

Although the coat is long and flowing, it rarely gets matted, and is easy to care for with occasional combing through.

PENALTIES

The Maine Coon is penalized for having a short or uneven coat; lack of undercoat; unbalanced proportions; delicate bone structure; long thin legs; short tail; wide set or flared ears; pronounced whisker pads; straight or convex profile; slanted, almond-shaped eyes.

KEY CHARACTERISTICS

- **CATEGORY** Longhair.

- **OVERALL BUILD** Medium to large.

- **COAT** Heavy and shaggy, with a silky texture. Short on the head, shoulders and legs, becoming gradually longer down the back and sides, shaggy on hind legs and belly fur; full ruff (frill).

- **HEAD** Medium sized with a squarish outline; gently concave in profile, with curved forehead and high, prominent cheekbones.

- **NOSE** Medium length.

- **CHIN** Firm, and in vertical alignment with the nose and upper lip.

- **EYES** Large, slightly oval but not almond shaped, set slightly slanted toward the outer base of the ear.

- **EARS** Large, wide at the base, moderately pointed and with lynx-like ear tufts, set high but well apart.

- **BODY** Long with substantial bone, large framed and well proportioned, muscular and broad chested. Males are larger than females.

- **LEGS** Medium length.

- **PAWS** Large, round, and tufted between the toes.

- **TAIL** At least as long as the body from shoulder-blade to the base of the tail; wide at the base tapering to the tip with full, flowing hair.

- **COLORS** The Maine Coon is recognized in all colors except the Himalayan and Burmese patterns, and chocolate, cinnamon, lilac or fawn. There is no relationship between coat color and eye color, though brilliant eye color is desirable. Any amount of white is allowed.

BLUE-CREAM AND WHITE
The Maine Coon originated in the state of Maine, where this cat would be known as the Dilute Calico variety.

GREEN-EYED WHITE
The Maine Coon is one of the few pedigree breeds in which the white variety may have green eyes.

THE STANDARD FOR solid colors insists on a coat that is sound to the roots and free from any shading, markings, or hair of another color. The nose leathers and paw pads match the eye rims.

WHITE The coat is pure glistening white; and the nose leather and paw pads are pink. The eye colors may be blue, orange, odd, or green.

BLACK The coat is dense coal black, sound from the roots to the tips of the hair; with no sign of rustiness of color on the tips, and no smoke undercoat. The nose leather is black; the pads are black or brown.

BLUE The coat is one even tone of gray-blue from nose to tail tip, and must be sound to the roots. Nose leather and paw pads are blue.

RED The coat is deep, clear, rich, brilliant red without any shading, markings, or ticking. The lips and chin must be the same color as the coat. Nose leather and paw pads are brick red.

CREAM The coat is one even shade of buff cream, without any markings, and must be sound to the roots. The nose leather and paw pads are pink.

TORTOISESHELL The color is black with unbrindled patches of red and light red, with the patches clearly defined and well broken on both the body and extremities. A blaze of red or light red on the face is desirable.

CALICO There must be white on the bib, belly, and all four paws. White on one-third of the body overall is desirable.

BLUE-CREAM The color is blue with clearly defined, unbrindled, well-broken patches of cream on the body and extremities.

BLUE-CREAM-AND-WHITE There must be white on the bib, belly, and all four paws. White on one-third of the body overall is desirable.

BICOLOUR This is a combination of a solid color with white. The colored areas predominate, with the white areas located on the face, chest, belly, legs, and feet. Colors accepted are black, blue, red, and cream.

SMOKE AND SHADED VARIETIES

ANY SOLID OR TORTIE color is accepted in this group. The base coat should be as white as possible, with the tips of the hairs shading to the basic color, darkest on the head, back, and paws. The Smoke is densely colored; while the shaded shows much more of the silver undercoat.

SHADED SILVER There is a white undercoat with a mantle of black tipping shading down the sides, face, and tail, with the color ranging from dark on the ridge to white on the chin, chest, stomach, and underside of the tail. The legs are the same tone as the face. The general effect is much darker than the Chinchilla. Eye rims, lips, and nose are outlined with black; nose leather is brick red; paw pads are black.

SHADED RED There is a white undercoat with red tipping shading down the sides, face and tail, with the color ranging from dark on the ridge to white on the chin, chest, stomach, and underside of the tail. Legs are the same tone as the face. Nose leather and paw pads are black.

BLACK SMOKE There is a white undercoat deeply tipped with black; in repose, the cat appears black; in motion, the white undercoat is clearly apparent. The points and mask are black, with a narrow band of white at the base of the hairs next to the skin. The ruff (frill) and ear tufts are light silver; the nose leather and paw pads are black.

BLUE SMOKE There is a white undercoat deeply tipped with blue; in repose, the cat appears blue; in motion, the white undercoat is clearly apparent. The points and mask are blue, with a narrow band of white hairs next to the skin. The ruff (frill) and ear tufts are white; nose leather and paw pads are blue.

RED SMOKE There is a white undercoat deeply tipped with red; in repose, the cat appears red; in motion, the white undercoat is clearly apparent. The points and mask are red, with a narrow band of white hairs next to the skin. The eye rims, nose leather, and paw pads are rose.

CREAM SMOKE This is a dilute version of the Red Smoke in which the red tipping is reduced to pale cream.

RED SHADED
In shaded varieties, the undercoat should be as white as possible, and the basic color should be deepest on the head, back, and the paws.

TABBY VARIETIES

BOTH THE CLASSIC TABBY and Mackerel Tabby patterned cats are accepted in any of the following colors.

SILVER TABBY The cat has a pale, clear silver base coat with dense black markings; white is allowed around the lips and chin. The nose leather is brick red; the paw pads are black.

BROWN TABBY The cat has a brilliant coppery brown base coat with dense black markings. The backs of the legs from the paw to the heel are black; white is allowed around the lips and chin. The nose leather and paw pads are black or brown.

BLUE TABBY The cat has a pale bluish-ivory base coat with very deep blue markings affording good contrast with the base color. There is a warm fawn patina over the whole coat. White is allowed around the lips and chin. The nose leather is old rose; the paw pads are rose.

RED TABBY The cat has a red base coat with deep rich red markings; white is allowed around the lips and chin. The nose leather and paw pads are brick red.

CREAM TABBY The cat has a very pale cream base coat with buff or cream markings sufficiently darker to afford good contrast with the base color. White is allowed around lips and chin. Nose leather and paw pads are pink.

BROWN MACKEREL TABBY

In the mackerel tabby pattern, the markings consist of fine lines running down the body.

MACKEREL TABBY AND WHITE

These markings are of the Mackerel rather than the Classic pattern.

SILVER TABBY
Cats with any either of the tabby patterns have similar head markings with the letter "M" etched on the forehead.

TORBIE
Full, round, and luminous eyes set off the glowing coat to perfection.

SILVER TORBIE and WHITE
Some of the most unusual of all the feline colors are found in the Maine Coon. This pretty little cat has pale tortoiseshell markings mixed with silver tabby, and white, creating a very attractive pattern.

CAMEO TABBY The cat has an off-white base coat with red markings; white is allowed around the lips and chin. The nose leather and paw pads are rose.

TORBIE TABBY A Torbie Tabby or patched tabby is a silver or brown tabby with patches of red and light red, or a blue tabby with patches of cream. Nose leather of Torbie Tabby brick-red or pink; paw pads black and/or pink. Nose leather and pads of Blue Tabby blue and/or pink.

TABBY-AND-WHITE The cat may be any tabby color as defined above – silver, brown, blue, red, or cream – with or without white on the face, but with white on the bib, belly, and all four paws; white on one-third of the body overall is desirable. The nose leather and paw pads are as for the color described above.

TORBIE TABBY-AND-WHITE The color is as described for the Torbie Tabby, but with white markings as defined for the Tabby-and-white (above). Colors accepted are silver, brown, and blue. The nose leather depends on basic color; paw pads are pink.

RAGDOLL

THE FIRST RAGDOLL cats were bred by an American, Ann Baker, whose white long-haired cat Josephine was involved in a road accident which left her with permanent injuries. When Josephine eventually had kittens, they were found to have particularly placid temperaments and would completely relax when picked up and cuddled, reminiscent of a rag doll.

The name was chosen and recognized in 1965 by the National Cat Fanciers' Association, and later by other associations. Although this breed's alleged inability to feel pain or fear, or to fight with other animals is claimed to be due to Josephine's accident, this goes against all genetic reasoning. The specialized temperament is almost certainly due to the fact that only cats of a loving disposition were selected in the first matings. The three patterns found in the breed could certainly have been produced by Josephine if the stud cat used had carried genes for the Himalayan pattern and long coat, and if either Josephine or her mate had also carried the gene for white spotting.

Though some controversy remains over the breed, the Ragdoll has gained popularity around the world, and it has become an interesting addition to the show scene.

BREAKDOWN OF 100 SHOW POINTS

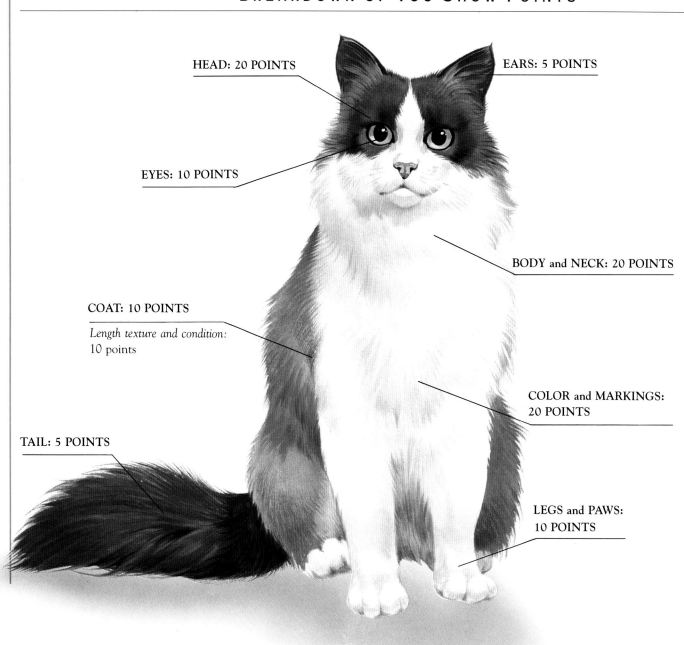

HEAD: 20 POINTS

EARS: 5 POINTS

EYES: 10 POINTS

BODY and NECK: 20 POINTS

COAT: 10 POINTS

Length texture and condition:
10 points

COLOR and MARKINGS:
20 POINTS

TAIL: 5 POINTS

LEGS and PAWS:
10 POINTS

Character and Care

The Ragdoll is an exceptionally affectionate, loving, and relaxed cat. Although it is generally calm and placid, with a quiet voice, it loves to play and to be petted. The thick coat does not form mats and is therefore quite easy to groom with regular gentle brushing of the body and combing through the longer hair on the tail and around the neck.

PENALTIES

The Ragdoll is penalized for having a narrow head, roman nose, too large a stop in profile, too small or pointed ears; almond-shaped eyes; a neck too long or too thin; cobby body; narrow chest; short legs; splayed feet; lack of toe tufts; short or blunt tipped tail; eye color other than blue.

KEY CHARACTERISTICS

- **CATEGORY** Longhair.

- **OVERALL BUILD** Large, solid appearance.

- **COAT** Medium long, dense, soft, and silky in texture, lying close to the body and breaking as the cat moves. Longest around the neck and framing the face; short on the face; short to medium length on the front legs; medium to long over the body.

- **HEAD** Medium size, broad modified wedge shape with a flat plane between the ears; well-developed cheeks; medium long muzzle.

- **NOSE** Slightly curved in the upper third.

- **CHIN** Well developed.

- **EYES** Large and oval, with the outer corners being level with the base of the ears.

- **EARS** Medium size, broad-based, with rounded tips, set wide apart and tipped slightly forward.

- **BODY** Long, with medium bone structure. Muscular, broad chest, muscular hindquarters.

- **LEGS** Medium in length and of medium bone. Hind legs slightly higher than forelegs.

- **PAWS** Large, round, and compact; with tufts between the toes.

- **TAIL** Long, but in proportion to the body, medium broad at the base and slightly tapered toward the tip; bushy.

- **COLORS** Seal point, blue point, chocolate point and lilac point, all with clear blue eyes.

73

MITTED

SEAL MITTED RAGDOLL

Mitted Ragdolls may have a narrow white facial blaze in addition to white on the chin, chest, bib, and underbody, and the obligatory four white paws.

BLUE MITTED RAGDOLL

In the mitted pattern of the Ragdoll breed, the four paws are white to the same degree as that found in the Birman.

THE BODY IS LIGHT in color and only slightly shaded; the points (except the paws and chin) should be clearly defined, matched for color and in harmony with the body color. The chin must be white, and a white stripe on the nose is preferred; white mittens on the front legs and back paws should be entirely white to the knees and hocks. A white stripe extends from the bib to the underside between the front legs to the base of the tail.

LILAC POINT The body color is glacial white; the points are frosty grey of a pinkish tone, except for the white areas.

SEAL POINT The body color is pale fawn or cream; the points are deep seal brown, except for the white areas.

BLUE POINT The body color is cold-toned bluish-white; the points are blue, except for the white areas.

CHOCOLATE POINT The body color is ivory; the points are milk chocolate, except for the white areas.

LILAC POINT The body color is glacial white; the points are frosty gray of a pinkish tone, except for the white areas.

BICOLOR

THE BODY IS LIGHT in color; the points – ears, mask, and tail – should be well-defined. The mask has an inverted white "V"; the stomach is white; and the legs are preferably white. No white is allowed on ears or tail.

SEAL POINT The body color is pale fawn or cream; the points are deep seal brown, except for the white areas.

BLUE POINT The body color is cold-toned bluish-white; the points are blue, except for the white areas.

CHOCOLATE POINT The body color is ivory; the points are milk chocolate, except for the white areas.

CHOCOLATE BICOLOR RAGDOLL

An inverted white "V" extending from the forehead to cover the nose is the identifying feature of the Colorpoint Ragdoll, in addition to the other required areas of white.

SEAL BICOLOR RAGDOLL

The Ragdoll is a large and very docile cat with a loving temperament and a sociable nature. Though long, its coat is easy to keep in good condition with little grooming.

COLORPOINT

THE BODY IS LIGHT in color and only slightly shaded; the points – ears, mask, legs, and tail – should be clearly defined, matched for color and in harmony with the body color. No white hairs allowed.

LILAC POINT The body color is glacial white; the points are frosty gray of a pinkish tone, except for the white areas.

SEAL POINT The body color is pale fawn or cream; the points are deep seal brown, except for the white areas.

BLUE POINT The body color is cold-toned bluish-white; the points are blue, except for the white areas.

CHOCOLATE POINT The body color is ivory; the points are milk chocolate, except for the white areas.

SEAL COLORPOINT
All the points are evenly matched, with no white markings anywhere.

BLUE COLORPOINT
The basic Himalayan colors of seal, blue, chocolate, and lilac are accepted in this breed.

LILAC COLORPOINT
Even in the lilac variety, good contrast between the body and points' color is required. The coat itself should be dense, of silky texture, and medium length.

SNOWSHOE

SNOWSHOE
Sometimes called Silver Laces, the Snowshoe is a very rare cat indeed and only recognized in a few associations. It is of the stocky build found in the American Shorthair.

THE SNOWSHOE OR Silver Laces is a rare cat, even in the United States where it was first bred. It combines the stocky build of the American Shorthair with the body length of the Siamese, and is Himalayan or Siamese in coloring, but with the white paws which are also found in the Birman.

Character and Care
The Snowshoe is a robust and lively cat. It is highly intelligent and loving and, like the Siamese, enjoys human company.

Its coat needs the minimum of grooming, and the white paws may be kept immaculate by dusting with grooming powder from time to time to prevent discoloration.

KEY CHARACTERISTICS
● **CATEGORY** Shorthair.
● **OVERALL BUILD** The Snowshoe is of medium size and well muscled.
● **COAT** Short, fine, close-lying coat.
● **COLORS** Any recognized points color.
● **OTHER FEATURES** The head is triangular with large pointed wide-based ears and large oval eyes of brilliant blue. The long body is well-muscled with a strong back, the legs are of medium bone with compact oval paws, and the tail is thick at the base, tapering to a pointed tip. There are no standards set either for the nose or for the chin.

NORWEGIAN FOREST CAT

KNOWN AS THE *Norsk Skaukatt* in its native Norway, the Norwegian Forest Cat is very similar to the Maine Coon in many ways. It is a uniquely Scandinavian breed whose origins are shrouded in mystery, and it is referred to in Norse myths and mid-nineteenth-century fairy stories. Having evolved naturally in the cold climate of Norway, it has a heavy, weather-resistant coat. The glossy, medium-length top coat hangs from the spine line, keeping out rain and snow, while the wooly undercoat keeps the body comfortably warm. Its strong legs, paws, and claws make the Forest Cat an extremely good climber in trees and on rocky slopes. It is highly intelligent, nimble, and an excellent hunter.

From these naturally evolved cats, a group of breeders set out in the 1930s to develop a pedigree breed, starting with some hardy farm cats. As a breed, the Forest Cat gained in popularity during the 1970s and was granted full Championship status in FIFe in 1977.

The ideal show cat differs from the Maine Coon in having hind legs longer than the forelegs, and the standard of points specifies a double coat, which is permitted but not desirable in the American breed.

BREAKDOWN OF 100 SHOW POINTS

EARS: 10 POINTS

Shape and placement.

HEAD: 20 POINTS

General shape, nose, profile, jaw and teeth, chin.

EYE SHAPE: 5 POINTS

BODY: 25 POINTS

Shape, size, bone structure, leg length, and height.

COAT: 25 POINTS

Quality, texture, and length.

TAIL: 10 POINTS

Shape and length.

CONDITION: 5 POINTS

Character and Care

Strong and hardy, the Forest Cat can be very playful while retaining the strongly independent character of its semi-wild ancestors. It enjoys human company and can be very affectionate, but dislikes too much cosseting. The trouble-free coat periodically needs combing through to keep the undercoat in good condition and to clean the flowing tail and full ruff or frill.

KEY CHARACTERISTICS

- **CATEGORY** Longhair.

- **OVERALL BUILD** Large.

- **COAT** Semi-long; a wooly undercoat is covered with a smooth, water-repellent upper coat. The glossy hair covers the back and sides. The cat has a full ruff or frill.

- **HEAD** Triangular, with a long, straight profile and no stop.

- **NOSE** Long and straight.

- **CHIN** Firm.

- **EYES** Large, open, and set slightly obliquely.

- **EARS** Wide-based, with lynx-like tufts, set high, the outer edges of the ears following the lines of the head down to the chin.

- **BODY** Long, strongly built, with solid bone structure.

- **LEGS** Long, the hind legs longer than the forelegs.

- **PAWS** Tufted.

- **TAIL** Long and bushy.

- **COLORS** All colors except chocolate, cinnamon, lilac, and fawn are accepted, though neither the Himalayan pattern nor the Burmese factor is allowed. Type always takes preference over color. No relationship between coat and eye color, but clear eye color is desirable.

SOLID VARIETIES

WHITE
In the Norwegian Forest Cat, any eye color is allowed, regardless of the coat color.

IN THE SOLID-COLORED varieties of the Norwegian Forest Cat, the coat should be sound in color and free from any shadings, markings, or color other than the basic one.

WHITE The coat is pure glistening white; and the nose leather and paw pads are pink.

BLACK The coat is dense coal black, sound from the roots to the tips of the hair; with no sign of rustiness of color on the tips, and no smoke undercoat. The nose leather is black; the pads are black or brown.

BLUE The coat is one even tone of gray-blue from nose to tail tip, and must be sound to the roots. Nose leather and paw pads are blue.

RED The coat is deep, clear, rich, brilliant red without any shading, markings, or ticking. The lips and chin must be the same color as the coat. Nose leather and paw pads are brick red.

CREAM The coat is one even shade of buff cream, without any markings, and must be sound to the roots. Both the nose leather and the paw pads are pink.

NORWEGIAN FOREST CAT
The coat is double, with a weatherproof, wooly undercoat covered by a smooth, almost waterproof top coat.

TABBY VARIETIES

ANY OF THE FOUR tabby patterns are accepted in the Norwegian Forest Cat, and a whole range of colors, except the chocolate and lilac series. Any amount of white on the body is also permitted.

SILVER TABBY The cat has a pale, clear silver base coat with dense black markings; white is allowed around the lips and chin. The nose leather is brick red; the paw pads are black.

BROWN TABBY Brilliant coppery-brown base coat with dense black markings. The backs of the legs from paw to heel are black; white allowed around lips and chin. Nose leather and paw pads are black or brown.

BLUE TABBY The cat has a pale bluish-ivory base coat with very deep blue markings affording good contrast with the base color. There is a warm fawn patina over the whole coat. White is allowed around the lips and chin. The nose leather is old rose; the paw pads are rose.

RED TABBY Red base coat with deep rich red markings; white allowed around lips and chin. Nose leather and paw pads are brick red.

CREAM TABBY The cat has a very pale cream base coat with buff or cream markings sufficiently darker to afford good contrast with the base color. White is allowed around lips and chin. Nose leather and paw pads are pink.

TABBY-AND-WHITE May be silver, brown, blue, red, or cream – with or without white on the face, but with white on the bib, belly, and all four paws; white on one-third of the body overall is desirable. The nose leather and paw pads are as above.

BLUE SILVER TABBY
Any amount of white is permitted on the paws, chest, or underbody, or as a facial blaze.

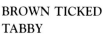

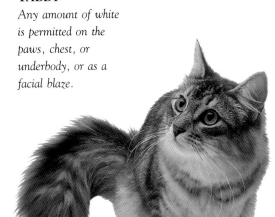

BROWN TICKED TABBY
All tabby patterns are accepted, including the Ticked as seen in this very full-coated cat.

BROWN TABBY
This handsome cat is marked with the Classic tabby pattern which shows clearly on the smooth semi-longhaired cat.

RED SILVER TABBY and WHITE
The addition of silver to other varieties adds to the range of pale, attractive shades.

RED AND WHITE
Although the amounts of white are not specified for this breed, this cat does look even more attractive, having neatly matching white paws and a small bib.

DEVELOPED FROM THE indigenous domestic cat, the Norwegian Forest Cat is found in a wide variety of coat colors and patterns. There is no relationship between coat color and eye color as expected in most other pedigree breeds.

TORTOISESHELL Black with unbrindled patches of red and light red, the patches clearly defined and well broken on body and extremities. A blaze of red on the face is desirable.

CALICO Color as for the Tortoiseshell with or without white on the face, but there must be white on the bib, belly, and all four paws. White on one-third of the body overall is desirable.

BLUE-CREAM The color is blue with clearly defined, unbrindled, well-broken patches of cream on the body and extremities.

BLUE-CREAM-AND-WHITE The color is as defined for the Blue-cream, with or without white on the face, but there must be white on the bib, belly, and all four paws. White on one-third of the body overall is desirable.

BICOLOR Combination of a solid color with white. Color predominates, with white areas located on the face, chest, belly, legs, and feet. Colors are black, blue, red, and cream.

TORTOISESHELL
All colors of torties are accepted in the breed and may be with or without white markings.

SMOKE AND CAMEO VARIETIES

THE LONG COAT OF the Norwegian Forest Cat is particularly attractive in the colors which have a silver undercoat, such as the smoke, shaded, tipped and cameo series in all colors.

CHINCHILLA There is a pure white undercoat, and the coat on the back, flanks, head, and tail is sufficiently tipped with black to give the characteristic sparkling silver appearance. The legs may be slightly shaded with tipping. The chin, ear tufts, stomach, and chest are pure white; eye rims, lips and nose are outlined with black. Nose leather and paw pads are black.

SHADED SILVER There is a white undercoat with a mantle of black tipping shading down the sides, face and tail, the color ranging from dark on the ridge to white on the chin, chest, stomach, and underside of the tail. The legs are the same tone as the face. The general effect is much darker than the Chinchilla. The eye rims, lips, and nose are outlined with black; nose leather is brick red; paw pads are black.

RED SHELL CAMEO There is a white undercoat, and the coat on the back, flanks, head, and tail is sufficiently tipped with red to give the characteristic sparkling appearance. The face and legs may be very slightly shaded with tipping. The chin, ear tufts, stomach, and chest are white; the eye rims, nose leather and paw pads are rose.

RED SHADED CAMEO There is a white undercoat with a mantle of red tipping down the sides, face, and tail, with the color ranging from dark on the ridge to white on the chin, chest, stomach, and underside of the tail. The legs are the same tone as the face. The nose leather and paw pads are black.

BLACK SMOKE There is a white undercoat deeply tipped with black; in repose, the cat appears black; in motion, the white undercoat is clearly apparent. The points and mask are black, with a narrow band of white at the base of the hairs next to the skin. The ruff (frill) and ear tufts are light silver; the nose leather and paw pads are black.

BLUE SMOKE There is a white undercoat deeply tipped with blue; in repose, the cat appears blue; in motion, the white undercoat is clearly apparent. The points and mask are blue, with a narrow band of white hairs next to the skin. The ruff (frill) and ear tufts are white; the nose leather, and paw pads are blue.

RED SMOKE There is a white undercoat deeply tipped with red; in repose, the cat appears red; in motion, the white undercoat is clearly apparent. The points and mask are red, with a narrow band of white hairs next to the skin. The eye rims, nose leather, and paw pads are rose.

BLACK SMOKE

The Forest Cat's eyes should be large and held well opened, set slightly obliquely, and may be of any color.

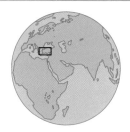

ANGORA

ONE OF THE MOST ANCIENT of cat breeds, originating in Turkey, the Angora was the first of the longhaired cats to reach Europe. In the sixteenth century, a naturalist called Nicholas-Claude Fabri de Peiresc imported several cats into France from Angora (now Ankara) in Turkey. They were described in contemporary literature as "ash-colored dun and speckled cats, beautiful to behold." The cats were bred from, and some of the kittens went to England, where they were highly prized and known as French cats. When another type of long-coated cat arrived in Europe from Persia (now Iran), the Angora and the Persian were intermated quite indiscriminately.

The Persian type gradually superseded the Angora type in popularity, and by the twentieth century the Angora breed was virtually unknown outside its native land.

During the 1950s and 1960s, North America, Britain, and Sweden imported cats from Turkey to start breeding programs for the development of the Angora breed. In the United States, the Turkish Angora was officially recognized and granted championship status by some associations in the early 1970s, but until 1978, the CFA only accepted the white variety. Eventually, however, a wide range of colors was accepted.

Character and Care
Precocious as kittens, Angoras are playful and athletic. They are generally affectionate with their owners, but can be aloof with strangers.

Angoras molt excessively in summer, and the loose hair should be combed out daily. The lack of a fluffy undercoat means that the coat does not become matted.

BREAKDOWN OF 100 SHOW POINTS

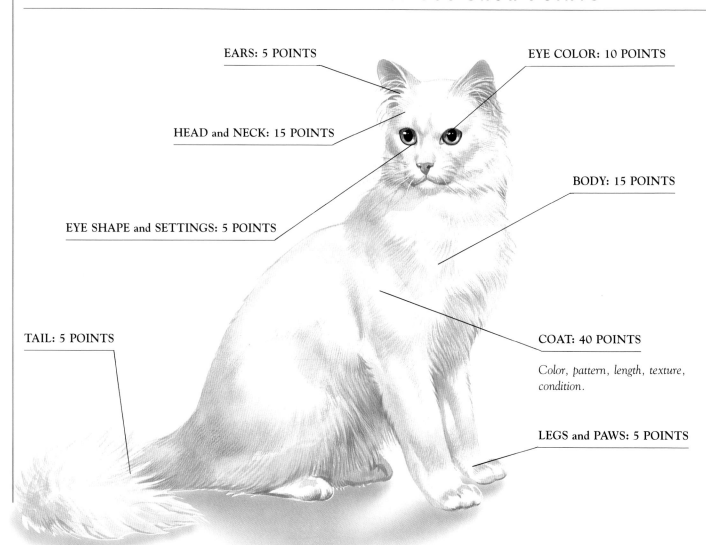

EARS: 5 POINTS

EYE COLOR: 10 POINTS

HEAD and NECK: 15 POINTS

BODY: 15 POINTS

EYE SHAPE and SETTINGS: 5 POINTS

TAIL: 5 POINTS

COAT: 40 POINTS

Color, pattern, length, texture, condition.

LEGS and PAWS: 5 POINTS

KEY CHARACTERISTICS

- **CATEGORY** Longhair.

- **OVERALL BUILD** Medium sized and well-proportioned, with males larger than females.

- **COAT** Medium length, silky and sleek, with no undercoat. Long at the ruff.

- **HEAD** Small to medium in size and wedge-shaped, wide at the top tapering toward the chin.

- **NOSE** Medium length, with a gentle slope and no stop or break.

- **CHIN** Gently rounded, the tip forming a perpendicular line with the nose.

- **EYES** Large, almond shaped, slanting slightly upward.

- **EARS** Long and pointed, wide at the base, well-furred and tufted.

- **BODY** Fine boned, with a light-framed chest and slender torso. Lithe, with the hind part higher than the front.

- **LEGS** Long, with hind legs longer than forelegs.

- **PAWS** Small, round, and dainty with tufts between the toes.

- **TAIL** Long and tapering, wide at the rump and narrow at the tip; well-furred. It is carried horizontally over the body, sometimes touching the head.

- **COLORS** White with amber, blue green, or odd eyes; black, blue, chocolate red, cream, cinamon, caramel, fawn, blue-cream tabby in standard and silver, in any pattern and all colors; tortie, torbie tabby, smokes and shaded in all colors.

PENALTIES

The Angora (Turkish Angora) is penalized for having a kinked or abnormal tail.

DISQUALIFICATION FEATURES
- Persian body type

ANGORA VARIETIES

ODD-EYED WHITE

In the Angora, unlike most other Odd-Eyed cats, one eye should be blue and the other eye green.

IN THE BRITAIN, the Angora has been granted preliminary show status as the longcoated equivalent of the Oriental, the cat called Javanese by the Cat Association of Britain and FIFe of Europe.

WHITE The coat should be pure white with no other coloring, and the nose leather and paw pads pink. There are three sub-varieties – Amber-eyed, Blue-eyed, and Odd-eyed.

BLACK The coloring must be dense coal black, sound from the roots to the tips of the hair and free from any tinge of rust on the tips, or a smoke undercoat. Nose leather is black and paw pads black or brown; eye color is amber.

BLUE The denser shades of blue are preferred, the coat should be one even tone from nose to tail tip with the color sound to the roots. The

nose leather and paw pads are all blue, and the eye color is amber.

RED A deep, rich, clear, brilliant red is required, without shading, markings, or ticking. Lips and chin should be the same color as the coat. Nose leather and paw pads are brick red; the eye color is amber.

CREAM One level shade of buff cream without markings must be attained, with the color sound to the roots. Lighter shades are preferred. Nose leather and paw pads should be pink, and the eye color is amber.

BLUE-CREAM Blue should be the predominant color with patches of solid cream. The patches should be clearly defined and well broken on both body and extremities. The eye color is amber.

TORTOISESHELL Black is the dominant color with unbrindled patches of red and light red. The patches should be clearly defined and well broken on both body and extremities. A blaze of red or light red on the face is desirable. The eye color is amber.

CALICO The coat should be mostly white, with unbrindled patches of black and red, and white predominant on the underparts. Eye color is amber. In the dilute calico, the dominant color is again white, with unbrindled patches this time of blue and cream; white is predominant on the underparts.

BICOLOR Varieties are black and white, blue and white, red and white, or cream and white.

WHITE

The white coat should be free from any staining, and a smudge of color is permitted in kittens but not in adult cats.

LILAC ANGORA

This is an excellent example of the variety, showing very good type and a true lilac coat, which should be as the standard describes – frosty gray with a distinct pinkish tone giving the overall appearance.

The muzzle, chest, legs, feet, and underparts should all be white in each. White under the tail and a white collar are permissible. An inverted V-shaped blaze on the face is desirable. Eye color is amber.

BLACK SMOKE The undercoat is white, deeply tipped with black. In repose the cat appears black, but in motion the white undercoat is clearly apparent. The narrow band of white hairs next to the skin may be seen only when the hair is parted. The mask and points, nose leather, and paw pads are black, and the eye color is amber.

BLUE SMOKE The white undercoat is deeply tipped with blue. The cat in repose appears blue, but in motion the white undercoat is clearly apparent. Blue mask and points with a narrow band of white hairs next to the skin may be seen only when the hair is parted. The mask and points, nose leather, and paw pads are blue, and the eyes amber.

Tabby

The following colors apply to both the Classic and Mackeral tabby patterns.

SILVER TABBY This cat has a pale, clear silver base coat including lips and chin, with dense black markings. Nose leather is brick red and paw pads black. The eyes are green or hazel.

BROWN TABBY The brilliant coppery brown base coat should have dense black markings. Lips and chin should be the same shade as the rings around the eyes, and backs of the legs black from paw to heel. Nose leather is brick red and paw pads black or brown. The eyes are amber.

BLUE TABBY The pale bluish-ivory base coat includes the lips and chin, with very deep blue markings affording a good contrast with the base color. A warm fawn patina should cover the whole coat. Nose leather is old rose, the paw pads rose, and the eyes amber.

RED TABBY The red base coat includes the lips and chin with deep, rich red markings. Nose leather and paw pads are all brick red; the eye color is amber.

BLACK

The jet black coat that is required in this variety is often difficult to produce, particularly in the young cat, for which judges make allowances in the show situation.

TURKISH

THE CAT KNOWN as the Turkish in Britain and the Turkish Van in Europe and the United States was first introduced to Britain and the cat fanciers of the world in 1955 by Laura Lushington. Traveling in the Lake Van district of Turkey, she and a friend were enchanted by these cats and eventually acquired the first breeding pair. Others of the breed were imported into Britain, and the necessary breeding programs were completed in order to apply for official recognition of the cats as a pure breed in their own right. This was achieved in 1969, and the cats attracted considerable attention.

Turkish Van cats were also introduced independently from Turkey directly to the United States, where they are now recognized by some associations.

Character and Care

The first cats imported from Turkey were inclined to be slightly nervous of human contact, but today's Turkish cats generally have affectionate dispositions. They are strong and hardy, and breeders were intrigued by the animals' natural liking for water – they will voluntarily swim if given the opportunity and have no objection to being bathed in preparation for show appearances.

The silky coat has no wooly undercoat, making grooming an easy task.

BREAKDOWN OF 100 SHOW POINTS

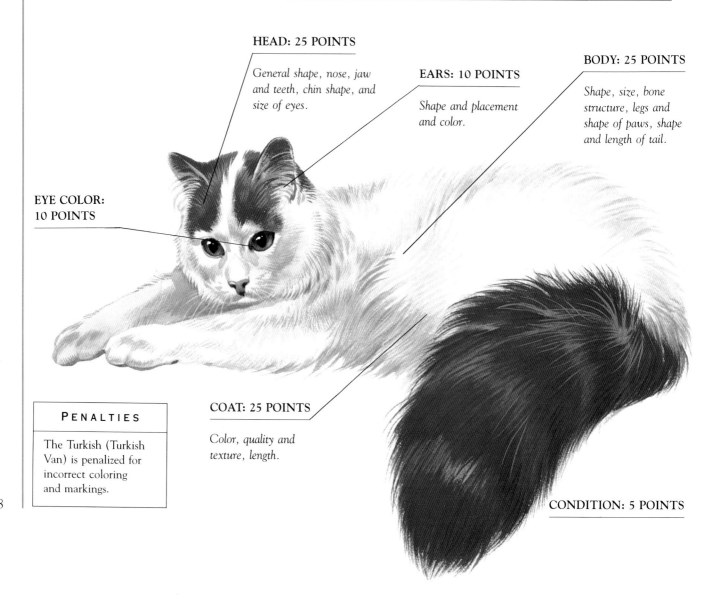

HEAD: 25 POINTS

General shape, nose, jaw and teeth, chin shape, and size of eyes.

EARS: 10 POINTS

Shape and placement and color.

BODY: 25 POINTS

Shape, size, bone structure, legs and shape of paws, shape and length of tail.

EYE COLOR: 10 POINTS

PENALTIES

The Turkish (Turkish Van) is penalized for incorrect coloring and markings.

COAT: 25 POINTS

Color, quality and texture, length.

CONDITION: 5 POINTS

AUBURN TURKISH

The markings of the Turkish Van cat are responsible for the "Van" designation in other varieties which are mostly white, with small and discrete areas of color.

KEY CHARACTERISTICS
● **CATEGORY** Longhair.
● **OVERALL BUILD** Of medium size and heavy build.
● **COAT** Fine and silky, semi-long on body, no wooly overcoat.   **Pattern** Predominantly white, with auburn or cream markings on the face, and a white blaze; the tail is auburn or cream. Small, irregularly placed auburn or cream markings on the body are allowed in an otherwise good specimen.
● **COLORS** Auburn – chalk-white coat with no trace of yellow; auburn markings on face with a white blaze; white ears. Eye rims, nose leather, paw pads, and inside ears are shell pink; eye color is amber (*UK*), plus blue and odd-eyed (*Europe*). Cream – chalk-white coat with no trace of yellow; cream markings on face with a white blaze; white ears. Eye rims, nose leather, paw pads, and inside ears shell pink; eye color amber, blue, and odd-eyed.
● **OTHER FEATURES** Short, blunt head, triangular in shape. Straight nose, of medium length, with firm chin. Eyes are large and oval, set slightly obliquely. Ears are large and well-furred, wide-based with slightly rounded tips, set high and erect on the skull. The body is long, but sturdy and muscular, with medium-length legs and medium-length tail, well-furred but without undercoat. Paws are round and dainty, and well-tufted.

CREAM TURKISH

The cream Turkish cat may have light amber eyes, or blue eyes, and the odd-eyed variety is also accepted where there is one blue eye and the other of light amber.

SHORTHAIRED
BREEDS

BRITISH SHORTHAIR

THIS BREED PROBABLY evolved from domestic cats introduced to the British Isles by the Roman colonists some 2,000 years ago. However, today's pedigree Shorthairs must conform to strict standards of points and differ quite considerably from the common domestic or farm cat.

Shorthairs appeared in substantial numbers in the first cat shows held toward the end of the nineteenth century, then seemed to lose their popularity in favor of the Persian and Angora cats which were specially imported for the show scene.

It was not until the 1930s that a general resurgence of the breed began, and selective breeding produced cats of good type and the desired range of colors. In the early days, solid colors were preferred to the patterned varieties, the most highly prized of all being the blue-gray, sometimes given solitary breed status as the British Blue.

British Shorthairs suffered a setback during World War II, when many owners had to give up breeding pedigree kittens and neutered their cats. In the post-war years, very few pedigree stud males remained, and the Shorthair's type suffered after outcrosses were made with short-haired cats of Foreign type. Matters were redressed during the early 1950s by careful matings with Blue Persians, and within a few generations the British Shorthair was brought up to the exacting standards existing today.

American stock came from the best of the British catteries. At first, the ACFA officially recognized only the blue and black varieties, and the CCA and CFF recognized only the British Blue. In 1976, the ACFA was the first to accept all colors, and it was followed by the remaining associations. In the United States, as in Britain, British Shorthairs are bred only to

BREAKDOWN OF 100 SHOW POINTS

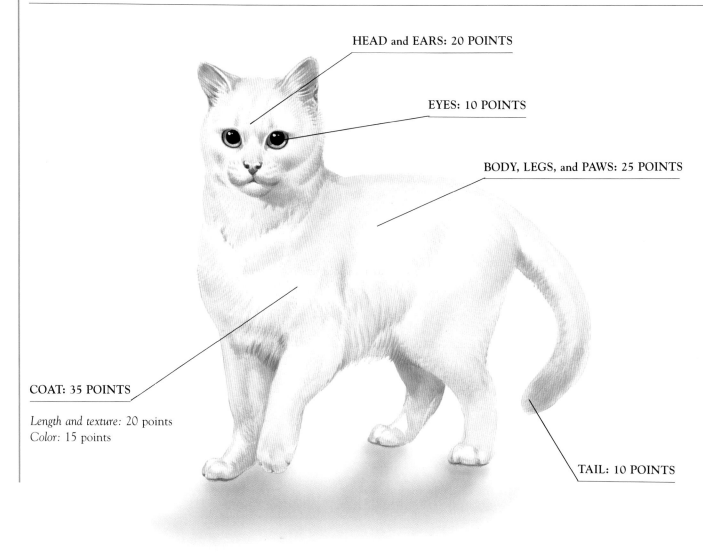

HEAD and EARS: 20 POINTS

EYES: 10 POINTS

BODY, LEGS, and PAWS: 25 POINTS

COAT: 35 POINTS

Length and texture: 20 points
Color: 15 points

TAIL: 10 POINTS

other British Shorthairs, and back-crossing to Persians is no longer allowed.

Character and Care

The typical British Shorthair has a sweet and gentle nature and makes an undemanding, quiet-voiced pet. It is generally calm and intelligent, and readily responds to affection.

Although it has a short coat, this is quite dense and needs regular grooming by brushing and combing right through to the roots every day. It is particularly important to accustom all kittens to this daily procedure from a very early age so that it is not resented later. The eyes and ears should be gently cleaned with a cotton swab whenever necessary, and the coat may be polished with a grooming mitt or a silk scarf.

KEY CHARACTERISTICS

- **CATEGORY** Shorthair.

- **OVERALL BUILD** Large and chunky (not coarse or overweight).

- **COAT** Short and dense, not double or wooly. Firm and resilient to the touch.

- **HEAD** Very broad and round with well-developed cheeks, set on a short, thick neck.

- **NOSE** Medium broad with gentle dip in profile.

- **CHIN** Firm and well-developed.

- **EYES** Large, round, and well opened.

- **EARS** Medium size, broad-based and round-tipped, set far apart.

- **BODY** Medium to large; powerful, with a level back and broad chest.

- **LEGS** Short to medium length, well boned.

- **PAWS** Round.

- **TAIL** Length in proportion to body, thick at the base and tapering to a rounded tip.

- **COLORS** White, black, blue, cream tortoiseshell, blue-cream, black smoke, bicolor, calico, tabby (Classic, Mackerel, and Spotted; all colors) chocolate, lilac, smoke (all colors), tipped (all colors), Himalayan or Colorpoint (all colors).

SOLID VARIETIES

THE MOST POPULAR of the British Shorthairs is the self-coloured British Blue, the color so well complemented by the orange or copper eyes. The Black and the British White have coats more difficult to produce to top show standard.

BLACK SHORTHAIR This is one of the oldest varieties known and is often mismarked with a white locket. In the show specimen, no white hairs are allowed anywhere. The true Black Shorthair must have a shining coat, jet black to the roots and with no rusty tinge. The nose leather is black, the paw pads black or brown, and the eye color gold, orange, or copper with no trace of green.

WHITE SHORTHAIR The White Shorthair of good show type is one of the most striking of British Shorthairs. The coat must be pure white with no sign of yellow tingeing; the nose leather and paw pads are pink. The Blue-eyed White has eyes of a deep sapphire blue and is penalized in the show ring for green rims or flecks in the eye. The Orange-eyed White has deep orange, gold or copper eye color,

BLACK

One of the oldest of the pedigree breeds, the Black British Shorthair is difficult to produce with the required black coat sound to the roots and with no white hairs.

BLUE-EYED WHITE

Occasionally found to be deaf, the Blue-Eyed White is a beautiful variety which, for showing, should have eyes of a deep blue.

CREAM BRITISH SHORTHAIR

The cream variety should be as free from tabby markings as possible and without any white hairs. The eye color may be copper, orange, or gold.

BLUE

The "British Blue" is by far the most popular and best known of all the Shorthairs. Its large round and glowing eyes of copper, orange, or gold perfectly complement the even blue coat.

CREAM SHORTHAIR A fairly rare variety, the Cream Shorthair is difficult to produce to the exacting show standard required without any shadowy tabby markings showing in the rich, light cream coat. There must be no white markings anywhere, and the cream color should be sound to the roots. The nose leather and paw pads are pink, and the eye color is orange or copper.

BLUE SHORTHAIR The British Blue is the most popular variety of the Shorthairs and is certainly the one that most closely meets the very exacting show standard. The coat should be very even in color and of a light to medium blue tone, lighter shades being preferred. No tabby or white markings are allowed anywhere. Nose leather and paw pads are blue, and the eye color is gold, orange, or copper.

BLUE-CREAM SHORTHAIR This is a female-only variety, being a dilute form of Tortoiseshell. It is bred from crosses between Blues and Creams, Creams and Tortoiseshells, or Blues and Tortoiseshells. In Britain, the standard calls for the coat to be softly intermingled with the two shades, but in the United States the variety is required to have a distinctly blue coat with cream patches. Nose leather and paw pads are blue and/or pink, and the eye color should be gold, orange, or copper.

BLUE-CREAM

A dilute variety of the tortoiseshell, the Blue-Cream British should have an evenly intermingled mixture of medium blue-gray and pale cream throughout its coat.

LILAC

A comparatively recent addition to the British Shorthair color list, the Lilac conforms to the usual standard for conformation, and has an even-colored, frosty gray coat with a distinctly pinkish cast.

BICOLOR VARIETIES

CREAM AND WHITE BICOLOR
Symmetry of coloring is desired in the British Bicolor, with not more than half of the cat white.

BLUE AND WHITE BICOLOR
This cat is very evenly marked, with a good shade of medium blue in the basic coat color.

BICOLOR SHORTHAIRS are cats of just two colors: a standard color with white. It is important for the markings to be as symmetrical as possible to present a balanced impression. The cats may be black-and-white, blue-and-white, red-and-white, or cream-and-white, and there must be no tabby markings in the self-colored areas. The markings which make up the self-colored portions should start immediately behind the shoulders around the barrel of the body and include the tail and hind legs, leaving the hind paws white. The ears and mask of the face should be in the self-color, while the shoulders, neck, forelegs and feet, chin, lips, and blaze should be white. The white area also extends as a blaze up the face and over the top of the head in the ideal specimen. The nose leather and paw pads are generally pink, and the eye color is gold, orange, or copper.

The Bicolor is penalized for brindling or tabby markings, and is disqualified if the white areas predominate.

TORTOISESHELL VARIETIES

BLACK AND RED markings, both dark and light, should be equally balanced over the cat's head, body, legs, and tail. Colors should be brilliant, free from blurring, brindling, and tabby patches, and with no white markings. A red blaze down the face is desired. The nose leather and paw pads should be pink and/or black. Eye color is gold, orange, or copper (hazel is also allowed by some associations).

This variety is penalized for brindling, tabby markings, unequal balance of color, and unbroken color on the paws, and is disqualified for any white markings.

TORTOISESHELL
Here the characteristic black and red colors are intermingled evenly.

CHOCOLATE TORTIE
Warm chocolate mixed with red and light red make up the bright coloring of the chocolate-tortoiseshell coat.

LILAC TORTIE
In the lilac tortoiseshell, there is an admixture of lilac and pale cream which produces a pleasing pastel effect over the body.

CALICO VARIETIES

OFTEN CALLED THE calico cat, the Tortoise-shell-and-white is very difficult to breed to top exhibition standard. It should be equally balanced in black and red, both light and dark on white. The colors must be brilliant, and the cat must have no sign of brindling or tabby markings. The patching should cover the top of the head, the ears and cheeks, the back and tail, and part of the flanks. There should be a white blaze down the face. The nose leather and paws are pink and/or black, and the eye color is gold, orange, or copper (hazel is also allowed by some associations).

This variety is penalized for brindling, tabby markings, unbroken color on the paws, and unequal markings, and it is disqualified if the white areas predominate.

CALICO

This cat is quite rare in the show rings since it is difficult to breed.

BLUE TORTIE AND WHITE

Bold areas of blue and cream patch the coat of this attractive cat and are highlighted by the white markings. In this variety, the eye color can be copper, orange, or gold.

TABBY VARIETIES

**BROWN
SPOTTED**

*Clearly defined black
spots on a brown
ground color is the
requirement for this
variety.*

THERE ARE THREE acceptable tabby patterns in
the British Shorthair – the Classic, the Mackerel, and the Spotted. All three are found in a
wide variety of colors, only some of which are
recognized for show purposes, although associations around the world differ considerably in
their rules. Tabby varieties are penalized for
incorrect eye color; white anywhere; and
incorrect tabby markings.

Patterns

In the Classic tabby, markings should be dense
and clearly defined; the legs evenly barred with
bracelets and the tail evenly ringed, and the cat
should have several unbroken necklaces on the
neck and upper chest. On the head, frown
marks form a letter "M," and an unbroken line
runs back from the outer corner of each eye.
There are swirl markings on the cheeks, and
vertical lines run over the back of the head to
the shoulder markings, which resemble a butterfly, with both upper and lower wings distinctly outlined and marked with dots within
the outlines. The back is marked with a spine

**RED MACKEREL
TABBY**

*Lines run down from
the spine in the
Mackerel Tabby, but
the markings on the
head are the same as
for the other tabbies.*

**BROWN CLASSIC
TABBY**

*This chunky British cat
shows the Classic
Tabby pattern, which
is also known as the
Marbled or Blotched
Tabby.*

BLUE SPOTTED

In the Blue Spotted, the pattern consists of blue-gray spots on a lighter background, with enough difference in color to afford a good contrast between the markings and the base coat.

line and a parallel line on each side, all three lines being separated by stripes of the coat's ground colour. A large solid blotch on each side of the body should be encircled by one or more unbroken rings, and the side markings should be the same on both sides of the body. A double row of "vest" buttons should run down the chest and under the stomach.

In the Mackerel tabby, markings should be dense and clearly defined and all resemble narrow pencil lines. The legs should be evenly barred with narrow bracelets, and the tail barred. There are several distinct narrow necklaces around the neck. The head is barred, with a distinct "M" on the forehead, and unbroken lines running back from the eyes. More lines run back over the head to meet the shoulder markings. Along the spine the lines run together forming a dark saddle, and fine, pencil-like markings run down each side of the body from the spine. Clear spotting is essential

in the Spotted tabby: the spots can be round, oval, oblong, or rosette-shaped. The head markings should be the same as those required for the Classic tabby. The legs should be clearly spotted, and the tail spotted or with broken rings. Spotted cats are penalized when the spots are not distinct, and for having bars, except on the head.

SILVER SPOTTED

Perhaps the clearest of all the spotted coats is that of the Silver, which has dense black markings on a background of very pale silvery-white hair.

RED TABBY
This richly colored Red Tabby has the typical Classic pattern on a slightly lighter red base. The desired unbroken "necklaces" can be seen quite clearly around the cat's neck.

SILVER TABBY
Like the Silver Spotted, the Silver Tabby's coat pattern shows up extremely well in black on pale silver. The necklaces and eye lines are easy to identify in this picture.

Colors

BROWN TABBY Ground color should be rich sable or brown with dense black markings. Lips and chin should be the same as the rings around the eyes. Backs of the legs should be black from heel to paw. Nose leather must be brick red and the paw pads black or brown. Eye color is gold, orange, or copper. (Some associations also allow green or hazel eye color.)

RED TABBY Ground color is red, including lips and chin. Markings are a deep, rich red, quite distinct from the ground color. Nose leather and paw pads are brick red. Eye color is gold, orange, or copper. (Some associations also accept hazel eye color.)

SILVER TABBY Ground color is a pale clear silver, including lips and chin, and markings are dense black. Nose leather is brick red; paw pads black. Eye color may be green or hazel.

BLUE TABBY Accepted by some associations. Ground color, including lips and chin, should be pale bluish-ivory, and markings a very deep blue, affording good contrast with the ground color. There should be an overall warm fawn patina. Nose leather is old rose; paw pads rose. Eye color is gold or copper.

CREAM TABBY Accepted by some associations. For this variety the ground color, including lips and chin, is very pale cream. Markings are of buff or cream sufficiently darker than the ground color to afford good contrast, while still remaining in the dilute color range. Nose leather and paw pads are pink. Eye color may be gold or copper.

BLUE TABBY
In dilute varieties like this blue tabby, the pattern is more diffused.

RED SILVER TABBY
The attractive base color of a pale silvery cream is a warm-toned color.

TORBIE
In the Torbie, the tabby pattern is patched with red, light red, or cream, depending on the main color of the cat's markings. This cat is a Tortie Silver Tabby.

OTHER VARIETIES

SMOKE-PATTERNED CATS are of standard feline colors, but instead of the color being sound to the roots, the undercoat is white or silver. In repose the cat at first appears to be self-colored, but in motion the white or silver undercoat is apparent, giving a shot-silk appearance. In each sub-variety, the nose leather, paw pads, and eye color required is the same as for that of the relevant self-color. British Shorthair Smoke cats are bred in a variety of colors, but the various associations each have a limited range of those which are officially recognized.

BLACK SMOKE The white or silver undercoat is deeply tipped with black. In repose the cat appears black; in motion the pale undercoat is clearly apparent. The nose leather and paw pads are both black, and the eye color may be either gold or copper.

BLUE SMOKE The undercoat is white or silver, deeply tipped with blue. The cat in repose appears blue; but as with the black, in motion the pale undercoat is clearly apparent. Nose leather and paw pads are blue, and the eye color may be gold or copper.

COLOR POINTED

The general type of this group of Shorthairs is the same for the British Shorthair. A range of points colors is accepted including the Lilac Point.

RED COLORPOINT

The mask, ears, legs, and tail should be clearly defined and well-matched.

CREAM COLORPOINT

There should be good contrast between the points and the body color, and any shading on the body should be of the same tone as the points.

BLUE CREAM COLORPOINT

Although the standard of points requires eye color in the Colorpoint to be a clear definite blue, this has proved difficult to achieve in most varieties.

BLACK TIPPED SHORTHAIR

A genetically silver variety, the color is restricted to the very tips of the hairs of the coat, while the undercoat is so pale that it appears to be pure white.

LILAC CREAM COLORPOINT

Also called the Lilac Tortie, this is a very ethereal color, the points being delicately mingled shades of palest lilac and delicate cream.

CHARTREUX

NATIVE TO FRANCE, the Chartreux is said to have been bred exclusively by Carthusian monks as long ago as the sixteenth century. The monks lived in the monastery near the town of Grenoble, world-famous for its unique liqueur, known as Chartreuse. The naturalist Georges Louis Buffon's work *Histoire Naturelle*, published in 1756, records details of the self-blue feline, and in the 1930s a French veterinarian suggested that the breed should have its own scientific name, *Felis catus cartusianorum*. Today's Chartreux should not be confused with the British Blue or the European Shorthaired Blue. It is massively built, with a very distinctive jowled head, more pronounced in the male than in the female, and is a blue-only breed.

Character and Care

Self-assured and affectionate, the Chartreux has always been considered a cat for the connoisseur. It is quiet-voiced and will happily live confined to the house. The dense coat needs regular combing to keep the wooly undercoat in good condition, and brushing enhances the way in which the coat stands away from the body – a breed characteristic.

BREAKDOWN OF 100 SHOW POINTS

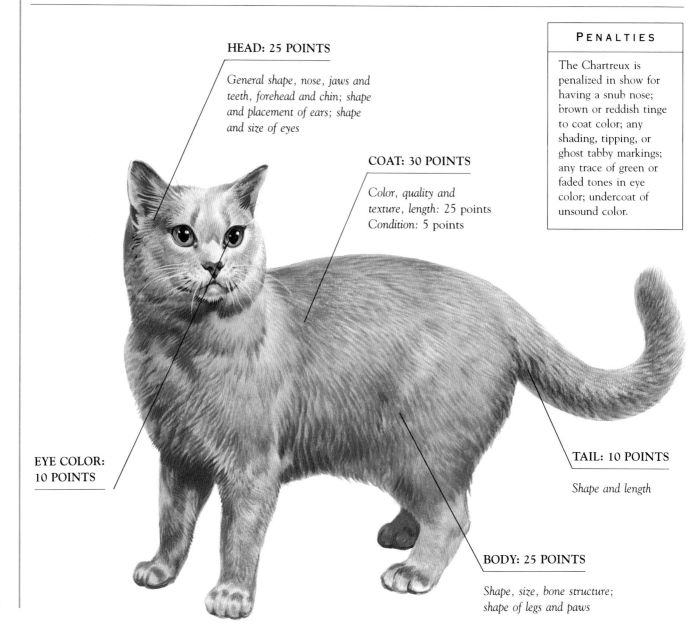

HEAD: 25 POINTS

General shape, nose, jaws and teeth, forehead and chin; shape and placement of ears; shape and size of eyes

COAT: 30 POINTS

Color, quality and texture, length: 25 points
Condition: 5 points

PENALTIES

The Chartreux is penalized in show for having a snub nose; brown or reddish tinge to coat color; any shading, tipping, or ghost tabby markings; any trace of green or faded tones in eye color; undercoat of unsound color.

EYE COLOR: 10 POINTS

TAIL: 10 POINTS

Shape and length

BODY: 25 POINTS

Shape, size, bone structure; shape of legs and paws

The strong head and broad skull of the blue cat known as the Chartreux.

KEY CHARACTERISTICS

- **CATEGORY** Shorthair.

- **OVERALL BUILD** Medium to large, firm and muscular.

- **COAT** Dense and with slightly wooly undercoat; double coat makes the hair stand out from the body; glossy appearance.

- **COLOR** Any shade of blue from pale blue-gray to deep blue-gray, paler shades preferred. Uniform tone essential.

- **OTHER FEATURES** A wide head, with a narrow flat plane between the ears, and wide jowls. The nose is broad and straight, and the chin firm and well developed. Eyes are large and open, not too rounded and with the outer corner slightly uptilted; eye color is vivid deep yellow to vivid deep copper. The most intense color is preferred. Ears are medium sized, set high on the head and slightly flaring, giving an alert expression. The body is solid and muscular with a broad chest; the legs are strong, medium length in proportion to the body. Paws are large, and the tail is medium length in proportion to the body; it may taper and has a rounded tip.

CHARTREUX

One of the true blue cats of the world, the Chartreux is a massive breed with a very gentle nature and a quiet voice.

MANX

LEGENDS AND FAIRY-TALES explaining the origins of this unique tailless breed abound, but modern science agrees that its appearance is due to a mutant dominant gene. The original mutation must have occurred many years ago, for Manx cats have been known since 1900, with a specialist breed club being first established in Britain in 1901.

Although it is an old breed, Manx cats remain rare. The females produce small litters as a direct result of the gene for taillessness. This factor is a semi-lethal gene, and the homozygous Manx – one that inherits the tailless gene from both parents – dies within the womb at an early stage of fetal development. The Manx that is born alive is the heterozygote – one that inherits only one gene for tail-

lessness, the other member of the gene pair being for a normal tail. Breeders usually cross tailless Manx with normal-tailed Manx offspring to retain the correct body type.

Character and Care

Manx cats are highly intelligent, playful and affectionate, and make ideal and unusual pets. A good specimen generally takes top awards in show when competing against other breeds, particularly if it is easy to handle and performs wells for the judges.

The Manx's double coat repays good feeding and regular grooming. It should be combed through to the roots over the entire body and given a final sheen by polishing with the hands, a grooming mitt, or a silk scarf.

BREAKDOWN OF 100 SHOW POINTS

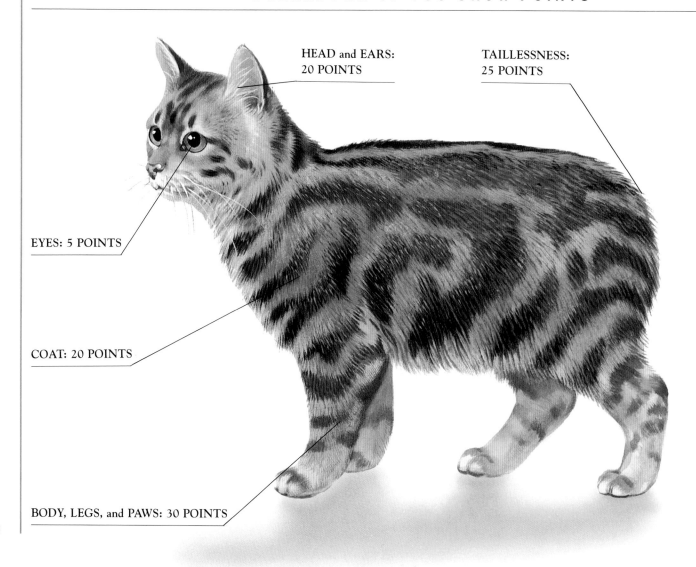

HEAD and EARS:
20 POINTS

TAILLESSNESS:
25 POINTS

EYES: 5 POINTS

COAT: 20 POINTS

BODY, LEGS, and PAWS: 30 POINTS

KEY CHARACTERISTICS

- **CATEGORY** Shorthair.

- **OVERALL BUILD** Medium sized with a general impression of roundness.

- **COAT** *Manx* Short, dense, and double, giving a padded quality due to the comparatively long, open outer coat and the close, cottony undercoat. *Cymric* Of medium length, with close dense undercoat and longer outer coat standing away from the body; full around the neck and on the breeches; tufted ears and toes.

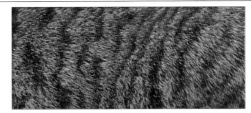

- **HEAD** Round, though slightly longer than it is broad, with a rounded forehead, prominent cheeks, and a jowly appearance. The definite whisker break enhances large, round whisker pads and the muzzle is well-developed.

- **NOSE** In profile there is a gentle nose dip.

- **CHIN** Firm and strong.

- **EYES** Large, round, and full.

- **EARS** Medium size, set wide apart, and turned slightly outward.

- **BODY** Solidly muscled and compact with sturdy bone structure. The chest is broad and the back short, forming a smooth, continuous arch from the shoulders to the rump, where it curves to give the desirable round look.

- **LEGS** The legs and feet are heavily boned. The hind legs are much longer than the forelegs, causing the rump to be higher than the shoulders in the standing cat.

- **PAWS** Neat and round.

- **TAIL** Taillessness is absolute in the perfect Manx, with a definite hollow at the end of the spine where, in a tailed cat, the tail would begin. A rise of bones at the end of the spine is not always penalized, depending on the amount of bone present.

- **COLORS** All colors and patterns are acceptable with the exception of the Himalayan (Siamese) coat pattern.

PENALTIES

The Manx cat is severely penalized in the show ring if the judge is unable to make it stand or walk properly.

DISQUALIFICATION FEATURES
- poor physical condition
- the incorrect number of toes
- color or pattern indicates hybridization

The cat is transferred from the Manx breed class to that for Any Other Varieties if it has long or silky fur, or there is a definite, visible tail joint.

MANX VARIETIES

THE MANX IS accepted in the following color varieties by most American associations. Each of the varieties listed has identical color requirements to its equivalent in the American Shorthair, with the exception of eye color. In American Shorthair varieties with brilliant gold eye color, the Manx should have eyes of brilliant copper.

The accepted varieties are: Black; Blue; Red; Cream; Tortoiseshell; Blue-cream; Calico; Dilute Calico; Chinchilla; Shaded Silver; Black Smoke; Blue Smoke; Classic and Mackerel Tabby in the following colors: Brown Tabby; Blue Tabby; Red Tabby; Cream Tabby; Cameo Tabby; Silver Tabby; Patched Tabby in Brown, and Blue and Silver.

Other Manx Colors

Any other colour or pattern with the exception of those showing hybridization resulting in the the Himalayan pattern. The eye color should be appropriate to the predominant color of the cat.

**TORBIE &
WHITE MANX**

This adorable little Manx kitten has adopted the typical natural stance of the breed. Manx kittens are precocious and very playful and inquisitive, making wonderful pets.

**RED SPOTTED
MANX**

All colors are accepted in the Manx except those in the Himalayan or Siamese pattern.

**BROWN TABBY &
WHITE MANX**
*All tabby patterns are
allowed, including
those with the addition
of white areas.
Taillessness is a high-
scoring feature.*

**BLUE TORTIE &
WHITE MANX**
*The solid compact
body and a short back
makes the typical
Manx a sturdy,
compact cat, and the
hind legs are longer
than the forelegs. The
rump is firm and
rounded.*

CYMRIC

IN THE LATE 1960S breeders of Manx cats in the United States were intrigued to discover that long-coated kittens occasionally appeared in otherwise normal litters from their Manx queens. Although there were no longhaired cats in any of the pedigrees, it is possible that the recessive gene for causing long hair had been inherited from some of the tailed short-haired cats used as outcrosses in past generations. Although the first reaction of the breeders was to let such kittens go as neutered pets, it was decided that the variety could be developed as a separate, very attractive breed in its own right. When choosing a name for the breed, some associations preferred Longhaired Manx, while others accepted Cymric (pronounced koom-rik), the Welsh word for "Welsh." The breed is recognized by some associations, and except for the coat, has the same standard requirements for show purposes as the Manx cat. The coat is of medium length, soft and full, giving a padded, heavy look to the body. The same coat colors and patterns are accepted as for the Manx.

**TORTOISESHELL
CYMRIC**
*The longcoated version
of the Manx cat is not
accepted by all
associations.*

111

SCOTTISH FOLD

A LITTER OF OTHERWISE normal kittens born on a farm in Scotland contained the first Scottish Fold in 1961. A shepherd, William Ross, noticed the kitten with the quaint, folded ears and expressed an interest in acquiring such a cat. Two years later, the mother cat, Susie, gave birth to two kittens with folded ears, and William Ross was given one. A breeding program was begun in Great Britain, but when it was discovered that a small proportion of cats with folded ears also had thickened tails and limbs, the governing registration body banned Scottish Folds from all shows. The British breeders, who were dedicated to breeding only sound cats, resorted to registering their cats in overseas associations, and the main center of activity for the breed switched to the United States. Today's Scottish Fold cats are bred to

British Shorthairs in Britain and to American Shorthairs in the United States, or back to the prick-eared offspring of Folds. The folded ears are due to the action of a single dominant gene, and all Scottish Folds must have at least one fold-eared parent.

Character and Care
The Scottish Fold is a loving, placid, and companionable cat which loves both humans and other pets. The female makes a superb mother, and the kittens are quite precocious.

The short, dense coat is kept in good condition with the minimum of brushing and combing, and the folded ears are kept immaculate by gently cleaning inside the folds with a moistened cotton swab.

BREAKDOWN OF 100 SHOW POINTS

EARS: 30 POINTS

EYES: 15 POINTS

COLOR: 10 POINTS

HEAD: 15 POINTS

TAIL: 20 POINTS

BODY: 10 POINTS

PENALTIES

The Scottish Fold is penalized in the show ring for lacking in type or for having a definite nose break.

DISQUALIFICATION FEATURES
- a kinked or foreshortened tail
- a tail that is lacking in flexibility due to abnormally thick vertebrae

**BLACK & WHITE
SCOTTISH FOLD**
*This cat illustrates the
caplike attitude of the
folded ears in a good
example of this breed.*

CALICO FOLD
*The color requirements
for the Scottish Fold
are the same as for the
American Shorthair.*

**A LONGHAIRED
VARIETY**
*This is one of the
longcoated cats which
have appeared from
time to time in litters
of Scottish Fold
kittens.*

**PATCHED SILVER
TABBY & WHITE**
*The ears of the
Scottish Fold are small
and fold forward and
downward on the top
of the head.*

KEY CHARACTERISTICS

- **CATEGORY** Shorthair.

- **OVERALL BUILD** Medium size, well rounded with medium bone.

- **COAT** Short, dense, and resilient.

- **COLORS** White, black, blue, red, cream, tortoiseshell, calico, dilute calico, blue-cream, chinchilla, shaded silver, shell cameo, shaded cameo, black smoke, blue smoke, cameo smoke, bicolor; Classic and Mackerel Tabby in brown, blue, red, cream, cameo, silver; Patched Tabby in brown, blue, silver; any other color or pattern with the exception of those showing evidence of hybridization resulting in the colors chocolate or lavender, the Himalayan pattern or these combinations with white. The eye color should be appropriate to the coat color. Each variety has identical color requirements to its equivalent variety in the American Shorthair.

- **OTHER FEATURES** Well-rounded head with a firm chin and jaw, and muzzle with well-rounded whisker pads. Short nose with a gentle curve, and with a slight stop at eye level. The ears are small and fold forward and downward, and are set in a caplike fashion to expose a rounded cranium. The ear tips are rounded. The eyes are large and round with a sweet expression. The firm body of medium size has legs of medium bone and neat round paws. The tail is medium to long, flexible and tapering.

113

EUROPEAN SHORTHAIR

THIS SHOW BREED has been naturally developed from the indigenous cat of continental Europe. Its standard of points is similar to that of the British Shorthair, and it is presumed to be totally free of any admixture of other breeds. The first European Shorthairs were descended from cats introduced to Northern Europe by invading armies of Roman soldiers, who brought their cats with them to keep down vermin in their food storage areas.

Character and Care
The European Shorthair is a placid, good-natured breed which makes an ideal family cat. It also accepts the time it spends in the show ring and the demands of being judged with a quiet, dignified tolerance.

The short dense coat is easy to maintain with a few minutes' daily combing to keep the undercoat in good condition. The eyes and ears should be cleaned regularly with a slightly moistened cotton swab.

BREAKDOWN OF 100 SHOW POINTS

EYE COLOR: 10 POINTS

HEAD: 25 POINTS

BODY: 25 POINTS

COAT: 35 POINTS

*Color, markings,
pattern: 25 points
Quality, texture,
length: 10 points*

CONDITION: 5 POINTS

KEY CHARACTERISTICS

- **CATEGORY** Shorthair.

- **OVERALL BUILD** Medium to large (not over-large).

- **COAT** Short and dense, tight and glossy, not wooly.

- **HEAD** Fairly large; it appears round, but is a little longer than its breadth; slightly rounded forehead and skull and well-developed cheeks. Neck muscular and of medium length.

- **NOSE** Medium length and straight.

- **CHIN** Firm.

- **EYES** Round and open, widely separated and set slightly obliquely.

- **EARS** Medium size, slightly rounded at the tips, set upright and well apart.

- **BODY** Robust, strong, and muscular with well-developed chest.

- **LEGS** Medium length, strong and sturdy, narrowing gradually to paws.

- **PAWS** Firm and round.

- **TAIL** Medium length, thick at the base, tapering gradually to a rounded tip.

- **COLORS** White with blue, green, yellow, orange or odd eyes; black, blue, red, cream, black torbie, blue torbie; smoke: black, blue, red, cream, black torbie, blue torbie; non-silver tabby: black, blue, red, cream , black torbie, blue torbie (all accepted in Classic, Mackerel, and Spotted); silver tabby: black, blue, red, cream, black torbie, blue torbie (all accepted in Classic, Mackerel, and Spotted); bicolor: black, blue, red, cream, black torbie, blue torbie (all accepted in van, harlequin, and bicolor).

PENALTIES

The European Shorthair is penalized in the show ring for being too large in overall size or being either too cobby or too slender.

DISQUALIFICATION FEATURES

- hanging jowl pouches
- a definite nose stop
- over-long or wooly appearance to coat
- any signs of crossbreeding in its ancestry

EUROPEAN SHORTHAIR VARIETIES

MANY EUROPEAN SHORTHAIRS have British Shorthair ancestors and are found in a similar range of coat colors and patterns. Tabbies are popular, particulady in the silver range, plus the typy reds and creams, and pretty bluecreams.

EUROPEAN WHITE There are three sub-varieties of the European White, and all must have pure white coats without any sign of yellow tingeing or colored hairs. The first sub-variety should have eyes of deep blue; the second may have either green, yellow, or orange eye color; the third, the White Odd-eyed, has one eye of deep blue and the other eye either green, yellow, or orange.

EUROPEAN SOLID The Solid-colored European may be black, blue, red, or cream. All must have a coat color sound to the roots. The eye color may be green, yellow, or orange.

EUROPEAN TORBIE These patched varieties may be either black and red, giving the Black Torbie, or blue and cream, giving the Blue Torbie. For both, the eye color may be green, yellow, or orange.

EUROPEAN SMOKE Cats in this group have a white or silver undercoat, and the six accepted varieties are Black Smoke, Blue Smoke, Red Smoke, Cream Smoke, Black Torbie Smoke, and Blue Torbie Smoke. All may have either green, yellow, or orange eye color.

Tabby Varieties

The non-silver tabby group may have a coat pattern blotched (also known as the Classic tabby), Mackerel, or Spotted. The six accepted varieties are Black Tabby, Blue Tabby, Red Tabby, Cream Tabby, Black Torbie Tabby, and Blue Torbie Tabby. All may have green, yellow, or orange eye color.

In the silver tabby group, the markings are of the main varietal color etched on a base color of pure pale silver. There should be no ticked hairs or brindling in the pattern. The three tabby patterns – Classic, Mackerel, and Spotted – are accepted, and the six accepted varieties are Black Silver Tabby, Blue Silver Tabby, Red Silver Tabby, Cream Silver Tabby, Black Torbie Silver Tabby, and Blue Torbie Silver Tabby. Eye color may be green, yellow, or orange, but green is preferred.

SILVER SPOTTED EUROPEAN
This typical European Shorthair shows the black version of the silver spotted, which is well-marked on the flanks, but with the pattern tending to form mackerel stripes over the ribs.

Non-tabby Bicolor Varieties

Three patterns are accepted, van, harlequin and bicolor. The markings may be black, blue, red, cream, black torbie, or blue torbie.

In van and harlequin, the eye color may be deep blue, green, yellow, or orange; or odd-eyed with one eye deep blue and the other green, yellow, or orange. In the Bicolor pattern, the eyes may be green, yellow, or orange. For judging purposes, the van and harlequin cats are grouped together by eye color.

Van-patterned cats are basically white, with two colored patches on the head, separated by a white blaze down the nose, and a tail colored from rump to tip. The ears may be colored, but white ears with a pink inner surface to the pinna are preferable; the chest and stomach must be white, but up to three small, irregularly distributed color patches on the body and/or legs are tolerated for judging purposes. There must be no white hairs in the colored areas of the coat.

Tabby Van cats have the same basic requirements and may have patches of any of the three basic tabby patterns – all Tabby Van cats are judged in the same class, regardless of pattern. Torbie Van cats also have the same basic requirements, but have torbie markings on the patched areas.

Nose leather may be pink or as expected for the color of the patterned areas. In the Tabby Van, the nose leather should be pink or pinkish-red outlined with the appropriate color for the patterned areas; in the Torbie Van, the nose leather should be patched with pink.

Harlequin-patterned cats are basically white with solid-colored patches over at least one quarter, but not more than one half, of the body surface. The colored parts should consist of various patches surrounded by white, and there must be no single white hairs present in the colored areas. Tabby and Torbie Harlequin cats are also accepted. The nose leather and paw pads are as for the Van pattern.

The bicolored cat is basically white with colored patches, which must be clearly separated from one another. At least one half, but not more than two-thirds, of the cat must be colored; the color must be even and harmoniously distributed over the cat's body. A white blaze down the face and some white on the back are desirable characteristics. There must be no single white hairs in the colored areas.

The Tabby Bicolor may be either Classic (blotched), Mackerel, or Spotted; the Torbie Bicolor should have large, well-defined patches of clear, bright colors. The nose leather and paw pads are as specified for the Van pattern.

CLASSIC TABBY

The Classic tabby pattern consists of a precise set of clearly defined, dense markings on a paler ground color.

MACKEREL TABBY

A beautiful example of a well-marked Mackerel tabby, this red cat has excellent type, matching the European Shorthair standards of points.

117

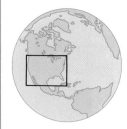

AMERICAN SHORTHAIR

AT THE BEGINNING of the twentieth century, an English cat fancier gave a pedigree Red Tabby Shorthair male to a friend in the United States, to be mated with some of the indigenous shorthaired felines. This cat was registered in the name of Belle and was the first pedigree cat to appear in the records of the Cat Fanciers' Association. Other British cats followed, including a male Silver Tabby named Pretty Correct, and the register grew with listings of "home-grown" cats as well as imports. At first, the breed was called the Shorthair, then its name was changed to Domestic Shorthair, and in 1966 it was renamed the American Shorthair. To gain it credence as a natural American breed, registration bodies accepted applications of non-pedigree cats and kittens conforming to the required breed standards, and in 1971 one such cat won the ultimate accolade of the best American Shorthair of the Year in CFA.

Despite the influence of the introduction of the British Shorthair imports in the breeding programs, the American Shorthair has retained its distinctive characteristics.

Character and Care

A cat of very even temperament, the American Shorthair makes an ideal family pet. It is an intelligent and good-natured animal which gets along well with other breeds and with dogs.

Its short, thick coat is quite easy to keep in good condition with a simple grooming routine. Combing keeps the coat neat, and stroking with the hand or a silk scarf imparts a healthy sheen. The eyes and ears are easily cleaned with a cotton swab, and a scratching post helps the indoor cat to trim its claws.

BREAKDOWN OF 100 SHOW POINTS

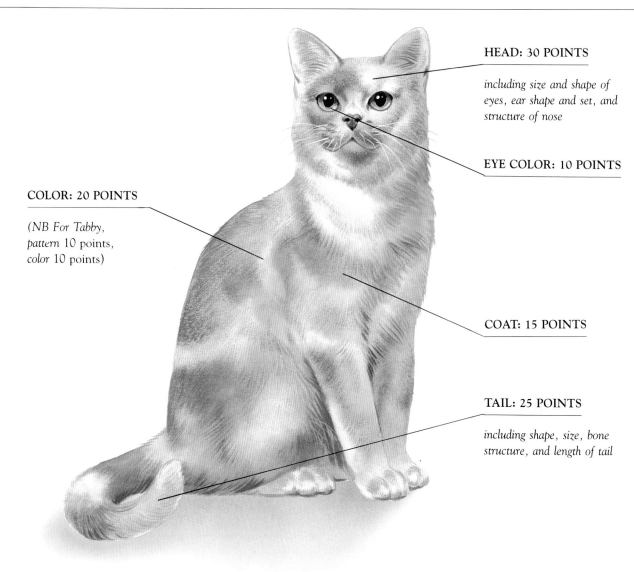

HEAD: 30 POINTS

including size and shape of eyes, ear shape and set, and structure of nose

EYE COLOR: 10 POINTS

COLOR: 20 POINTS

(NB For Tabby, pattern 10 points, color 10 points)

COAT: 15 POINTS

TAIL: 25 POINTS

including shape, size, bone structure, and length of tail

KEY CHARACTERISTICS

- **CATEGORY** Shorthair.

- **OVERALL BUILD** Medium to large, well-knit and powerful, not excessively cobby or rangy.

- **COAT** Short, thick, and even, hard in texture, somewhat heavier and thicker in winter.

- **HEAD** Large, with full cheeks giving an oblong effect, head very slightly longer than it is wide, with square muzzle. Set on a medium-length, muscular neck.

- **NOSE** Medium length.

- **CHIN** Firm and well developed.

- **EYES** Round, wide-set, with a very slight slant to the outer aperture.

- **EARS** Medium size with rounded tips, set wide apart.

- **BODY** Well-knit, powerful body with well-developed chest and heavy shoulders.

- **LEGS** Firm-boned and heavily muscled.

- **PAWS** Firm, full, and rounded paws with heavy pads.

- **TAIL** Medium length, heavy at the base, tapering to an apparently blunt end.

- **COLORS** White, black, blue, red, cream, chinchilla, shaded silver, shell cameo, shaded cameo, black smoke, blue smoke, cameo smoke, tortoiseshell smoke, brown patched tabby, blue patched tabby, silver patched tabby, silver tabby, red tabby, brown tabby, blue tabby, cream tabby, cameo tabby, tortoiseshell, calico, dilute calico, blue-cream, bicolor, van bicolor, van calico, van blue-cream-and-white.

PENALTIES

The American Shorthair is penalized in the show ring for excessive cobbiness or ranginess in conformation; for obesity or boniness; or for having a very short tail.

DISQUALIFICATION FEATURES

- long or fluffy fur
- a kinked or abnormal tail
- a deep nose break in profile
- the incorrect number of toes.

AMERICAN SHORTHAIR VARIETIES

AMERICAN SHORTHAIR

Developed from the American domestic "working" cat, the American Shorthair has been refined and standardized into an attractive and viable breed of show cat in a wide variety of coat colors and patterns.

IN THE CFA STANDARD of points, the American Shorthair is lovingly described. It says that some naturalists believe the breed to be the original domestic cat, which has, for centuries, adapted itself willingly and cheerfully to the needs of man, without allowing itself to become effete, or its natural intelligence to diminish.

The standard goes on: "Its hunting instinct is so strong that it exercises the skill even when well provided with food. This is our only breed of true working cat ... This is a cat lithe enough to stalk its prey, but powerful enough to make the kill easily. Its reflexes are under perfect control. Its legs are long enough to cope with any terrain, and heavy and muscular enough for high leaps. The face is long enough to permit easy grasping by the teeth with jaws so powerful they can close against resistance. Its coat is dense enough to protect from moisture, cold, and superficial skin injuries, but short enough and of sufficiently hard texture to resist matting or entanglement when slipping through heavy vegetation. No part of the anatomy is so exaggerated as to foster weakness. The general effect is that of the trained athelete, with all muscles rippling easily beneath the skin, the flesh lean and hard, and with great latent power held in reserve."

Because the American Shorthair was developed from domestic cats in all colors and coat patterns, which were crossed with show-quality imported British Shorthairs, today's cats are seen in a wide variety of accepted coats.

The best known and most popular of the American Shorthair varieties is undoubtedly the silver tabby, with the Classic, Marbled, or Spotted pattern being the favorites among fanciers. Other tabby colors are also very popular, but each of the accepted varieties has its own following of ardent fans.

TABBY VARIETIES

AMERICAN SHORTHAIR TABBY varieties may have the Classic or Mackerel pattern. In the Classic tabby, markings should be dense and clearly defined, the legs evenly barred with bracelets and the tail evenly ringed; and the cat should have several unbroken necklaces on the neck and upper chest. On the head, frown marks form a letter "M," and an unbroken line runs back from the outer corner of each eye. There are swirl markings on the cheeks, and vertical lines run over the back of the head to the shoulder markings, which resemble a butterfly, with both upper and lower wings distinctly outlined and marked with dots within the outlines. The back is marked with a spine line and a parallel line on each side, with all three lines separated by stripes of the coat's ground color. A large solid blotch on each side of the body should be encircled by one or more unbroken rings, and the side markings should be the same on both sides of the body. A double row of "vest" buttons should run down the chest and under the stomach.

In the Mackerel tabby, markings should be dense and clearly defined and all resemble narrow pencil lines. The legs should be evenly barred with narrow bracelets, and the tail barred. There are several distinct narrow necklaces around the neck. The head is barred, with a distinct "M" on the forehead and unbroken lines running back from the eyes. More lines run back over the head to meet the shoulder markings. Along the spine, the lines run together forming a dark saddle, and fine, pencil-like markings run down each side of the body from the spine.

BLUE TABBY Base color of coat for the blue tabby, including lips and chin, is pale bluish-ivory with very deep blue markings. The whole coat color has warm fawn overtones. Nose leather "old rose" in color; paw pads are rose, and the eye color is brilliant gold.

BLUE TABBY AMERICAN

This classic tabby with its typical full-cheeked face is showing a good example of the "M" on the forehead, formed by the clearly marked frown lines.

**MACKEREL
TABBY**

*In the mackerel tabby,
the body markings take
the form of clear
narrow pencil lines
running down from the
spine and with narrow
bracelets on the legs.*

CLASSIC TABBY

*The classic, blotched,
or marbled tabby has
markings in a
standardized patterns
on the head, body,
legs, and tail, which
show judges assess with
great care when selecting
the final winners.*

BROWN TABBY Base color of coat is a brilliant coppery brown with dense black markings. Lips and chin should be the same shade as the rings around the eyes, and backs of legs black from paw to heel. Nose leather is brick red; paw pads black or brown. Eye color is brilliant gold.

RED TABBY Base color of coat, including lips and chin, is red with deep rich red markings. Nose leather and paw pads are brick red and the eye color brilliant gold.

CREAM TABBY Base color of coat, including lips and chin, is very pale cream with buff or cream markings sufficiently darker than the base color to afford good contrast. Nose leather and paw pads are pink, and the eye color is brilliant gold.

CAMEO TABBY Base color of coat is off-white with red markings. Nose leather and paw pads are rose-colored, and the eye color is brilliant gold.

CAMEO TABBY

The Cameo is a soft and delicate color. This Classic tabby exhibits the intricacies of the pattern on the sides and flanks, and shows good contrast between the colors of the base coat and markings.

RED TABBY

This fine cat is very well-marked in the Classic pattern, and the red color of both the base coat and the markings is correctly defined.

123

BROWN TORBIE
The tortoiseshell tabbies are often called "torbies" for convenience, and in the United States some associations refer to the coloration as patched tabby.

SILVER TABBY
Perhaps the most striking of all the tabbies is the Classic or marbled silver tabby with its dense black markings clearly etched on a pale silver base coat.

SILVER TABBY Base color, including lips and chin, is pale clear silver with dense black markings. Nose leather brick red, paw pads black, and eye color may be green or hazel.

PATCHED TABBY or TORBIE The Patched Tabby or Torbie is similar to the established varieties of tabby, but with the addition of patches of red and light red, or cream.

BROWN PATCHED TABBY Base color of coat is brilliant coppery brown with Classic or Mackerel markings of dense black and patches of red and/or light red clearly defined on both body and extremities; a blaze of red or light red on the face is desirable. Lips and chin to be the same shade as the rings around the eyes; the eye color is brilliant gold.

BLUE PATCHED TABBY Base color of coat, including lips and chin, is pale bluish-ivory, with Classic or Mackerel markings of very deep blue and patches of cream clearly defined on both body and extremities; a blaze of cream on the face is desirable, and warm fawn overtones suffuse the whole body. The eye color is brilliant gold or hazel.

SILVER PATCHED TABBY Base color, including lips and chin, is pale clear silver with Classic or Mackerel markings of dense black and patches of red and/or light red clearly defined on both body and extremities; a blaze of red and/or light red on the face is desirable. Eye color may be hazel or brilliant gold.

BLUE TORBIE
Still clearly marked, but with paler coloring, the blue patched tabby or torbie is the dilute version of the brown torbie, having blue and cream markings instead of black and red.

125

AMERICAN WIREHAIR

I N VERMONT, IN 1966, one of a litter of farm kittens was born with an unusual sparse and wiry coat. An experienced cat breeder acquired the kitten and one of its plain-coated litter-mates and sent hair samples from both for analysis by a British expert in feline genetics. The coat was of a different type to anything previously encountered in the domestic cat, and a breeding program was soon established to develop the wirehaired trait.

The first wirehaired cat was a red and white male named Adam. He was first mated to his normal-coated litter-mate, and then to other unrelated shorthaired cats, and from these beginnings a new breed was born. All Amer-

ican Wirehair cats are descended from Adam, and breeding stock has been very carefully selected over the years to guarantee refinement and viability of the breed. Championship status was granted by the CFA in 1977.

Character and Care
The Wirehair is said by its owners to rule the home and cats of other breeds with an "iron paw," but to make a devoted parent. They are affectionate and playful, with a strongly independent character.

The unusual wiry coat is easy to maintain in peak condition by correct feeding and needs a minimum of grooming.

BREAKDOWN OF 100 SHOW POINTS

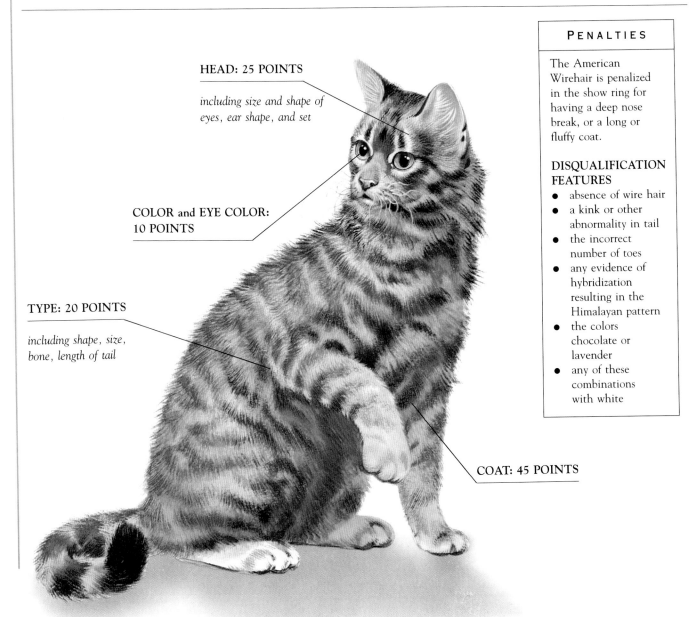

HEAD: 25 POINTS

including size and shape of eyes, ear shape, and set

COLOR and EYE COLOR: 10 POINTS

TYPE: 20 POINTS

including shape, size, bone, length of tail

COAT: 45 POINTS

PENALTIES

The American Wirehair is penalized in the show ring for having a deep nose break, or a long or fluffy coat.

DISQUALIFICATION FEATURES
- absence of wire hair
- a kink or other abnormality in tail
- the incorrect number of toes
- any evidence of hybridization resulting in the Himalayan pattern
- the colors chocolate or lavender
- any of these combinations with white

KEY CHARACTERISTICS

- **CATEGORY** Wirehair.

- **OVERALL BUILD** Medium to large, with medium bone. Males larger than females.

- **COAT** Springy, dense, and resilient, feels coarse and hard. The hairs are crimped and wiry, hooked at the tips. The facial hairs and whiskers are crimped and often set at odd angles.

- **COLORS** Requirements as for the American Shorthair (see pages 146–153). White, black, blue, red, cream, tortoiseshell, calico, blue-cream, dilute calico, chinchilla, shaded silver, shell cameo, shaded cameo, black smoke, blue smoke, cameo smoke, bicolor; Classical or Mackerel tabby in brown, blue, red, cream, cameo, silver.

- **OTHER FEATURES** Round head with prominent cheekbones and a well-developed muzzle with a slight whisker break. Nose shows a gentle, concave curve in profile. The chin is firm, and the eyes are large, round, bright and clear, set wide apart, with a slightly tilted aperture. The ears are medium sized with rounded tips, set wide apart on the head. Body is medium to large with a level back and well-rounded rump. Legs are well muscled and paws oval and compact. Length of tail in proportion to body, tapering from the rump to a rounded tip, neither blunt nor pointed.

BLACK AND WHITE
This cat is very well marked and with an inverted "V" on the forehead and the white area continuing right over the chin onto the chest.

AMERICAN WIREHAIR
All colors accepted for the American Shorthair are accepted in the Wirehair.

EXOTIC SHORTHAIR

I N THE DEVELOPMENT of British and American Shorthairs, and during the introduction of alternative color factors in the Persians, breeders occasionally mated together pedigree cats of longhaired and shorthaired varieties. This was generally done as a single exercise, the offspring being back-crossed to the main breed in successive generations to strengthen the desired traits.

During the 1960s, cats of mixed Shorthair and Persian lineage were, with the approval of the board of the CFA, given the breed name Exotic Shorthair. The breed is, in essence, a short-coated version of the typical Persian, with the conformation of the latter, but the added bonus of a coat that is relatively easy to

care for. The coat stands out from the body and is longer than that of the British or American Shorthair cat breeds.

Character and Care

In temperament the Exotic Shorthair is quiet, gentle, and placid. It is an ideal show cat, easy to prepare for the show ring, and enjoys being handled and admired.

The medium-length coat is quite easy to comb through, and being groomed from the tail toward the head encourages the plush fur to stand away from the body. Body condition and shining fur is achieved by correct feeding, and the eyes and ears are kept immaculate by gentle cleaning with a cotton swab.

BREAKDOWN OF 100 SHOW POINTS

HEAD: 30 POINTS

including size and shape of the eyes; ear shape and set

EYE COLOR: 10 POINTS

COLOR: 20 POINTS

COAT: 20 POINTS

TYPE: 20 POINTS

including shape, size, bone, and length of tail

KEY CHARACTERISTICS

- **CATEGORY** Shorthair.

- **OVERALL BUILD** Medium to large, cobby.

- **COAT** Medium length, dense and plush, soft-textured, standing well away from the body due to its density, never flat or close-lying.

- **HEAD** Round and massive, with great depth of skull, set on a short, thick neck. Round face, full cheeks, broad and powerful jaws.

- **NOSE** Short and stubby with a definite "break."

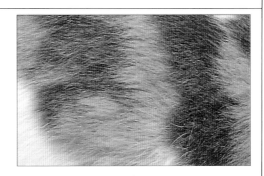

- **CHIN** Full and well developed.

- **EYES** Large, round, and set wide apart.

- **EARS** Small, round-tipped, set wide and low on the head.

- **BODY** Cobby, with a deep chest, massive shoulders and rump and a level back.

- **LEGS** Short and thick.

- **PAWS** Large and round.

- **TAIL** Short.

- **COLORS** White (blue eyed and orange red), black, blue, chocolate, lilac, red, cream: tabby in Classic or Mackerel pattern: silver, brown, blue chocolate, lilac, red, cream: torbie tabby: black, chocolate, lilac: torbie, blue-cream, chocolate tortie, lilac-cream. Calico, blue calico, chocolate calico, lilac calico; bicolor and Van Bicolor and Tricolor: any recognized color with white; spotted tabby: brown, blue chocolate, lilac, red, cream, silver; smoke: any recognized color with silver-white undercoat; tipped: any recognized color with white undercoat and color restricted to very tips of hair.

PENALTIES

DISQUALIFICATION FEATURES

- undesirable white markings such as a locket
- a kink or other abnormality in the tail
- the incorrect number of toes

SOLID VARIETIES

CREAM EXOTIC
The coat of the Exotic Shorthair is very dense and plush, soft in texture, and stands out and away from the body.

BLUE EXOTIC
The head type of the Exotic Shorthair is almost identical to that of a show-standard Persian.

SELF-COLORED EXOTIC cats are bred to a very exacting standard and are penalized at shows for having incorrect or extremely pale eye colors or for flecks of incorrect color in either of the eyes' irises. Oriental or almond-shaped eyes or those set on a slant are also unacceptable.

WHITE The color is pure, glistening white with pink nose leather and paw pads. Eye color is deep blue or brilliant copper. Odd-eyed Whites should have one blue and one copper eye of equal color intensity.

BLACK The dense coal-black coat should be sound from roots to tips of fur. Nose leather is black and paw pads black or brown. Eye color is brilliant copper.

BLUE An even tone of blue stretches from the nose to the tip of the tail, and is sound to the roots. Lighter shades are preferred. Nose leather and paw pads are blue, and the eye color is brilliant copper.

RED A deep, rich, brilliant red is required, without any shading, markings, or ticking. Lips and chin should be the same color as the coat. The nose leather and paw pads are brick red, and the eye color is brilliant copper.

CREAM One even shade of buff cream throughout should have no shading or markings, with lighter shades preferred. The nose leather and paw pads are pink, and the eye color is brilliant copper.

CHOCOLATE The coat is warm-toned medium to dark chocolate, free from shading or markings. The nose leather and paw pads are chocolate. Eye color is copper or orange.

LILAC The warm-toned lilac coat is sound and even in color. Lilac nose leather and paw pads, and copper or orange eye color.

TABBY AND BICOLOR VARIETIES

THE EXOTIC SHORTHAIR is accepted in the Classic and Mackerel patterns with the following colors allowed: silver, brown, blue, chocolate, lilac, red, and cream. They have identical color requirements to the equivalent varieties in the British Shorthair, except for eye color, which in the Exotic Shorthair is brilliant copper.

Torbie tabbies are accepted in brown, blue, chocolate, and lilac. The Spotted Tabby Exotic, in the same color range as the Classic and Mackeral Tabbies, is very attractive with numerous well-defined round, oval, or rosette-shaped marks clearly etched in distinct color on the lighter base coat.

BICOLOR The coat of the Bicolor is white with unbrindled patches of either black, blue, red, or cream, as seen in the American Shorthair. Nose leather and paw-pad color corresponds with the basic coat color. The eye color is brilliant copper.

VAN BICOLOR The coat of the Van Bi-color is white with unbrindled patches of either black, blue, red, or cream confined to the head, tail and legs, although one or two small colored patches on the body are allowed.

VAN TRICOLOR The coat of the Van Tricolor is white with unbrindled patches of both black and red confined to the head, tail, and legs, although up to three small colored patches on the body are allowed.

VAN BLUE-CREAM-AND-WHITE The coat of this variety is white with unbrindled patches of both blue and cream confined to the head, tail, and legs, although one or two small colored patches on the body are allowed.

BLUE AND WHITE EXOTIC
Bicolored Exotic cats should have clear and well-distributed patches of color, as in this fine blue and white. The face should be patched with color and with white.

BLUE TABBY COLORPOINT EXOTIC
In the colorpointed range of the Exotic, the six main points colors are accepted.

OTHER VARIETIES

BLUE TORTIE AND WHITE EXOTIC

Well-distributed patches of light to medium blue, pale cream, and white form the pattern of this color variety, known as the dilute calico in the USA.

THE EXOTIC SHORTHAIR is the ideal breed for the owner who craves for a cat with true Persian type, but does not have the time necessary to care correctly for the demanding Persian coat. Exotics are indeed a short-coated version of their Persian ancestors, and show standards for the two breeds, apart from the coat, are almost identical

TORTOISESHELL The coat is black with clearly defined, well-broken, unbrindled patches of red and light red on the body and extremities. A red or light red blaze on the face is desirable. Eye color is brilliant copper.

CALICO The coat is white with unbrindled patches of black and red, with white predominant on the underparts. Eye color is brilliant copper.

BLUE-CREAM The coat is blue with clearly defined, well-broken patches of solid cream on the body and the extremities. The eye color is brilliant copper.

BLUE-CREAM-AND-WHITE The coat is white with unbrindled patches of blue and cream, with white predominant on the underparts. Eye color is brilliant copper.

CHINCHILLA The undercoat is pure white. The coat on the back, flanks, head, and tail is sufficiently tipped with black to give a characteristic sparkling silver appearance. The legs may be slightly shaded with tipping. Chin, ear tufts, stomach, and chest are pure white, and the rims of the eyes, lips, and nose are outlined with black. Nose leather brick red, paw pads black, eye color green or blue-green.

SHADED SILVER The undercoat is pure white and the coat heavily shaded with black to form a mantle over the spine, sides, and on the face and tail, gradually shading from very dark on the spine to white on the chin, chest, stomach, and under the tail. Legs are the same tone as the face. The general effect is much darker than the Chinchilla. Rims of the eyes, lips, and nose are outlined with black. Nose leather brick red, paw pads black, eye color green or blue-green.

CHINCHILLA GOLDEN The undercoat is a rich warm cream. The coat on the back, flanks, head, and tail is sufficiently tipped with seal brown to give a golden appearance. The legs may be slightly shaded with tipping. Chin, ear tufts, stomach, and chest are cream, and the rims of the eyes, lips, and nose are outlined with seal brown. Nose leather is deep rose, paw pads are seal brown, and the eye color green or blue-green.

SHADED GOLDEN The undercoat is a rich, warm cream, and the coat is heavily shaded with seal brown to form a mantle over the spine, sides, and on the face and tail, gradually shading from dark on the spine to cream on the chin, chest, stomach, and under the tail.

BROWN TABBY EXOTIC

The head has the frown lines created by the dark "M" marking on the forehead.

CHOCOLATE SMOKE CORNISH REX
The short plush coat is dense and has uniform narrow waves extending from the top of the head across the back, sides, and hips, and continues to the tip of the tail.

WHITE CORNISH REX
The head should be narrow with a flat skull. A straight line can be seen from the center of the forehead to the end of the nose.

CHOCOLATE TORTIE CORNISH REX
The eyes of the Cornish Rex are medium sized and oval, with a full eye's-width between them.

TORTIE SMOKE AND WHITE
The Cornish Rex stands tall, appearing to walk on tiptoe.

133

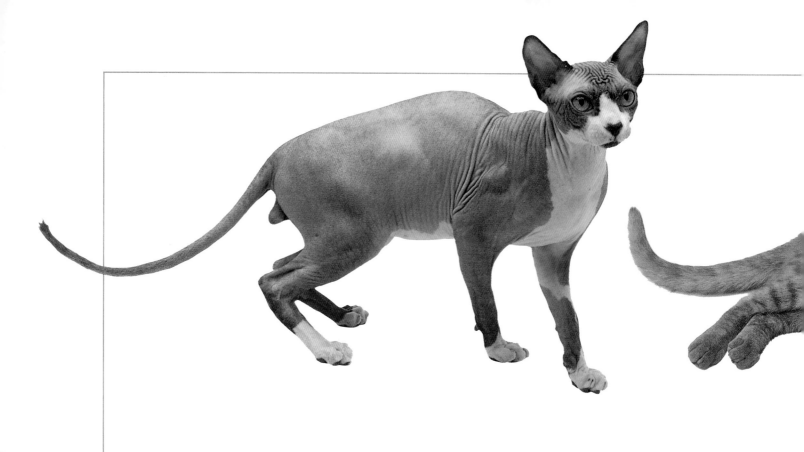

FOREIGN
SHORTHAIRED
BREEDS

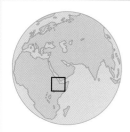

ABYSSINIAN

NO EVIDENCE EXISTS to connect an Abyssinian cat, recorded as having been taken from Ethiopia to England in 1868, with today's pedigree cats. Recognized as a true breed in 1882, the Abyssinian was also known as the Spanish, Russian, Ticked, Hare, or Bunny Cat – it was once thought that it had resulted from a cross between a cat and wild rabbit!

The modern Abyssinian is a well-established breed worldwide. It has been referred to' as the Child of the Gods because of its close resemblance to the sacred cats of the Ancient Egyptians. Whatever their color, all Abyssinian cats have unusual ticked coats, known as the agouti, or wild-type pattern. Selective breeding over many generations has resulted in a reduction of the natural tabby bars normally found on the face, neck, tail, and underparts, so that today's show cat has a clear, glowing, ticked coat, rather like that of a Belgian hare.

The Abyssinian is another foreign shorthaired breed which is judged by slightly different standards in Europe and North America. The American Abyssinian has a shorter head and a more rounded profile than its European counterpart. In the allocation of show points, the American fancy gives most weight by points to body type, while the European standards place more emphasis on coat color.

BREAKDOWN OF 100 SHOW POINTS

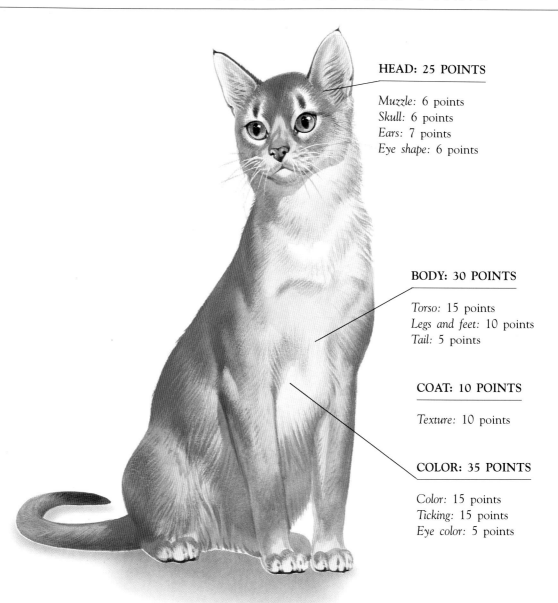

HEAD: 25 POINTS

Muzzle: 6 points
Skull: 6 points
Ears: 7 points
Eye shape: 6 points

BODY: 30 POINTS

Torso: 15 points
Legs and feet: 10 points
Tail: 5 points

COAT: 10 POINTS

Texture: 10 points

COLOR: 35 POINTS

Color: 15 points
Ticking: 15 points
Eye color: 5 points

Character and Care

The Abyssinian cat is typically quiet and gentle. It can be shy and reserved, mistrusting strangers, but it generally gets along well with other cats and adores its owner.

The coat is simple to keep immaculate with the minimum of grooming, and the large ears must be kept clean at all times, by regular use of moistened cotton swabs.

PENALTIES

Abyssinian cats are penalized in the show ring for having incorrect head type, barring on the legs, rings on the tail, incorrect color of paw pads, or cold gray tones in the coat.

DISQUALIFICATION FEATURES
- a white locket
- white anywhere other than in the region of the nostrils, chin, or upper throat
- a dark, unbroken necklace
- a gray undercoat close to the skin extending over a large portion of the body

KEY CHARACTERISTICS

- **CATEGORY** Foreign Shorthair.

- **OVERALL BUILD** Medium size, lithe and muscular.

- **COAT** Soft, silky, fine textured; medium in length to accommodate two or three bands of ticking.

- **HEAD** Slightly rounded and wedge shaped with gentle contours, gently curved in profile. The muzzle is neither pointed nor square.

- **NOSE** Medium length.

- **CHIN** Firm.

- **EYES** Almond-shaped, large, brilliant and expressive.

- **EARS** Large and alert.

- **BODY** Long, lithe, and graceful.

- **LEGS** Slim and fine-boned.

- **PAWS** Small and oval.

- **TAIL** Thick at the base, fairly long and tapering.

- **COLORS** Usual, blue, red or sorrel, chocolate, lilac, cream, beige-fawn, torbie in all these colors. (Note that not all varieties are recognized by all associations.)

ABYSSINIAN VARIETIES

THE USUAL OR RUDDY is the normal coat color for the Abyssinian, and is genetically black – the rich golden hairs having two or three bands of black ticking. The Red or Sorrel is produced by the action of the light-brown gene.

RUDDY (USA, Europe) **USUAL** (UK–GCCF) The coat is warm ruddy brown with black ticking; the base color deep apricot or orange. The tail tip, ear tips, and eye rims are black; the nose leather brick red (may be outlined with black). Paw pads, back of feet, and toe tufts are seal brown or black. The eye color is gold or green; rich deep colors are preferred.

BLUE The coat is warm blue-gray with dark, steel blue-gray ticking; the base color pale fawn/cream. The tail tip and ear tips are dark steel blue-gray; the eye rims blue-gray. Nose leather is old rose (may be outlined with blue-gray); paw pads are old rose/blue-gray; backs of feet and toe tufts are deep steel blue-gray. Eye color is as Ruddy Abyssinian.

SORREL or RED The coat is a bright, warm, copper red with chocolate-brown ticking; the base color deep apricot. The tail tip, ear tips, eye rims, backs of feet, and toe tufts are red-brown. Nose leather is pale red (may be outlined with red-brown); paw pads cinnamon to chocolate. Eye color is as Ruddy Abyssinian.

USUAL ABYSSINIAN

The rich golden brown coat ticked with bands of black gives the Usual Abyssinian its unusual appearance. It is known as the Ruddy Abyssinian in Europe and America.

BEIGE-FAWN The coat is dull beige with deep, warm, fawn ticking; the base color pale cream. The tail tip, ear tips, backs of feet, and toe tufts are dark warm cream; the eye rims old rose. Nose leather is pink (may be outlined with old rose); paw pads are pink. Eye color is as Ruddy Abyssinian.

BLACK SILVER The coat is pure silver-white with black ticking; the base color pure silver-white. The tail tip and eye rims are black; the ear tips, paw pads, backs of feet, and toe tufts are black or seal brown. Nose leather is brick red (may be outlined with black). Eye color is as Ruddy Abyssinian.

BLUE SILVER The coat is pure silver-white with dark steel blue-gray ticking; the base color pure silver-white. The tail tip, ear tips, eye rims, backs of feet, and toe tufts are dark steel blue-gray. Nose leather is old rose (may be outlined with dark steel blue-gray); paw pads are old rose or blue-gray. Eye color is as Ruddy Abyssinian.

FAWN ABYSSINIAN

Beige with bands of warm fawn ticking makes up the rare and attractive coat of this variety.

BLUE ABYSSINIAN

Abyssinians with this coloring turned up in otherwise usual litters from time to time, but until recent years were not accepted for showing.

SORREL ABYSSINIAN

Bright copper red and warm chocolate bands of ticking give the Sorrel or Red Abyssinian its rich glowing appearance.

139

SOMALI

THIS BREED IS the longhaired version of the Abyssinian cat, and its coat color is typically Abyssinian. It was thought that the long coat was due to a spontaneous mutation occurring within the Abyssinian breed, but genetic investigation of the history of the Somali showed that the gene for long hair was probably introduced when cats of Abyssinian type and lineage were outcrossed to others in the early days of breeding and showing.

When the first long-coated kittens appeared in otherwise normal litters of Abyssinian kittens, they were discarded and given away as pets, but later, having seen some of these cats at maturity when the full beauty of the ticked longhaired coat was apparent, breeders decided to develop the longhaired Abyssinian as a separate variety. A worldwide network of breeders – in North America, Europe, New Zealand, and Australia – worked together and agreed on Somali as the cats' name. The breed was granted full championship status by the CFA in 1978.

Character and Care
Like the Abyssinian, the Somali is gentle and receptive to quiet handling and affection. It is soft-voiced, playful, and athletic, and makes a perfect companion pet.

The coat, though full, is not wooly and is therefore very easy to groom. The full ruff (frill) and tail need regular combing through, and the large ears must be gently cleaned and kept free from dust.

BREAKDOWN OF 100 SHOW POINTS

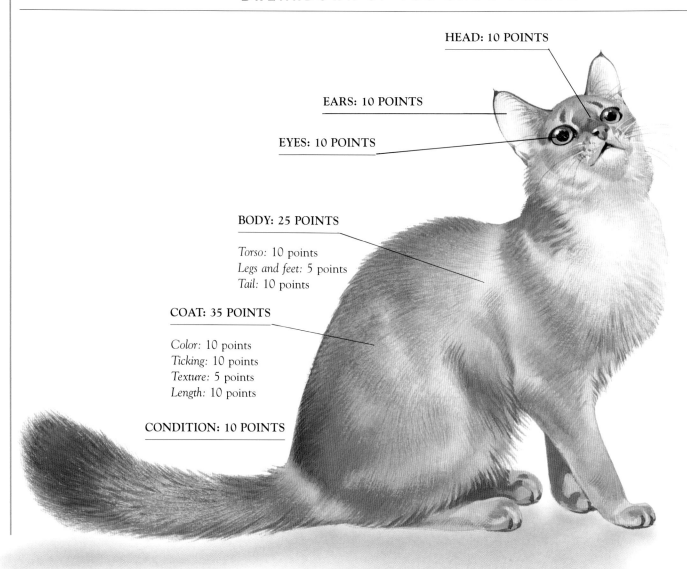

HEAD: 10 POINTS

EARS: 10 POINTS

EYES: 10 POINTS

BODY: 25 POINTS

Torso: 10 points
Legs and feet: 5 points
Tail: 10 points

COAT: 35 POINTS

Color: 10 points
Ticking: 10 points
Texture: 5 points
Length: 10 points

CONDITION: 10 POINTS

KEY CHARACTERISTICS

- **CATEGORY** Foreign Longhair.

- **OVERALL BUILD** Medium to large.

- **COAT** Extremely fine and very dense, of medium length but shorter on the shoulders. A well-developed ruff (frill) and breeches are desirable.

- **HEAD** Wedge-shaped and of medium proportions; wide at the top with soft contours.

- **NOSE** Medium long with a soft curve in profile, with neither a stop nor a straight nose.

- **CHIN** Firm and well developed.

- **EYES** Large, almond-shaped, and set well apart.

- **EARS** Large and broad at the base, slightly rounded at the tips, with lynx-like tufts, set well apart and pricked.

- **BODY** Of medium length. Bone structure firm, lithe, and muscular.

- **LEGS** Long and fine-boned, in proportion to the body.

- **PAWS** Small and oval.

- **TAIL** Fairly long and tapering; broad at the base and well-furred.

- **COLORS** As for the Abyssinian: ruddy, blue, red, or sorrel, beige-fawn, black, silver, blue silver, sorrel silver, beige-fawn silver.
  Note Not all associations recognize all color varieties.

PENALTIES

The Somali is penalized for having a cold gray or sandy tone to the coat color; mottling or speckling in unticked areas; black roots to body hair; incorrect markings; a white locket or white anywhere other than the upper throat, chin or nostrils; incorrect color of paw pads and/or nose leather; Siamese type and a whip tail.

NON-SILVER VARIETIES

ALTHOUGH DIFFERENT CAT associations have their own rules for acceptance of new varieties, the Somali is recognized in most of the regular Abyssinian color varieties by most registering bodies. In the United Kingdom, the Cat Association of Britain accepts all colors, while the GCCF has granted full Championship status to the Usual and Sorrel in the non-Silver group, and has given preliminary status only to the blue, chocolate, lilac, and fawn non-Silvers, and to all the Silver Somali cats in the full range of colors.

LILAC USUAL The coat is rich and glowing golden brown ticked with black. The tail is tipped with black; the ears with black or dark brown. Nose leather is tile red; the paw pads and heels, and toe tufts are black or dark brown.

BLUE Any shade of blue ticked with darker blue is allowed, and the base hair is cream or oatmeal. The ears and tail are tipped with the same color as the ticking. The nose leather is blue-mauve, and the blue-mauve paw pads have deeper blue between the toes and extending up the heels. The toe tufts are deep blue.

CHOCOLATE The coat is rich golden coppery

BLUE SOMALI

In this variety, the ticking may be any shade of blue on a base coat of cream or oatmeal, complemented by the delicate mauve-pink nose leather.

USUAL SOMALI

This variety's other name of "Ruddy" sums up its appearance very well. The black ticking on the rich apricot base coat combines to give a rich golden and ruddy overall glow.

CHOCOLATE SOMALI

Somali kittens are slow to mature both in size and in developing the full ticked effect of the typical coat.

brown ticked with dark chocolate, with paler base hair. The ears and tail are tipped with the same shade as the ticking. The nose leather is pinkish chocolate. The paw pads are chocolate with darker chocolate between the toes and extending up the heels. The toe tufts are dark chocolate.

LILAC The pinkish dove-gray coat is ticked with a deeper shade of the same color and a paler base coat. This variety has a powdered effect to the coat. The ears and tail are tipped with the same color as the ticking. The nose leather is pinkish mauve; the pinkish-mauve paw pads have deeper dove gray between the toes and extending up the heels. The toe tufts are deep dove gray.

SORREL The warm, glowing copper coat is ticked with chocolate and a base coat of deep apricot. The ears and tail are tipped with chocolate. The nose leather is pink; the paw pads are pink with chocolate between the toes and extending up the heels; the toe tufts are chocolate.

FAWN The warm fawn coat is ticked with a deeper shade of the same color and a paler base coat. The ears and tail are tipped with the same color as the ticking. The nose leather is pink; the pinkish-mauve paw pads have deep fawn between the toes and extending up the heels. The toe tufts are deep fawn.

FAWN SOMALI

A diluted version of the red or sorrel, the fawn Somali has an attractive "powdered" effect to its warm fawn coat, ticked with a deeper fawn color. This is an elegant young kitten.

SILVER VARIETIES

A YELLOWISH EFFECT on the body, known as "fawning," is an undesirable trait in the Silver series of Somali cats. It occurs particularly in the usual silver, and in blue silver varieties especially on the face and paws.

USUAL SILVER The white base coat is ticked with black; the tail and ears are tipped with black. The nose leather is light brick red. The paw pads are black or brown with black between the toes and extending up the heels with black toe tufts.

BLUE SILVER The white base coat is ticked with blue, giving an overall sparkling silver-gray effect. The ears and tail are ticked with blue. The nose leather is blue-mauve. The blue-mauve pads have blue between the toes, extending up the heels; the toe tufts are blue.

USUAL SILVER
The coat gives an overall appearance of silver produced by black ticking on a white base coat.

RED SILVER
The Sorrel or Red Silver has a sparkling coat of a silvery peach shade. The ticking is a medium chocolate shade.

CHOCOLATE SILVER The white base coat has dark chocolate ticking, giving an overall sparkling silvery chocolate effect. The nose leather is pinkish chocolate, and the ears and tail are tipped with dark chocolate. The paw pads are chocolate with dark chocolate between the toes and extend up the heels. The ear tufts are dark chocolate.

LILAC SILVER The white base coat is ticked with dove-gray giving an overall sparkling dove-gray effect. The nose leather is pinkish mauve; pinkish-mauve pads have dove gray between the toes and extending up the heels. The toe tufts are dove-gray.

SORREL SILVER The white base coat has chocolate ticking, giving the overall sparkling silvery peach effect. The ears and tail are tipped with chocolate. The nose leather is pink. The pink paw pads have chocolate brown between the toes and extending up the heels. The toe tufts are dark chocolate.

FAWN SILVER The white base coat is ticked with fawn, giving an overall sparkling silvery fawn effect. The ears and tail are tipped with fawn. The nose leather is pink. The pinkish-mauve paw pads have fawn between the toes and extending up the heels. The toe tufts are fawn.

BLUE SILVER

Another striking color in the Silver Somali range, where the white base coat is ticked with blue giving a sparkling silvery blue-gray coat pattern. As in all Somali varieties, the ears and tail color should match that of the ticking.

145

RUSSIAN BLUE

THE VERY HANDSOME and unique Russian Blue is a natural breed with a unique combination of conformation, color, and coat that make it a striking animal.

The first Russian Blue cats are thought to have originated near the White Sea port of Archangel, just outside the Arctic Circle, and were carried as trade goods by merchant sailors on ships trading with England. The cats were shown extensively in England during the latter part of the nineteenth century, but differed from those of today in having bright orange eyes. The breed was exhibited under a number of names, including the Spanish Blue, the Archangel, and the Maltese. In the first cat shows, all shorthaired blue cats competed in one class, regardless of type. In 1912, the Russian Blue was given its own classes, but during World War II, the breed almost became extinct, being saved only by outcrossing to Siamese. Cats of foreign type were then shown as Russian Blues, but eventually breeders made a coordinated attempt to return to the prewar characteristics of the breed, and in 1966 the show standard was changed to state specifically that Siamese type was undesirable in the Russian Blue.

BREAKDOWN OF 100 SHOW POINTS

PENALTIES

The Russian Blue is penalized in the show ring for any white or tabby markings, or for having a kinked or abnormal tail.

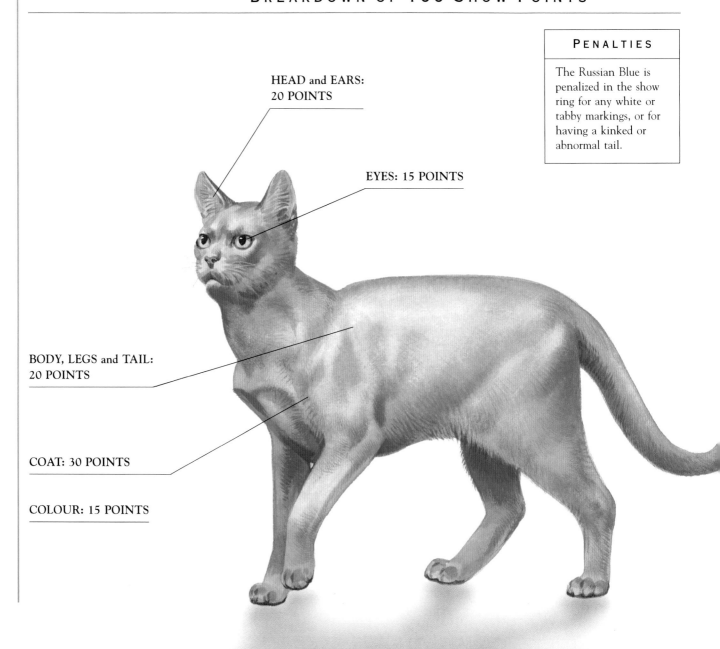

HEAD and EARS:
20 POINTS

EYES: 15 POINTS

BODY, LEGS and TAIL:
20 POINTS

COAT: 30 POINTS

COLOUR: 15 POINTS

Maltese or Russian Blue cats are recorded in the United States as long ago as 1900, but only in 1947 did breeders really start work with these unique cats, and even today the breed is rare in the show rings of the world.

Character and Care

The Russian Blue has a delightful temperament, being quiet-voiced and very affectionate. It does not like to be left alone for long periods and needs the company either of a human being, or other pets.

The unique coat, with its short, thick double fur, should be regularly combed through and may be stroked both ways without exposing the blue skin. The sparsely furred ears must be kept clean at all times.

KEY CHARACTERISTICS

- **CATEGORY** Foreign Shorthair.

- **OVERALL BUILD** Medium in size, lithe and muscular.

- **COAT** Short, fine, and plush, its density causes the double-textured coat to stand out from the body.

- **COLOR** Blue only (some associations in Australia and New Zealand recognize a Black Russian and a White Russian.) A clear, even blue, the guard hairs being silver-tipped giving the cat an overall lustrous silvery sheen. Lighter blue shades are preferred in the United States, and medium blue shades in Britain. Nose leather is slate gray; paw pads, lavender-pink or mauve; eye color, vivid green.

- **OTHER FEATURES** Wedge-shaped head with flat skull, broad at eye level with nose of medium length and level chin. Wide-based ears with very little hair inside or out. In the United States, the ears should be set far apart on the head; in Britain, the ears must be set vertically. Wide-set eyes of vivid green and a rounded aperture in the United States, but almond-shaped in Britain. Fine-boned, long and muscular body with long, slender legs and small paws. The tail should be long and tapered.

RUSSIAN BLUE
A natural breed with a long and interesting history, the Russian Blue standard has developed differently on each side of the Atlantic.

147

KORAT

THE BREED ORIGINATED in Thailand where it is called Si-Sawat, a descriptive compound word referring to its silver gray coat and luminous, light green eyes. The thirteenth-century *Book of Cat Poems* in the National Library of Bangkok illustrates the breed with the caption: "The cat Mal-ed has a body like Doklao, the hairs are smooth with roots like clouds and tips like silver, the eyes shine like dewdrops on a lotus leaf." *Mal-ed* refers to the seed of the Look Sawat, a silvery gray fruit lightly tinged with green. *Dok* is a flower, and *lao* a plant with silver-tipped flowers. Highly prized in its native land, the Si-Sawat is considered a harbinger of good fortune, and a pair of these cats is a traditional wedding gift, intended to bring longevity, wealth, and happiness to the couple.

First exhibited in London in 1896, the Korat was disqualified, being judged as a Siamese cat and not having the desired fawn coat, dark points, and blue eyes! In 1959 Korat cats arrived in the United States, where they were officially recognized in 1966. The cat fanciers of South Africa and Australia officially accepted the breed in 1968 and 1969 respectively, but Britain's Governing Council of the Cat Fancy delayed recognition until 1975 and then withheld championship status. In 1983, the Cat Association of Britain finally accepted the Korat for full status, and Britain's first champion was chosen by judges from England, Belgium, and Australia.

Character and Care

The Korat is a dainty, quiet-voiced little cat, generally alert, inquisitive, and affectionate.

Its short, dense coat is easily cared for with a weekly brushing and buffing with a silk scarf.

BREAKDOWN OF 100 SHOW POINTS

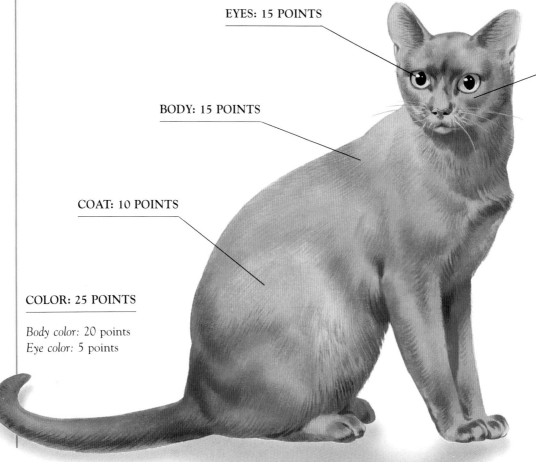

EYES: 15 POINTS

BODY: 15 POINTS

COAT: 10 POINTS

COLOR: 25 POINTS

Body color: 20 points
Eye color: 5 points

HEAD: 20 POINTS

Broad head: 5 points
Profile: 6 points
Breadth between eyes: 4 points
Ear set and placement: 5 points

PENALTIES

The Korat is penalized if it is any color but silver blue; has a visible tail kink; or white spot or locket. Kittens and young cats are not penalized for incorrect eye color; this is not set until maturity in the Korat.

KEY CHARACTERISTICS

- **CATEGORY** Foreign Shorthair.

- **OVERALL BUILD** Small to medium size.

- **COAT** Short to medium length, fine textured and glossy.

- **COLOR** Blue only. Silver blue tipped with silver. Nose leather and lips, dark blue or lavender; paw pads, dark blue ranging to lavender with a pinkish tinge. Eye color, luminous green preferred, amber acceptable.

- **OTHER FEATURES** Heart-shaped head with large, round-tipped ears set high, giving an alert expression. Slight stop in profile of nose and a firm chin, lion-like in profile. The eyes are luminous and oversized for the face, and with an Asian slant when closed. The body is muscular and supple, midway between the Shorthair and the Siamese in type, with females being daintier than males. Well-proportioned legs with neat oval paws, and a tail of medium length heavier at the base and tapering to a rounded tip.

PROFILE
Always blue and with a fine short coat, the Korat is a dainty, quiet little cat.

KORAT
A natural breed discovered in Thailand, the Korat was considered as a good luck charm and often given as a wedding gift.

HAVANA BROWN

THIS UNIQUE, MAN-MADE breed came into being when British breeders were working with Russian Blue and Shorthair cross-matings during the early 1950s, and self-colored chocolate brown kittens were occasionally produced. At that time, the science of feline color genetics was in its infancy, but it was soon established that chocolate kittens could only occur when both parents carried the chocolate factor, and when two chocolate cats were mated, chocolate kittens always resulted.

Cats from these early matings were developed in Britain as the Chestnut Brown Foreign Shorthair and were outcrossed to Siamese to establish Oriental type and conformation. Others were sent to the United States to establish a new breed and were bred to a unique standard of points as the Havana Brown.

Character and Care
This breed is highly intelligent, affectionate, and very agile. Less vocal than the Siamese, it is playful and craves human company. It makes a superb pet.

The coat is easy to maintain in good condition with the minimum of grooming. Combing removes any loose hairs, and buffing with the hand or a silk scarf produces a sheen on the glossy brown coat.

BREAKDOWN OF 100 SHOW POINTS

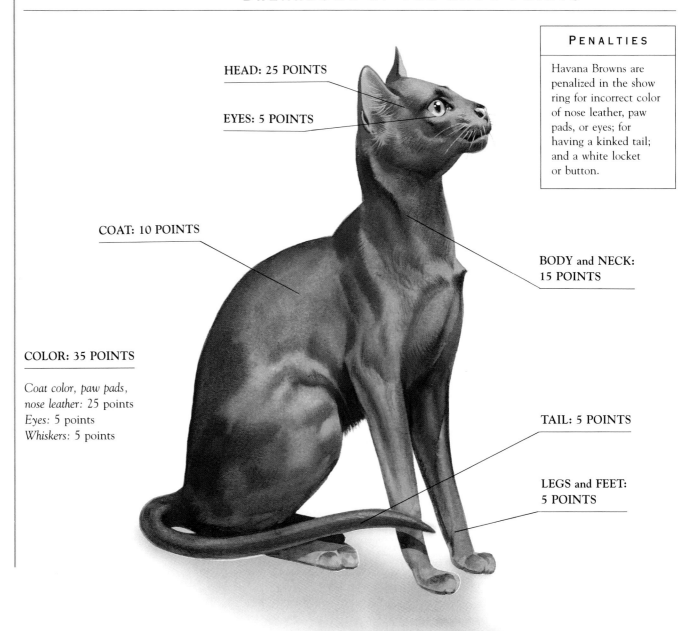

HEAD: 25 POINTS

EYES: 5 POINTS

COAT: 10 POINTS

COLOR: 35 POINTS

*Coat color, paw pads,
nose leather:* 25 points
Eyes: 5 points
Whiskers: 5 points

BODY and NECK:
15 POINTS

TAIL: 5 POINTS

LEGS and FEET:
5 POINTS

PENALTIES

Havana Browns are penalized in the show ring for incorrect color of nose leather, paw pads, or eyes; for having a kinked tail; and a white locket or button.

HAVANA BROWN

The Havana Brown as shown in the United States was developed from early imports of Chestnut Brown Foreign Shorthairs from Britain. It is a unique breed and bears very little resemblance to the Havana, or Oriental Chocolate, found in Europe and Britain.

KEY CHARACTERISTICS
● **CATEGORY** Foreign Shorthair.
● **OVERALL BUILD** Medium size, muscular build.
● **COAT** Short to medium length coat, smooth and lustrous.
● **COLOR** Warm brown only. Coat of a rich and even shade of warm brown throughout. Kittens are not penalized for showing ghost tabby markings. The nose leather is brown with a rosy flush; the paw pads must have a rosy tone. The eye color is a vivid green.
● **OTHER FEATURES** Head slightly longer than it is wide, with a distinct change in slope or "stop" at eye level when viewed in profile. The rounded muzzle has a definite break on each side behind the whisker pads, well-developed chin. Large round-tipped ears, wide set but not flaring and slightly pricked forward, giving an alert appearance. Oval eyes of vivid green. Firm muscular body of medium length with legs in proportion, and neat oval paws. A medium length tail, tapering gently to a slightly pointed tip.

HAVANA BROWN

Large pricked ears and vivid green oval eyes give the face of the Havana Brown its typical, sweet expression. The smooth, lustrous coat is evenly colored in warm brown.

EGYPTIAN MAU

NOT TO BE CONFUSED with cats of the same name bred experimentally in Britain during the 1960s and now called Oriental Tabbies. The Egyptian Mau was bred in the United States, and came from foundation stock brought there from Egypt via Rome in 1953. It is a spotted cat, very similar to those pictured in ancient Egyptian scrolls and cartoons. It gained official recognition from the CFF in 1968 and finally from the CFA in 1977.

Character and Care
Rather shy but very loving, the Mau tends to attach its affections to only one or two people. It is naturally active and may be taught one or two tricks.

Although the short coat is easy to keep in good condition, regular combing is required to remove dead hair.

BREAKDOWN OF 100 SHOW POINTS

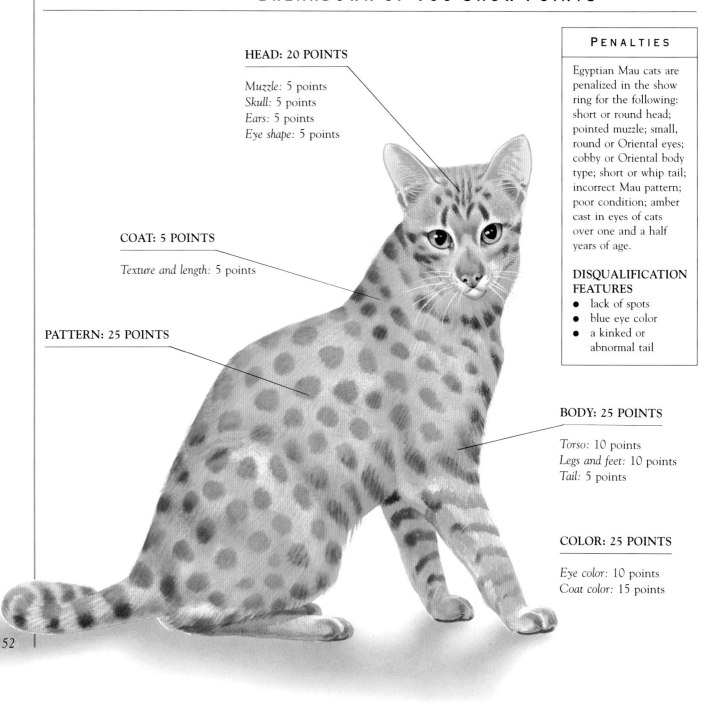

HEAD: 20 POINTS

Muzzle: 5 points
Skull: 5 points
Ears: 5 points
Eye shape: 5 points

COAT: 5 POINTS

Texture and length: 5 points

PATTERN: 25 POINTS

BODY: 25 POINTS

Torso: 10 points
Legs and feet: 10 points
Tail: 5 points

COLOR: 25 POINTS

Eye color: 10 points
Coat color: 15 points

PENALTIES

Egyptian Mau cats are penalized in the show ring for the following: short or round head; pointed muzzle; small, round or Oriental eyes; cobby or Oriental body type; short or whip tail; incorrect Mau pattern; poor condition; amber cast in eyes of cats over one and a half years of age.

DISQUALIFICATION FEATURES
- lack of spots
- blue eye color
- a kinked or abnormal tail

SILVER MAU

The silver Egyptian Mau has clear markings in dark charcoal on a pale silver ground color. The green eyes complete the rather exotic effect.

BRONZE MAU

The Bronze Egyptian Mau is perhaps the cat that most resembles the color of the cats of the ancient Egyptians. Dark brown markings show up clearly on the light bronze base coat. The whole coat has a warm glowing appearance.

SMOKE MAU

Unusual black markings on a charcoal gray base and with a silver undercoat give this unusually colored cat the appearance of shot silk, the color changing almost imperceptibly as it moves.

KEY CHARACTERISTICS

- **CATEGORY** Foreign Shorthair.

- **OVERALL BUILD** Medium size, long and graceful; muscular strength.

- **COAT** Silky and fine coat, dense and resilient to touch, with a lustrous sheen. Medium length hair, two or more bands of ticking, separated by lighter bands.

- **COLORS**
  Silver Pale silver ground color; dark charcoal markings contrasting with ground color. Backs of the ears are grayish pink tipped in black; the nose, lips, and eyes are outlined in black. The upper throat, chin, and around the nostrils is pale clear silver, appearing white. Nose leather is brick red; paw pads are black; eye color is light green. *Bronze* Light bronze ground color with creamy ivory underparts, dark brown markings against the ground color. Backs of the ears are tawny pink tipped in dark brown; the nose, lips, and eyes are outlined in dark brown, with ocher on the bridge of the nose. The upper throat, chin, and around the nostrils are pale creamy white. Nose leather is brick red; paw pads are black or dark brown; eye color is light green. *Smoke* Charcoal gray ground color with silver undercoat, the jet black markings plainly visible. Nose, lips, and eyes outlined in jet black; upper throat, chin, and around the nostrils are lightest in color. Nose leather and pads black: eye color light green.

- **OTHER FEATURES** Slightly rounded wedge head of medium length. Muzzle neither short nor pointed. Medium to large ears alert and slightly pointed. Inner ear delicate shell pink. Ears tufts accepted. Legs in proportion to body, with higher hind legs and small, slightly oval paws. Medium long tail thick at the base, slightly tapered.

OCICAT

THE FIRST KITTEN of this breed appeared in the litter of an experimentally bred hybrid queen, from an Abyssinian-pointed Siamese breeding program, mated with a chocolate-pointed Siamese male. The kitten, which was called Tonga, reminded its breeder of a baby ocelot, and she decided to produce similar cats, which were eventually recognized as a separate breed called Ocicats.

Apart from the Ocicat itself, outcrosses to Abyssinian, American, and Siamese are allowed in the pedigree. The Ocicat is a rather large, but well-proportioned cat, muscular and agile, with a typically "wild-cat" appearance. It is remarkable for its very clear spotted pattern and its striking golden eyes.

Character and Care

Ocicats are loving and gentle, inquisitive and playful, and make excellent pets.

Their coats are groomed by gentle brushing and combing through on a regular basis to remove dead hair.

TYPICAL OCICAT
All the hairs except for those at the tip of the tail are banded. Within the markings, each hair is tipped with darker color. The overall effect is that of a small spotted and graceful wild cat.

BREAKDOWN OF 100 SHOW POINTS

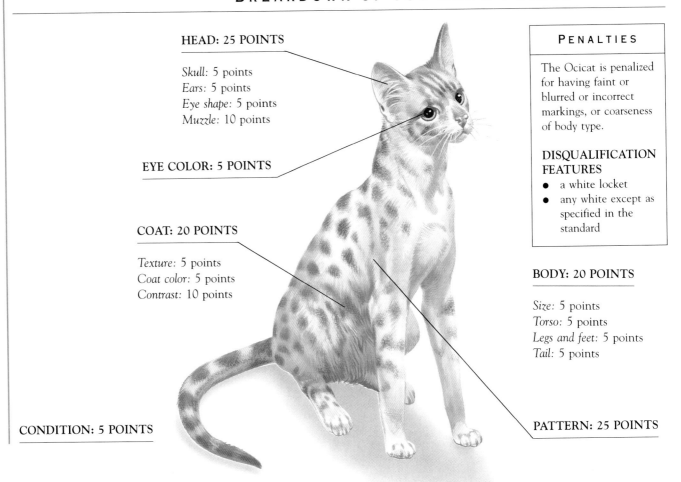

HEAD: 25 POINTS

Skull: 5 points
Ears: 5 points
Eye shape: 5 points
Muzzle: 10 points

EYE COLOR: 5 POINTS

COAT: 20 POINTS

Texture: 5 points
Coat color: 5 points
Contrast: 10 points

CONDITION: 5 POINTS

PENALTIES

The Ocicat is penalized for having faint or blurred or incorrect markings, or coarseness of body type.

DISQUALIFICATION FEATURES
- a white locket
- any white except as specified in the standard

BODY: 20 POINTS

Size: 5 points
Torso: 5 points
Legs and feet: 5 points
Tail: 5 points

PATTERN: 25 POINTS

CHOCOLATE SILVER

In this variety, the tabby markings are in a warm shade of chocolate on a pure silver base coat.

KEY CHARACTERISTICS

- **CATEGORY** Foreign Shorthair.

- **OVERALL BUILD** Medium to large, athletic build.

- **COAT** Short smooth coat, satiny and lustrous, yet long enough to accommodate the necessary bands of color.
  Ticking All hairs except those on the tip of the tail are banded. Within the markings, hairs are tipped with the darker color; hairs in the ground color are tipped with a lighter color.
  Markings Distinctive markings must be clearly seen from any angle. Markings on the face, legs, and tail may be darker than those on the body. The ground color may be darker on the saddle and lighter on the underside, chin, and lower jaw.
  Pattern The pattern is that of a spotted cat. This breed is noted for its powerful, graceful "wild cat" appearance.

- **COLORS** Black spotted; blue spotted; chocolate spotted; lavender spotted; cinnamon spotted; fawn spotted; black silver spotted; blue silver spotted; chocolate silver spotted; lavender silver spotted; cinnamon silver spotted; fawn silver spotted. All colors should be clear. The lightest color is on the face, around the eyes, on the chin, and the lower jaw; the darkest color is at the tip of the tail.

- **OTHER FEATURES** Modified wedge-shaped head with a broad, well-defined muzzle and strong chin. Alert, moderately large ears preferably with ear tufts, set fairly wide apart on the head. Large, almond- shaped eyes. Long solid body, athletic with substantial bone and muscle structure; medium long legs with compact oval paws and a fairly long, slightly tapered tail.

BLUE SPOTTED

Markings on the face, legs, and tail may be darker than those on the body, and the ground color may be darker on the saddle.

BLACK SILVER

This kitten is very well patterned with clear spots the correct head markings and pleasing type.

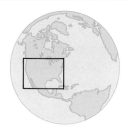

BENGAL

BASED ON CROSSES between Asian leopard cats which live wild in southeastern Asia, and domestic cats, the Bengal was first produced in the United States. It seems to have preserved the self-assurance and confidence of the Asian Leopard Cat in conjunction with the affectionate disposition of the domestic, producing a miniature leopard with a loving nature. The appearance of the Bengal should be as close as possible to that of the first cross, but without the possibility of its being mistaken for an actual Asian leopard cat. The texture of this breed's coat is unique, having the feel of satin or silk, and a glittering appearance as if sprinkled with gold dust or fragments of pearl.

Its cooing or chirruping call is quite different from that of the ordinary domestic cat, which adds to the impression the ideal Bengal gives of being a truly wild cat.

Character and Care
Self-assured and as confident as its leopard cat ancestors, the Bengal has acquired an affectionate disposition and a loving, dependable temperament.

The thick, luxuriant coat is kept in good condition with a well-balanced diet, and regular brushing and combing.

BREAKDOWN OF 100 SHOW POINTS

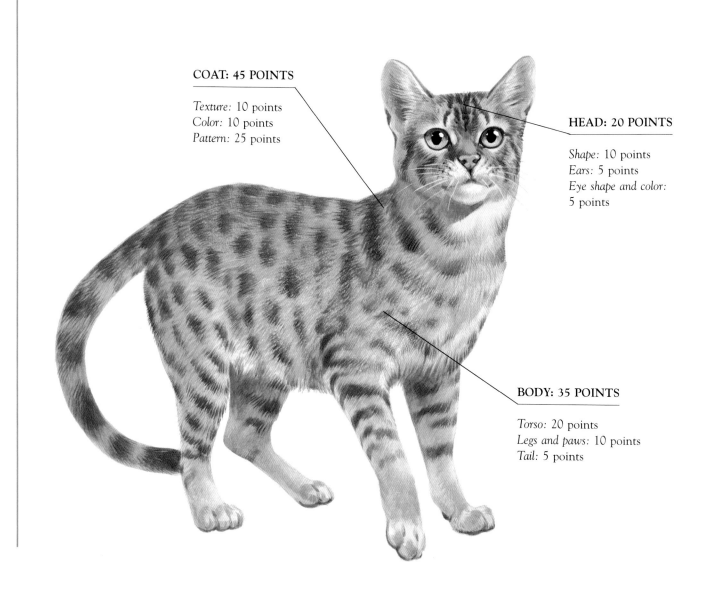

COAT: 45 POINTS

Texture: 10 points
Color: 10 points
Pattern: 25 points

HEAD: 20 POINTS

Shape: 10 points
Ears: 5 points
Eye shape and color: 5 points

BODY: 35 POINTS

Torso: 20 points
Legs and paws: 10 points
Tail: 5 points

KEY CHARACTERISTICS

- **CATEGORY** Foreign Shorthair.

- **OVERALL BUILD** Large, robust, and muscular.

- **COAT** Short to medium length, dense, luxuriant and unusually soft to touch.

- **HEAD** Broad, medium wedge with rounded contours, rather small in proportion to the body. Profile has a gentle curve from the forehead to the bridge of the nose; prominent brow.

- **NOSE** Large, broad nose with a puffed nose leather. Full broad muzzle and pronounced whisker pads.

- **CHIN** Strong.

- **EYES** Oval or slightly almond-shaped, large but not bold, set on the slant toward base of ear.

- **EARS** Medium to small, rather short with a wide base and rounded tips; set as much on the side as the top of the head; pointing forward in profile.

- **BODY** Large and robust with a broad chest. Very muscular, but long and sleek, with hindquarters slightly higher than the shoulders.

- **LEGS** Medium length, strong and muscular.

- **PAWS** Large and rounded.

- **TAIL** Of medium length, thick and even with a rounded tip.

- **COLORS** Leopard spotted or marble markings in brown tabby, blue-eyed snow, or blue.

PENALTIES

The Bengal is penalized for having a long, rough, or coarse coat; a ticked coat; incorrect color of the tail tip or paw pads; a whip tail; an unspotted stomach; and white patches or spots other than the *ocelli* (light spots on the backs of the ears).

DISQUALIFICATION FEATURES

- Aggressive behavior which threatens to harm.

BENGAL VARIETIES

IN BOTH THE Leopard Spotted and Marble Patterned, the spectacles which encircle the eyes should extend into vertical streaks which may be outlined by an "M" on the forehead. Broken streaks in the Marble, and streaks or spots in the Leopard, run over the head on each side of a complex scarab marking, down the neck onto the shoulders. A bold "chinstrap" and "mascara" markings, unbroken or broken necklets, and blotchy horizontal streaks are desirable in the Marble streaks, or spots in the Leopard.

The Marble should have a distinct pattern with large swirled patches or streaks, clearly defined but not symmetrical, giving a marble-like impression, preferably with a horizontal flow. The pattern should be formed of distinct shapes and sharp outlines with sharp contrast between the base coat, and the markings should bear no similarity to that of the Classic Tabby.

The Leopard Spotted should have generally large, well-formed, and randomly distributed spots. Extreme contrast between the ground color and the spots, which should be arrow-shaped, or rosetted in the case of larger spots. The cat's stomach must be spotted, and the legs may show broken horizontal lines and/or spots along its length with a solid dark-colored tip. It is important that the spots do not run vertically into a mackerel tabby pattern.

BROWN TABBY All variations are allowed in both Leopard Spotted and Marble Bengals, but a high degree of reddish-brown yielding a yellow, buff, golden, or orange ground color is preferred. The overall appearance should be of a cat dusted with gold glitter. The markings may be black or various shades of brown, and there may be *ocelli* – light-colored spots on the backs of the ears. The whisker pads and chin must be very pale, and the chest, underbody, and inner legs should be pale compared with the general ground color. The eye rims, lips, and nose leather are outlined in black; the center of the nose leather is brick red. Paw pads and tail tip are black; eye color is gold, green, or hazel, with deep shades preferred.

BROWN SPOTTED BENGAL
This kitten exhibits the arrowhead spots favored in the Leopard Spotted variety of the Bengal cat.

SNOW BENGAL
This variety shows the Burmese/Tonkinese coat pattern, where the most intense color is at the points, but the pattern is still visible on the body and has a special glittering appearance.

MARBLE BENGAL
Striking markings easily identify Bengals with the Marble pattern, with its complex whorls, distinct shapes, and sharp outlines. The pattern bears little or no resemblance to the Classic Tabby.

BLUE-EYED SNOW This variety is of the Himalayan type, with the pattern restricted to the points. The ground color is ivory to cream, with the overall appearance being that of a cat dusted with pearl glitter. The pattern varies in color from charcoal to dark or light brown; there are light-colored spectacles, whisker pads, and chin; and *ocelli* are preferred on each ear. The eye rims, lips, and nose leather are outlined in black; the center of the nose leather is brick red. The paw pads are rosy-toned brown; the tail tip is charcoal or dark brown; the eye color is blue.

BROWN SNOW This variety shows the Burmese/Tonkinese restriction of coat pattern. The ground color is cream to light brown, with the overall appearance being that of a cat dusted with pearl glitter. The clearly visible pattern varies in color from charcoal to light brown; there are light-colored spectacles, whisker pads, and chin; and *ocelli* are preferred on each ear. The eye rims, lips, and nose leather are outlined in black; the center of the nose leather is brick red. The paw pads are rosy-toned brown; the tail tip is charcoal or dark brown; the eye color is gold, green, or blue-green.

BLUE The ground color is pinkish mushroom to warm oatmeal, with the overall appearance being that of a cat dusted with pearl glitter. The clearly visible pattern is pale blue to blue-gray; there are light-colored spectacles, whisker pads, and chin; and *ocelli* are preferred on each ear. The eye rims, lips, and nose leather are outlined in slate gray; the center of the nose leather is dark pink. The paw pads are mauvish pink; the tail tip is dark blue. The eye color is gold, green, or blue-green.

CORNISH REX

I N 1950 A CURLY-COATED kitten was born in an otherwise normal litter at a farm in Cornwall in southwestern England. Microscopic examination by a geneticist of the kitten's hair samples showed they were similar to those of the Rex rabbit. When the kitten, named Kallibunker, matured, he was mated with his mother, and two of the resulting three kittens had Rex coats. The male, Poldhu, eventually sired a stunning Rex female called Lamorna Cove, which was exported to the United States to found the Cornish Rex breed on the other side of the Atlantic. British Shorthairs and Burmese cats were used as foundation stock in the early days of Cornish Rex breeding, and eventually there were enough curly-coated cats to establish an acceptable breed which could be registered. In Britain, the Cornish Rex achieved full breed status in Britain in 1967 and in the United States, in 1979.

Character and Care

The Cornish Rex cat is intelligent, affectionate, and rather extrovert by nature. Playful and mischievous, it makes a wonderful pet.

The unique curled coat does not shed hair, making it extremely easy to groom with hand stroking and the occasional use of a comb.

BREAKDOWN OF 100 SHOW POINTS

COAT: 40 POINTS

Texture: 10 points
Length: 5 points
Wave, extent of wave: 20 points
Close-lying: 5 points

HEAD: 25 POINTS

Size and shape: 5 points
Muzzle and nose: 5 points
Eyes: 5 points
Ears: 5 points
Profile: 5 points

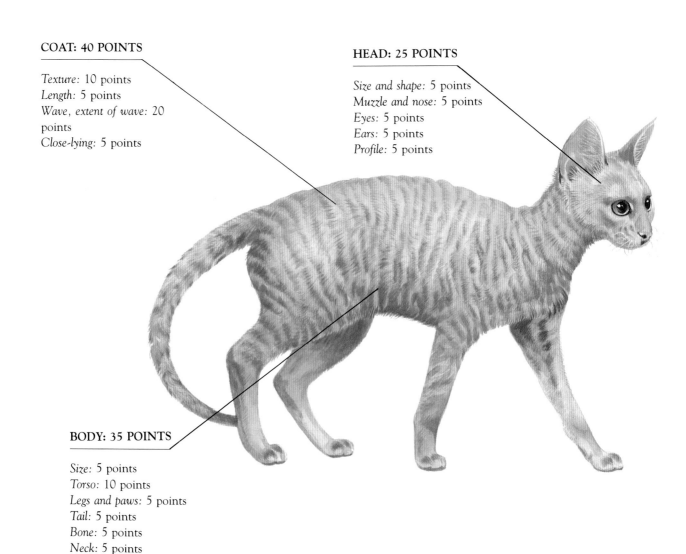

BODY: 35 POINTS

Size: 5 points
Torso: 10 points
Legs and paws: 5 points
Tail: 5 points
Bone: 5 points
Neck: 5 points

KEY CHARACTERISTICS

- **CATEGORY** Foreign Shorthair, curled.

- **OVERALL BUILD** Medium sized, slender build.

- **COAT** Short plush coat without guard hairs. Curls waves or ripples over the body particularly on the back and tail. Whiskers and eyebrows crinkled.

- **HEAD** Medium size, wedge shaped. About one third longer than it is wide.

- **NOSE** Rounded muzzle. In profile, a straight line is seen from the center of the forehead to the end of the nose.

- **CHIN** Strong.

- **EYES** Medium to large, oval shaped.

- **EARS** Large, set high on the head.

- **BODY** Medium length. Slender, hard, and muscular.

- **LEGS** Long and straight.

- **PAWS**

- **TAIL** Long, slender, and tapering.

- **COLORS** Most associations accept virtually all colors and patterns except white markings on Siamese patterned cats.

PENALTIES

Cornish Rex cats are penalized in the show ring for having a shaggy coat or one that is too short, a head of Shorthair type, or too wedge-shaped, small ears, a cobby body, slack muscles, a short tail or a tail with bare areas. Bare patches are considered a fault in kittens and a serious fault in cats.

CORNISH REX VARIETIES

IN ORDER TO widen the gene pool and to insure stamina in the Cornish Rex as a breed, it was necessary for the pioneer breeders to outcross to other breeds having the desired conformation. Foreign breeds were selected in the main, including Havana and Oriental lilac, and Burmese as well as Siamese of various colors. All the offspring of Cornish Rex to non-rexed cats resulted in cats with normal coats, all carrying the recessive gene for the Cornish curly coat, and when such cats matured, and were mated with similar cats, or back to Cornish Rex, curly-coated kittens were produced. The various colors and coat patterns of the cats selected for the original outcrosses resulted in a wide range of color varieties in the Cornish Rex breed, and breeders soon began to show their preferences for certain colors and combinations of colors. Though conformation

BLACK SMOKE & WHITE CORNISH
The tail of the Cornish Rex is long, fine, and tapered, and must be well covered with waved fur.

BLACK SMOKE VAN PATTERN
Virtually all the feline coat colors and patterns are found in the Cornish Rex. Perhaps one of the most unusual is the Van pattern, in which the cat's coat is basically white, with color restricted to the head and tail.

RED CORNISH REX
The Cornish Rex is medium sized, lithe, and muscular, with long slender legs and small oval paws.

CHOCOLATE SMOKE CORNISH REX

The short plush coat is dense and has uniform narrow waves extending from the top of the head across the back, sides, and hips, and continues to the tip of the tail.

WHITE CORNISH REX

The head should be narrow with a flat skull. A straight line can be seen from the center of the forehead to the end of the nose.

CHOCOLATE TORTIE CORNISH REX

The eyes of the Cornish Rex are medium sized and oval, with a full eye's-width between them.

TORTIE SMOKE AND WHITE

The Cornish Rex stands tall, appearing to walk on tiptoe.

163

DEVON REX

TEN YEARS AFTER the discovery of the first Cornish Rex kitten, another curly-coated kitten was discovered in the neighboring English county of Devon. The kitten, named Kirlee, was eventually mated with some Cornish Rex queens. To everyone's surprise, all the resulting kittens were flat-coated, and it was concluded that Kirlee's curls were caused by a different gene. More breeding tests confirmed this. The gene for the Cornish coat was labeled Rex gene [i]; the gene for the Devon coat Rex gene [ii]. The two rex-coated varieties were developed quite separately and are quite distinct breeds. The Devon Rex would look rather unusual even without its wavy coat, having a quizzical, pixie-like expression and huge bat-like ears.

In Britain, a popular sub-variety of Devon Rex is known unofficially as the Si-Rex. It combines all of the characteristics of the typical Devon Rex with the Siamese coat pattern and colors.

Character and Care

The Devon is said to be the cat for the connoisseur. It is demanding as a pet, constantly craving human attention, loving, playful, and intelligent.

The cat is very easy to groom with hand stroking and occasional combing. It often shows sparse areas on the body, and when it does, the cat needs extra warmth. The large ears need regular cleaning.

BREAKDOWN OF 100 SHOW POINTS

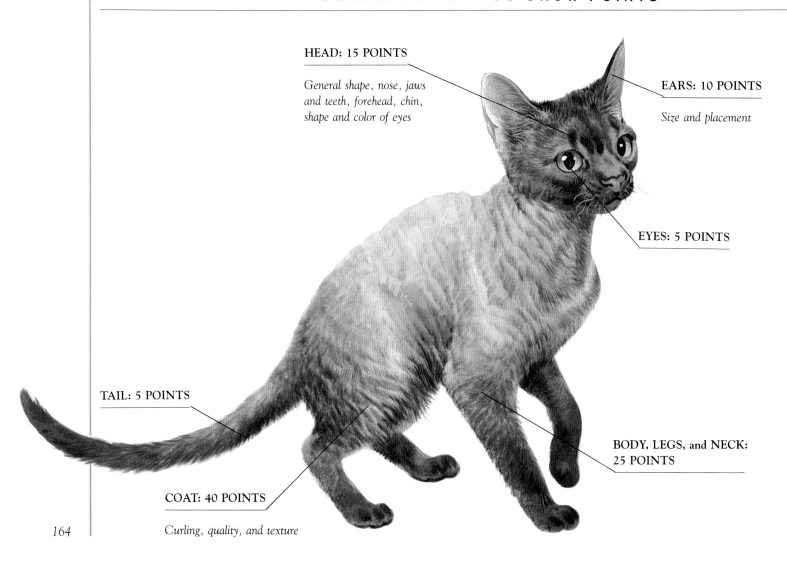

HEAD: 15 POINTS

General shape, nose, jaws and teeth, forehead, chin, shape and color of eyes

EARS: 10 POINTS

Size and placement

EYES: 5 POINTS

TAIL: 5 POINTS

BODY, LEGS, and NECK: 25 POINTS

COAT: 40 POINTS

Curling, quality, and texture

KEY CHARACTERISTICS

- **CATEGORY** Foreign Shorthair, curled.

- **OVERALL BUILD** Medium size, hard and muscular, slender but with a broad chest.

- **COAT** Very short, soft, fine coat without guard hairs; curly or wavy particularly on the body and tail.

- **HEAD** Small, modified wedge shaped with short muzzle and prominent cheekbones.

- **NOSE** No standards set.

- **CHIN** No standards set.

- **EYES** Large, oval and set wide apart, giving a unique "elfin" look.

- **EARS** Large, set low down.

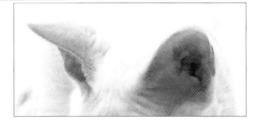

- **BODY** Long and straight with a broad chest.

- **LEGS** Long and slim.

- **PAWS** Small and oval

- **TAIL** Long, fine and tapered.

- **COLORS** All recognized colors or patterns except white markings on Siamese patterned cats.

PENALTIES

Devon Rex cats are penalized in the show ring for having incorrect head type; a short, bare, or bushy tail; a straight or shaggy coat; a cobby body; small ears or ears set high and upright on the head; slack muscles or bare patches (a fault in kittens and a serious fault in cats).

DISQUALIFICATION FEATURES

- baldness
- a kinked or abnormal tail
- a squint
- weak hind legs

DEVON REX VARIETIES

WHATEVER THEIR COLOR or coat pattern, all Devon Rex must conform to the same stringent show standard of points. The coat of the Devon Rex is quite different from that of the Cornish, and in some cats the fur may be sparse and downy on the underparts, often causing the coat color to look indistinct. Like the Cornish Rex, the first Devons were outcrossed to cats of other Foreign breeds in order to widen the gene pool of available breeding stock. Siamese cats were extensively used, and the resulting curled cats were called Si-Rex in the beginning. Si-rex is not now an accepted as correct terminology for the Siamese-patterned Devon Rex, and white markings are not permitted in cats with the Himalayan or Siamese coat pattern, where the color is restricted to the cat's points.

Apart from this requirement, all colors and patterns accepted in the feline standards are recognized in the Devon Rex, with or without white areas.

ODD-EYED WHITE
White Devon Rex cats are accepted with blue eyes, golden eyes, or odd eyes.

CHOCOLATE TORTIE POINT
The Devon Rex appears in a range of Siamese-patterned colors. At one time these cats were called Si-rex.

BLACK SMOKE DEVON REX
The Devon Rex is totally different from the Cornish. It is of similar size, but has a unique head type and unusual bodily conformation.

**TORBIE &
WHITE**
*Tortoiseshells of all
colors may have white
markings and can be
very bright and
attractive, like this
alert young cat.*

**LILAC POINT
DEVON REX**
*Siamese patterns are
quite usual, but the
eye color is generally
paler in the Rex breeds
than in the true
Siamese.*

TORBIE
*All feline colors are
accepted in this breed,
though some
associations disallow
any white markings
except in tortoiseshell
varieties.*

167

SPHYNX

ALTHOUGH IT APPEARS SO, the Sphynx is not truly hairless. The skin has the texture of soft leather and may be covered with a fine down which is almost imperceptible to the eye. A fine covering of hair is sometimes apparent on the ears, muzzle, feet, tail, and scrotum.

The first Sphynx appeared as a spontaneous mutation in a litter born to a black and white domestic cat in Ontario, Canada, in 1966. A breeder of Siamese cats took the hairless kitten, and with other breeders worked on the development of a new breed. The CFA gave the Sphynx provisional status, then revoked it. The CCFF recognized the breed for champion-ship status in 1971, and the first champion was chosen in 1972. Today the Sphynx is accepted only by a few feline associations, and it remains a rare and unique breed.

Character and Care

People-orientated and not fond of other cats, the Sphynx does not like being held or strongly petted. It often stands with one foreleg raised, and resists lying with its body touching the ground, preferring a warm surface.

It never needs brushing, but the suede-like body must be kept in good condition by hand grooming and rubbing down with a soft cloth.

BREAKDOWN OF 100 SHOW POINTS

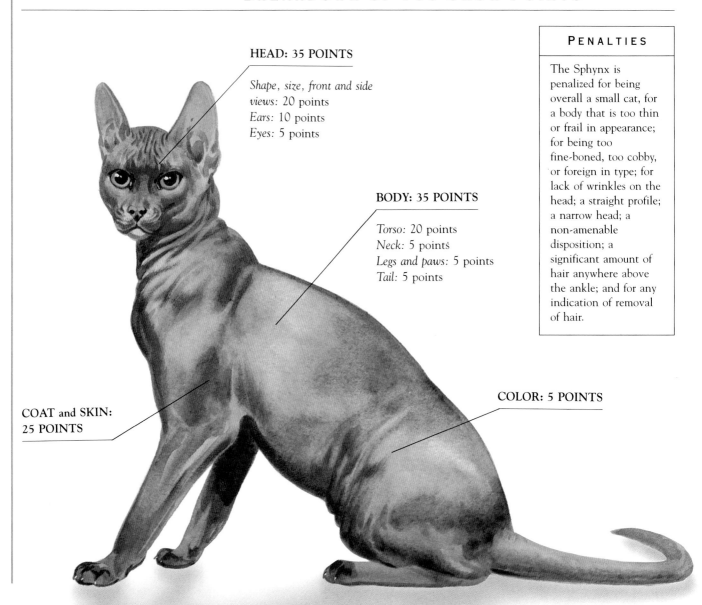

HEAD: 35 POINTS

Shape, size, front and side views: 20 points
Ears: 10 points
Eyes: 5 points

BODY: 35 POINTS

Torso: 20 points
Neck: 5 points
Legs and paws: 5 points
Tail: 5 points

COAT and SKIN: 25 POINTS

COLOR: 5 POINTS

PENALTIES

The Sphynx is penalized for being overall a small cat, for a body that is too thin or frail in appearance; for being too fine-boned, too cobby, or foreign in type; for lack of wrinkles on the head; a straight profile; a narrow head; a non-amenable disposition; a significant amount of hair anywhere above the ankle; and for any indication of removal of hair.

KEY CHARACTERISTICS

- **CATEGORY** Foreign.

- **OVERALL BUILD** Medium size, hard and muscular.

- **COAT** Appears hairless; may be covered with short fine down. Kittens have wrinkled skin; adults should retain some wrinkles.

- **COLORS** All colors and patterns are acceptable; white lockets and buttons are also accepted.

- **OTHER FEATURES** Medium-sized head is a modified wedge with rounded contours, skull is slightly rounded, forehead is flat, cheekbones are prominent. There is a slight stop at the bridge of the nose, and the muzzle is rounded, with a distinct whisker break. Chin is firm; eyes are large and almost round, slanting toward the outer corner of the ear; ears are broad based and very open, set upright on the head, hairless inside and slightly haired on the back. The medium long body has a broad chest and well-rounded abdomen; it is hard and muscular with medium bone. Legs are in proportion to the body and of medium bone; hind legs longer than forelegs, which are widely set and muscular. Paws are medium sized, oval, with long, slender toes and thick paw pads; tail is whip-like, tapering from the body to the tip. A lion tail (with a tuft of hair on the tip) is acceptable.

PROFILE
The head of the Sphynx is a modified wedge with rounded contours.

BLACK & WHITE SPHYNX
The Sphynx may appear to be hairless, but it is usually covered with a very short, fine down.

JAPANESE BOBTAIL

A NATURAL BREED, WHICH has existed in its native Japan for centuries, the Japanese Bobtail is considered to be a symbol of good luck in the home, and the tricolored variety, known as the *mi-ke* (meaning three colors), is particularly favored.

The Bobtail first came to the attention of cat fanciers in the Western world when an American cat show judge visiting Japan became captivated by the breed. Five years later, in 1968, three Bobtails were exported from Japan to the United States. More were to follow, and Bobtails were accepted for provisional status by the CFA in May 1971.

After five years of careful breeding, the Japanese Bobtail became well established in the United States and gained full recognition and Championship Status in the CFA in May 1976. It is also recognized in Britain by the Cat Association.

Character and Care

The Japanese Bobtail has an endearing personality and loves human company. It is a vocal cat, and has a soft melodious voice with a range of sounds. As a house cat, the Bobtail is well-behaved, intelligent, and playful; and as a show cat it is easy to handle.

The silky coat is easy to maintain in perfect condition with gentle brushing and combing, finishing with the hands or a silk scarf. The pompom on the tail is combed into shape, and the wide ears are kept in pristine condition by wiping daily with a cotton swab.

BREAKDOWN OF 100 SHOW POINTS

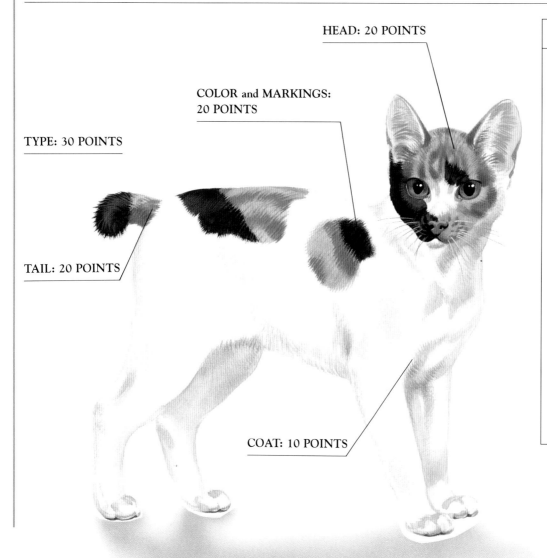

HEAD: 20 POINTS

COLOR and MARKINGS: 20 POINTS

TYPE: 30 POINTS

TAIL: 20 POINTS

COAT: 10 POINTS

PENALTIES

The Bobtail is penalized in the show ring for having a short round head or cobby build.

DISQUALIFICATION FEATURES

- tail bone absent, or extending too far beyond the body
- tail bone lacking a pompom or a fluffy appearance
- the delayed pompom effect, apparent when the pompom is preceded by an inch or two of normal tail with close-lying fur, rather than appearing to start at the base of the spine.

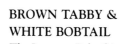

BROWN TABBY & WHITE BOBTAIL

The Japanese Bobtail is loving and talkative, and so makes a perfect pet.

BLUE-EYED VAN

The silky coat is very easy to groom by regular brushing and polishing with a silk scarf.

BLACK & WHITE VAN PATTERN

The unique tail of the Bobtail is short and may be straight or bent into one or more curves, with the hair fanning out to create a pompom effect.

KEY CHARACTERISTICS

- **CATEGORY** Shorthair.

- **OVERALL BUILD** Medium size, lean and well-muscled.

- **COAT** Soft and silky, medium length; no noticeable undercoat and relatively little shedding of hair.

- **COLORS** White, black, red, black and white, red and white, *mi-ke* (tricolor – black, red, and white), tortoiseshell. Other colors include any other color or pattern or combination of colors and patterns except coloring that is restricted to the points, such as Himalayan, or unpatterned agouti, such as Abyssinian ticking. Patterned categories include any variety of tabby with or without areas of solid unmarked color, preference being given to bold dramatic markings and rich vivid coloring.

- **OTHER FEATURES** Long fine head forming a perfect equilateral triangle with gentle curving lines, high cheek bones, and a noticeable whisker break. The muzzle is fairly broad, rounding into the whisker break. The ears are large and upright, set wide apart and at right angles to the head, and the eyes are large and oval, wide and alert. The medium-sized body is lean but well-muscled, and the legs are long and slender with neat oval paws. The short tail is said to resemble a bunny tail with the hair fanning out to create a pompom effect. If straightened, the tail bone could be four or five inches in length. It is usually jointed only at the base and may be either straight or composed of one or more curves and angles.

BURMESE

ALL MODERN BURMESE cats can trace their ancestry back to a Siamese hybrid female named Wong Mau, who was taken from Rangoon to the United States in 1930. Wong Mau was almost certainly a cat of the type known as Tonkinese today. At first she was mated with Siamese males; then her offspring were inter-mated, and some back-crossed to Wong Mau herself. From these matings three distinct types of kittens emerged – some identical to Wong Mau, some Siamese, and some much darker than Wong Mau. These cats were the foundation of the Burmese breed, which was officially recognized in 1936 by the Cat Fanciers' Association, and was the first breed of pedigree cats to be developed completely in the United States.

Due to the lack of suitable Burmese cats, outcrosses to Siamese were made from time to time. Because of this, registration was suspended by the CFA from 1947 to 1953, but the breed soon became stabilized, with a strict standard of points ensuring that it maintained its unique physique and character.

Burmese cats were exported to Britain and accepted at shows during the 1950s. Since then, the breed has developed to slightly different standards on opposite sides of the Atlantic.

Character and Care
The Burmese is a highly intelligent, active cat which can be strong-willed, but repays firm, kind handling with affection.

Its short, glossy coat needs very little grooming to keep it in top condition.

BREAKDOWN OF 100 SHOW POINTS

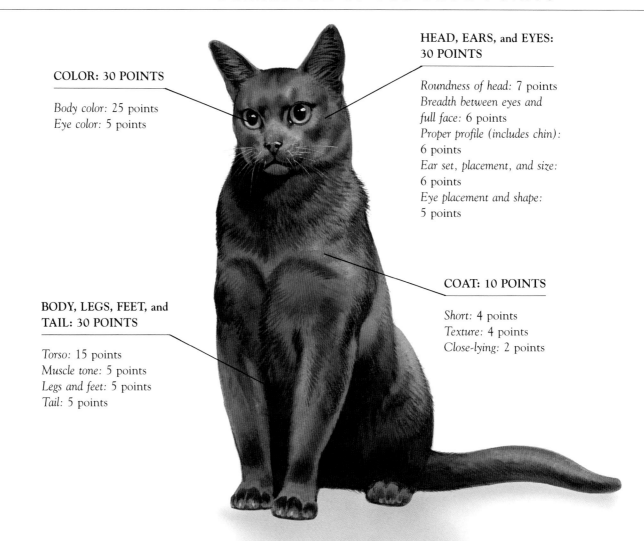

COLOR: 30 POINTS

Body color: 25 points
Eye color: 5 points

HEAD, EARS, and EYES: 30 POINTS

Roundness of head: 7 points
Breadth between eyes and full face: 6 points
Proper profile (includes chin): 6 points
Ear set, placement, and size: 6 points
Eye placement and shape: 5 points

COAT: 10 POINTS

Short: 4 points
Texture: 4 points
Close-lying: 2 points

BODY, LEGS, FEET, and TAIL: 30 POINTS

Torso: 15 points
Muscle tone: 5 points
Legs and feet: 5 points
Tail: 5 points

KEY CHARACTERISTICS

- **CATEGORY** Foreign Shorthair.

- **OVERALL BUILD** Medium size with substantial bone structure and good muscular development. The cat is surprisingly heavy for its size.

- **COAT** Very short and close lying, fine and glossy with a satin-like texture.

- **HEAD** Pleasingly rounded, with no flat planes whether viewed from the front or in profile. The face is full with a broad, short muzzle.

- **NOSE** In profile there is a definite nose break.

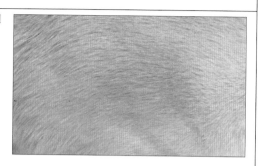

- **CHIN** Firm and rounded.

- **EYES** Large, set wide apart, with a rounded aperture.

- **EARS** Medium size, set well apart and tilted slightly forward, giving an alert expression.

- **BODY** Muscular, compact, with strong shoulders and hips.

- **LEGS** Well proportioned.

- **PAWS** Round.

- **TAIL** Medium length and straight.

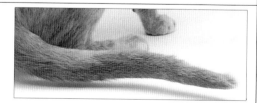

- **COLORS** *USA* In some US associations, only the sable or brown varieties are classed as Burmese. The blue, champagne or chocolate, platinum or lilac are classed as dilute division Burmese in some associations, and as Malayan in others. *UK* All accepted colors in Burmese and Malayan compete as Burmese.

PENALTIES

The Burmese is penalized in the show ring for having green eyes.

DISQUALIFICATION FEATURES

- blue eyes
- a kinked or abnormal tail
- a white locket or button

SOLID VARIETIES

STANDARDS FOR THE ideal Burmese cat differ on each side of the Atlantic Ocean. The American Burmese has a rounder head and a slightly heavier body than its British counterpart. America's Burmese also tend to have better eye color, but as this breed was originally developed in the United States, this is probably to be expected. Eye color is very difficult to assess under the artificial light of a show hall, and judges often take Burmese entrants to a window with natural light if the eye color is at all suspect.

RED The coat is actually a light tangerine color as even as possible, though very slight tabby markings are allowed on the face. Ears are darker than the body. Nose leather and paw pads are pink; eye color is yellow to gold, with deeper shades preferred.

CREAM The coat is pastel cream, with ears slightly darker than the body. Nose leather and paw pads are pink; eye color is yellow to gold, with deeper shapes preferred.

SABLE or BROWN The rich, warm, sable brown coat shades almost imperceptibly to a lighter tone on the underparts, otherwise without any shading, barring, or markings of any kind. Kittens may be ligher in color. The nose leather and paw pads are brown; the eye color ranges from yellow to gold, with the deeper shades preferred.

BLUE The coat is soft silver gray, very slightly darker on the back and tail. There should be a distinct silver sheen on the ears, face, and feet. Nose leather and paw pads are blue-gray; eye color is yellow to gold.

CHOCOLATE or CHAMPAGNE The warm milk chocolate coat should be as even as possible, though the mask and ears may be very slightly deeper in color. Nose leather is chocolate brown; paw pads are cinnamon to chocolate brown; eye color is yellow to gold, with deeper shades preferred.

LILAC or PLATINUM The pale delicate dove-gray coat has a pinkish tone, as even as possible. though the mask and ears may be very slightly deeper in color. Nose leather and paw pads are lavender pink; eye color is yellow to gold, with deeper shades preferred.

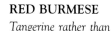

RED BURMESE

Tangerine rather than red in color, this variety is bright and very attractive, particularly when it has the desired golden eyes.

SABLE BURMESE

It is interesting to compare this American cat with those raised in Britain, when the slight differences encouraged by the slightly differing show standards become apparent.

BROWN BURMESE

Known as the Sable Burmese in the US where the breed was first developed, this variety has a rich dark brown coat and gold eye color.

CREAM BURMESE

The paler colors in the Burmese often show a very slight Himalayan effect, with darker color on the points – the face, ears, legs, paws, and tail.

LILAC BURMESE
Lilac Burmese appeared in litters when cats which carried both the chocolate and blue color genes were mated together. At first they were considered "poor Blues," but were later accepted as a new variety.

CHOCOLATE BURMESE
With its warm chocolate coat and slightly darker points, this variety is very attractive.

BLUE BURMESE
A simple dilute of the usual brown color, the Blue Burmese was the first additional variety to be recognized and accepted.

176

TORTOISESHELL VARIETIES

THE ORANGE (RED) gene was first introduced into the Burmese in Britain from three sources, a shorthaired ginger tabby, a red-pointed Siamese, and a calico domestic cat. From these beginnings, a breeding program was set up; and by the mid-1970s, clear-coated red Burmese, cream Burmese, and the invariably female tortoiseshells had been produced in considerable numbers, most of which were of very good Burmese type.

SEAL TORBIE Seal brown, red and/or light red, patched and/or mottled. Nose leather and paw pads are plain or mottled, seal brown and/or pink. The eye color is yellow to gold, with deeper shades preferred.

BLUE-CREAM or BLUE TORBIE Pale tones of blue and cream, patched and/or mottled. Nose leather and paw pads are plain or mottled, pink and/or blue-gray. The eye color is yellow to gold, with deeper shades preferred.

CHOCOLATE TORBIE Milk chocolate, red and/or light red, patched and/or mottled. Nose leather and paw pads are plain or mottled, milk chocolate and/or light red or pink. The eye color is yellow to gold, with the deeper shades preferred.

LILAC-CREAM or LILAC TORBIE Lilac and pale cream, patched and/or mottled. Nose leather and paw pads are plain or mottled, pale pink and/or lavender pink. The eye color is yellow to gold, with deeper shades preferred.

Painted Varieties

The "points" are the mask (face), ears, legs and paws, and the tail. The color of the points is the same as the body color, and show little contrast, but should be as equal in color density as possible.

BLUE TORTIE OR BLUE-CREAM

Tortoiseshells have mixed colors in their coats, the Blue Tortie being blue and cream. There are four colors of Tortie Burmese – brown, blue, chocolate, and lilac.

In all varieties, the body color will be paler on the underparts than on the back and legs.

The eye color is in the yellow/gold range with deeper shades preferred. In non-tabby varieties, allowance is made in kittens and adolescent cats for an overall paler body color, and for faint tabby barring or ghost tabby markings. Tabby markings in adult cats of non-tabby varieties and white hairs are faults.

CHOCOLATE TORTIE BURMESE

After the introduction of the red or orange gene into the breed, a range of tortoiseshell Burmese soon began to appear.

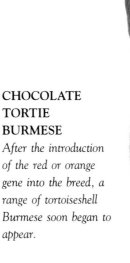

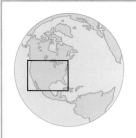

TIFFANIE

TIFFANIE

The Tiffanie is a long-coated cat of Burmese type and is accepted in all colors found in the Burmese and Malayan range.

THIS BREED COMBINES the conformation and coloring of the typical Burmese with an attractive coat of long silky hair. First developed in the United States from long-coated kittens which appeared from time to time in otherwise normal litters of pedigree Burmese, the Tiffanie was later developed as a breed in its own right. The American breeders concentrated on the sable Tiffanie, born a pale *café au lait* color, and gradually developing the long sable coat with maturity. In Britain, long-coated cats of good Burmese conformation came from the Burmilla breeding programs and were refined by back-crosses to Burmese, which resulted in Tiffanie kittens of all colors found in the Burmese and Malayan ranges. At the time of writing (1995), no association officially accepts this breed, and no standard of points is available, including penalties.

Character and Care

Just like its Burmese ancestors, the Tiffanie is playful and affectionate with an extrovert nature, making it a good pet.

The long coat is quite easy to care for with regular grooming.

BROWN SMOKE

In Britain, the Tiffanie is a product of the Burmilla breeding plan and is found in a variety of Smoke colors.

KEY CHARACTERISTICS
• **CATEGORY** Semi-longhair.
• **OVERALL BUILD** Medium size with substantial bone; it is surprisingly heavy for its size.
• **COAT** Of medium length, fine and silky, longer at the ruff (frill) and with a flowing plume-like tail.
• **COLORS** USA Sable UK All colors found in the Burmese and Malayan range.
• **OTHER FEATURES** Head is pleasingly rounded with no flat planes; face is full with a broad, short muzzle; nose is short with a break in profile. Chin is strong; eyes large, set wide apart, the top line showing a straight, Oriental slant toward the nose, the lower line rounded. Ears are medium size, broad based with rounded tips, set wide apart with a slight forward tilt. Body is medium length, hard, compact and muscular, with a strong, rounded chest and straight back. Legs are slender, and in proportion to the body; paws small and oval; tail medium length, not thick at the base and tapering only slightly to a rounded tip, well covered with flowing silky hair.

SINGAPURA

A N AMERICAN CAT breeder, Tommy Meadows, developed the Singapura from cats she discovered in Singapore. She decided to import some into the United States, and drew up a careful programme for the development of the breed. Her work has been rewarded by the production of an attractive, viable feline breed with considerable esthetic appeal. The Singapura has a ticked coat, similar to that of the Abyssinian, and is of moderate Foreign Shorthair bone structure and conformation.

Character and Care

The Singapura is a happy, friendly cat with a playful nature.

The short, fine coat is extremely easy to keep in good condition with very little grooming. A light combing removes dead hairs, and occasional brushing tones the skin. Hand grooming or stroking with a silk scarf imparts a healthy looking sheen to the coat.

KEY CHARACTERISTICS
● **CATEGORY** Foreign Shorthair.
● **OVERALL BUILD** Small to medium in size, moderately stocky and muscular.
● **COAT** Very short and fine; each hair should have at least two bands of dark ticking separated by light bands of colour. Each individual hair is light next to the skin and dark at the tip.
● **COLORS** Sepia Agouti. The ground color is warm ivory; the ticking is dark brown. The muzzle, chin, chest and stomach are the color of unbleached muslin; the ears and bridge of the nose are salmon toned. The nose leather is pale to dark salmon pink, outlined with dark brown; the paw pads are rosy brown; the eye rims are dark brown; the eye color is hazel, green or yellow.
● **OTHER FEATURES** Head is rounded, with a definite whisker break; nose short and blunt; chin well developed; eyes large and almond shaped; ears large and slightly pointed, set fairly wide apart, giving an alert expression. Body is stocky and muscular; legs are heavy; paws small and oval; tail of medium length with a blunt tip.

BROWN TICKED SINGAPURA

With its short, fine, ticked coat and happy, friendly nature, this rare breed makes a perfect pet.

TONKINESE

A HYBRID OF Burmese and Siamese cats, the Tonkinese has physical features of both these breeds. A mating between a Burmese and a Siamese gives all Tonkinese kittens, whereas the mating of two Tonkinese cats produces, on average, two Tonkinese kittens to one Burmese and one Siamese.

Tonkinese cats have dark points which merge gradually into the body color, which is intermediate between the typical pale Siamese and the dark Burmese coloring. Tonkinese eye color is blue-green or turquoise, never Siamese blue or Burmese gold.

Character and Care

The Tonkinese is a friendly and affectionate cat, with a strong sense of mischief. Extrovert and intelligent, it is generally good with other cats, as well as with dogs and children. It is less vocal than the Siamese.

The coat is very easy to keep in good condition with very little grooming. Regular combing to remove dead hair, and buffing with a silk scarf or grooming mitten imparts a healthy sheen.

BREAKDOWN OF 100 SHOW POINTS

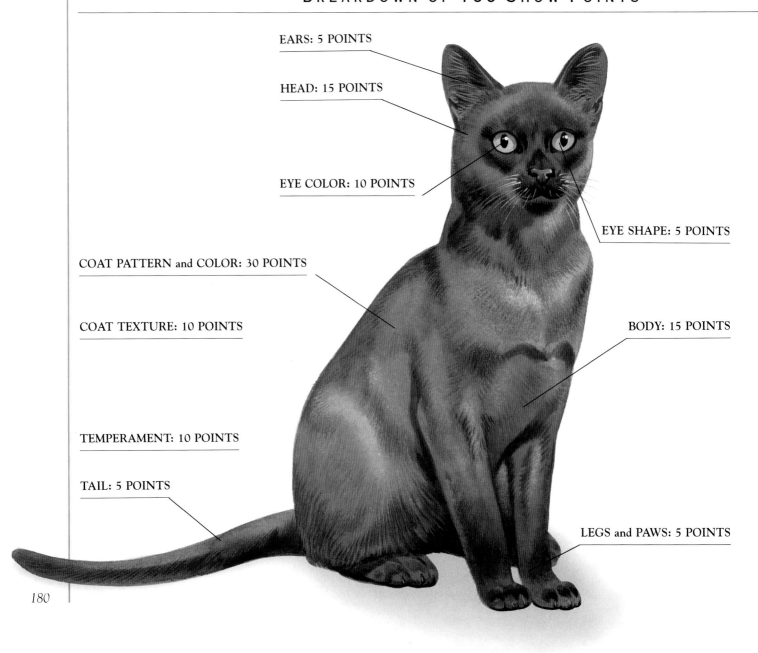

EARS: 5 POINTS

HEAD: 15 POINTS

EYE COLOR: 10 POINTS

EYE SHAPE: 5 POINTS

COAT PATTERN and COLOR: 30 POINTS

COAT TEXTURE: 10 POINTS

BODY: 15 POINTS

TEMPERAMENT: 10 POINTS

TAIL: 5 POINTS

LEGS and PAWS: 5 POINTS

KEY CHARACTERISTICS

- **CATEGORY** Foreign Shorthair.

- **OVERALL BUILD** Medium size, muscular and surprisingly heavy for its size.

- **COAT** Short, fine and close-lying with a soft, fur-like texture.

- **HEAD** Modified wedge shape, longer than it is wide, with high, gently planed cheekbones and strong contours to the brow, cheek and profile. In profile there should be a slight stop at eye level; a definite break is undesirable. The muzzle is blunt, with a definite whisker break.

- **NOSE** No standards available.

- **CHIN** Firm but not massive.

- **EYES** Almond shaped, slanted along cheekbone toward outer edge of ear.

- **EARS** Medium size with oval tips, set wide apart and tilted slightly forward. The hair on the ears is very short.

- **BODY** Medium length, muscular but not coarse, with tight abdomen.

- **LEGS** Slim.

- **PAWS** More oval than round.

- **TAIL** Medium to long, tapering.

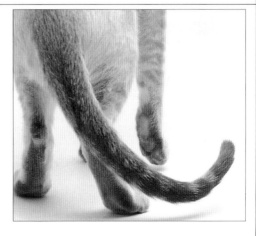

- **COLORS** Natural mink, blue, champagne mink, platinum mink, red, cream, natural mink torbie, blue torbie, champagne mink torbie, platinum mink torbie.

PENALTIES

Tonkinese cats are penalized in the show ring for having a palpable tail fault.

DISQUALIFICATION FEATURES
- yellow eyes
- a white locket or button
- a visible kink in the tail

MINK VARIETIES

THE TONKINESE IS bred from Burmese and Siamese, and as would be expected, is intermediate to those breeds in both conformation and coloring. As a pet it suits those people who find the show-type Siamese to be too extreme, but do not favour the typical chunkiness and almost uniform coloration of the Burmese. Indeed, a typical Tonkinese is very similar to the "old-fashioned" type of Siamese cat that many people today desire as pets.

NATURAL MINK A medium-brown coat shades to a lighter tone on the underparts. The points and nose leather are dark brown; the paw pads are medium to dark brown; the eye color is blue-green.

BLUE A soft gray-blue color shades to a lighter tone on the underparts. The points are slate blue (distinctly darker than the body color). Nose leather and paw pads are blue-gray; eye color is blue-green.

CHAMPAGNE MINK The buff-cream body has medium brown points. Nose leather is cinnamon-brown; paw pads are cinnamon-pink to cinnamon-brown; eye color is blue-green.

RED The golden cream coat has apricot underparts. The points are light to medium ruddy brown; the nose leather and paw pads are caramel-pink; the eye color is blue-green.

PLATINUM MINK The pale silvery gray coat has warm overtones (not white or cream). The points are pewter gray – distinctly darker than the body color; nose leather is lavender pink to lavender gray; paw pads are lavender pink; eye color is blue-green.

Pointed Varieties

The "points" are the mask (face) ears, legs and paws, and the tail. The points are densely marked, but gradually merge into the body color. The color of the points is the same as the body color, but denser and darker.

The body color in the adult cat should be rich and even, and shade almost imperceptibly into a slightly lighter color on the underparts. There is a distinct contrast between the points and body color whatever the color variety. The eye color is blue-green (aquamarine), with depth, clarity and brilliance.

N.B. Allowance is made for lighter body color in kittens and adolescent cats, and for slight barring in the coat; colors darken with maturity – full coloration may take up to 16 months to develop, particularly in the dilute color varieties.

BROWN TONKINESE

The darkest color variety with a medium brown coat. As in other Tonkinese varieties, the eye color is blue–green.

**CHOCOLATE
TONKINESE**
*The product of
Siamese and Burmese,
the Tonkinese has
coloring between the
two breeds.*

**LILAC
TONKINESE**
*Equivalent to the Lilac
Burmese and Lilac
Point Siamese, this cat
has a pale silvery gray
coat with warm
overtones.*

183

NEW VARIETIES

MEMBERS OF THE Cat Association of Britain, working with new colors in Burmese and Siamese cats, decided to introduce these into the Tonkinese, and the breeding programs were provisionally accepted by CA prior to its becoming the British member of FIFe in 1990. The Cat Association of Britain therefore offers special awards for Tonkinese in the following color varieties: seal, blue, chocolate, cinnamon, lilac, fawn, caramel, beige, red, cream, apricot, indigo, and all these colors as tortoiseshell, tabby, and torbie.

**CREAM
TONKINESE**
*This cat should be a
rich warm cream with
slightly darker points,
except for the legs
which may be paler
than in other colors.*

RED TONKINESE
*Red and Cream
Tonkinese are often
quite similar and can
be difficult to tell apart
as kittens.*

BLUE TORTIE
Bluish silver-gray either patched or mingled with shades of cream produce this pretty variety.

CHOCOLATE TORTIE
The introduction of the red or orange gene into Tonkinese breeding soon gave rise to an entire range of tortoiseshells.

LILAC TORTIE TONKINESE
A paler version of the Blue Tortie with pale dove gray patched or mingled with pale cream. Like its darker cousin, the Lilac Tortie has blue-green eyes.

BOMBAY

BECAUSE OF ITS looks, the Bombay cat has been referred to as the "patent-leather kid with new-penny eyes," an apt description for this shining jet-black feline. Developed from outstanding specimens of black American Shorthair and sable Burmese, the desired type was quickly achieved, and Bombays were found to breed true. Full recognition and championship status was granted by the CFA in 1976.

Although the cat looks like a black American-style Burmese, the early pioneers of the breed thought it looked like a miniature version of the Indian (Asian) black panther and so, after much deliberation, chose Bombay as the breed name.

Character and Care

The Bombay has a very even temperament. It is generally strong and healthy, affectionate and playful, making it a good pet.

The coat is easy to maintain with a balanced diet and minimal grooming. Buffing with a silk scarf or velvet grooming mitt enhances the typical patent-leather gloss.

BREAKDOWN OF 100 SHOW POINTS

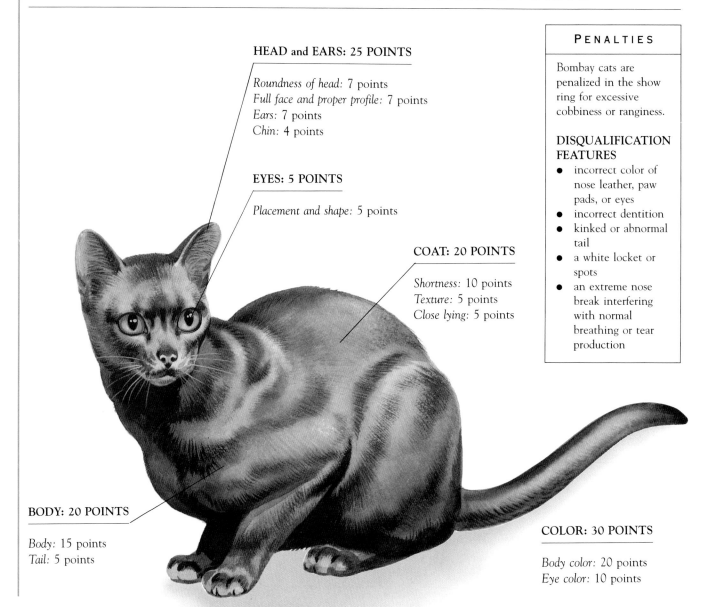

HEAD and EARS: 25 POINTS

Roundness of head: 7 points
Full face and proper profile: 7 points
Ears: 7 points
Chin: 4 points

EYES: 5 POINTS

Placement and shape: 5 points

COAT: 20 POINTS

Shortness: 10 points
Texture: 5 points
Close lying: 5 points

BODY: 20 POINTS

Body: 15 points
Tail: 5 points

COLOR: 30 POINTS

Body color: 20 points
Eye color: 10 points

PENALTIES

Bombay cats are penalized in the show ring for excessive cobbiness or ranginess.

DISQUALIFICATION FEATURES

- incorrect color of nose leather, paw pads, or eyes
- incorrect dentition
- kinked or abnormal tail
- a white locket or spots
- an extreme nose break interfering with normal breathing or tear production

BOMBAY

The true Bombay from the United States was produced from Sable Burmese and American Shorthairs, and is a unique, shiny jet black cat with large golden eyes.

KEY CHARACTERISTICS

- **CATEGORY** Foreign Shorthair.

- **OVERALL BUILD** Medium size, muscular, surprisingly heavy for size.

- **COAT** Fine and short with satin-like texture, close lying and with a sheen like patent leather.

- **COLOR** Black only. Coat-jet black to the roots with a patent-leather sheen. Nose leather and paw pads, black. Eye color, gold to copper; deeper shades preferred.

- **OTHER FEATURES** Pleasingly round head with no sharp angles, full face with good width between the eyes, tapering to a short, strong muzzle. In profile there is a visible nose break. Medium sized ears with slightly rounded tips set wide apart and tilting slightly forward giving an alert expression. Muscular, medium sized body with legs in proportion, round paws, and a straight, medium length tail.

BOMBAY (ASIAN BLACK)

In Britain, the black Asian, a product of Burmese and Shorthair, is known as the Bombay.

187

BURMILLA

AN ACCIDENTAL MATING between a lilac Burmese female and a Chinchilla Silver male in 1981 resulted in the birth of four black-shaded silver female kittens. All were of foreign conformation, and had short dense coats. They looked so spectacular and caused so much interest that similar matings were carried out. In 1983, the Cat Association of Britain accepted breeding programs and a standard of points for the breed to be known as Burmilla, to be developed as a shorthaired silver cat of medium foreign type, showing a striking con-trast between the pure silver undercoat and the shaded or tipped markings. FIFe granted international breed status to the Burmilla in 1994.

This elegant cat is of medium foreign type with a muscular body, long sturdy legs, and a moderately thick, long tail. The head is a medium wedge, with large ears, a short nose, and large expressive eyes. Its most impressive feature, however, is the sparkling shaded or tipped ("shell") coat. The ground color is pure silver white, with shading or tipping in any of the recognized solid or tortoiseshell colors,

BREAKDOWN OF 100 SHOW POINTS

NB Annotated points are those set in Europe.

HEAD: 50 POINTS

Shape, nose and chin:
20 points
Ear placement and shape:
10 points
Eye placement, shape and colour: 20 points

BODY: 25 POINTS

Shape and structure; legs and paws; tail shape and length

COAT: 20 POINTS

Length and texture: 10 points
Evenness of shading/tipping:
10 points

CONDITION: 5 POINTS

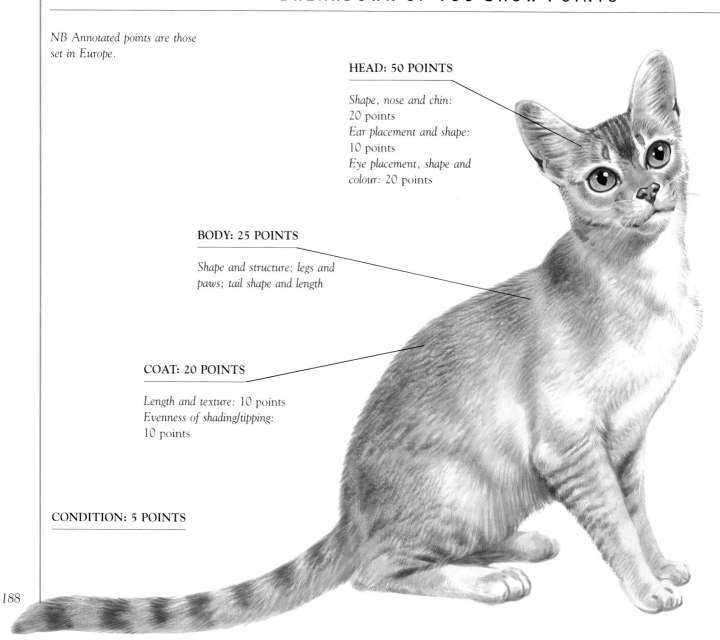

which must be uniformly distributed. The eyelids, lips, and nose leather are rimmed with the basic color, and delicate tracings of tabby markings are present on the points, which are more clearly defined on the shaded Burmilla than on the tipped varieties.

Character and Care

The Burmilla is easy-going and relaxed, has a playful nature, and is very affectionate.

The dense coat is best groomed with a rubber brush to loosen dead hairs before being given a thorough combing.

PENALTIES

The Burmilla is penalized for having a weak chin; incorrect eye color in adults; a cobby or oriental type body in adults; and a coat that is too long or shaggy.

KEY CHARACTERISTICS

- **CATEGORY** Foreign Shorthair.

- **OVERALL BUILD** Medium size and build.

- **COAT** Short and dense with a silky texture; with enough undercoat to give a slight lift to the coat.

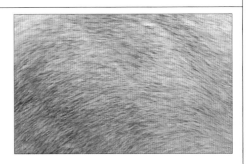

- **HEAD** Gently rounded at the top with medium width between the ears; wide at eye level and tapering to a short, blunt wedge.

- **NOSE** The profile shows a gentle nose break.

- **CHIN** Firm, level with the tip of the nose.

- **EYES** Large, set well apart and slightly oblique, luminous and expressive.

- **EARS** Medium to large, broad-based and with rounded tips. Set with a slightly forward tilt.

- **BODY** Medium length, with a straight back and rounded chest.

- **LEGS** Slender, with strong bone; the hind legs are slightly longer than forelegs.

- **PAWS** Neat and oval.

- **TAIL** Medium to long, fairly thick at the base and tapering slightly to a rounded tip.

- **COLORS** Shaded or tipped in the following colors: black, blue, brown, chocolate, lilac, red, cream, red tortoiseshell, blue tortoiseshell, brown tortoiseshell, chocolate tortoiseshell, lilac tortoiseshell.

BURMILLA VARIETIES

BLACK TIPPED
The pure silver white coat of the Burmilla is lightly tipped with black in this variety.

ELEGANT CATS OF medium foreign conformation, the Burmilla male is larger and more stocky than the dainty female. Any tendency to the fine bone of the Siamese, or the cobby type of the Shorthair, is regarded as a fault.

BLACK SHADED or TIPPED The coat is pure silver white, shaded or tipped with black. The nose leather is brick red; the paw pads and soles are black; the eye color is green.

BLUE SHADED or TIPPED The coat is pure silver white, shaded or tipped with blue-gray. The nose leather is brick red; the paw pads and soles are blue-gray; the eye color is green.

BROWN SHADED or TIPPED The coat is pure silver white, shaded or tipped with dark brown. The nose leather is brick red; the paw pads and soles are dark brown; the eye color is green.

CHOCOLATE SHADED or TIPPED The coat is pure silver white, shaded or tipped with milk chocolate. The nose leather is brick red; the paw pads are chocolate tinged with pink; the soles are chocolate; the eye color is green.

CHOCOLATE TIPPED BURMILLA
In the Chocolate Tipped, the pure silver undercoat is tipped with milk chocolate at the ends of each hair.

BROWN SHADED BURMILLA
The shaded varieties are more heavily tipped than the tipped varieties, producing a stronger color. In the Brown Shaded, the shading is dark brown on the silver base coat.

BROWN TIPPED BURMILLA
This Brown Tipped Burmilla is typical of the breed, playful and affectionate.

LILAC SHADED or TIPPED The coat is pure silver white, shaded or tipped with lilac (light gray with a pinkish tinge). The nose leather is brick red; the paw pads are lavender pink; the soles are gray tinged with pink; and the eye color is green.

RED SHADED or TIPPED The coat is pure silver white, shaded or tipped with red. The nose leather and paw pads are pink; the soles are red; the eye color is green or amber.

CREAM SHADED or TIPPED The coat is pure silver white, shaded or tipped with pale cream. The nose leather and paw pads are pink; the soles are cream; the eye color is either green or amber.

RED TORTOISESHELL SHADED or TIPPED The coat is pure white, shaded or tipped with a patchwork of black and red. The nose leather and paw pads are black, pink, or mottled black and pink; the soles are black and/or red; the eye color is green or amber.

BLUE TORTOISESHELL SHADED or TIPPED The coat is pure white, shaded or tipped with a patchwork of blue-gray and cream. The nose leather and paw pads are blue-gray, pink, or mottled blue-gray and pink; the soles are blue-gray and/or cream; the eye color is either green or amber.

191

**BLUE SHADED
BURMILLA**

*A silver white coat
shaded with blue-gray,
set off by a brick red
nose and large,
luminous green eyes.*

**BROWN TORTOISESHELL SHADED or TIP-
PED** The coat is pure white, shaded or tipped
with a patchwork of dark brown and red or
light red. The nose leather and paw pads are
dark brown, pink, or mottled dark brown and
pink; the soles are dark brown and/or red; the
eye color is green or amber.
**CHOCOLATE TORTOISESHELL SHADED or
TIPPED** The coat is pure white, shaded or
tipped with a patchwork of milk chocolate and
light red. The nose leather and paw pads are
chocolate, pink, or mottled chocolate and
pink; the soles are chocolate and/or light red;
the eye color is green or amber.

**LILAC TORTOISESHELL SHADED or TIP-
PED** The coat is pure white, shaded or tipped
with a patchwork of lilac (light gray with a
pinkish tinge) and cream. The nose leather and
paw pads are lavender pink, pink, or mottled
lavender pink and pink; the soles are gray
tinged with pink; the eye color is either
green or amber.
Note In all colors, the Tipped Burmilla is
lighter overall than the Shaded Burmilla.

**BLACK SHADED
BURMILLA**

*As in all Burmilla
cats, the paw pads and
soles (the area from
the paw to the hock)
match the color of the
shading or tipping on
the silver coat.*

ASIAN

The Burmilla is just one variety in a larger family of cats known as the Asian Group. All of the variants are of Burmese type and basic conformation, but do not have the Burmese coat color or slight restriction of color to the "points" area as found in the usual Burmese cat.

TICKED TABBY
Each hair of the coat is ticked with two or three bands of color which produces the effect commonly seen in a wild rabbit. All ticked tabby Asian cats should have clear tabby bars marking the legs and tail.

Rather the cats of the Asian Group bear the same relationship to Burmese as the Orientals do to Siamese. Within the Asian Group are found a range of cats with unusual and very attractive coats for color pattern and texture. It includes the Burmilla, Asian Smoke, Asian Tabby, Bombay, and Tiffanie. The Burmilla is by far the most successful in terms of numbers and popularity, and, in fact, most of the other Asians have arisen as off-shoots of the carefully controlled programs designed to breed the Burmilla in a wide variety of colors, and with the creation of a broad and viable base from which to select second and third generation crosses.

ASIAN EYES
All varieties of Asian cats have characteristically large, full, and expressive eyes which are set well apart. They are slightly Oriental in setting, but are neither Oriental nor round in shape.

193

ORIENTAL BREEDS

SIAMESE

PROBABLY THE BEST KNOWN of all pedigree breeds, the Siamese cat of today is quite different from that seen in the early 1900s, though it still retains its points, caused by the Himalayan factor, the gene which restricts the true coloring to the animal's face, ears, legs, paws, and tail.

Seal-pointed cats were presented by the Royal Court of Siam to British and American diplomats toward the end of the nineteenth century, and the breed gained public interest which has continued to grow.

Although the original Royal Cats of Siam were seal-pointed, some had lighter brown points and were eventually recognized as being a separate color variety which was called Chocolate Point. A naturally occurring dilute factor also became apparent when the almost black coloration of the seal point gave rise to

cats with slate-gray extremities. These were eventually accepted as the color variety Blue Point.

With increasing knowledge of feline color genetics, breeders of Siamese cats realized that they could increase the range of color varieties by first making judicious outcrosses, then back-breeding the offspring to Siamese of excellent type. The red series of points colors was added by outcrossing to red, red tabby, and tortoise-shell cats, and a range of colors in tabby-pointed cats was developed from out-crosses with tabbies.

Britain's GCCF and the CA recognize all short-coated pointed cats of Oriental type as Siamese, as do some foreign associations, in particular FIFe. Others such as America's CFA accept only the four original, naturally occurring colors as Siamese, and register the .red

BREAKDOWN OF 100 SHOW POINTS

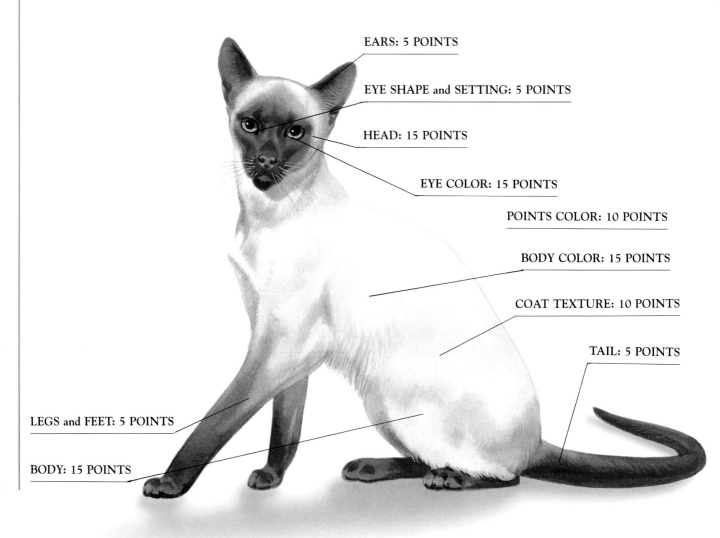

EARS: 5 POINTS

EYE SHAPE and SETTING: 5 POINTS

HEAD: 15 POINTS

EYE COLOR: 15 POINTS

POINTS COLOR: 10 POINTS

BODY COLOR: 15 POINTS

COAT TEXTURE: 10 POINTS

TAIL: 5 POINTS

LEGS and FEET: 5 POINTS

BODY: 15 POINTS

series and the tabby (or lynx point) series as Colorpoint Shorthairs.

Character and Care

The typical Siamese cat has an extrovert personality. It is very affectionate with people and pets that it likes, is lively and intelligent, and can be very vocal. Siamese cats do not like being left alone for long periods, and do better as pets when kept in pairs or small groups. They are naturally fastidiously clean and make perfect house pets.

The short fine coat is kept in good condition by stroking with clean hands or buffing with a silk scarf. The large ears need regular cleaning, and Siamese should be provided with a scratching post and lots of toys.

PENALTIES

The Siamese is penalized for having belly spots or spots on the flanks; white or lighter colored hairs, or ticked hairs in the points; bars and stripes in the points, except in Tabby-pointed varieties; insufficient contrast in color between the body color and the points; white patches or white toes; any eye color other than blue; a kinked tail; and malocclusion resulting in either an undershot or overshot jaw.

KEY CHARACTERISTICS

- **CATEGORY** Foreign Shorthair.

- **OVERALL BUILD** Medium size, long and svelte.

- **COAT** Very short and fine, glossy, silky and close-lying.

- **HEAD** Medium sized in proportion to the body; wedge-shaped with straight lines, the wedge starting at the nose and gradually increasing in width in straight lines on each side to the ears. No whisker break.

- **NOSE** Long and straight without any break.

- **CHIN** Medium size, the tip forming a vertical line with the tip of the nose.

- **EYES** Medium size and almond shaped, set slightly slanting toward the nose in harmony with the lines of the wedge.

- **EARS** Large and pointed, wide at the base, placed to continue the line of the wedge.

- **BODY** Long and svelte, well muscled but still dainty and elegant. The shoulders should not be wider than the hips.

- **LEGS** Long and fine, in proportion to the body.

- **PAWS** Small and oval.

- **TAIL** Very long, thin at the base and tapering to a fine point.

- **COLORS** Seal point, blue point, chocolate point, lilac point, red point, cream point, seal torbie point, blue torbie point, chocolate torbie point, lilac torbie point, seal tabby point, blue tabby point, chocolate tabby point, lilac tabby point, red tabby point, cream tabby point, seal torbie tabby point, blue torbie tabby point, chocolate torbie tabby point, lilac torbie tabby point (lilac (frost) torbie point).

SIAMESE VARIETIES

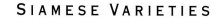

THE BODY MUST be even in color with subtle shading when allowed in the color variety. The points – mask, ears, legs, feet, and tail – must be all of the same shade and clearly defined. The mask should cover the entire face including the whisker pads and be connected to the ears by traced markings. There should be no ticking or white hairs in the points. The eye color of all the following varieties is deep, vivid blue.

SEAL POINT The body color is beige to cream or pale fawn; the points color dark seal brown. The nose leather and paw pads are dark seal brown; the eye color is deep, vivid blue.

RED POINT The body color is creamy white; the points color bright, warm orange. Nose leather pink; paw pads pink and/or red.

BLUE POINT The body color is bluish-white of a glacial tone; the points color blue-gray. The nose leather and paw pads are blue-gray.

CHOCOLATE POINT The body color is ivory;

RED POINT SIAMESE
This is a cat of extreme show type with its large flared ears following the lines of the wedge-shaped head. The body is creamy white, and the matching points are a warm orange.

SEAL POINT SIAMESE
The original color, once known as the Royal Cat of Siam. This cat has a pale fawn body and dark seal-brown points, which may appear to be black.

BLUE POINT SIAMESE
Blue Point Siamese often show more shading on the body than cats with other points' color.

the points color milk chocolate. The nose leather is milk chocolate; the paw pads are cinnamon to milk chocolate.

LILAC POINT (FROST POINT) The body color is glacial white (magnolia); the points color frosty gray with a slight pinkish tone. The nose leather and paw pads are lavender pink.

CREAM POINT The body color is creamy white; the points color pastel cream. The nose leather and paw pads are pink.

SEAL TORTIE POINT The body color is beige shading to fawn; the points color seal, patched or mingled with red and/or light red. The nose leather and pads are seal brown or pink.

CHOCOLATE POINT SIAMESE
The Chocolate Point has an ivory body and points of a warm milk chocolate.

199

LILAC POINT SIAMESE

This is the palest of the Siamese, with a magnolia-colored coat and points of a pink-toned frosty gray. It is known as the Frost Point in some cat associations.

BLUE TORTIE POINT The body color is bluish-white; the points color blue-gray patched or mingled with pastel cream. The nose leather and paw pads are blue-gray and/or pink.

CHOCOLATE TORTIE POINT The body color is ivory; the points color milk chocolate patched or mingled with red and/or light red. The nose leather is milk chocolate and/or pink; paw pads are cinnamon to milk chocolate and/or pink.

FROST TORTIE POINT The body color is glacial white (magnolia); the points color frosty gray with a pinkish tone patched or mingled with pale cream. Nose leather and paw pads lavender pink and/or pale pink.

SEAL TABBY POINT The body color is beige; the points color dark seal tabby; the rims around the eyes and nose are seal brown. The nose leather is brick red, pink or seal brown; the paw pads are seal brown.

BLUE TABBY POINT The body color is bluish white; the points color blue-gray tabby; the rims around the eyes and nose are blue-gray. The nose leather is old rose or blue-gray; the paw pads are blue-gray.

CHOCOLATE TABBY POINT The body color is ivory; the points color milk chocolate tabby; the rims around the eyes and nose are milk chocolate. The nose leather is light red, pink, or milk chocolate; the paw pads are cinnamon to milk chocolate.

FROST TABBY POINT The body color is glacial white (magnolia); the points color lilac tabby – frosty gray with slightly pinkish-toned tabby markings – the rims around the eyes and nose are lavender pink. The nose leather is lavender pink or pink; the paw pads are lavender pink.

RED TABBY POINT The body color is off-

CREAM POINT SIAMESE

The creamy white body of this variety is accented by points of a delicate pastel cream.

white with a slight red tinge; the points color warm orange tabby; the rims around the eyes and nose are dark pink. The nose leather is brick red or pink; the paw pads are pink.

CREAM TABBY POINT The body color is creamy white; the points color cream tabby with a cold tone; the rims around the eyes and nose are dark pink. The nose leather and paw pads are pink.

SEAL TORBIE POINT The body color is beige; the points color has seal tabby markings patched or mingled with red or light red torbie markings. The nose rims are seal; the nose leather and paw pads are seal, brick red, or pink, or seal mottled with brick red and/or pink.

BLUE TORBIE POINT The body color is bluish white; the points color has blue tabby markings, patched or mingled with cream torbie markings. The nose rims are blue-gray; the nose leather is blue-gray, old rose, or pink, or blue-gray mottled with old rose and/or pink; the paw pads are blue-gray and/or pink.

CHOCOLATE TORBIE POINT The body color is ivory; the points color has milk chocolate tabby markings, patched or mingled with red or light red torbie markings. The nose rims are chocolate; the nose leather milk chocolate, pale red, or pink, or milk chocolate mottled with pale red or pink; the paw pads are cinnamon to milk chocolate and/or pink.

FROST TORBIE POINT The body color is glacial white (magnolia); the points color has lilac tabby – frosty gray with slightly pinkish toned tabby markings – patched or mingled with pale cream torbie markings. The nose rims are lavender pink; the nose leather and paw pads are lavender pink, pale pink, or lavender pink mottled with pale pink.

BLUE TABBY POINT SIAMESE
Originally called Lynx Points, Tabby Point Siamese were produced by breeders entranced by a litter of kittens which resulted from a mismating.

RED TABBY POINT SIAMESE
In this variety, the off-white body has a slightly red tinge, and the points are a warm orange tabby.

COLORPOINT SHORTHAIR

WHEN SIAMESE CATS were mated with cats of other varieties, such as the tabby shorthair, in order to achieve new colors and patterns, the Colorpoint Shorthair was the result. As the gene which restricts the color to the points in Siamese is recessive, the resulting kittens were colored all over.

When these cross-bred cats were mated back to high-quality Siamese, however, Siamese patterned offspring were produced, and successive back-crossing to Siamese upgraded the "new" Siamese to conform to the rigorous standards set by various associations. In Britain, the new colors were gradually accepted as additions to the Siamese varieties, but in the United States, some associations decided to accept such cats as Colorpoint Shorthairs.

Character and Care

Siamese in everything but name, the Colorpoint Shorthair is a delightfully intelligent, agile, and affectionate pet.

It is very easy to maintain in top condition by feeding a good diet and needs minimal grooming, just combing through to remove any dead hair and buffing the fine coat either with the hands or a silk scarf.

BREAKDOWN OF 100 SHOW POINTS

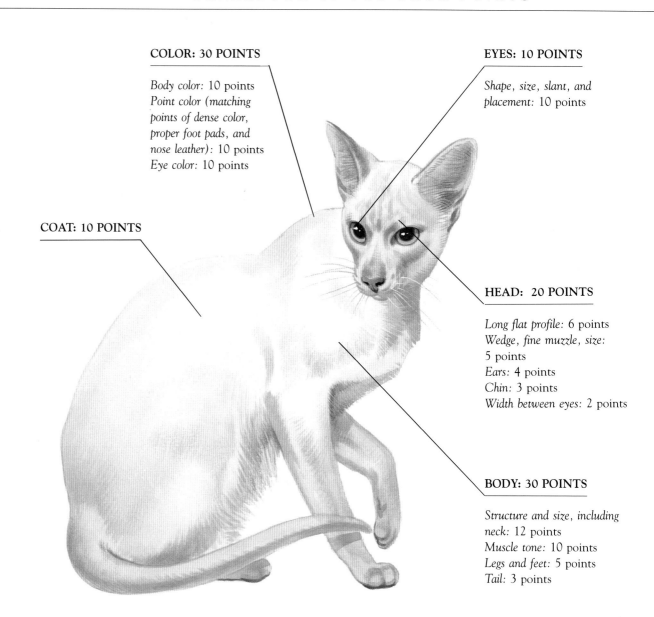

COLOR: 30 POINTS

Body color: 10 points
Point color (matching points of dense color, proper foot pads, and nose leather): 10 points
Eye color: 10 points

COAT: 10 POINTS

EYES: 10 POINTS

Shape, size, slant, and placement: 10 points

HEAD: 20 POINTS

Long flat profile: 6 points
Wedge, fine muzzle, size: 5 points
Ears: 4 points
Chin: 3 points
Width between eyes: 2 points

BODY: 30 POINTS

Structure and size, including neck: 12 points
Muscle tone: 10 points
Legs and feet: 5 points
Tail: 3 points

KEY CHARACTERISTICS

- **CATEGORY** Foreign Shorthair.

- **OVERALL BUILD** Medium size, svelte and dainty.

- **COAT** Short, fine-textured, glossy and close-lying.

- **HEAD** Long, tapering, and wedge-shaped, with a fine muzzle.

- **NOSE** Long and straight.

- **CHIN** Tip of chin lines up with tip of nose.

- **EYES** Medium sized and almond shaped, slanting toward the nose.

- **EARS** Strikingly large and pointed, continuing the line of the wedge-shaped head.

- **BODY** Long and slender, with fine bones, firm muscles, and a tight abdomen. Slim shoulders and hips.

- **LEGS** Long and slim.

- **PAWS** Small and oval.

- **TAIL** Long and thin, tapering to a fine point.

- **COLORS** Red point, cream point, seal lynx point, blue lynx point, chocolate lynx point, lilac lynx point, red lynx point, seal torbie point, chocolate torbie point, blue-cream point, lilac-cream point.

COLORPOINT VARIETIES

SIAMESE CATS UNDER a different title in some American associations, the Colorpoint Short-hair group embraces all the Siamese varieties produced by outcrossing to others breeds to introduce the orange (red) and tabby genes.

RED POINT The body is clear white, with any shading toning with the points, which should be bright apricot to deep red. Deeper shades are preferred, with no barring. Nose leather and paw pads are flesh or coral pink; and the eye color a deep, vivid blue.

CREAM POINT The body is clear white, with any shading toning with the points, which should be pale buff to light, pinkish cream with no barring. Nose leather and paw pads are flesh or coral pink; eye color a deep vivid blue.

SEAL LYNX POINT The body is cream or pale fawn, shading to a lighter color on the stomach and chest. Ghost striping is allowed as body shading. The points are distinct seal brown bars, separated by the lighter background color. Ears are seal brown with a paler thumb-print in the center. Nose leather is seal brown, or pink edged in seal brown; paw pads are seal brown; eye color a deep, vivid blue.

BLUE LYNX POINT The body is bluish-white to platinum gray, cold in tone, shading to a lighter color on the stomach and chest. Ghost striping is allowed as body shading. The points

are distinct deep blue-gray bars, separated by the lighter background color. Ears are deep blue-gray with a paler thumb-print in the center. Nose leather is slate-colored or pink-edged in slate; paw pads are slate; eye color a deep, vivid blue.

CHOCOLATE LYNX POINT The body is ivory. Ghost striping is allowed as body shading. The points are distinct warm milk chocolate bars, separated by the lighter background color. Ears are warm milk chocolate with a paler thumb-print in the center. Nose leather is cinnamon, or pink edged in cinnamon; paw pads are cinnamon; eye color is deep blue.

LILAC LYNX POINT The body is glacial white. Ghost striping is allowed as body shading. The points are frosty gray with distinct pinkish-toned bars, separated by the lighter background color. Ears are frosty gray with a paler thumb-print in the center. Nose leather is lavender pink or gray edged with lavender pink; paw pads are lavender pink; eye color is a deep, vivid blue.

RED LYNX POINT The body is white. Ghost striping is allowed as body shading. The points are distinct deep red bars, separated by the lighter background color. Ears are deep red with a paler thumb-print in the center. Nose leather and paw pads are flesh or coral pink; eye color is a deep, vivid blue.

SEAL TORTIE POINT The body is pale fawn to cream, shading to a lighter color on the stomach and chest. It may be mottled with cream in older cats. The points are seal brown-uniformly mottled with red and light red. A blaze is desirable. Nose leather is seal brown; flesh or coral pink mottling is permitted where there is a facial blaze. Paw pads are seal brown; flesh or coral mottling is permitted where the points' color mottling extends into the paw pads. Eye color is a deep, vivid blue.

CHOCOLATE TORTIE POINT The body is ivory and may be mottled in older cats. The points are warm milk chocolate uniformly mottled with red and/or light red. A blaze is desirable. Nose leather is cinnamon; flesh or coral mottling is permitted where there is a facial blaze. Paw pads are cinnamon; flesh or coral mottling is permitted where the points' color mottling extends into the paw pads. Eye color is a deep, vivid blue.

BLUE-CREAM POINT The body is bluish white to platinum gray, cold in tone, shading to a lighter color on the stomach and chest. The body color is mottled in older cats. The points are deep blue-gray, uniformly mottled with cream. A blaze is desirable. Nose leather is

CHOCOLATE TORTIE POINT SIAMESE

Tortie Point Siamese are found in a full range of colors and appeal to those who like to have a completely unique cat – no two tortie points have the same markings.

SEAL TABBY POINT SIAMESE

The body is often shaded with ghost tabby markings. The points are patterned with tabby bars and stripes of the main color. In the Seal Tabby, the markings are deep seal brown.

slate; flesh or coral pink mottling is permitted where there is a facial blaze. Paw pads are slate; flesh or coral mottling is permitted where the points' color mottling extends into the paw pads. Eye color is a deep, vivid blue.

LILAC-CREAM POINT The body is glacial white and may be mottled in older cats. The points are frosty gray with a pinkish tone uniformly mottled with pale cream. A blaze is desirable. Nose leather is lavender pink; flesh or coral pink mottling is permitted where there is a facial blaze. Paw pads are lavender pink; flesh or coral mottling is permitted where the points' color mottling extends into the paw pads. Eye color is a deep, vivid blue.

SEAL TORTIE POINT

In the Seal Tortie Point, the points are patterned in a mixture of black and red or light red, and the cat, like this one, may have a red or light red blaze down the face.

BALINESE

THE LONG-COATED kittens that appeared from time to time in otherwise normal litters of Siamese cats were developed into the Balinese. At first such kittens were quickly discarded and sold as pets, but in the 1940s two breeders in New York and California began to work toward the development of a separate breed. The name was chosen because of the cats' gracefulness and svelte lines, reminiscent of the dancers on the island of Bali. The breed soon gained a lot of admirers, but it was not until 1970 that the CFA first recognized it and granted it championship status. The long coat is nothing like that of the Persian. It has no wooly undercoat and lies flat against the body.

Character and Care

As might be expected from their ancestry, Balinese are very similar to Siamese in character – affectionate, demanding of attention, extremely active, and inquisitive.

The coat is relatively easy to care for with regular gentle combing, and brushing of the ruff (frill) and plumed tail.

BREAKDOWN OF 100 SHOW POINTS

COLOR and COAT:
50 POINTS

Eye color: 15 points
Points color: 10 points
Body color: 10 points
Coat Texture and Length: 15 points

TYPE: 50 POINTS

Head: 15 points
Ears: 5 points
Eye shape: 5 points

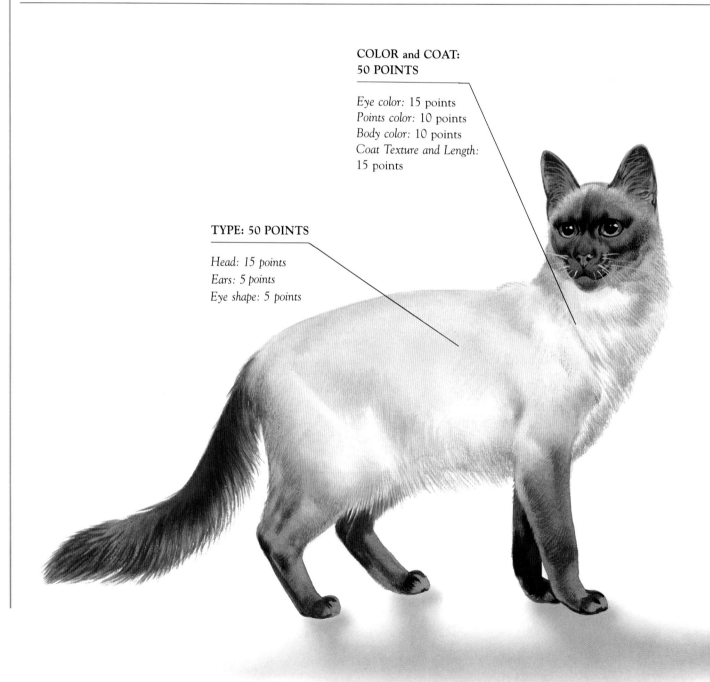

KEY CHARACTERISTICS

- **CATEGORY** Longhair.

- **OVERALL BUILD** Medium size, svelte and elegant.

- **COAT** Fine and silky.

- **HEAD** Medium size, a long tapering wedge shape which starts at the nose and gradually increases in width in straight lines on each side, as far as the ears. No whisker break.

- **NOSE** Long and straight, continuing the line from the forehead without any break.

- **CHIN** Medium size, the tip forming a vertical line with the tip of the nose.

- **EYES** Medium size and almond shaped, set slightly slanted toward the nose.

- **EARS** Large and pointed, wide-based, placed to continue the lines of the wedge.

- **BODY** Long, svelte, well-muscled but dainty. The shoulders should be no wider than the hips.

- **LEGS** Long and fine, in proportion to the body.

- **PAWS** Small, dainty, and oval.

- **TAIL** Very long and thin, tapering to a fine point; the tail hair spreads out like a plume.

- **COLORS** All the colors found in the Siamese (and Colorpoints): Seal point, blue point, chocolate point, lilac (frost) point, red point, cream point, seal tortie point, blue tortie point, chocolate tortie point, lilac (frost) tortie point, seal tabby point, blue tabby point, chocolate tabby point, lilac (frost) tabby point, red tabby point, cream tabby point, seal tortie tabby point (seal torbie point), blue tortie tabby point (blue torbie point), chocolate tortie tabby point (chocolate torbie point), lilac (frost) tortie tabby point (lilac (frost) torbie point). Some associations accept only seal point, blue point, chocolate point, and lilac (frost) point.

PENALTIES

The Balinese is penalized for lack of pigment in the nose leather or paw pads; and for having crossed eyes.

DISQUALIFICATION FEATURES

- any evidence of poor health
- weak hind legs
- mouth breathing due to nasal obstruction
- kinked tail
- eye color other than blue
- white toes and/or feet
- downy undercoat

BALINESE VARIETIES

CREAM BALINESE
The Balinese is a long-coated version of the Siamese. It is accepted in the same range of points' colors.

THE BODY MUST be even in color with subtle shading when allowed in the color variety. The points – mask, ears, legs, feet, and tail – must be all the same shade and clearly defined. The mask should cover the entire face, including the whisker pads, and be connected to the ears by traced markings. There should be no ticking or white hairs in the points. Eye color for all varieties is deep, vivid blue.

SEAL POINT The body color is beige to cream or pale fawn; the points color dark seal brown. The nose leather and paw pads are dark seal brown.

BLUE POINT The body color is bluish-white of a glacial tone; the points color blue-gray. The nose leather and paw pads are blue-gray.

CHOCOLATE POINT The body color is ivory; the points color milk chocolate. The nose leather is milk chocolate; the paw pads are cinnamon to milk chocolate.

LILAC POINT The body color is glacial white (magnolia); the points color frosty gray with a slight pinkish tone. The nose leather and paw pads are pink.

RED POINT The body color is creamy white; the points color bright, warm orange. The nose leather is pink; the paw pads pink or red.

CREAM POINT The body color is creamy white; the points color pastel cream. The nose leather and paw pads are pink.

SEAL TORTIE POINT The body color is beige shading to fawn; the points color seal, patched or mingled with red and/or light red. The nose leather and paw pads are seal brown and/or pink.

BLUE TORTIE POINT The body color is bluish white; the points color blue-gray patched or mingled with pastel cream. The nose leather and paw pads are blue-gray and/or pink.

CHOCOLATE TORTIE POINT The body color is ivory; the points color milk chocolate patched or mingled with red and/or light red. The nose leather is milk chocolate and/or pink; the paw pads are cinnamon to milk chocolate and/or pink.

LILAC TORTIE POINT The body color is glacial white; the points color frosty gray with a slight pinkish tone patched or mingled with pale cream. The nose leather and paw pads are lavender pink and/or pale pink.

SEAL TABBY POINT The body color is beige; the points color dark seal tabby; the rims around the eyes and nose are seal brown. The nose leather is brick red, pink, or seal brown;

BLUE POINT BALINESE
As only top quality Siamese cats were used in the breeding programs for Balinese, most of today's Balinese cats are of outstanding type.

the paw pads are seal brown.

BLUE TABBY POINT The body color is bluish white; the points color blue-gray tabby; the rims around the eyes and nose are blue-gray. The nose leather is old rose or blue-gray; the paw pads are blue-gray.

CHOCOLATE TABBY POINT Body color is ivory; the points color milk chocolate tabby; the rims around the eyes and nose are milk chocolate. The nose leather is light red, pink, or milk chocolate; the paw pads are cinnamon to milk chocolate.

LILAC TABBY POINT The body color is glacial white; the points color lilac tabby – frosty gray with slightly pinkish-toned tabby markings – the rims around the eyes and nose are lavender pink. The nose leather is lavender pink or pink; the paw pads are lavender pink.

RED TABBY POINT The body color is off-white with a slight red tinge; the points color warm orange tabby; the rims around the eyes and nose are dark pink. The nose leather is brick red or pink; the paw pads are pink.

CREAM TABBY POINT The body color is creamy white; the points color cream tabby with a cold tone; the rims around the eyes and nose are dark pink. The nose leather and paw pads are pink.

SEAL TORBIE POINT The body color is beige; the points color has seal tabby markings patched or mingled with red or light red tortie markings. The nose rims are seal; the nose leather and paw pads are seal, brick red, or pink, or seal mottled with brick red and/or pink.

BLUE TORBIE POINT The body color is bluish-white; the points color has blue tabby markings, patched or mingled with cream tortie markings. The nose rims are blue-gray; the nose leather is blue-gray, old rose or pink, or blue-gray mottled with old rose and/or pink; the paw pads are blue-gray and/or pink.

CHOCOLATE TORBIE POINT The body color is ivory; the points color has milk chocolate tabby markings, patched or mingled with red or light red tortie markings. The nose rims are chocolate; the nose leather milk chocolate, pale red or pink, or milk chocolate mottled with pale red or pink; the paw pads are cinnamon to milk chocolate and/or pink.

CHOCOLATE TORTIE POINT BALINESE

Patched or mingled points of milk chocolate and light red allied with an ivory coat make this an unusual and attractive variety.

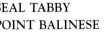

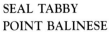

SEAL TABBY POINT BALINESE

This cat epitomizes the Balinese breed, conforming almost exactly to the standard of points.

ORIENTAL

CATS OF THE DISTINCTIVE Siamese body conformation, but without having the true color restricted to the points, are recognized by some associations as Orientals.

In the main, the Oriental is identical to the Siamese in all respects except for not having its color restricted to the points and not having blue eyes. It has a slightly quieter voice than the Siamese, but is equally talkative. Oriental cats have been known for many years, but first became popular in the early 1960s when a small number of fanciers began to breed them in a wide variety of colors, some individuals specializing in just one or two colors or patterns, but each taking extreme care with the selection of their foundation stock to give strength, stamina, and good temperament in their cats, as well as beauty. Some Orientals were produced as offshoots to the breeding programs for the red-, tortie- and tabby- or lynx-pointed Siamese, and others were developed after much genetic research.

A light-brown gene was recognized and gave rise to a whole new series of attractive feline colors, and a pure white Oriental, in fact a Siamese with white masking its points, entranced show visitors with its sapphire eyes. Britain's GCCF designates the self-colored cats of Siamese type "Foreign," and so they are known as the Foreign White, Foreign Black, Foreign Blue, Foreign Lilac, and so on, yet the "Foreign Chocolate" is called the Havana, the name having been changed from Chestnut Brown Foreign in the 1950s. Europe's FIFe and its British member, the Cat Association of Britain, recognize the entire group as Oriental, as does the largest of the American associations, the CFA.

Color terminology varies, too, black being called ebony, chocolate chestnut, lilac lavender, and there is some controversy over the cinnamon, caramel, and fawn colors. The showing system in the CFA proved the most helpful to breeders of Orientals, dividing the

BREAKDOWN OF 100 SHOW POINTS

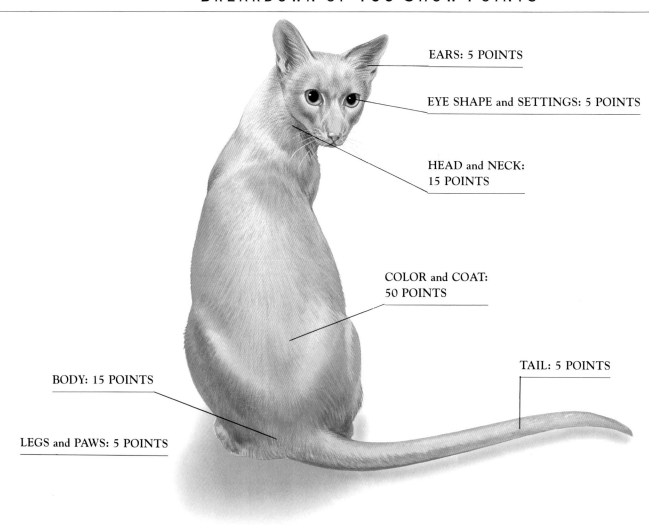

EARS: 5 POINTS

EYE SHAPE and SETTINGS: 5 POINTS

HEAD and NECK:
15 POINTS

COLOR and COAT:
50 POINTS

TAIL: 5 POINTS

BODY: 15 POINTS

LEGS and PAWS: 5 POINTS

breed into five groups: solid colors; shaded; smokes; tabbies, and particolors. In this way the Orientals reached championship status level in 1977, and the following year a number of Orientals featured among the CFA's top twenty. In Britain, each color variety had to work separately toward a breed number, and in 1995 their status as a group is still in confusion in the GCCF.

Character and Care

The Oriental is extroverted, intelligent, and very affectionate with its own family and friends. It is active and playful, and hates being left alone for long periods.

They are naturally very clean cats, and the very short, fine coat can be kept in good condition with daily hand grooming and buffing with a silk scarf. The large ears need regular cleaning, and Orientals should be provided with a scratching post and plenty of toys to play with.

PENALTIES

The Oriental is penalized for any evidence of ill health; weak hind legs; mouth breathing due to nasal obstruction; a visible kink in the tail; miniaturization; a white locket or button; and tabby barring or striping in non-agouti varieties.

KEY CHARACTERISTICS

- **CATEGORY** Foreign Shorthair.

- **OVERALL BUILD** Medium size, long and svelte.

- **COAT** Very short and fine, glossy, silky and close-lying.

- **HEAD** Medium sized in proportion to the body; wedge-shaped with straight lines, the wedge starting at the nose and gradually increasing in width in straight lines on each side to the ears. No whisker break.

- **NOSE** Long and straight without any break.

- **CHIN** Medium size, the tip forming a vertical line with the tip of the nose.

- **EYES** Medium size and almond shaped, set slightly slanting toward the nose in harmony with the lines of the wedge.

- **EARS** Large and pointed, wide at the base, placed to continue the line of the wedge.

- **BODY** Long and svelte, well muscled but still dainty and elegant. The shoulders should not be wider than the hips.

- **LEGS** Long and fine, in proportion to the body.

- **PAWS** Small and oval.

- **TAIL** Very long and thin, thin at the base, and tapering to a fine point.

- **COLORS** Black, white, blue, havana chocolate, lilac, cinnamon, caramel, fawn, red self, cream, black tortie, blue tortie, chocolate tortie, lilac tortie, cinnamon tortie, caramel tortie, fawn tortie, black smoke, blue smoke, chocolate smoke, lilac smoke, cinnamon smoke, caramel smoke, fawn smoke, red smoke, black tortie smoke, blue tortie smoke, chocolate tortie smoke, lilac tortie smoke, cinamon tortie smoke, caramel tortie smoke, black shaded, blue shaded, chocolate shaded, lilac shaded, cameo, black tabby, blue tabby, chocolate tabby, lilac tabby, red tabby, cream tabby, cinnamon tabby, fawn tabby, silver tabby. Tipped: all recognized colors.

SOLID VARIETIES

This variety is, in fact, a Siamese disguised by its pure white coat. It has eyes of Siamese blue, and a separate standard of points from the rest of the Orientals.

AS SIAMESE CATS without the gene which restricts the color to the points; the first Orientals to appear in half-Siamese litters were blacks and blues. Later, the elusive chocolate gene produced the Chestnut Brown Foreign, a self chocolate-colored cat, which is now known as the Havana in the UK, and the Oriental Chesnut elsewhere. Some of the early Chestnut Browns were exported to the US, where they formed the nucleus of a totally different breed with its own characteristic features known as the Havana Brown. When the gene for dilution was also present in the cats used for breeding, chocolate, lilac, or lavender kittens began to appear.

ORIENTAL WHITE, FOREIGN WHITE, SIA-MESE WHITE The coat color is pure white without markings or shadings of any kind. The nose leather and paw pads are pink; the eye color is deep, vivid blue.
Note: In the CFA, the Oriental White should have green eyes. Blue eye color is also accepted, but odd-eyed cats are not.
BLACK The coat color is dense coal black, sound from the roots to the tips of the hair, free from any rusty tinge, and without any white hairs or other markings. There should be no gray undercoat. The nose leather is black; the paw pads are black or seal brown; the eye color is vivid, intense green.
BLUE The coat color is any shade of blue-gray, but lighter shades are preferred. The color must be sound and even throughout, without any white hairs, shadings, or other markings. Nose leather and paw pads are blue-gray; eye color is vivid, intense green.

ORIENTAL BLUE
Any shade of blue is permitted in this variety, but lighter shades are preferred.

CHOCOLATE (CHESTNUT) The coat color is any shade of warm chocolate (chestnut) brown, sound and even throughout without any white hairs, shadings, or other markings. There should be no gray undercoat. The nose leather is milk chocolate; the paw pads are cinnamon to milk chocolate; the eye color is vivid, intense green.

LILAC The coat color is faded lilac with a slight pinkish tinge, sound and even throughout without any white hairs, shadings, or other markings. The nose leather and paw pads are lavender pink or faded lilac; the eye color is vivid, intense green.

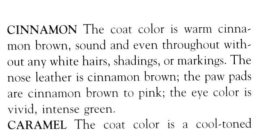

CINNAMON The coat color is warm cinnamon brown, sound and even throughout without any white hairs, shadings, or markings. The nose leather is cinnamon brown; the paw pads are cinnamon brown to pink; the eye color is vivid, intense green.

CARAMEL The coat color is a cool-toned bluish fawn, sound and even throughout without any white hairs, shadings, or markings. Nose leather and paw pads are bluish fawn; the eye color is vivid, intense green.

ORIENTAL CINNAMON

This beautiful, unusual color variety excited geneticists when it first appeared in recent years.

HAVANA BROWN

The name Havana was originally chosen to describe the rich tobacco-brown color of this breed's coat, likened to that used for making the best of the Havana cigars. It is far more descriptive than other names used for the warm brown coat.

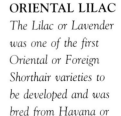

ORIENTAL LILAC

The Lilac or Lavender was one of the first Oriental or Foreign Shorthair varieties to be developed and was bred from Havana or Oriental Chocolates.

FAWN The coat color is a warm beige fawn (buff), sound and even throughout without any white hairs, shadings, or markings. The nose leather is pinkish fawn; paw pads are pink or pinkish fawn; eye color is vivid, intense green.

RED SELF The coat color is deep, rich, clear and brilliant red, sound and even throughout, without any white hairs, lighter shadings, or markings. The nose leather and paw pads are brick red or pink; the eye color is vivid, intense green.

Note: Slight shading is allowed on the face and legs, and dark whiskers are permitted.

CREAM The coat color is pale, pure pastel cream, with no warm tone, sound and even throughout without any white hairs, shadings, or markings. There must be no light or white undercoat. The nose leather and paw pads are pink; the preferred eye color is vivid, intense green.

Note: Slight shading is allowed on the face and legs, and dark whiskers are permitted.

ORIENTAL RED

The type of the Oriental is exactly the same as the Siamese; in fact, Oriental cats are merely Siamese without the factor restricting the color to the points of the body. With the loss of the Himalayan factor comes the change of eye color from blue to green.

ORIENTAL CREAM

Tabby markings may be evident in the coat of the cream Oriental, and an otherwise good cat will not be penalized for this excusable fault.

ORIENTAL TORTIE

The base color in all of the Oriental Tortoiseshell varieties must be sound to the roots and totally free from tabby markings.

WITH THE INTRODUCTION of the sex-linked gene which produced the red and the cream, litters included female kittens of various combinations of colors in the pattern called tortoiseshell.

BLACK TORTIE The coat color is black patched or mingled with red and/or light red. The nose leather and the paw pads are black, brick red or pink, or black mottled with brick red and/or pink.

BLUE TORTIE The coat color is light blue-gray patched or mingled with pale cream. The nose leather and paw pads are blue-gray or pink, or blue-gray with pink.

CHOCOLATE TORTIE The coat color is milk chocolate patched or mingled with red or light red. The nose leather is milk chocolate, pale red, or pink, or milk chocolate mottled with pale red and/or pink; the paw pads are cinna-mon to milk chocolate, pale red, or pink, or cinnamon to milk chocolate mottled with pale red and/or pink.

LILAC TORTIE (LAVENDER-CREAM) The coat color is faded lilac with a slight pinkish tinge, patched or mingled with pale cream. The nose leather and paw pads are lavender pale pink, or lavender pink mottled with pale pink.

CINNAMON TORTIE The coat color is warm cinnamon brown patched or mingled with red or light red. The nose leather and paw pads are cinnamon brown, pinkish red or pink, or cinnamon brown mottled with pinkish red and/or pink.

CARAMEL TORTIE The coat color is cool-toned bluish fawn patched or mingled with rich beige and/or cream. The nose leather and paw pads are bluish fawn or pink; or bluish fawn mottled with pink.

TABBY

CARAMEL SPOTTED TABBY

A young Oriental tabby with a nicely spotted coat pattern, good overall type, and a lovely color.

chest. The head should be barred, with an "M" on the forehead. For the Spotted, the spots on the body may vary in size and shape, but those that are round and evenly distributed are preferred. They must not run together to form a broken mackerel pattern. A dorsal stripe runs the length of the body to the tip of the tail and is ideally composed of spots.

The body hairs are clearly ticked, and there are no other spots, bars, or stripes on the body. Typical tabby markings including the forehead "M" are found on the face, and thumb prints on the backs of the ears.

BLACK TABBY (EBONY TABBY) The base coat is brilliant coppery brown; the markings are dense black. The lips and chin should be the same color as the rings around the eyes. The backs of the legs from paw to heel are black; the nose leather is black or brick red rimmed with black; the paw pads are black or seal brown; the eyes are green.

BLUE TABBY The base coat, including the lips and chin, is pale bluish-ivory, or warm gray in the ticked tabby, with markings any shade of blue-gray affording a good contrast with the base color. The backs of the legs from paw to heel are a darker shade of blue-gray; the nose leather is blue or old rose rimmed with blue; the paw pads are blue-gray or rose; the eyes are green.

CHOCOLATE TABBY (CHESTNUT TABBY) The base coat, including the lips and chin, is warm fawn, or sandy beige in the ticked tabby, with markings a rich chocolate brown. The

ORIENTAL TABBY CATS may have any of the following four tabby patterns – Classic, Mackerel, Spotted, or Ticked. In the Classic, there should be dense and clearly defined broad markings; the legs should be evenly barred with bracelets coming up to join the body markings. The tail should be evenly ringed; and there should be several unbroken necklaces on the neck and upper chest. Frown marks on the forehead form a letter "M." In Mackerel tabbies, there should be dense and clearly defined stripes like narrow pencil marks; the legs should be evenly barred with narrow bracelets coming up to join the body markings. The tail should be barred; and there should be distinct chain-like necklaces on the neck and

CHOCOLATE CLASSIC TABBY

The classic tabby pattern is shown to perfection by this superbly marked Oriental cat.

CHOCOLATE SPOTTED TABBY
Although all the tabby markings are correct on the head, legs, and tail, this cat needs to develop better spotting on the body.

backs of the legs from paw to heel are chocolate brown; the nose leather is chocolate or pale red rimmed with chocolate; the paw pads are cinnamon to chocolate; the eyes are green.

LILAC TABBY (LAVENDER TABBY) The base coat is off-white to palest lilac, with markings rich lilac (lilac gray with a pinkish tinge) or lavender, affording a good contrast with the base color. The backs of the legs from paw to heel are a darker shade of lilac; the nose leather is lavender or pink rimmed with lavender; the paw pads are lavender pink; the eyes are green.

RED TABBY The base coat is red, with markings a deep rich red. The backs of the legs from paw to heel are dark red; the nose leather is brick red or pink; the paw pads are pink (Europe); brick red (USA), the eyes are any shade of copper to green, green preferred.

CREAM TABBY The base coat, including the lips and chin, is very pale cream, with markings buff or cream, affording a good contrast with the base color. The backs of the legs from paw to heel are dark cream; the nose leather and paw pads are pink, the eyes are any shade of copper to green, green preferred.

CHOCOLATE TICKED ORIENTAL
The ticked Orientals have two or three bands of ticking on each hair. The basic color also shows at the heels of the hind legs and at the tip of the tail.

217

CINNAMON TICKED ORIENTAL

A superb specimen with a perfectly ticked cinnamon coat which is similar to that of a sorrel Abyssinian.

CINNAMON TABBY The base coat is deep apricot, with markings clear, warm, cinnamon brown. The backs of the legs from paw·to heel are cinnamon brown; the nose leather is pale pink; the paw pads are cinnamon brown to pinkish brown.

CARAMEL TABBY The base coat is cool-toned beige; cool-toned bluish fawn markings; back of leg from paw to heel is a darker bluish fawn; the nose leather is bluish fawn, or pink rimmed with bluish fawn; the paw pads are pink to bluish fawn.

FAWN TABBY The base coat is dull beige, with markings any shade of beige-brown, affording a good contrast with the base color. The backs of the legs from paw to heel are a darker beige-fawn; the nose leather is pink; the paw pads are pinkish fawn.

SILVER TABBY The base coat, including the lips and chin, is pure pale silver, with dense black markings. The backs of the legs from paw to heel are black; the nose leather is black or brick red with black rims; paw pads are black. **Note** There are other colors in the Silver Tabby series – Blue Silver Tabby, Chocolate Silver Tabby, Lilac Silver Tabby, Red Silver Tabby, Cream Silver Tabby, Cinnamon Silver Tabby, Caramel Silver Tabby, Fawn Silver Tabby. In these varieties the color of the markings is as for the non-silver varieties, but on a base coat of pale silver.

CINNAMON SPOTTED ORIENTAL

The effect of the tabby pattern, whether it is spotted or ticked, is to brighten the normal base color.

TORTIE TABBY (PATCHED TABBY) Any color recognized in the Oriental group; the coat patched or mingled with areas of red or light red in the non-dilute colors; rich beige or cream in the Caramel and the Fawn. The nose leather is the solid basic color, pink-rimmed with the basic color, or basic color mottled with pink; the paw pads are basic color mottled with pink. The eyes are any shade of copper to green, green preferred.

BLACK SILVER SPOTTED

Ideally, this cat should have more clearly marked spots, though the rest of its tabby markings are excellent. Spotting often improves with maturity.

CHOCOLATE TORTIE SILVER TICKED

An amazing combination of color and pattern combined in a typical Oriental.

SMOKE, SHADED, AND TIPPED VARIETIES

CHOCOLATE SILVER SHADED ORIENTAL
This variety has chocolate markings on a paler, silvery chocolate ground.

BLACK SMOKE ORIENTAL
Looking like a black in repose, the smoke undercoat becomes apparent as the cat moves.

THE INTRODUCTION OF silver to the Oriental breeding programs excited many Oriental fanciers, and before long, cats with short, fine silvery-white coats were bred with various amounts of colored tipping. The most heavily tipped are the smokes, the lightest tipped are just called "tipped," and the intermediates are known as "shaded."

In the Smoke, the hairs are tipped with the appropriate color and have a narrow silver-white band at the roots which can only be seen when the hair is parted. The undercoat is silver-white. In repose, the cat appears to be of solid color, but in motion the silver-white undercoat is clearly visible. In the Shaded, the hair is tipped to about one-third of its length and the undercoat is white, producing the characteristic sparkling appearance of this color group. The face and legs may be shaded with tipping. In the Tipped, the hair is tipped just at its extremity, and the tipping is evenly distributed over the cat's body. The face and legs may be shaded, but in adults, ghost tabby markings are considered a serious fault. The tipped cat is considerably lighter in overall color than the shaded.

SEYCHELLOIS

FOLLOWING A BREEDING program approved by the Cat Association of Britain, the Seychellois was developed by a small group of breeders interested in Oriental cats. It is of medium size and typical Oriental conformation, with a long svelte body, slim legs, and dainty paws. The head is wedge-shaped with very large pointed ears and almond-shaped eyes. It is unusual in having a predominantly white coat, with splashes of color on the head, legs, and body, and a colored tail. Seychellois markings are classified into three groups. The Seychellois Longhair is identical in every respect to the Shorthair except in its coat, which is of medium length, soft and silky in texture, and longer on the frill or ruff. It has ear tufts and a full, plume-like tail.

SEYCHELLOIS NEUVIÈME Almost entirely white with a colored tail and a few tiny colored markings on the head.

SEYCHELLOIS HUITIÈME Mainly white with a colored tail and splashes of color on the head and legs.

SEYCHELLOIS SEPTIÈME White with a colored tail and splashes of color on the head, legs and, body.

KEY CHARACTERISTICS
● **CATEGORY** Foreign Shorthair (Oriental).
● **OVERALL BUILD** Medium size, long and svelte.
● **COAT** *Shorthair* Very short and fine, glossy, silky and close-lying. *Longhair* Of medium length, fine, silky and longer on the ruff (frill) and tail.
● **COLORS** Any color or combination of colors is allowed.
● **OTHER FEATURES** Head medium sized, in proportion to body, wedge shaped with straight lines starting at nose and gradually increasing in width to ears, no whisker break. Nose is long and straight; chin medium sized, the tip forming a vertical line with tip of nose; eyes are medium sized, almond shaped, and set slightly slanting toward nose to follow lines of wedge; ears are large and pointed, wide at base and placed to continue lines of wedge. Body is long and svelte, well muscled but dainty and elegant; shoulders should not be wider than hips. Legs are long and fine boned, in proportion to body; paws small and oval; tail very long and thin, tapering to a fine point. *Longhair* Tail hair spreads out like a plume.

SEYCHELLOIS SHORTHAIR
This rare breed is of Oriental type and is a predominantly white cat with splashes of color on the head, tail, and body.

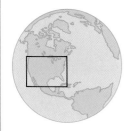

JAVANESE

THE LONGHAIRED ORIENTAL, now known as the Javanese, was selectively bred from Oriental cats and long-coated cats of exceptional Oriental type. In the CFA, the name Javanese was given to Balinese cats not conforming to the four main Siamese colors (seal point, blue point, chocolate point and lilac point). These were the red- and tabby-based colors which in the short-coated varieties are termed Colorpoints by the CFA. In New Zealand, where the red- and tabby-, or lynx-pointed cats with long coats are accepted, along with the four main Siamese colors, as Balinese, it is the spotted and self-coated varieties which are called Javanese. In the UK, the CA, as a member of FIFe, accepts all long-coated colors of Orientals as Javanese.

Medium long on the body, and without an undercoat, the coat of the Javanese cat is fine, with a silky texture. It flows over the body and forms a ruff around the shoulders and chest. The cat has a full, plume-like tail.

Character and Care
Active, always alert, and very inquisitive, the Javanese has an extrovert personality, and is intelligent and quite vocal. It is a very affectionate cat and loves human company, hating to be left alone for long periods.

Regular gentle brushing keeps the coat in good condition; the ruff (frill), underparts and tail can be combed gently with a broad-toothed comb.

BREAKDOWN OF 100 SHOW POINTS

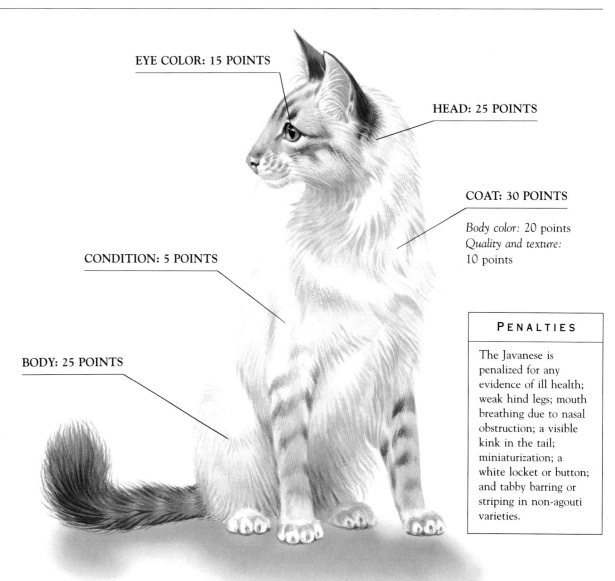

EYE COLOR: 15 POINTS

HEAD: 25 POINTS

COAT: 30 POINTS

Body color: 20 points
Quality and texture:
10 points

CONDITION: 5 POINTS

BODY: 25 POINTS

PENALTIES

The Javanese is penalized for any evidence of ill health; weak hind legs; mouth breathing due to nasal obstruction; a visible kink in the tail; miniaturization; a white locket or button; and tabby barring or striping in non-agouti varieties.

SEAL LYNX POINT JAVANESE
In the United States, the Javanese is the name given to the longcoated variants of the Siamese colors which they call Colorpoints.

KEY CHARACTERISTICS

- **CATEGORY** Semi-longhair (Foreign Longhair).

- **OVERALL BUILD** Medium size, svelte and elegant.

- **COAT** Fine and silky.

- **COLORS** *(UK and Europe)* As for the Oriental Shorthair – black, blue, chocolate, lilac, red, cream, cinnamon, fawn, tortoiseshell (all colors), smoke (all colors), tabby (all colors), tabby-tortoiseshell or torbie (all colors). The eye color for all color varieties is vivid, intense green.

- **OTHER FEATURES** Medium-sized head, a long, tapering wedge which starts at the nose and gradually increases in width in straight lines on each side to the ears, with no whisker break in these lines. Long, straight nose, continuing the line from the forehead without a break; medium-sized chin, its tip lining up with the nose in the same vertical plane; medium-sized eyes, almond shaped, and set slightly slanted toward the nose; ears are wide-based, large and pointed, placed to continue the lines of the wedge; body is long, svelte, well muscled but dainty, with the shoulders no wider than the hips. Legs are long and fine, in proportion to the body, ending in small, dainty, oval paws; tail is very long and thin, tapering to a fine point, with the hair spreading out like a plume.

BLUE LYNX POINT JAVANESE
The Javanese has the same type and conformation as Siamese and Orientals, and is long and svelte with fine bones. The coat is fine and silky, and very easy to care for.

223

CHARACTERISTICS OF THE CAT

THE BODY BEAUTIFUL

The cat is perfectly adapted to life as a hunter. Its agility, well-coordinated movements and acute senses makes it one of the most successful predators in the wild. The domestic cat, despite living in a totally different environment, still retains many of the physical characteristics of its near relatives.

IN GENERAL SHAPE and overall size, all breeds of domestic cats have retained the same basic structure as their ancestors, unlike dogs, which have been selectively bred to produce very wide variations of shape and height. Cats are therefore free from many of the skeletal abnormalities that can affect dogs. Some defects are occasionally encountered. These include shortened, bent or kinked tails, cleft palates, flattened chests, and polydactylism (extra toes). In the main, evolution seems to have been particularly kind in designing the cat, proceeding along such a well-ordered path of natural selection that it remains an efficient and perfect carnivore of convenient size, still well capable of hunting and killing small animals and birds. The cat's frame permits fluid, coordinated, and graceful movements at all speeds. It's taut-muscled body and legs enable it to make impressive leaps and bounds. The retractable nature of the sharp claws allows fast sprinting over short distances, holding and gripping of prey, and fast climbing of convenient trees when danger threatens. The cat's brain is large and well-developed, enabling it to assimilate facts rapidly and react quickly. Its adaptable eyes can cope with extremes of lighting conditions, allowing perfect vision in both bright light and dim twilight. The mobile ears work to catch the faintest sound, and the sensitive nose, allied to the perceptive Jacobsen's organ in the mouth, can identify the faintest of scents imperceptible to humans.

Pedigree breeds of domestic cats have been developed to fit certain standards of conformation,

STRUCTURE OF A CAT

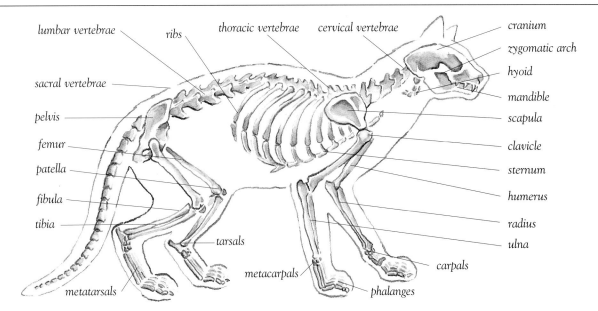

The skeletal system of the cat is comprised of approximately 244 bones, with over 21 in the tail alone. The tail is, in fact, part of the vertebral column; between individual vertebra are discs that act as shock-absorbers. At birth the bones are not fully ossified, but are composed partly of cartilage, which is replaced by bone. Over 500 different skeletal muscles are attached to the bones. Those in the hindlimbs, neck and shoulder are particularly well developed. In addition to these skeletal muscles are smooth muscles, which are involved in the functioning of various organs.

Modern cats eventually developed from early climbing carnivores, the Miacids. *Some, like the prehistoric sabre-tooth tigers, died out leaving no descendants; others continued to evolve into today's family of cats, the* Felidae. *The* Felidae *can be divided into three genera: the cheetah (*Acinonyx*), the great cats (*Panthera*) and the smaller cats (*Felis*) – from which our domestic cats are descended.*

color and coat pattern. This has been done over many generations of domestic cats, with dedicated breeders first working out exactly what the desired feline end-product would look like. Then they set out to achieve this look with careful and selective breeding. Today there are two main types of pedigree cats: those with chunky, heavyweight bodies and large round heads, and a lighter, finer type with lighter bone and a longer head.

Cats of the heavier type come in a wide variety of colors and coat patterns and may be longhaired or shorthaired. The former include Persians and similar breeds, while the shorthairs cover cats such as the British, American, European and Exotic Shorthairs. Lightweight cats are more variable in their characteristics. The Orientals, including the distinctive Siamese, are at the furthest extreme from the heavier types. The Siamese varieties have very fine bones, very long bodies, legs and tails, together with long, wedge-shaped heads and large ears. Less extreme are the Foreign Shorthairs and Rex cats, each variety having its own very recognizable features. Some breeds have come about from mixtures of heavy and lightweight types. These breeds these have intermediate features.

THE SELF-RIGHTING REFLEX

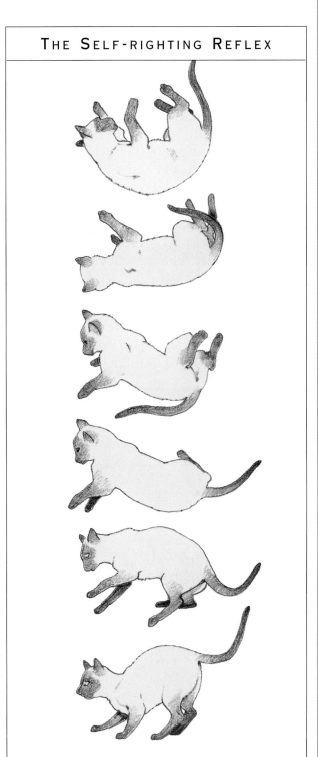

The famous feline attribute of always being able to land on its feet is not wholly accurate, but a falling cat is often able to reposition its body during falling to avoid serious injury on landing. A set of information that reaches the brain from the eyes is combined with impulses from the vestibular apparatus in the ears to transmit an orienting signal to the animal's neck muscles. The head is twisted into an upright and horizontal position, and the rest of the body twists and lines itself up accordingly before landing. Kittens soon acquire this agility.

227

Physical Adaptations

Cats, as members of the *Felidae*, are adapted to a unique carnivorous existence among mammals. As hunters, their movements are agile and their musculo-skeletal system is adapted both for power and to allow a high degree of maneuvrability. The flexible backbone enables them to swivel their bodies into a wide range of postures, impossible in other species. An arching of the back, associated with stretching after a period of rest or as a threat gesture, is achieved by this means. Cats can curl up into a tight ball to sleep, and then roll over onto their backs before twisting.

Powerful hindlimbs provide the major thrust for running, with the forelegs offering stability and direction. Cats are not suited to prolonged running, but can outpace prey over short distances before launching into a jump if necessary. The claws are held in a retracted position by ligaments.

RETRACTABLE CLAWS

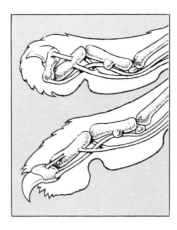

The domestic cat (right) shares many characteristics with its wild counterparts. The cheetah (*Acinonyx jubatus*), however, is unique in lacking retracting claws. In all other cats, the claws are attached to the bones of the toe and can be retracted by means of ligaments, which are under muscular control (above). The muscles exert their effect through tendons, attached to the bones.

The cat's gait can be broken down into distinct stages, as shown in this sequence taken by the Victorian photographer Eadweard Muybridge (1830–1904). Muybridge was interested in the

analysis of motion and published the results of his experiments in 1887. In the cat, the hindlimbs are especially powerful, providing the major thrust for running and enabling the cat to leap on prey.

THE ANATOMY OF SIGHT

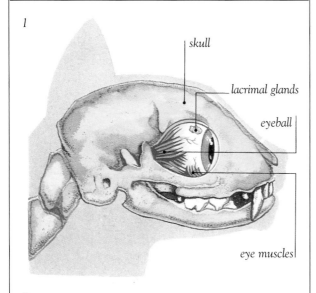

1

skull

lacrimal glands

eyeball

eye muscles

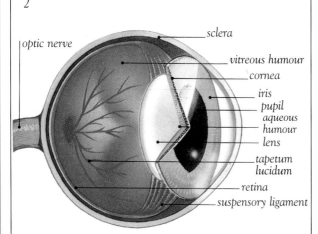

2

optic nerve

sclera

vitreous humour

cornea

iris

pupil

aqueous humour

lens

tapetum lucidum

retina

suspensory ligament

The eyes of the cat are set well forward in sockets in the skull, positioned to give efficient three-dimensional vision (1). The actual structure of the eye does not differ significantly from that of other mammals, except for the *tapetum lucidum*, a special feature designed to increase the intensity of light falling on the retina (2). The light-sensitive retina is the part of the eye where the image actually registers, and impulses from here are then conveyed along the optic nerve to the appropriate part of the brain. Because the eyes are set in slightly different positions, the cat's field of view is overlapping. This binocular vision enables the position of the prey to be judged very accurately. Without such information, the cat would strike slightly off-target, allowing the prey to escape. By contrast, and befitting the cat's role as hunter rather than hunted, its peripheral vision is poor: the cat can only see in a fairly restricted field on either side of its head.

All the senses of the cat, as a true hunter, need to be highly developed, and vision is correspondingly acute. A cat's eyes differ from ours in several ways. They observe less of the color spectrum, having fewer cones, but more rod sensors allow the perception of more brightness in dim light. The iris of the cat's eye opens and closes to a greater extent, and the eyeball is more spherical and, in relation to body size, very much larger than in the human.

The cat's eyes are effective over a wide range of light intensities. The pupils of the eyes adapt to the available light, narrowing to just a slit in bright light, yet widening to their maximum diameter to make best use of any light under conditions of almost complete darkness. Another adaptation of nocturnal vision is provided by the *tapetum lucidum*, located behind the retina in the posterior chamber of the eye. This serves to reflect light back to the retina so increasing the available intensity, and it is for this reason that a cat's eyes can appear to glow at night.

In order to catch prey, cats have developed binocular vision. The eyes pick up slightly different images by virtue of their differing positions, and these are fed back by each optic nerve to the brain. This overlapping field of vision enables prey to be located with pinpoint accuracy. The ability is not as pronounced in some breeds, such as Siamese, and these may not prove such successful hunters as a result. Kittens, being born blind, are unlikely to be able to use the sense of vision fully until they are at least 12 weeks old.

VISION

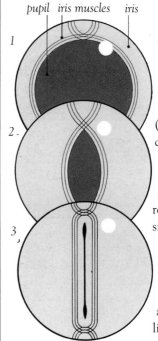

pupil   iris muscles   iris

1

2.

3,

The diameter of the cat's pupils changes with its facial expression. When the cat is frightened, the pupils will be dilated (1), whereas they contact to a slit when the cat is angry (3). Changes in the available light also result in changes in the size and shape of the pupils. In dim light, the pupils are enlarged and circular (1); in moderate light, they are oval (2); in bright light, they contract (3).

The cat, as a hunter, needs to have acute senses for tracking and catching prey. While hearing, taste, touch and smell all contribute to the cat's natural ability as a predator, vision is perhaps the cat's most important sense, and the eyes are correspondingly the most noticeable feature. The cat can see over a very wide range of light conditions, although in dim light it cannot pick out much detail. At night, the tapetum lucidum, at the back of the eye, reflects light back onto the retina, enabling the cat to see in the dark.

231

Wild cats, such as this leopard, drink in a similar manner to their domestic relatives.

TASTE AND SMELL

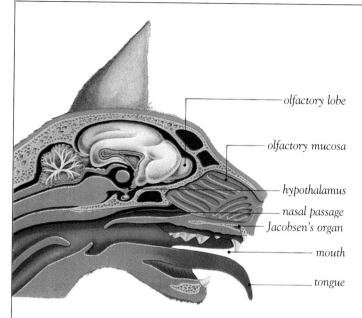

olfactory lobe

olfactory mucosa

hypothalamus

nasal passage

Jacobsen's organ

mouth

tongue

The senses of taste and smell are closely associated in the cat, since the nasal passage opens into the mouth, with impulses registering in the olfactory lobe of the brain. Jacobsen's organ, located in the roof of the mouth, also demonstrates this link: molecules of scent are actually detected by the taste-buds, and the information is then passed on to the brain via this organ.

The cat's tongue is an effective muscular ladle. When lapping fluid, the tongue becomes curled at its tip. The surface of the tongue is rough because of the presence of abrasive papillae, backward hooks which enable the cat to hold food, or prey, in its mouth. They also help the cat to remove loose fur during grooming. These rough papillae are located in the middle of the tongue, while other papillae around the perimeter and at the back carry the tastebuds.

HEARING

Structures in the ears provide the cat with the means to hear and also serve to maintain a sense of balance. Nerve impulses convey the vibrations caused by sound to the brain, while the semicircular canals help to give the cat an indication of its position relative to gravity.

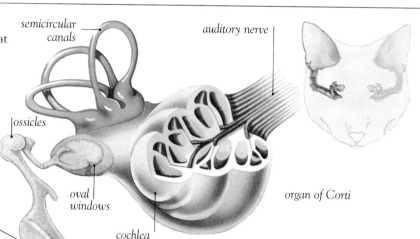

semicircular canals

auditory nerve

ossicles

oval windows

cochlea

organ of Corti

ear drum

Cats can detect higher pitched sounds than the human ear, but deaf individuals will not respond to their kittens' calls. This condition affects Blue-eyed Whites in particular, which often congenitally lack the organ of Corti within the ear.

The cat's tongue is adapted for lapping fluids, forming a shape reminiscent of a ladle for this purpose. After several successive laps, the cat swallows the collected fluid in one gulp. The rough feel of the tongue results from the presence of papillae, which serve to hold prey in the mouth when necessary. There are various types of papillae distributed over the tongue, each of which have a distinct morphology. Taste-buds are also present on the tongue; unlike other mammals, cats do not appear to respond to sweet items, but actively recognize pure water. Smell is related to taste, which is particularly important in the case of the cat. It is likely to refuse all but the strongest smelling foods if this sense is impaired. This impairment is commonly due to a respiratory infection.

There is an additional organ of sense in the cat which does not exist in humans. This is known as Jacobsen's organ, and it is present in the upper surface of the mouth. Molecules of a scent are picked up from the air on the tongue, which is then pressed against Jacobsen's organ. A connection is made with the hypothalamic region of the brain, which triggers an appropriate response.

The hairs of a cat can be divided into various groups, with the longest being classified as "guard" hairs; these form the outer coat. The undercoat beneath is comprised of shorter, softer fur. Certain hairs have become modified for sensory purposes, such as those behind the forelegs and the whiskers.

BEHAVIOR

Understanding a cat is a question of appreciating the natural instincts that help to direct its behavior. An insight into the cat's complex psychology can enhance owners' appreciation of their pets. One important factor is territory. Scratching, spraying and even fighting are all ways in which the cat marks and defends its territory.

WHEN BADLY FRIGHTENED or angry, the cat may resort to spitting, as well as calling out loudly. Such behavior is often linked to an arching of the back, and raising of the fur along the spine. Another indication of discontent will be signalled by the tail movements. Rapid waving of the tail is an expression of annoyance, whereas an upright tail that twitches only slightly is suggestive of an alert demeanor.

The eyes and ears are also used to communicate a cat's state of mind. When the ears are erect, the cat is expressing annoyance, and the pupils of the eyes are likely to be narrowed to a vertical slit. Flattened ears suggest fear or submission, and are typically evident in the weaker of two cats disputing an area of territory. When actually hunting for prey, the ears are drawn back slightly, contributing to the cat's watchful appearance. A contented cat sits with its eyes semi-closed, while the ears are maintained in an upright position. There are known to be more than 20 different muscles controlling ear posture in the cat.

EXPRESSION AND GESTURE

Cats indicate moods using a variety of gestures and postures. Contentment will be shown by alert, upright ears, relaxed whiskers and a tranquil pose (1).

Fear is demonstrated by a lowered head, with the ears and whiskers flattened (2). Anger is expressed by an arched back, raised fur along the spine, bristling whiskers and pricked ears pulled back (3).

A cat under threat first freezes, staring at the aggressor with wide eyes. Its muscles are poised for either fight or flight (right).

frightened cat

In an aggressive encounter, the dominant cat is the one in the higher position (far right) and will deter an opponent by making an appropriate threat gesture.

aggressive cat

FACIAL EXPRESSIONS

A contented cat has upright ears and relaxed whiskers.

When nervous or apprehensive, ears start to go back and whiskers tense slightly forward.

A frightened or very angry cat has flat ears, narrowed eyes and forward-facing whiskers.

This cat is alert and ready to pounce on its prey.

Half-closed eyes and relaxed whiskers indicate a relaxed and contented cat.

Feline "vocabulary" includes growls, hisses, screeches, purrs, and just plain meows – a wide variety of sounds used mainly to communicate with other cats (right), but sometimes also with their owners. Siamese cats are particularly vocal and will often have "conversations" with their owners.

Cat's ears are erect if alert (above) but pulled down flat if angry or scared (right). Hearing in cats is far more acute than ours, and the trumpet-shaped ear flaps can be used to direct as much sound as possible into the ear.

The tail is an obvious indicator of the mood of your cat. It is held high when happy and alert (above), twitches at the end when mildly irritated and is bushy and fully erect when spoiling for a fight.

FELINE BODY LANGUAGE

Cats are masters in the art of body-language, conveying their moods and intentions by a series of well-defined postures, clearly understood by humans, as well as fellow felines.

Cats use a variety of sounds to communicate. The cat above is voicing feelings of nervousness.

This Blue Smoke Persian is obviously upset and emitting an extremely loud yowl.

An unhappy Lilac Burmese squats into a defensive posture with wide eyes and flattened ears.

A long, slow blink from a cat is a sign of relaxed contentment and may be used as a greeting.

The hair of a cat is unconsciously controlled by the autonomic nervous system, and if the cat is angry or frightened the hormone adrenaline is activated, making its hair fully erect so that it appears as large as possible (below).

Other Means of Communication

Purring is the sound most closely associated with domestic cats, yet the actual means by which this noise is produced has never been fully disclosed. It is thought that the additional membranes close to the vocal cords are responsible, and purring results from their vibration. The sound is not audible in all members of the Felidae, however, but is typically confined to the smaller species. While purring is normally accepted as a sign of contentment, very sick cats will continue to purr, and so the sound should not be taken as an indication of good health.

Cats are quieter than dogs, but they possess a distinctive range of vocal sounds, as well as purring. Their calls have been divided into three basic categories. Murmuring sounds, often made with the mouth closed, are reserved for times of intimate contact. The soft calls emitted while being stroked are typical of this group. The second set are specific calls, made with an open mouth, and with a closing of the mouth appearing to act as punctuation. Such calls are normally used to attract the owner's attention. The third group of sounds provide a means of communicating with their fellow cats and can be regarded as being more aggressive, with the teeth constantly visible. Facial characteristics alter, but the mouth itself remains open throughout the encounter.

There are two other types of call that do not fit into the above categories. Cats occasionally open their mouths as if to make a sound, but none is emitted. Such behavior is normal and not indicative of ill health. This gesture is made especially when asking for food or milk, and can be interpreted as a sign of submission. Another call, actually uttered while hunting, is a quiet yet definite clicking sound, indicating to any other cats nearby that the individual is in pursuit of prey.

Cats occasionally groom each other, especially if they have been reared together from kittenhood. This mutual grooming is the sign of a close bond; such contact also gives the opportunity to groom inaccessible areas.

Close contact with another cat may result in the whole body being used to communicate. When ready to accept a mate, the female cat indicates this by crouching in a distinctive, recognized position described as lordosis. Grooming can also be a means of communication. Mutual grooming serves to reinforce a bond between two cats, whereas in some situations a cat will start to groom itself for no reason, perhaps when threatened or under stress.

SELF-GROOMING

Cats are fastidious about grooming, spending long periods cleaning their coats each day. Licking serves many functions: it removes dead hair from the coat, it enables the cat to ingest Vitamin D (which is produced on the fur by exposure to sunlight), and evaporation of saliva cools the cat down in hot weather, fulfilling the same function as sweat. Sweat glands are confined to the feet in cats, so it has to rely on grooming and panting to cool itself. The head is normally cleaned using the front paws.

Compared to other animals, cats spend relatively long periods of their lives asleep.
The usual pattern consists of many short "catnaps" spaced throughout the day.

Sleeping

Cats sleep, on average, twice as long as other mammals, and this behavior is especially noticeable in both very young and very old animals. They may spend nearly three-quarters of the day asleep. The pattern of sleep is nevertheless variable. A cat left on its own tends to sleep more.

The cat's method of sleeping has been extensively studied by attaching external electrodes to the head and monitoring brain waves. The resulting trace on the machine is known as an electroencephalogram (EEG). During the day in particular, light sleep prevails; the cat does not relax its muscles completely and wakes readily, giving rise to the description "cat-naps". After a period of light sleep, however, the cat may enter a phase of deep sleep; this gives a characteristic change in the pattern of EEG. The eyes move rapidly in brief bursts during deep sleep, although the eyelids remain closed, and this has given rise to the alternative name of "rapid eye movement" sleep, or REM sleep. There is usually an accompanying change of posture during REM sleep, and the body becomes more relaxed. Conversely, brain activity is actually increased during REM sleep, despite the way that the cat appears to be more soundly asleep. Periods of REM sleep alternate with light sleep once the cycle has started, until the cat wakes up.

KITTENS

Kittens are constantly learning, from their earliest encounters with their fellows onward. As soon as the kittens have established themselves at their mother's teats, a rudimentary social structure will begin to develop. Each kitten usually has its own nipple, with the liveliest often winning the best position and the weaker individuals relegated to the teats where the milk flow is not as plentiful. Kittens are born blind and need to learn how to use the sense of sight as it develops. About the third week after birth, once they have become proficient in this respect, they begin to show a degree of independence from their mother. Early games will simply consist of jumping on each other or on their mother, but as the kittens grow and become more mobile, their play routine becomes more complex. Although such behavior is commonly referred to as "play," it is in fact vital training.

Learning to Be a Cat

A social structure begins to form in a litter of kittens almost immediately as each seeks out its own nipple, and a distinct pattern is formed by the third day after birth. Kittens are born blind, so a sense of smell is of particular importance at this early stage, to the extent that kittens will become confused if their mother's teats are washed. Sometimes they become side-tracked to their mother's feet, where the odour of perspiration may be strong.

Kittens start playing with objects and each other from three weeks old. Studies show that in a litter comprised partly of males, female kittens tend to play more with objects than those in litters comprised solely of females. This habit of playing, developed during kittenhood, is vital to the cat's subsequent survival as a hunter. At first, kittens simply jump on their fellow kittens and mother, but gradually a more sophisticated routine becomes evident. They start side-stepping and chasing each other more frequently, but do not actually bite at this stage. Under natural conditions, queens will teach their kittens to recognize prey from the age of six weeks onwards. They watch her kills, and she brings them injured prey for killing.

One interesting study into the killing habit of cats, carried out during the 1930s, found that kittens reared with hunting mothers nearly all became killers in turn. It has also been found that prey taken during the formative stages of hunting remains favored throughout the cat's life. On the other hand, only half of a litter reared by a mother who never preyed on mice would attack these creatures in later life. Kittens actually reared alongside mice hardly ever kill their early associates. All cats will play long after they have grown out of kittenhood.

There is some evidence to suggest that while stalking and pouncing are instinctive procedures, triggered by the movement of prey, administering the final bite must be taught. Mothers who do not hunt themselves will not teach this skill to their kittens.

Mock battles between kittens can become quite rough, but the infliction of real injuries is very rare (top right). Such behavior has little to do with actual aggression, and is more often a way of practising hunting routines – stalking, pouncing and capturing.

Imitative and curious, the interest of one kitten in a particular scent will often serve to attract another to the same spot (center right).

Kittens are fairly adept at climbing from an early age. If this is not feasible, they can support themselves on their hindlimbs to investigate something out of reach that looks intriguing (below right).

The inquisitiveness and playfulness of young cats are particularly appealing, but such traits are actually part of the process of learning to be a hunter. Kittens learn the routine of hunting from their mother, with prey often being presented to the litter for practising. This teaching by example normally only occurs if the mother is a hunter herself.

Like any other young animal, a kitten learns by exploring and investigating the outside world, gradually honing its senses and reactions in readiness for life as a hunter. The sense of smell is particularly important in encounters with strange, new objects – kittens will sniff cautiously before approaching closer.

TERRITORIES

Each cat has its own clearly defined territory. The center of this territory is known as the "home base," from which the "home range" extends. This is the region over which the cat normally roves and can be as large as 60 acres (24 hectares), sometimes more. In colonies of feral cats, the availability of food appears to be the feature which determines the area of home range. The hunting range may extend outside the home range, but is rarely established by domestic cats.

When a new cat is acquired it must establish itself, possibly at the expense of another. While tom cats may not object to the apparent intrusion of a female on their territory, neutered cats and queens will often actively resent a newcomer's presence. They will defend their relatively small territories vigorously, whereas toms tend to range over a much wider area which cannot be defended so easily. A new tom will be challenged by others in the area and will almost

A newcomer in the neighborhood will almost certainly be challenged by others in the area.

TERRITORIAL MARKING

Toms do not appear to resent new females, but a new tom will probably have to establish his position. Although domestic cats are much less aggressive than wild cats, neutered cats and females will also defend their territories against the intrusion of a newcomer. Many of these confrontations do not end in a fight but merely consist of ritual threat gestures, aggressive postures and vocalizations. To mark out their territories clearly, cats leave a variety of visual and olfactory signs. Spraying is just one such method (above). Urine is a powerful and individual scent; toms will spray repeatedly around their territory to establish their boundaries. In the confines of the home, however, such activity is bound to be a problem, with the pungent smell lingering on furniture and surroundings. Many owners prefer to have their toms neutered in order to eliminate

this habit as far as possible. Other territorial markers include scent, produced by glands on the cat's body. Rubbing the chin, or head, and tail along fences and boundaries deposits scent from the glands located in these parts of the body (above top). Scratching posts or tree trunks is another way of visibly marking out a particular area, and also leaves scent behind (above).

certainly have to fight rivals to gain a place in the social hierarchy. Queens will also attack others, without warning, if their kittens are threatened. Fighting only occurs in the last resort, however, as there exists a series of well-defined gestures that may be used to resolve the matter without bloodshed.

In a confrontation, ear and tail movements coupled with constriction of the pupils serve to indicate the aggressive demeanor of a potential combatant, forcing the other to adopt a defensive posture. The actual challenge follows an eye-to-eye meeting, and the weaker individual may then simply back off. If it cannot escape, or wishes to resist the challenge, then it moves into a position to resist the threat. It curls its tail and positions its body to emphasize its size, although the pupils remain dilated and the ears are down. The aggressor may then choose to advance on its crouched, hissing rival, who rolls over to meet the challenge with the claws of all

four feet tensed and its sharp teeth ready. After a brief encounter of this nature, when one cat has had enough, it will escape, pursued by its opponent.

A subsequent challenge may have a different outcome. Domestic cats, partly because a high proportion are neutered, usually prove less aggressive towards a newcomer on their territory than their wild counterparts. They mark their territory by a variety of means. Urine provides a pungent scent, while rubbing the head and tail on a favored spot fulfils a similar role. Scratching provides both a visual and olfactory means of staking out a claim on a particular region.

The high density of domestic cats in some areas has led them to evolve various methods for sharing a region without coming into conflict. They will have distinct recognized paths for crossing each other's territory, while a favored spot may be shared, according to the time of day.

Fighting is always a last resort and is often of short duration. The main reasons for fighting are disputes over territory and competition over a mate. Occasionally queens will attack to defend their kittens from intruders.

LOOKING AFTER
YOUR CAT

A ginger kitten up an apple tree.

BASIC CAT CARE

The domestic cat is quite easy to care for within the confines of the home. It must be provided with some basic equipment, such as feeding and drinking bowls, a comfortable bed, a litter tray, and scratching post.

KEEPING YOUR CAT healthy is mainly a matter of commonsense and proper husbandry. In the first place, the cat needs to have been properly reared as a kitten and should be regularly vaccinated against the most dangerous feline diseases such as panleukopenia, or infectious enteritis, rhinotracheitis and calicivirus, often called cat 'flu, and feline leukemia virus. All cats should be fed a well-balanced diet and receive regular courses of anthelmintics to make sure that they are free from internal parasites. External parasites such as fleas should be controlled by the application of pest powder or sprays when necessary, or by dosing with a product designed to curtail the fleas' breeding cycle. The cat's toilet tray must be maintained in spotless condition at all times, as must its food and water bowls. Given such care, and lots of love and attention, the cat should always remain in good health.

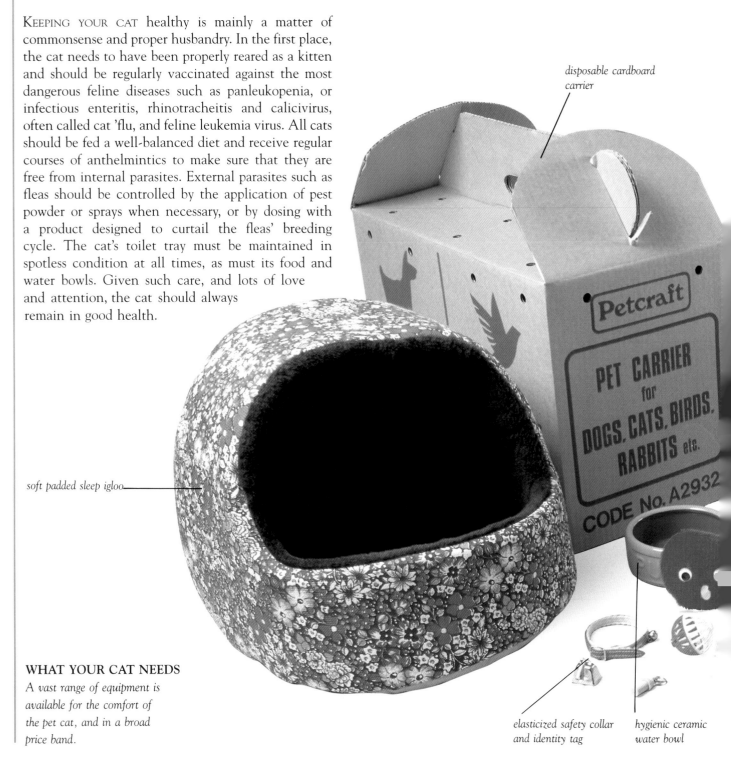

disposable cardboard carrier

Petcraft

PET CARRIER for DOGS. CATS. BIRDS. RABBITS etc.

CODE No. A2932

soft padded sleep igloo

WHAT YOUR CAT NEEDS
A vast range of equipment is available for the comfort of the pet cat, and in a broad price band.

elasticized safety collar and identity tag

hygienic ceramic water bowl

LIFESPAN OF A CAT

The length of a cat's life varies enormously. Those living wild as strays may only survive for two years or so, while a cherished pet may live well into its teens, a senior citizen in human terms.

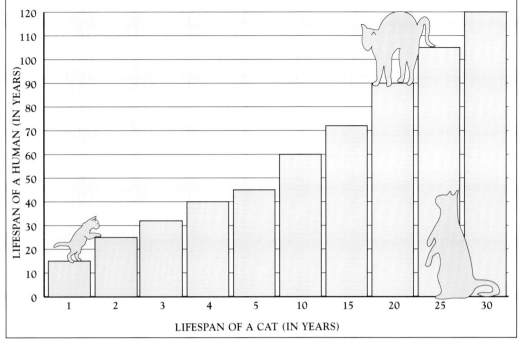

LIFESPAN OF A HUMAN (IN YEARS)

LIFESPAN OF A CAT (IN YEARS)

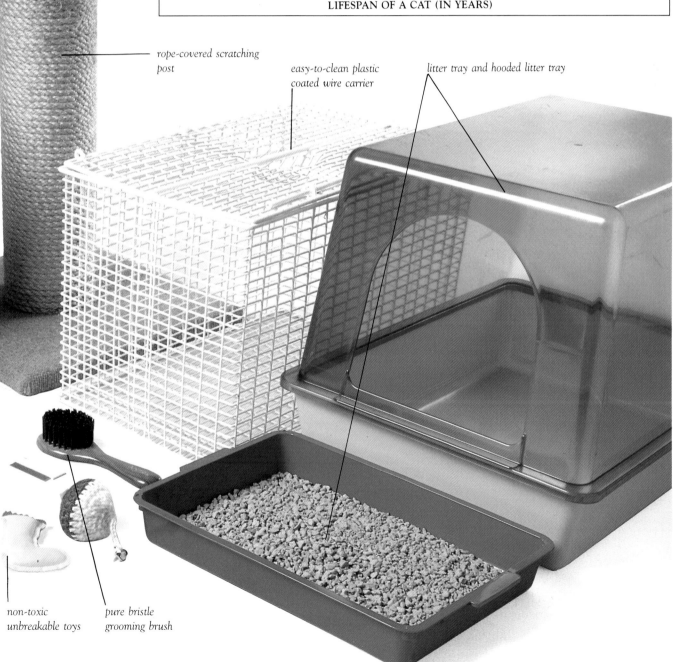

rope-covered scratching post

easy-to-clean plastic coated wire carrier

litter tray and hooded litter tray

non-toxic unbreakable toys

pure bristle grooming brush

255

GROOMING

Most cats benefit from grooming, and longhaired breeds such as the Persian must be groomed daily to keep the full coat in good condition and to prevent the soft undercoat from matting. Start grooming routines when the cat is very young. Weaning kittens should be gently brushed and handled all over so that they never resent being groomed in later life. It is essential to make the grooming routine a pleasant one, making sure that the cat never becomes resentful, particularly when its tender parts, such as the inside of the thighs, are being combed through. Different coat types need different grooming tools, and these should be reserved for the cat's own use. A wide variety of equipment is available, and items of better quality are less likely to damage the cat's coat or skin.

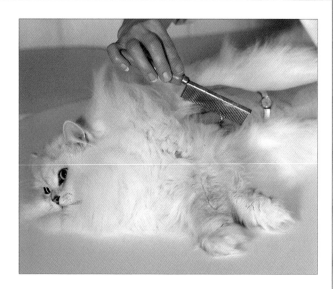

GROOMING A LONGHAIRED CAT

1 Apply grooming powder to the coat.
2 Rub powder into the coat starting from the tail and working toward the head.
3 Brush the coat thoroughly, removing the powder and lifting the coat away from the skin.

4 Use a wide-toothed comb from tail to head to make sure there are no tangles; pay particular attention to the underparts.
5 Clean the eyes, nostrils, and inside the ear flaps with a series of moist swabs or small brush.

  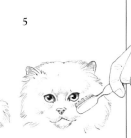

GROOMING A SHORTHAIRED CAT

1 Remove dust, loose hairs, and any debris or parasites, using a metal fine-toothed comb from head to tail.
2 A rubber brush may be used for cats with thick short coats.

3 A soft bristle brush is best for cats with very fine short coats.
4 Buff the coat with a special grooming mitt, a piece of silk or velvet, or a chamois leather.

wire and bristle brush

slicker brush

wide- and fine-toothed comb

toothbrush

HEALTH

Though basically strong, healthy, and built for survival, the cat is susceptible to a host of diseases. Luckily, the most deadly of these may be guarded against by means of effective vaccines, generally given from kittenhood.

GIVING A CAT the correct care is basically a question of common sense. A cat must be given a clean, warm environment in which to live; the correct amount of suitable, nourishing food; constant access to fresh, clean drinking water; and facilities for play and exercise.

A cat should have a bed of its own in a quiet, secluded place, and it should be left in peace to sleep for undisturbed periods during the day. Meals should be fed regularly, on clean dishes, and any food not eaten within a reasonable time, should be removed and disposed of. Cats will not eat stale food. Fresh water should be provided every day and left down for the cat to drink whenever it wishes.

Even if the cat has access to the outdoors, it should be provided with a toilet tray and fresh litter at all

WATCHING OUT FOR PROBLEMS

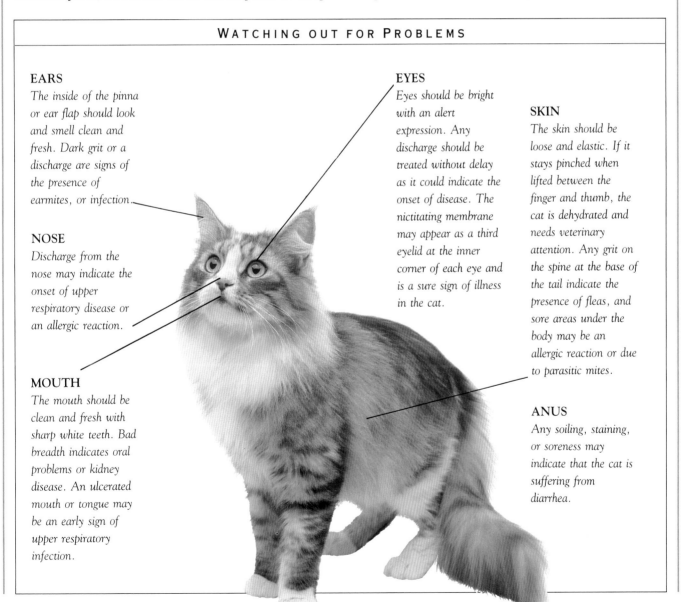

EARS

The inside of the pinna or ear flap should look and smell clean and fresh. Dark grit or a discharge are signs of the presence of earmites, or infection.

NOSE

Discharge from the nose may indicate the onset of upper respiratory disease or an allergic reaction.

MOUTH

The mouth should be clean and fresh with sharp white teeth. Bad breadth indicates oral problems or kidney disease. An ulcerated mouth or tongue may be an early sign of upper respiratory infection.

EYES

Eyes should be bright with an alert expression. Any discharge should be treated without delay as it could indicate the onset of disease. The nictitating membrane may appear as a third eyelid at the inner corner of each eye and is a sure sign of illness in the cat.

SKIN

The skin should be loose and elastic. If it stays pinched when lifted between the finger and thumb, the cat is dehydrated and needs veterinary attention. Any grit on the spine at the base of the tail indicate the presence of fleas, and sore areas under the body may be an allergic reaction or due to parasitic mites.

ANUS

Any soiling, staining, or soreness may indicate that the cat is suffering from diarrhea.

257

SIGNS OF ILL HEALTH

Pain Often the first sign of disease. Locating the site of pain may need diagnosis. Pain from skin, muscle, or bone damage is easier to detect than that from the deeper structures.

Fever A rise in body temperature generally indicates infection, but may be caused by heatstroke. A cat's normal temperature at rest is 101.5° F, but 102.5° F is not uncommon.

Change in Behavior Often the first sign of a serious illness, a change in the personality or behavior of a cat should be monitored.

Loss of Balance or Body Control Lameness is detected fairly easily, denoting an injury to a muscle, tendon, or bone; other signs of painful movement may be more difficult to detect – the cat may just stop jumping up to or down from a chair.

Breathing Labored breathing, wheezing, coughing, or sneezing must not be ignored. Note changes in the cat's voice. Any of these symptoms could denote the onset of respiratory disease.

Defecation and Urination Any changes such as the presence of blood in the feces or urine must be taken seriously. A cat straining on its litter tray without producing any results must see a veterinarian without delay.

Eating and Drinking A change in appetite may be transitory, but should not be disregarded. Constant drinking, vomiting, or dribbling are all symptoms of feline diseases. Take note of the cat's behavior pattern and if it persists, seek veterinary advice. It may point to a dental problem or indicate the onset of illness.

Skin and Fur Most cats normally shed their coats twice a year, but any severe hair loss, perhaps leaving bald patches, should be reported to your veterinarian. If the cat scratches at its neck, it may have a parasitic infestation of fleas, ticks, or mites, which need to be treated. Ear mites infest the inside of the ear and must not be neglected. Ringworm, a fungal infection, often produces circular lesions and is transmissable to humans. Cats are also susceptible to various allergies from such things as household disinfectants and flea bites. A skin condition should never be neglected.

CALL THE VET IMMEDIATELY IF THE CAT IS:
- Shocked or hemorrhaging
- Thought to have ingested a poisonous substance
- Partially or completely unconscious
- Falling about, with uncoordinated movements, or appears partly or completely paralyzed
- Obviously injured
- Vomiting frequently or has constant diarrhea

times. It is more hygienic for the cat's wastes to be disposed of than for it to soil the yard. Various types of litter boxes are available, some with hooded lids, and the wide choice of cat litter includes some made from fresh smelling wood chips, as well as the original products made from Fuller's earth. The litter tray should be washed and dried when the litter is changed, and sterilized with diluted household bleach or a safe disinfectant recommended by the vet.

Cats need to strop their claws from time to time, to keep them in good condition and to remove any loose scale. Various types of scratching posts are available, from simple cardboard strips to ingenious constructions of shelves and posts covered with rope or carpet. A cat prefers to strop its claws on an upright post rather than one laid flat on the floor.

Although most cats which are correctly cared for and properly fed, housed, and vaccinated remain fit and well, it is important to be able to recognize the first signs of infection or trauma. Any change in a cat's normal behavior patterns should be treated with suspicion, for while this may be caused by something as simple as a change in the weather, it could also point to the first stages of a specific illness. All signs and symptoms should be carefully noted, and if necessary, veterinary advice should be sought. It is important to avoid any delay in seeking advice in the event of one of the more serious feline diseases, when early treatment is most effective.

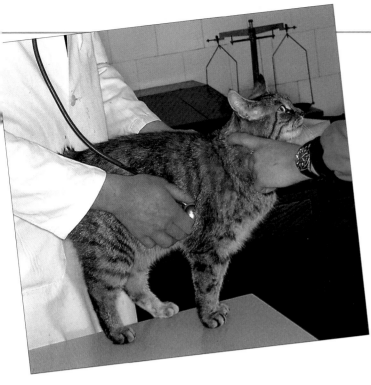

The veterinarian should be a cat's best friend, diagnosing and treating any problems and providing preventative care in the form of feline vaccinations and constructive advice.

FELINE DISORDERS

	Gynecological disorder FP	Pregnancy	Queen in distress; "calling"	Trauma: fracture, dislocation, etc.	Ear infection	Conjunctivitis	Dental problems	Incorrect diet	Fleas and other external parasites	Intestinal worms	Heat stroke	Kidney disease	Hairball	Gastroenteritis	Urolithiasis FUS	Feline infectious peritonitis FIP	Feline leukemia virus FeLV	Feline infectious anemia FIA	Respiratory virus infection – cat 'flu, FOV, FVR	Feline infectious enteritis FIE
Vomiting	?	?		?				*		?		×	*	*	×	?	?	?		×
Diarrhea		?						*		?			?	*		?	*	?		×
Apparent constipation				?				×					?	?	*					?
Excessive thirst	×											*	?	?		?		?		?
Loss of appetite	×	×	×	×			?	*	×		?	?	×	×	×	×	×	×	?	*
Abnormal urination	?			?								*			*					
Dehydration	?											×				?	×		×	*
Coughing/sneezing							?				?		?	?		?			*	
Breathing problems		?		×			?				?	*				×	×	?	?	
Fever	?				?						*		?			×		?	×	?
Lowered temperature	×	?		?								?		?	?	×	?	?	?	*
Pale lips/gums	?			×				?				×				?	?	*		×
Abdominal swelling	×	*		?				?		×			?			×	*	?		
Shaking head				?	*		?		?											
Scratching head/neck				?	×		×	?	*											
Apparent pain	?		*	*	×		×					?	?	×	?				×	
Lameness				*				?				?								
Salivation				?			*	×			*		×	?						?
Localized discharge	*			×	*	*	*	?											*	
Noticeable weight loss	?							?				?			*		*	*	?	?

SYMPTOMS
* MAJOR
× COMMON
? POSSIBLE

KEEPING YOUR CAT HEALTHY

A regular regime of care for your cat will help it to stay in good condition and be less likely to become ill.

DAILY

- Observe the cat's general appearance and behavior; any dramatic change may indicate the need for immediate veterinary attention.
- Feed a well-balanced diet of good-quality food.
- Provide fresh water in a clean container.
- Dispose of soiled litter; clean toilet tray; check cat's stools (and urine if possible) for any sign of abnormality.
- Groom the cat according to its requirements in respect of coat type and hair length.
- In free-ranging cats, check the coat for the staining which could indicate diarrhea and for foreign bodies such as grass seeds or parasites such as ticks; check the feet for sore or cracked pads and for foreign bodies such as splinters or thorns; check all over the head, body, underparts, and legs for signs of fighting – bites and scratches can lead to abcesses if not treated with an antiseptic wash.

WEEKLY

- Examine ears and coat for parasites. If present, check with the veterinarian for appropriate treatment.
- Check mouth and throat; clean teeth if necessary.

MONTHLY

- Check the cat all over from head to tail with your fingertips, feeling for any lumps, bumps, lesions, or foreign bodies. Any worrying anomalies should be discussed with the vet.

SIX-MONTHLY

- Check the cat's records to see if blood tests or vaccinations are due and mark the dates in your diary: free-ranging cats should have a sample of feces analyzed for the presence of parasitic worms, and treatment administered where appropriate.

YEARLY

- Have a complete veterinary check carried out. This can be arranged in conjunction with an annual booster vaccination program.

A QUESTION OF FOOD

A cat's general appearance is the best guide to whether or not its diet is suitable for its size and lifestyle. The signs of a poor diet include dull eyes; a warm, dry nose; bad breath; a dry, scurfy coat; flaky claws; and diarrhea or offensive-smelling stools.

WHAT KINDS OF FOODS should I feed my cat? How much? How often? Can cats be vegetarians? Can they eat dog food? Why does my cat go crazy when it smells catnip? Can I put my overweight cat on a diet? This section answers some of the questions that cat owners often ask about feeding their pets.

A balanced diet will ensure that your cat remains alert, stealthy and playful.

A HEALTHY DIET

Cats are like miniature lions in that they are carnivores. Their nutritional requirements in terms of sustenance and essential vitamins and minerals, can only be derived from meat, fish and animal fats such as milk.

Is it better to cook fresh food for my cat rather than feed it prepared foods?

There is nothing wrong with feeding your cat with a balanced diet of freshly prepared foods, but it is not essential. The manufacturers of the reputable brands of commercial cat foods put a lot of work into insuring that they contain a balance of all the essential nutrients your cat needs. By far the largest proportion of cat food sales in the United States are of dried foods, with approximately 90 per cent of cat owners feeding it at least once a week. Surprisingly, the most popular brand is also one of the most expensive. You may be able to fool your dog into frugal eating habits, but cats are notoriously selective as to what they will and will not eat – very often only the best will do!

Cats also seek more variety in their diets than dogs and will become bored with the same diet day after day. However, most are content with a regular change of the flavor of canned foods offered. If you are one of the many owners who get pleasure from carefully preparing fresh food for your cat, then you may rest assured that you can feed your cat a perfectly healthy diet by taking care to provide a reasonably wide variety of food, including some animal protein and fat and a reputable vitamin and mineral supplement. Next time you take your cat to your vet for a health check or routine vaccinations, take the opportunity to discuss any dietary matters you might be unsure about.

Is it healthy to feed dry cat foods?

Dry cat foods are convenient and hygienic to feed; they help to exercise the teeth and are ideal to put out if you have to leave the cat alone in the house for a period. Unlike so many of their owners, most cats are pretty good at regulating their food intake and avoiding middle-age spread.

However, dry cat food seems to be highly popular with many cats and can easily overcome their natural weight control mechanisms, leading to obesity. In addition, many cats do not seem to drink enough extra water to make up for what they are not getting in the food, causing them to produce concentrated urine. This may lead to urinary problems, especially in neutered male cats. Dry foods are fine as an occasional treat, but they should be avoided if your cat has had a past history of urinary problems, such as cystitis, or is so enthusiastic that it tends to become "hooked" on them and refuses to eat other foods.

A fat cat is not necessarily a contented one. Although most cats seem to be able to eat just enough food to maintain a normal body weight, weight control in cats can be a problem in those few cats that do not regulate their own intake sensibly, particularly if they are able to find food elsewhere. It is not uncommon for one cat to be fed at two homes. Attempting to fill up the cat's stomach with high fibre foods may be an answer, but your cat may not agree!

How often should I feed my cat?

Since cats are generally good at regulating their weight, it is usually all right to feed a little and often on request. Your cat will quickly have you trained to respond to his or her demands for food! Be sure the bowl is always cleaned out before food is put into it – most cats will only eat food that is fresh and wholesome and will object to the smell of stale food.

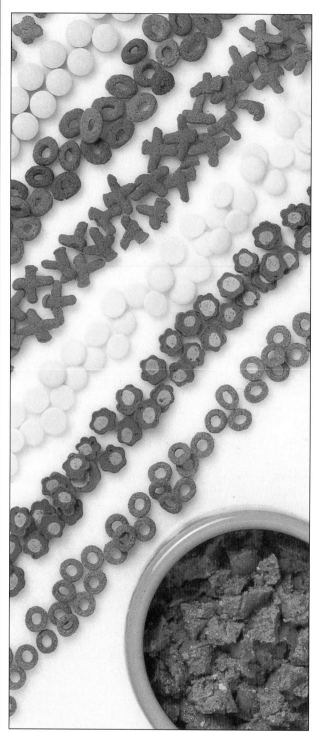

Canned food does contain carefully balanced amounts of protein, fat, carbohydrate, fiber and mineral and vitamin supplements that mimic a cat's natural prey. If your cat only eats dried food, ensure that it drinks plenty of water as well.

What can I do if my cat is overweight?

Often there is not a lot that you can do, unless your cat is an indoor cat and you are prepared to withstand persistent demands for food. In this case it is relatively easy to simply feed your cat smaller amounts of its normal diet. Unfortunately, most owners have little control over their cat's food intake, since it will seek food elsewhere if not enough is provided at home. Keep away from the more fattening items such as dry cat foods and milk and try to fill the cat's stomach with bulking agents such as bran. Playing with your cat will help to increase the speed at which food is burned up. The chart below shows the approximate energy value (kcals) per 100g of different food types.

ENERGY REQUIREMENTS

An adult cat needs 200 to 300 calories a day, depending on its size and amount of exercise. Kittens have a higher demand in relation to their body weight due to their rapid growth rate. Neutered cats need less energy in relation to their body weight as they are not reproducing and generally lead rather sedentary lives.

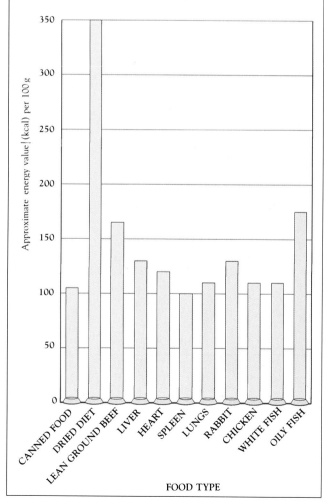

What should I give my cat to drink?

Always be sure that fresh water is available for your cat, but don't be surprised if it chooses to drink elsewhere. Many perfectly normal cats drink very little, getting the fluids they need from their food. Other cats prefer to drink outdoors, or from less conventional sources, such as a running tap, hot bath water, or even from the toilet. Our simple human palates seem inadequate to appreciate the subtle differences in flavor that are so important to our feline friends!

Should I offer milk?

It is not essential for cats to drink milk, but some cats are very fond of it. Too much milk may cause diarrhea and encourage obesity, so do not allow your cat to drink to excess. Of course, milk can turn sour very quickly, so be sure that it is not left out too long.

Are there any foods which can be harmful to cats?

As is often the case, too much of a good thing can cause problems. In particular, an excess of liver in the diet can result in severe bone disease due to the large amounts of vitamin A it contains. And a diet of canned fish only can cause pansteatitis or "yellow fat disease," a painful inflammation of the fatty tissues due to vitamin E deficiency. Raw fish contains an enzyme that breaks down vitamin B1 and can lead to a deficiency. In general it is best to cook fresh foods and remove any bones.

Why does my cat eat grass?

We're not sure of the reason, but it seems to be quite a common habit. It might be an attempt to take in extra roughage or an attempt to clear the stomach of

Milk and cream are appealing to most cats, but some are unable to digest it very well. These cats may develop diarrhea if they drink too much of these products.

Chewing grass is a popular pastime with many healthy cats, although sometimes it may be a sign of an impending digestive upset. Housebound cats should be offered pots of grass.

Meat or meat-derived products form the staple diet of most cats as they are generally fairly conservative in terms of taste. However, some cats do have more adventurous palates (such as this cat on the left), and they will eat vegetables or starchy foods. This kind of variety should be encouraged.

265

AGE TO WEIGHT CHART			
CAT DETAILS		FOOD REQUIREMENTS	
AGE OF CAT	WEIGHT OF CAT	FEEDS	OUNCES PER FEED
KITTEN			
NEWBORN	$3^3/_4$ oz	10	1
5 WEEKS	16 oz	6	3
10 WEEKS	32 oz	5	5
20 WEEKS	$4^1/_2$ lb	4	6
30 WEEKS	$6^1/_2$ lb	3	7
ADULT			
MALE/FEMALE	$6^1/_2$–10 lb	1–2	6–$8^1/_2$
PREGNANT	7–8 lb	2–3	$8^1/_2$
LACTATING	$5^1/_2$ lb	4	14
NEUTER	8–10 lb	1–2	6–$7^3/_4$

hairballs. Or perhaps cats simply like the taste! In any case, it is a good idea to offer housebound cats some grass in a pot and to discourage them from chewing houseplants, which can be poisonous.

Why do many cats like catnip?

Nepeta mussinii, otherwise known as catnip or catmint, is very popular in the feline world. It contains a chemical called nepetalactone, which seems to have a similar effect to that which a large gin and tonic would have on their owners – releasing their inhibitions and making them more playful than normal. Some toys are also impregnated with this chemical. While the effects seem to be pleasant in most cats, some cats seem to react aggressively, sometimes to the extent of attacking their owners. This reaction is very uncommon, but it would be worth removing anything containing catnip if aggression is a problem.

Can my cat be vegetarian?

It is not advisable since they are obligate carnivores. In other words, they have to eat meat in the wild. Some other carnivores, such as dogs, can manage in the wild on a mixed diet if meat is in short supply. Cats have lost the ability to make certain essential amino acids not found in protein of vegetable origin. A deficiency of amino acid, taurine, can cause progressive blindness. Cats also require a much higher fat content in their diet than most other animals, and vegetarian diets tend to be low in fat. In the wild, their diet would be composed of small rodents, frogs, toads, birds and insects – so be sure that at least a third of the diet is protein of animal origin. Vegetarianism is fine for humans and all right for dogs, but cats need meat!

Can I feed my cat dog food?

No. While it will not do any harm to give cat food to a dog, dog food will probably not contain all the essential nutrients your cat needs. Additionally, some of the dog foods contain preservatives that are poisonous to cats.

Should I worry if my cat does not eat for a day or two?

You will quickly become familiar with your cat's habits – some cats will go without food for a couple of days for no apparent reason, whereas others are absolutely regular in their eating habits and will alert you quickly if something is amiss. Remember, however, that in the warmer months particularly your cat's predatory instincts will come to the fore, and it may get food elsewhere. Even if your cat is too lazy to pose a threat to the local wildlife, a friendly neighbor may be offering food. If your cat is otherwise well, do not worry if it is off its food for a couple of days. However, should your cat seem at all unwell, or not eat for more than 48 hours, it's time for a visit to your vet.

A healthy appetite is often a sign of a healthy cat, although some cats are prone to fads. Watch out for any change in your cat's habits, since it may give a warning of an impending problem.

Two ginger kittens (brothers) scoffing cat food. Whichever gets he food first is the boss!

REPRODUCTION

REPRODUCTION

Cats are by nature highly sexed animals. Even if owners do not want their cats to breed, an understanding of the way the cat's reproductive cycle works is important.

THOUSANDS OF UNWANTED cats are born each year. Many of these are destroyed or live for only a brief time as strays. It is part of the responsibility of every cat owner not to add to this suffering.

The Reproductive System of the Male

The reproductive anatomy of the male cat is not very different from that of other mammals, in spite of its internal penis. This organ deposits semen in the female's reproductive tract, swelling with blood in periods of sexual excitement to facilitate penetration of the vagina. The penis of the cat, however, is barbed with small spines around the tip, or glans. These may serve to keep the erect penis in position, but also appear to stimulate ovulation in the female.

The testes, where the semen is produced, are located outside the body because body temperature is too high for spermatozoa to mature successfully. Prior to birth, the testes develop first in the abdomen of the kitten and then descend into the scrotal sac. On some occasions this may not occur and one or, rarely, both testes are retained in the body. Such cats are

Care and nurturing of kittens is almost exclusively the concern of the female cat: this is true in the domestic species (above) and in the case of wild felids, such as lions (left). For the first three weeks, the mother (dam) will devote all of her time and energies to her kittens, rarely leaving the nest.

By about the third week, kittens acquire a measure of independence and begin to explore the world outside their nest (above). At this stage, the mother will often refuse to suckle them on demand and will leave the nest herself for longer periods.

273

known as cryptorchids. The testicle will need to be removed surgically if it has not descended by the age of eight months. Castration alone is no use because the cat will continue to display the typical signs of male behavior, including spraying.

In the testes, semen is produced in the seminiferous tubules, while the neighboring interstitial cells are responsible for producing the sex hormone testosterone. This is sometimes known as the "male" hormone, but can also be detected in females, who correspondingly possess relatively higher levels of oestrogen, the "female" hormone, than males. Testosterone is responsible for the development and maintenance of the secondary sexual characteristics which, in the case of the cat, include the presence of thicker skin in the region of the neck and prominent jowls around the face.

The Reproductive System of the Female

The uterus of the female cat has two relatively long "horns", which connect to the ovaries by tubes known as oviducts. The horns meet to form the body of the uterus, which terminates in the cervix and connects to the vagina, or birth canal, where the male inserts his penis. The reproductive cycle in the queen cat differs from that of the human female, and indeed most mammals, in several fundamental respects. The most important of these is the fact that the actual release of eggs, or ovulation, is brought about by mating.

Ovulation, as with other reproductive processes, is mediated by hormones released under the control of part of the brain called the hypothalamus. It triggers an adjoining region, known as the anterior pituitary, which in turn then produces and liberates follicle stimulating hormone (FSH) into the circulation.

As they reach puberty, kittens will often show the first signs of sexual gestures in their usual greeting and play behavior.

BOYS AND GIRLS

FEMALE

kidney
ovary
fallopian tube
uterus
cervix
ureter
bladder
vagina

MALE

kidney
ureter
bladder
spermatic cord
testicle
penis

The hormone acts on the ovaries, stimulating the development of fluid-filled follicles containing ova. The ovaries contain masses of minute ova from birth, but only a relatively small proportion of these will develop and be released during the individual's lifetime. Oestrogen is produced within the follicles and this produces characteristic signs of "heat" or sexual activity, as well as preparing the uterus to receive the fertilized ova.

The process of fertilization, when a male sperm fuses with an ovum, normally occurs in the uterine horns, with the sperm swimming up through the cervix from the vagina. The number of ova released will determine the maximum number of kittens that can be born; this number is usually between three and six. The fertilized ovum then moves down into the uterine horns where the process of implantation, or attachment to the uterine wall, occurs, giving rise to the development of a placenta.

Although only one sperm can fertilize an ovum, it is possible for a queen to bear kittens by different sires in one litter if matings occur very closely together. Certain queens will also mate while pregnant and can even conceive during this period, although such behavior is unusual. The second set of kittens may be born prematurely at the same time as those from the initial mating. Under controlled conditions such events are not likely to occur.

MATING

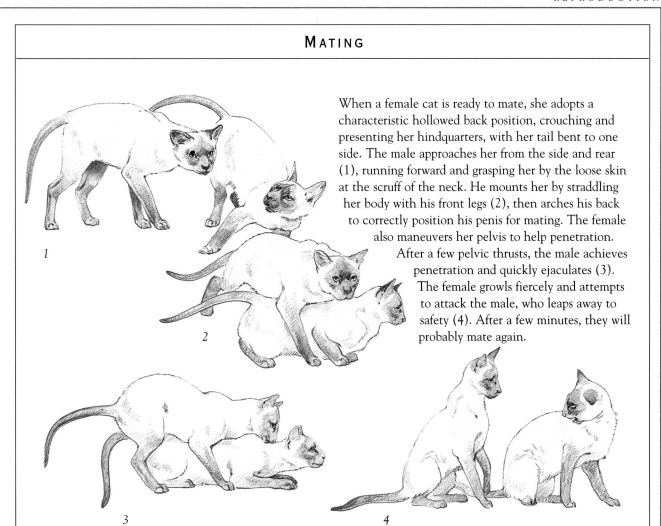

When a female cat is ready to mate, she adopts a characteristic hollowed back position, crouching and presenting her hindquarters, with her tail bent to one side. The male approaches her from the side and rear (1), running forward and grasping her by the loose skin at the scruff of the neck. He mounts her by straddling her body with his front legs (2), then arches his back to correctly position his penis for mating. The female also maneuvers her pelvis to help penetration. After a few pelvic thrusts, the male achieves penetration and quickly ejaculates (3). The female growls fiercely and attempts to attack the male, who leaps away to safety (4). After a few minutes, they will probably mate again.

The Breeding Period and Mating

The female cat may start having oestrus cycles when only three and a half months old, although this is quite unusual. Seven months is more likely, even later in the case of some longhairs. Siamese as a general rule mature early, but other factors such as climate, can also be significant. Kittens born in a spring that precedes a cold summer may not start their cycles until they are one year old. Tom cats are unlikely to be mature before one year and in some instances may not reach puberty until their second year.

The breeding period, during which time a queen may cycle continuously, extends over the greater part of the year, from the end of December until the beginning of the following September. Most kittens are born during July and August, although later litters are not unknown if the weather remains mild. When in oestrus, the queen is said to be "calling." This description results from the noise made by certain cats, notably Siamese, during this period. Reliance on calling alone to detect oestrus is not reliable in all cases. Many foreign breeds, such as the Russian Blue, may not be noticeably vocal. It is also difficult to detect oestrus by changes in the vulval region, as only a very slight swelling may be evident around the vulval lips. Other behavioral signs are much more helpful. Queens on heat become restless and often abnormally affectionate; they also rub and lick the area around their vulvas repeatedly.

The oestrus period in the cat supposedly lasts for three weeks, but signs of oestrus will be particularly

Prior to mating, the female will adopt a characteristic posture, known as lordosis.

A good stud tom should complement the queen, not reinforce her strengths and weaknesses. The kittens resulting from the mating should then show an overall improvement on both parents.

noticeable for one week. Several males will make advances before one is finally accepted. This stage lasts from 12 hours to four days as a rule, during which time the queen, if she is allowed out, may not return home. Once the female has decided on a mate, repeated episodes of copulation over a day or so usually occur. The protracted courtship is thought to bring the ovarian follicles up to the point of rupture, when the enclosed ova are liberated and can then be fertilized.

Mating itself is a relatively brief procedure, with the male stalking around the female as a preliminary while she moves and displays to him. Mating can only take place with the female's cooperation, as she must raise her hindquarters to a virtually horizontal position, displaying her vulva to the male. He will grab the scruff of her neck in his mouth and may actually bite her during mating.

There is no "tie," or locking, as occurs with dogs, but the spines on the male's penis prove traumatic to the vaginal walls, especially on withdrawal. The significance of these spines is not completely understood, but they may serve to stimulate the release of luternizing hormone (LH) from the pituitary of the female, which in turn ensures that

the follicles rupture. At these sites structures known as corpora lutea develop and begin secreting progesterone. This hormone ensures that the uterus will be ready to accept the fertilized ova and, with declining levels of oestrogen in the circulation, the queen's sexual drive diminishes accordingly. Releasing ova in response to coitus appears to have particular benefits for creatures that are only drawn together for mating purposes. Regular release of ova, as occurs monthly in human females, provides no guarantee for solitary creatures that a male would be in the vicinity to effect fertilization when the ova are released, and thus the future of the next generation would be threatened.

Stud Mating

For the ordinary mating, there is rarely any financial benefit to be gained from keeping and breeding from a pedigree queen – bloodlines are only established over a period of years, with considerable work and effort. Many owners, however, prefer to pay a stud fee to have their cats mated to another pedigree, particularly if any of the kittens are to be kept. If an intact pedigree queen is allowed to roam free, the litters will almost certainly be crossbred.

Choosing the right stud cat is an important decision for the pedigree breeder. Visiting cat shows is a good way of studying the characteristics of a particular breed, noting type and color of regular winners and making contact with other breeders. Pedigree studs are advertised in cat magazines. Before selecting a particular stud, it is useful to visit the breeder's premises to see the tom and inspect the quarters. The premises should be clean, and all the cats should be in good health. At this stage, the fee should be decided, together with any other contractual conditions. Many breeders are pleased to give advice on the selection of the stud cat.

Siamese cats mature earlier than many breeds and may begin calling at three and a half months old.

The advice of an experienced breeder is invaluable when selecting a stud or a queen for breeding purposes. The stud tom should complement the particular queen, balancing out her own strengths and weaknesses so that the kittens show improvement overall. Visits to shows will give opportunities to assess type and bloodlines, and cat magazines can be studied to keep in touch with regular winners.

Championship winners are not often for sale, but most breeders are prepared to part with kittens with good pedigrees. When starting a stud, breeders often begin with one or two queens and increase numbers as the stud develops around the kittens. Indeed, it is often more satisfactory to obtain young cats as breeding stock, rather than buying a mature individual, unless its past history is known. Such cats often prove liabilities and may turn out to be poor mothers. Kittens from a relatively large litter are sought by many breeders because it appears that they, in turn, may produce slightly more offspring per litter than is average for the breed concerned.

It is usual practice to mate a queen at her second – rather than first – heat, although problems can arise with precocious breeds. Siamese may commence calling before four months of age, but should not really be mated until eight months, preferably later. Unfortunately, the follicles on the ovaries may develop into cysts if the cat is not allowed to mate. Veterinary advice will be necessary to deal with this condition if the cat fails to mate or conceive.

Visiting the stud gives an opportunity to see the tom and view the premises. The stud quarters should be kept extremely clean and thoroughly disinfected between queens. It is also important to establish the stud fee; this will be influenced by the status of the male, with championship winners commanding correspondingly higher fees. There is no guarantee that mating will produce any kittens and some owners will permit a second mating period free of charge in the event of an initial failure.

When the queen starts calling, an appointment

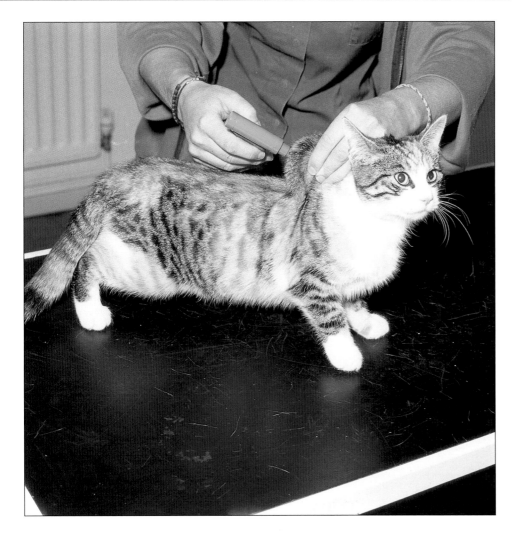

can be confirmed by telephone with the stud owner. The queen should then be taken to the stud with minimum disturbance, especially in the case of an uninitiated cat. Relevant papers must also be taken: the queen's pedigree, and vaccination certificates both for feline infectious enteritis and respiratory viruses are likely to be required, possibly together with the result of screening for feline leukemia virus. Many stud owners also like a diet sheet for the queen, as she will remain in residence for several days.

It is quite normal for the stud owner to examine the incoming queen for any signs of illness and even to take her temperature. This is often slightly raised as a result of the journey. If the queen appears at all off-color, it is preferable from all points of view to defer mating until a later date.

Mating quarters consist of pens with a connecting door. The queen, still in her box, is introduced to one side of the partition and then released. The tom will already be on the opposite side; at first the door between the two will be kept closed. Some queens become very wild at the scent of a male and may scratch and struggle violently; they should never be carried free into the enclosure for this reason.

After a period adjusting to her environment, the queen will begin to acknowledge the male by rubbing along the bars to attract his attention. On rare occasions, the journey may have disturbed a queen so much that mating will have to be postponed until the next oestrus. The time taken to settle down in breeding quarters will vary greatly; with previously unmated animals, it may take eight hours or so before they feel comfortable in their surroundings.

Once the signs of wanting to mate are evident, the cats can be allowed to mix together. After mating, the queen is likely to strike out at her mate, and he must be allowed space to withdraw to a safe distance. A shelf is often provided in stud quarters for this reason. The female's apparent resentment is normally brief; subsequently, mating may take place again.

The violent episodes that can occur during mating necessitate the constant yet discreet presence of the stud owner. Difficulties often arise with inexperienced cats of either sex; pairings are usually arranged so that at least one partner knows the routine.

The queen is normally separated after one mating. Once she has settled down, she will be reintroduced to the tom for further matings. This procedure is carried out daily and should ensure successful fertilization. Most studs keep queens for at least three days and often longer, if the queen is left for a short period with the tom following the third mating.

PREGNANCY AND BIRTH

On her return home, the female cat should be kept isolated from other cats if possible and not allowed outside in case mating with another sire takes place. The follicles rupture about a day after coitus and, once the ova are fertilized, they reach the uterus within five days. Implantation occurs about two weeks after mating. The placentae, or "afterbirths" develop; these provide the kittens with oxygen and nourishment via the blood and remove toxic waste products by the same route.

The gestation period is approximately 63 to 66 days following mating. Survival of kittens born prematurely – a week or more early – is rare. Like human babies, such kittens will be unable to inflate their lungs and breathe atmospheric air.

It may be possible for an experienced breeder or vet to detect the developing fetuses by gentle palpation of the abdomen about three weeks after mating. This should not be undertaken by the inexperienced; unintentional injury, either to the dam or the kittens, may result.

An external indication of pregnancy that appears about the same time is the development of the nipples, especially in cats giving birth for the first time. They enlarge and turn pink; this change is sometimes referred to as "pinking up." Three weeks after mating, the fetuses are about the size of peas, but will be causing a noticeable distension of their mother's abdomen a fortnight later. From day 49 of the pregnancy, it is possible to feel the distinct outline of the kittens in the uterus, although the actual number present is hard to detect accurately. Their developing skeletal systems will also appear on X-rays from this stage onwards, although

DEVELOPMENT OF THE FETUS

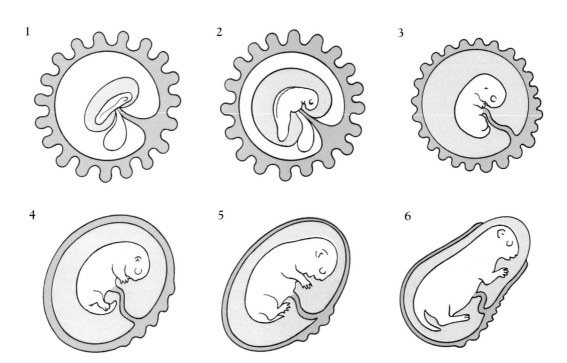

In the first stage, known as implantation, a connection is made with the uterine wall about two weeks after mating (1).

The embryo is nourished by a yolk sac until the placental connection is fully operational and the umbilical cord has developed (2, 3). This is achieved by day 22 of the pregnancy; at the same time the head and limbs are becoming apparent (4). At four weeks old, the fetus is about 1in (2.5cm) in length and its organ systems are fully formed (5).

Five weeks after mating the fetuses will be causing a swelling of their mother's abdomen. The fetus may double in size within a week, reaching its final size of about 5in (12.5cm) (6).

unnecessary exposure to such radiation should be avoided if possible. The major period of the kittens' physical growth takes place during the last third of pregnancy.

Taking Care of the Pregnant Cat

The queen will not require significantly increased amounts of food until the kittens rapidly increase in size, from about six weeks onward. She can he fed to appetite, and in the latter stages may be taking twice her usual amount of food. This should be offered as three or four meals a day, while milk, a good source of calcium and other minerals, must also be freely available. For cats that cannot digest even goat's milk, alternative sources of calcium will need to be provided. Comprehensive supplements for all queens can be obtained from a vet.

There is no need to restrict the activity of a pregnant cat, although she will need to be handled with extra care during the latter stages of pregnancy. The kittens, each weighing perhaps 1/4lb (0.09kg), will be a considerable burden on a creature that normally only weighs 10lb (5kg) or so. About a week before the kittens are due, it is sensible to worm the queen so that she is less likely to be a source of infection. Treatment should be continued every week through the suckling phase.

At least 10 days before the kittens are due, cardboard boxes lined with paper toweling should be distributed in various warm, secure locations around the home. One side of each box should be cut away to allow easy access; later it can be taped back to prevent the kittens from walking off unsupervised. Paper toweling is preferable for bedding purposes because it can be easily discarded when soiled, and there will be no risk of young kittens being accidentally smothered. The queen will probably investigate all the boxes, before concentrating on one or two. As the time of birth approaches, she should be encouraged to select a suitable site by closing her in the room concerned; otherwise she may wander away or even adopt a bed for the purpose.

The pregnant queen is not sick in the mornings, neither does she have a craving for crazy food. Nature does not allow for such luxuries. Cats are exceptionally healthy creatures. The majority will sail through pregnancy without difficulty.

The Birth

Cats do not normally have difficulty in giving birth, but it is advisable to notify the vet of the likely date of the kittens' arrival, in case problems do arise. Immediately before giving birth, the contractions of the uterus will be visible against the cat's flanks and she will probably appear anxious and restless. However, even queens of the same breed can vary greatly in their reaction to giving birth. Once the movements in her sides are apparent, she must be confined to the room where the chosen box is located. Signs of a discharge in the vulval region may be evident; she will also start treading the paper to form a bed.

After the first stage of labor, the cat will then actively strain and may cry out. This is quite usual and not a cause for concern. She should be left without interference throughout the whole birth process unless difficulties arise. The period of straining before the first kitten is born can vary, and is often longer in cats giving birth for the first time, but will normally be about 30 to 45 minutes. The kittens should be presented (born) head first; occasionally breech presentations, with the hindquarters emerging first, are encountered. This can be dangerous, since the head may become stuck; the kitten concerned is likely to start breathing while still in the vagina and may choke as a result. Careful manipulation, using a clean towel or piece of cotton sheeting, will be necessary to free the kitten. It must be handled gently, preferably as close to the shoulders as possible, to minimize risk of injury.

The third or final stage of labor entails the passing of the placentae, one for each kitten. This may be interspersed with the birth of subsequent kittens, but more commonly the young cat emerges still attached to its placenta. The connecting umbilical cord should be cut by the queen and she may then eat the afterbirth. This behavior is quite normal, but it is perhaps preferable to remove the placentae if she shows no interest in them. Most litters consist of about four kittens but larger or smaller numbers are not uncommon. The kittens are usually born at intervals of between 10 minutes and an hour.

If the queen is very tired after giving birth, she might not cut the cord or break the amniotic sac

STAGES OF LABOUR

Cats normally give birth without any difficulty. The first signs that a queen is about to give birth include general restlessness and heaving movements of her flanks, indicating that contractions have begun. At this point, she should be confined to the room where the nesting box is located. After a period of straining, the first kitten will appear. The mother will free it from any retaining membranes and rupture the umbilical cord. After each kitten is born, its placenta, or afterbirth, will be passed and the mother may eat it if it is not taken away. It is important to check that one afterbirth has been passed for each kitten. Once all the kittens have arrived, the mother will clean them thoroughly while they feed.

1. A general restlessness indicates the approaching birth.

4. Kittens will be licked to encourage them to breathe.

5. The mother may eat the placenta, or afterbirth.

enveloping the kitten. Without rapid assistance the young cat is likely to die. In such an emergency the sac can be broken with clean fingers and then, most importantly, the kitten's nose and mouth must be wiped clear of any debris, which may otherwise stop it breathing. Opening the jaws slightly with a finger should stimulate inflation of the lungs. If the kitten still does not respond after having been held upside down, its rib-cage should be rubbed repeatedly. Applying pressure to the chest is not recommended in case internal organs are damaged. The remaining alternative is artificial resuscitation.

If the cord has not been cut by the queen, a piece of cotton, previously boiled in water, should be tightly knotted around the cord about 1in (2.5cm) from the body. Hands should be washed thoroughly in cetrimide before performing this operation. Cut the cord on the side of the knot furthest from the body. A few drops of blood may appear but this is no cause for alarm if the cord is tied off adequately. The kitten should then be returned to its mother so that it can start suckling. The remains of the cord will eventually dry up and drop off.

After giving birth, the queen usually settles down and starts cleaning her kittens while they suckle. Some queens stay with their offspring constantly for the first day. In rare cases, after the queen appears to have finished giving birth, she may show signs of second-stage labor again and produce more kittens. This can occur up to a day later.

Complications

There are several instances when veterinary assistance will be required. The first indication that all is not well will be if no kittens appear after the queen has been straining for an hour or more. The first kitten is probably in an incorrect position with its head causing an obstruction. Unfortunately, the birth canal of the cat is too small for a major manual correction of presentation. A Caesarean section may be required; providing surgery is begun without undue delay, there is usually a good prognosis for both mother and kittens. In some cases, such as a female with a fractured pelvis, the vet may recommend simultaneous spaying, removing both kittens and uterus via an incision made in the

2. Each kitten appears as a protrusion from the vagina.

6. Kittens may begin suckling before the last is born.

3. The kittens will be born at regular intervals.

7. Most litters consist of four kittens.

abdominal wall. Abnormally large kittens are not common, but can sometimes be the cause of a hold-up in the birth process.

It is important to check that the number of afterbirths passed corresponds to the number of kittens. If any are retained within the body, the cat is likely to become ill. They can be detached by suitable drugs, often given in the form of an injection. Any signs of a brownish discharge from the vagina, coupled with a raised temperature, must also be treated seriously. The cat will appear sick and dull and rapidly lose interest in her kittens. Antibiotic therapy will prove effective in most cases.

Once the kittens are suckling, the mammary glands should be observed for any signs of mastitis. The glands most commonly involved are those nearest the tail, but often only one will be affected. It will appear painful, hot and swollen, as a result of the accumulation of pus within, and the queen will resent any kittens attempting to suckle from it.

Apart from antibiotic treatment, some protection must be given to gland itself to minimize discomfort.

Perhaps the most serious condition to affect a cat that has recently given birth is prolapse of the uterus. This is where the uterus is expressed through the vagina. It is typically associated with a prolonged birth cycle or excessive straining; the uterus will hang out as a red, inflamed mass of tissue. Rapid veterinary attention is required to clean the uterus and reinsert it back in the abdominal cavity.

A disturbing disorder of the lactating queen is lactation tetany, or milk fever, seen mostly in cats nursing large litters. Shaking, muscle tremors and collapse typically occur, but rapid treatment with calcium borogluconate, given by a vet, will lead to a spectacular recovery. If possible, reduce the number of kittens being suckled by placing a few with a foster mother, but they should stay with their mother for the first few days in order to obtain the "first milk," or colostrum, a fluid containing vital antibodies.

CARE OF KITTENS

If kittens are orphaned the use of a foster mother is to be recommended if at all possible. Rearing kittens by hand is an extremely time-consuming, albeit rewarding, task especially during the early weeks. Cats will readily foster other kittens alongside their own without difficulties, providing their litter is relatively small. One or two kittens from a large litter could be transferred usefully to a queen with only a couple of kittens herself. This is a potential advantage of having two cats expecting litters at approximately the same time. A vet may be able to help find a foster mother.

If a foster mother cannot be found, the necessary milk substitute powder can be obtained from a vet. Complete products that correspond exactly to the queen's milk are now available. Alternatively, other general rearing foods sold in pet stores can be used. Cow's milk alone is inadequate because it contains insufficient protein to support the growing kittens. Special feeding bottles for kittens are also produced, but in an emergency a simple eye-dropper or a 5ml syringe without a needle can be used.

Good hygiene plays a very important part in successful rearing. Feeding bottles must always be kept scrupulously clean – and should be thoroughly washed and rinsed between feeds. The milk powder should be mixed fresh each time according to the instructions and offered at a temperature of 100°F (38°C). It is vital never to rush a feed; otherwise there is a significant risk of choking the kitten. Fluid entering the lungs is likely to lead to the development of inhalation pneumonia, with serious, often fatal, consequences. Kittens rapidly learn to suck and the feeding mixture should only be given a drop or so at a time.

Young kittens take small quantities of fluid at first, perhaps only 3ml per feed. They must be fed every two hours around the clock. Their food intake should have doubled by the age of a week and four-hourly feeds, certainly through the night, should then prove adequate. At three weeks old, they can be offered a little solid food on a spoon, such as a finely chopped

HAND-REARING

An orphan kitten is best fostered. But if there is no alternative to hand-rearing, a milk substitute should be given. Encourage the kitten to suck by only releasing small amounts at a time.

boiled fish mixed with gravy. As soon as the kitten starts to lap, feeding will become much easier.

Kittens need to be kept warm, at a temperature of about 86°F (30°C) at first, which can then be lowered carefully in stages to 70°F (21°C) by the age of six weeks. A hot-water bottle in the bed will encourage the kitten to snuggle up, as it would to its mother, while an infrared lamp should be suspended above the box. Models specifically produced for use with livestock, which emit predominantly heat rather than light, should be used if possible. The temperature on the surface of the bedding should be monitored with a thermometer; it is possible to overheat the kitten if the lamp is placed too close.

In order to stimulate the mother's habit of licking her kittens after they have fed, hand-reared kittens should be wiped over with a damp cloth wetted with warm water. This in turn will encourage them to urinate and defecate, and their bedding will then have to be changed.

Normal Development

Kittens normally start suckling soon after birth. Each will adopt a particular nipple. Any that appear to be having difficulty in suckling should be examined for the presence of a cleft palate. This is a developmental abnormality affecting the roof of the mouth and is often shown up by milk running down the nostrils. In such cases, no treatment is really possible, and the kitten will have to be painlessly destroyed by a vet.

After a few days in her box, the queen may decide to move her litter to another location, carrying each kitten in turn by the scruff of its neck. The box should be transferred accordingly, although there is no guarantee that she may not decide to move on again. The kittens are likely to be growing at the rate of 1/2oz (15g) daily, which puts a considerable burden on the mother, who needs to be fed accordingly. She is likely to drink more when lactating, because of the loss of fluid in her milk.

Mineral and vitamin supplements may be advisable, depending on the diet concerned, and advice on this should be obtained from a vet. Food must be offered three or four times a day during this period, to prevent the queen having to draw on her own body resources to nourish the kittens.

The kittens, born blind, start to open their eyes from five days onward depending on the breed. Siamese, as always, are precocious in this respect. This is a gradual process extending over several days. Gentle bathing, using cottonwool soaked in warm water, may be necessary to remove any discharge. If the eyes become sealed again, they may be infected, and an antibiotic ophthalmic preparation will be required to prevent any serious and lasting damage.

At the age of three weeks, the kittens will have begun to take their first tentative steps, and weaning can start in earnest about a week later. There are now complete canned foods produced especially for kittens, and these should be used if possible. Other palatable items for young cats include finely chopped mince and boiled fish. Milk, or a suitable substitute, should also be freely available. Kittens will often eat more readily at first from a plate rather than a bowl. Feeding periods should be supervised to ensure that one or two individuals do not dominate at the expense of their littermates. Nor must their mother be allowed to eat all the food. By five weeks old, each kitten should be consuming about 3oz (70g) of food, as well as milk, spread over four daily sittings.

The litter will be virtually independent of their mother when two months old, although certain longhairs, such as Persians, may need to be left with their mother for another month. The queen's milk will dry up naturally once the kittens stop suckling. She must be kept separate from toms throughout the whole kittening period; it is not unknown for queens to conceive again about 10 days after giving birth. During this period calling is often not obvious and courtship will only be brief if she mates while caring for kittens.

KITTEN DEVELOPMENT

Newborn

One week

Two weeks

Three weeks

Six weeks

Vaccination and Registration

The first vaccination is normally given at about nine weeks of age, followed by another three weeks later. Worming around the same time is also to be recommended. No further vaccinations are generally likely to be required for a further year.

Pedigree kittens should be registered at around six weeks of age, once their sexes are known. The registration procedure varies according to the association concerned. It may be advantageous to register them with more than one organization. Breeders can simply register the entire litter, or each kitten can be registered separately. In the former instance, the individuals may then be registered independently for new owners.

The purpose of registration is to ensure that any particular member of the breed could be traced at a later date, and for this reason all registered cats must have a unique name. Most breeders have a prefix, usually relating to their stud, which they register for their own exclusive use. All kittens bred by them are then listed with this description, followed by another name. Advice on such matters should be sought from the organization concerned prior to submitting a formal registration application. Pedigrees trace the bloodline of a specific cat back over at least four generations, showing the ancestry of both parents. When a cat changes hands, it may be possible to add the suffix of the new owner, but there can be no confusion as to who initially bred the cat in question.

REPRODUCTIVE PROBLEMS

Female cats allowed to roam free will often disappear while in oestrus and may not return home for a few days, until after mating. Toms stay out for longer periods and suffer particularly during the latter part of the breeding season, often reappearing in poor condition during August. They have usually lost considerable weight and their relatively large kidneys may be evident as swellings in the abdominal region, either side of the vertebral column. They should, however, respond well to good feeding, and soon put on weight again.

Spontaneous abortion is very rare in cats, although it can occur in conjunction with FeLV infection. This is more likely to cause resorption of the fetuses before they have developed to maturity. Repeated small litters are usually indicative of the same problem. Another possible cause could be endometritis, or inflammation of the lining of the uterus, which is often linked with a vaginal discharge. If the uterus becomes full of pus, the condition is referred to as pyometra. This is more commonly seen in older cats, 14 or 15 years old, which are not actually breeding yet still cycling regularly. The only treatment for pyometra is a rapid ovarohysterectomy (spaying). Providing surgery is carried out without delay, then the chances of recovery are likely to be good.

Neutering

Such surgery is not only carried out to prevent unwanted kittens, but also serves to facilitate the integration of a cat kept solely as a pet into domestic life. The spraying and wandering of mature tom cats are unpleasant and troublesome habits. The sensible owner will opt for surgery to overcome such difficulties, giving the cat itself a less stressful existence. Neutered individuals live longer than their intact counterparts, and obesity is not likely to be a significant side-effect of the operation, particularly if the diet is controlled accordingly.

Spaying

Ovarohysterectomy, or spaying, entailing removal of both the ovaries and uterus, is to be recommended for all queens not kept for breeding purposes. While there is a risk of sexual alopecia developing, spaying removes the threat of ovarian cysts and pyometra in later life. Surgery is normally carried out at the age of four and a half months before kittens are likely to be sexually mature, and so is less complex. In older

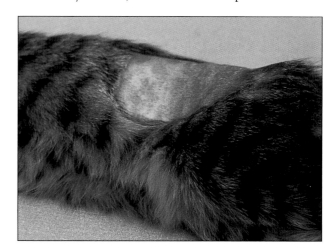

Spaying is the removal of both ovaries and uterus in a female cat to prevent breeding. This operation, best carried out at the age of four and a half months, is recommended for all queens not kept for breeding purposes. Spaying not only prevents unwanted kittens, but also serves to integrate the cat better into a domestic environment. Before surgery, the area where the incision is to be made is shaved of fur and thoroughly cleaned to give a sterile site for the operation (above).

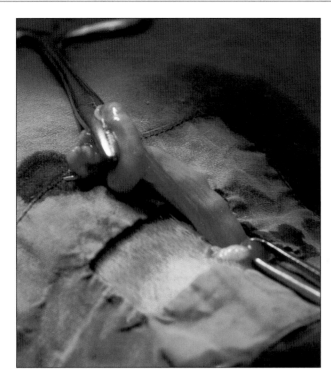

Before operating, the vet will administer an anesthetic, usually by gas or intravenously. The incision is usually made on the flank although in some cases it may be made on the underside of the body. (left)

The horns of the uterus are then removed. The site of the incision is then sutured. (below)

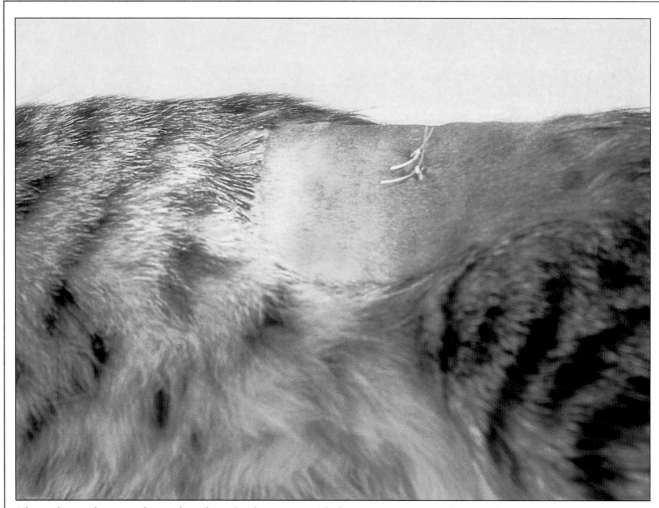

The stitches can be removed around ten days after the operation. The hair soon regrows over the site of the surgery.

cats showing signs of oestrus, spaying is not recommended until a later date. The hormonal changes resulting from oestrus mean that the tissue is receiving a larger blood supply, and the uterus itself is more fragile and prone to rupture.

The operation can either be carried out through an incision in the flank, or via the mid-line of the abdomen, underneath the body. The area has to be clipped of fur to ensure a sterile environment around the site of the incision, and the fur may grow back paler, particularly in the case of Siamese. For this reason, providing there are no veterinary objections, owners often prefer to have their cat spayed via the mid-line where the change will be less noticeable.

It is routine for cats to be kept overnight by the vet after surgery. Very few complications result from spaying. The sutures are always removed about a week after surgery, by which time the site of the incision should be healing well. For the first few days at home the cat should be kept indoors.

Castration

In the case of the male cat, surgery, referred to as castration, can be carried out at virtually any time, although five months is perhaps the best age. At this stage, the blood supply to the testes is relatively small, and the risk of post-operative haemorrhage is significantly reduced. Some pedigree breeds, such as the Abyssinian, may need to be left intact until they are slightly older. Signs of masculinization of the head will be apparent if the operation is deferred for several months, as some owners prefer, but spraying of urine around the home will have already begun.

Castration, even in young cats, necessitates the use of an anesthetic. This may be given either as an injection or in the form of gas. Recovery from gaseous anesthetic is quicker than recovery from the intravenous method – as cats can often be conscious again within 10 minutes after gas – but other factors will also influence the vet's decision in this regard. It is preferable to castrate an adult cat outside the breeding season, between September and December. The operation will be less traumatic then, both psychologically and physically, since blood flow to the testes will be reduced at this time. After castration, sexual drive will be lost, but the cat's hunting instinct will not be affected. The risk of abscesses resulting from fights is also significantly reduced. Sexual alopecia, or hair loss, may result from the loss of testosterone from the circulation, but can be corrected by implants if necessary.

NEUTERING

Unless a cat is destined for breeding purposes, it should be neutered in order to make it a loving and carefree pet. Neutered cats can be shown in most cat associations and are easier to maintain in peak show condition than their entire male and female counterparts.

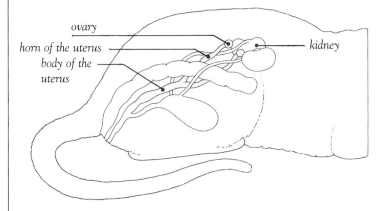

ovary
horn of the uterus
body of the uterus
kidney

Spaying
Spaying involves the surgical removal of most of the female cat's sex organs – the ovaries, fallopian tubes and uterus. Spaying may be carried out at a very early age in the female cat and is better performed before she has her first period of oestrus.

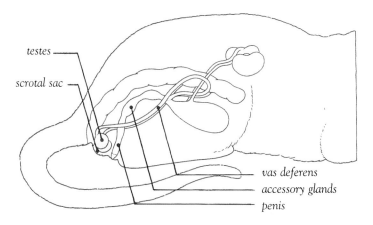

testes
scrotal sac
vas deferens
accessory glands
penis

Castration
The reproductive system of the entire male comprises the testes, which lie inside the scrotal sac, the vasa deferentia (the tubes that carry the sperm), the accessory glands that supply fluid to the ejaculate, and the penis. A castrated male has part of the vasa deferentia and both testes removed.

AFTER THE OPERATION
After spaying, the wound is closed with sutures, or stitches. Most cats behave as if nothing had happened within a couple of days of the operation. Stitches are removed about a week after the operation, by which time the wound should be healing. The hair will already have begun to regrow.

Castration is best carried out just before the male kitten reaches sexual maturity, when he has formed his masculine character, but has not shown signs of being interested in the opposite sex. A small cut is made at the base of the scrotal sac and the vasa deferentia are tied and cut. Then the testes are removed. For most tom cats, no stitches are needed. In time the scrotal sacs recede (bottom picture).

Before

After

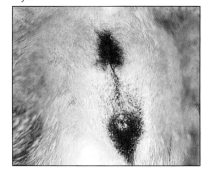

THE FIVE AGES OF
THE CAT

THE FIVE AGES OF THE CAT

The five ages of a cat make an interesting study. Just as in Shakespeare's slightly longer version dealing with man, the cat at the beginning and at the end of its life is a relatively helpless creature.

Kittens need more care than older cats, but are probably a better choice for first-time pet owners. Inquisitive by nature, they should not be allowed outside without supervision; otherwise, they may wander away.

THE NEWLY-BORN KITTEN and the fading great-great-grandfather still have a lot going for them. They may be relatively helpless, but the kitten has the advantage of a doting mother to guide it into early adolescence, and the very elderly cat has experience on its side. They have something else in common: proportionately large heads that tend to wobble. This is common to all new-born kittens and aged cats who die of nothing other than old age. How can that short and skinny neck, which contains seven cervical bones, carry the weight? The first two bones are so modified that the cat can turn its head from side to side as easily as it can turn it up and down. And they are supported by muscles that any other species would envy. It seems miraculous that a mother cat can carry a kitten that weighs almost as much as she does over big fences and for long distances, but physiologically they are well-geared for that sort of task.

The newly-emerged kitten has limbs that are about as useful as fins. It flounders and paddles, a reminder that we all evolved from creatures that once lived in water. The kitten gradually becomes more sure-footed. Its limbs begin to act like arms and legs, but are still quite pliant. The logic of that evolutionary plasticity is simple. The growing animal is prone to all sorts of accidents. Pliant bones don't fracture easily. And, if they do, they heal very easily. The exceptions are those cats which are not allowed a natural diet that includes bones or bone meal.

During the middle stages of development – late kittenhood, adolescence and maturity – the cat's shape gradually changes according to geometric principles. The athletic youngster is roughly triangular, with a broad back that tapers into a very tiny abdomen. All muscle up and above and a tiny abdomen underneath. Later, the adult becomes rectangular. As the cat becomes elderly, the muscles at the top tend to waste and the waist below becomes more prominent. The triangle has become inverted. This simple rule of thumb is an aid to telling the difference in ages between cats, and shows a cat that has prematurely aged through serious illness.

YOUTH AND AGE.

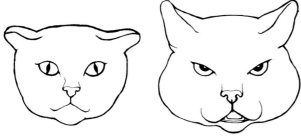

The face of youth   *The face of age*

CHANGING FACES

The shape of the kitten's head (far left) changes dramatically as it matures. The kitten's ears gradually become more pointed and move upward from the side of the head. As the cat grows into an adult, the face becomes more stretched and, in the case of the tom cat, widens around the jowls.

THE FIVE AGES

The newly-emerged kitten's limbs are virtually useless, and it can only drag itself about (1). As it grows up it is much more sure footed (2). Its body shape changes as it reaches adolescence. This athletic youngster has a triangular shape, all muscle above and a tiny abdomen below (3). Later, the adult becomes rectangular (4). Old age brings a complete reversal as the triangle of youth is inverted, the muscles at the top tending to diminish and the waist becoming more prominent (5).

1. The very young kitten

2. The kitten

3. The adolescent

4. The adult cat

5. The elderly cat

THE SUCKLING KITTEN

The kitten at birth is deaf and blind, and almost completely helpless. It can move only a limited distance by using a sort of rock-and-roll shuffle accompanied by a characteristic head shaking.

However, it has an acute sense of feeling. The mother licks the kitten and by instinct it orientates itself from the mother's mouth toward the nursing area. The kitten crawling about in a haphazard manner usually has first contact with the outstretched legs of the mother. The kitten follows the legs upward until it finds a nipple.

The feeding behavior of the new-born kitten has two instinctive elements. The first is the search for the nursing area and the second is the response to the nipple. Sometimes kittens seem to burrow underneath the mother. But they won't suffocate. They know what they are doing. The mother has two rows of nipples, and each kitten knows on which side it customarily feeds.

There are three major phases in the relationship of the nursing kitten and its mother. During the first phase the mother initiates the whole feeding process. During the second, the relationship is more reciprocal. The kittens waddle toward the mother, and she assists the odd laggard. During the third phase, the kittens actively demand to be fed. They will follow the mother about until she stands or lies and allows them to feed. Even at this last stage the most callous of mothers will quickly respond to the pitiful call of a lost kitten. She will not rest until she has found it and carried it to a place of safety.

A nursing mother may reject one or more of her litter that appear to her to be sub-standard. Often these are smaller and weaker than the rest. They are known as runts. It is also possible that these kittens have congenital defects. This rejection is almost always irreversible. Nothing will persuade the mother to accept a once-rejected kitten, and the hapless owner must undertake the round-the-clock job of hand-rearing. However, she may accept and rear a creature quite unlike herself, like a puppy. This behavior, stimulated by hormones, is a physiological and not a psychological reaction.

Kittens, like many young animals, lick their mother's mouth. In this way, she passes on antibodies that help to fight disease. The habit also reinforces the links between the mother and her young. No kitten can be expected to go from the coddled security of milk and nest directly into the skilled activity of hunting for food.

To conserve body heat, the young kittens huddle closely together (left). If the kittens are too warm, they will spread out to become cooler.

Not until their eyes are open (right) do the kittens have any semblance of independence, and even then they will need their mother for some weeks to come. Fortunately for them, her maternal instincts are very strong, and they reciprocate with an equally strong instinct to survive.

LEARNING BEHAVIOR

During kittenhood and adolescence, the young cat learns the skills that in maturity become second nature. The highest form of learning is insight learning, which is the conscious consideration of a problem. In the laboratory it is difficult to devise experiments that simulate problems in the field, but it can be shown that higher animals are capable of insight learning. Chimpanzees, for example, will pile boxes one on top of another so that they can reach a reward of fruit. Cats do not learn through insight; their instinctive behavior is modified through experience, habituation and inhibited play.

It is difficult to distinguish between learned and instinctive behavior. A litter of kittens may be left on their own for some hours while the mother goes off hunting. If they are left in a relatively cold nest they will instinctively cuddle together. The group can keep itself warm, whereas a kitten on its own might rapidly lose body warmth and die. The same litter, left in a very warm area, will spread themselves out. This is almost certainly instinct.

A kitten learns through experience, or trial and error. This means that if a cat accidentally performs an action that is rewarded, it may then deliberately do it again in the expectation that the reward too will be repeated. This is how many cats gradually learn the difference between the many possible expressions of their family of fellow cats, dogs and people. They will learn that every time they approach an individual who is not interested in play they receive a painful bite, scratch or kick. After a while, even the most energetic kitten learns that it is best to take stock before rushing in. Similarly, a kitten, while jumping about, might accidentally open a cupboard door. It may learn to open the same cupboard door by imitating the mother. A world of forbidden tidbits is revealed. By trial and error, the cat learns to avoid punishment or receive reward.

Habituation is the simplest and most common form of learning. This results from the loss of an old response. In the same way that crows tend not to be scared of scarecrows, a cat soon learns that falling leaves or shadows carry neither punishment nor reward. These are among the things that can safely be ignored.

It is quite obvious, when a kitten plays with a ping-pong ball, that something important is being learned. The kitten makes a tentative approach and gives the strange object a small pat. The ball moves and in effect is saying to the kitten, "I am running away and must be chased." The kitten quickly learns to dribble the ball. Scientists call this inhibited play. Later, the kitten will go through exactly the same motions while pursuing a mouse. At this stage, it knows it should keep the object in control, but has neither the knowledge nor the experience for the quick kill.

In the wild, almost every outsider is a cat's potential enemy. This certainly includes men and dogs. So why do kittens reared in an urban society ignore these primitive "enemies"? They have learned through their mother's lack of response that these creatures represent no threat. They may be welcomed or ignored. In this way the animal's instinctive behavior has been tempered by what it has learned.

The human-oriented cat may have chosen to rear her litter in a bedroom, despite the fact that the people who open the tins continue to feed her in the kitchen. No matter how clever the cat, she is simply not designed to carry a bowl of milk. This cat has solved the problem. She carries her litter to the bowl in the kitchen, and they follow her example and lap the milk provided for them.

The kitten must learn the limits of its own body by its own efforts. Where is that sound coming from? Is that strange object worthy of note? Can I move fast enough and pounce quickly enough to catch it and not do myself an injury?

THE SPIRIT OF ADVENTURE

Ogden Nash once said, "The trouble with a kitten is that it grows up to be a cat." The period in between is called adolescence.

As with young humans, this difficult time may be protracted by a mother who is over-protective, or cut short by her flinging the youngster into the adult world too soon.

The kitten in a good home can take as long as six months to learn the game of life. The less fortunate grow up much more quickly. Skills learned in play must soon become established routine for simple survival. Like underprivileged children, neglected kittens have neither the time nor the place in which to enjoy luxuries.

In bodily terms, the adolescent cat is certainly one of nature's great successes. It is aware, alert and totally receptive. Its reflexes will never be better and its sensory apparatus works in perfect harmony. All that is lacking is adult strength of muscle and, of course, experience.

At this stage, the young cat will start to make tentative forays into the neighborhood. The adolescent is on the

Life is an adventure to the adolescent cat, but it is still a game, and will be treated as such at every opportunity.

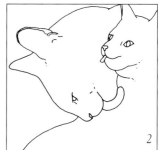

LEARNING TO GROOM
The young cat is quite capable of grooming itself (1), although it has not get gained the poise of the adult. At this stage it will also groom another youngster (2) in the hope that the other will respond by joining in a mutual wash (3).

edge of a vast, unknown world and its steps will be exploratory and highly inquisitive, but it does not have the confidence to wander too far. This wary animal always seems to keep one eye on the rear view mirror and is very easily frightened away. In the domestic situation, the adolescent is unlikely to challenge established neighborhood cats for either territorial or social rights. At this stage, it is still obliged to rely on the charitable tolerance granted by adults to the offspring of their own and other species.

The transmission from adolescence to adulthood is often marked when the kitten does stake out its own territorial claim. Its elders and betters are then left in no doubt that "this is my place... get out and keep out."

The growing cat has all the energy requirements of the active adult, in addition to the needs of the immature body. Many owners know only too well how expensive this can be. There are authenticated reports of healthy adolescent kittens who swallow half a pint of milk and two eggs for breakfast, a large tin of food for lunch, steak for dinner – and then sit begging at the family dinner table.

Male adolescents develop an early interest in the opposite sex, although they may not be able to do anything about it until after their first birthday. They will indulge in the most outrageous, and fruitless, display activities to attract the attention of the queen. Nature does not similarly restrain the young female, for she can quite easily become pregnant at the age of only four or five months.

The mature cat displays all those qualities of

Although curiosity can get some cats into trouble, cats also exhibit a cautious side to their personalities that could well save their lives. Strange objects and situations are always thoroughly examined from a safe distance before the cat will venture any closer.

THE THINKING CAT

independence and self-sufficiency that its human family finds so compelling. It spends less time playing and more time in activities that have a clearly defined purpose. As the cat advances into fully fledged adulthood, it gradually gains confidence and tends to fall into an ordered routine of day-to-day living. It accommodates itself to its household's way of life and the limitations of territory.

Cats gradually get to know their neighbors and they evolve a social order. One male cat will wait at a crossroads for another to pass. This could be a recognition of territorial rights. It could also be a sign of respect for superior strength.

Cats recognize and tolerate those that they know. Strangers are fought off. They soon learn that the fat, old King Charles spaniel next door can be safely and completely ignored. The nasty little terrier across the street, however, must be kept in a state of constant fear. Each and every time it shows its ugly, snarling face it must be met by a formidable display of ruffled fur, enlarged tail and a threatening hiss that can he heard in hell. Further down the street lives a tired old tortoiseshell that likes to bask in the sun while lying on the window sill – she might respond to a greeting in passing by wearily lifting one eyelid.

The cat has acquired skills and techniques in order to adapt to its environment. As well as protecting itself and its territory, the cat is now a hunter. The first step, of course, is to gain access to the hunting grounds. This poses no problem for farmyard cats or their feral cousins. But the hearthside cat may have to wait patiently by the door to the basement or garden for several hours until it is given the opportunity to make a furtive dash to begin an exploration.

Cats learn in kittenhood that certain actions result in either reward or punishment. Some are particularly quick to learn that by swinging on door

handles, for instance, doors open, making hunting grounds more accessible.

The mature cat may take control of its own existence. Many are the tales of cats being fed in more than one household, exacting affection and attention wherever they go. The family with which a cat normally lives will be greatly concerned when the pet stays away from home for more than twenty-four hours. It may have been in some difficulties, but more often it is exercising the independence that is so attractive. A feline assignation or an equally warm fire elsewhere, a moonlight hunting trip or extra-rich morsels from a neighbor's table are just some of the possible reasons for its absence.

The average lifespan of the domestic cat is now

One obvious benefit to the mature cat of early exploratory behavior is physical fitness. The muscles become stronger. The lungs increase in capacity and efficiency to accommodate the needs of the muscles. The heart and circulation respond to the increased demands. And, of course, reflexes become razor-sharp.

Hunting is a major activity. Much of the cat's play as a kitten and adolescent has led to finely-honed instincts for the kill. It may not need its prey in order to feed but the veneer of domestication is sufficiently thin for it to continue to exercise these drives, which ensure the continuation of the species.

OLD AGE

The average lifespan of the domestic cat is now considered to be about 14 years. This average has gradually increased as infectious diseases become more readily controlled and treated.

Many cats are old at the age of seven. At the other extreme, there are cats in their twenties that appear to be as lively as they did in their younger days. Any article in the Press about long-living cats will provoke a spate of letters from people claiming to have cats of 28 and 30.

People spend an average of one third of their lives growing up, a third as adults, and the remaining third in the gentle decline of old age. Cats, on the other hand, spend about a tenth of their lives growing up, eight-tenths in vigorous maturity, and a further tenth on the final slide.

Animals born to long-living parents are more likely to live longer themselves. It is also thought that a kitten born to a relatively old mother may have more defects and a shorter lifespan than those of younger mothers.

It is obvious that a cat with a stable home, regular meals and inoculations against disease, is more likely to reach a ripe old age than the unfortunate alley cat.

The vet can make a quick assessment of the elderly cat's condition by simply glancing at it. There are four signals that will be obvious before the patient has even been settled on the table: general alertness, muscular tone, brightness of eye, and the condition of the coat.

Closer examination will reveal the other signs of old-age deterioration, such as a dry, scaly nose, receding gums, blunted claws, harsh coat, and difficulty in manipulating the spine, head and neck.

In their prime, cats are able to leap at least five times their own height. However, the elderly cat will move slowly and reluctantly. Instead of leaping onto a chair, it will either climb slowly, or wait for a trusted human friend to lift it.

Many owners simply do not notice any of these signs, mainly because the disabilities of old age do not seem to affect the cat's appetite. In fact, many senile cats eat with more gusto than ever.

Elderly cats tend not to groom as regularly as they once did, because stiffening joints make the process difficult, and because self-interest seems to lessen with the advancing years. The owner must give the cat regular grooming in order to help it restore its own pride in appearance. Also, the diet must be high in protein to maintain the wasting cells.

As their joints stiffen, so do their minds. Change of any sort is resented. Therefore, it is useless to try to brighten up your elderly pet's life by introducing a kitten or puppy. The cat will hate this.

Moving house is, of course, a real trauma for the aged cat. As long as familiar objects are available, it will settle comfortably within the confines of the house. It is the outdoor aspect of the move that causes problems. In its old home, it probably spent several years establishing superiority over the neighborhood animals. It cannot do this in its new environment, for it is sure to lose any territorial fights with younger cats.

It is always sad when a much-loved pet is approaching the final phase of its life. The following chapter takes a closer look at how best to care for an elderly cat and answers some of the questions that owners often ask.

As with all creatures, cats tend to become less active as they grow older, and it will be normal for them to spend relatively long periods resting and sleeping (left).

Cats left to fend for themselves have a much shorter lifespan than those kept as pets. (right).

THE ELDERLY CAT

THE ELDERLY CAT

Although an elderly cat may not be quite so active anymore, he or she may still give you several more years of pleasure.

A CAT KEPT LOVINGLY in your home will live to be much older than a cat living in the wild, and may, therefore, need rather special care and attention in later years. As in humans, the onset of old age can vary tremendously – some cats may be showing distinct signs of old age at 12, whereas others are still behaving like kittens at 16. An owner can learn to recognize some of the diseases that are common in old age, and even learn to diagnose some of the common problems in their early stages. Ultimately, the question of euthanasia arises and this is a problem that many pet owners may have to tackle.

Relaxing and sleeping become important pastimes for older cats. This brown tabby has chosen a warm and cozy spot.

LOOKING AFTER AN ELDERLY CAT

HOW OLD IS YOUR CAT – AS OLD AS YOU?

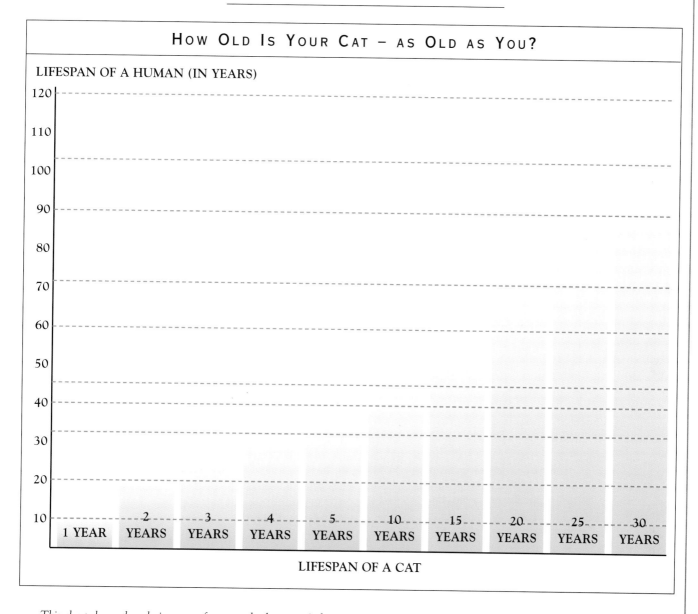

LIFESPAN OF A HUMAN (IN YEARS)

LIFESPAN OF A CAT

This chart shows the relative ages of a cat and a human. A direct comparison is difficult to make because the rate of aging slows down as the cat gets older. The first year is roughly equivalent to 15 human years but, in the later years of life, each cat year is only comparable to about 3 human years.

I've heard about cats living twenty years or more. Is this true?

The domestication of cats has greatly increased the number of years they are likely to survive. While a feral cat will be very lucky to live to the age of 10 years, pet cats treated to all the creature comforts have a considerably longer life expectancy. The "average" lifespan is normally about 14 years, but it is certainly not unusual for cats to live to be 16 or 17 years old. Those cats that survive even longer than that are the exception rather than the rule, but cats of over 20 years are reported fairly regularly. The absolute maximum lifespan for a domestic cat is between 25 and 30 years.

What are the signs that may tell me that my cat is getting old?

Many cats are surprisingly resistant to the effects of old age, but you will probably find that your cat will gradually become less active and sleep for long hours in a favorite warm spot. Some cats may put on weight, but most older cats tend to slowly lose weight and may well develop an increased thirst. Failing eyesight and deafness are common in old cats, but these problems do not necessarily mean that the cat has to be put to sleep. With a little extra care and attention, cats that are afflicted with deafness and blindness can adjust and learn to cope very well in familiar surroundings.

OVERGROWN CLAWS

 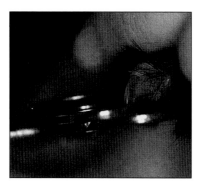

Elderly cats may not wear down their nails by scratching and climbing, and they may overgrow, even to the point where they curl around and grow into the toe (far left). It is important to keep an eye on the nails and clip them before they become overlong, taking care not to cut into the sensitive pink quick (left).

What extra care will my elderly cat need?

Regular veterinary check-ups are always a good idea. In this way problems that may otherwise be serious can be picked up early. Many elderly cats will need more grooming than when they were younger and will be less able to cope with the hair they swallow. The nails of an elderly cat may well overgrow, even to the point where they begin to curl around and grow back into the pads of the feet. If necessary, they should be regularly clipped well before they reach that state. Be sure that your elderly cat has a warm and draft-free bed to go to, and try to discourage it from staying outside for too long in very cold weather. Older cats will often drink more water than when they were younger, and a plentiful supply of fresh water must be available at all times.

Is there any special diet I should feed my cat when he gets older?

While many cats can be pretty fussy eaters at the best of times, you can probably expect your cat to become even more choosy in his eating habits as he ages. Good quality, easily digested sources of protein should be fed, such as fish, rabbit, chicken and cooked eggs, together with a reputable balanced mineral supplement. If your cat appears to be losing weight, you should try to encourage him to eat starchy foods as well as meat. This is not very popular with many cats, but you could experiment with foods such as rice, pasta with butter, bread and butter, potato chips and potatoes. Older cats will often want to eat smaller and more frequent meals, and should be fed on demand.

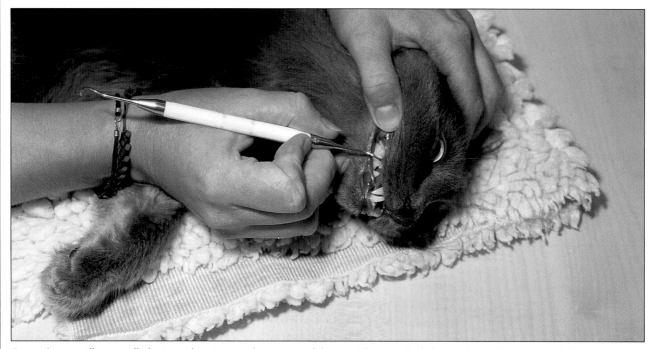

Signs of aging will eventually begin to show in even the most cared-for cat. They may include muscle wasting, increased thirst, general lethargy, and gradual diminishing of the senses especially eyesight and hearing. Regular veterinary check-ups are advisable to try and treat any disease problems, slow down any deterioration, and insure that your pet is not in pain.

DISEASES OF OLD AGE

Age makes an old cat vulnerable to many diseases that a younger animal can shrug off, and there are a number of veterinary problems that are special to the elderly cat. There are several disease problems that can occur in elderly cats, and owners should be on their guard for signs of them. It is always wise to turn to your vet for advice as soon as you notice a problem – the use of home or pet shop remedies can be harmful and will probably allow the condition to become more firmly entrenched before effective treatment is started.

Why is my cat losing weight and always thirsty?

It is very common for elderly cats to lose weight gradually and drink more fluids. This may be a part of your cat's natural aging process, but could be due to a specific disease that requires treatment. Regular veterinary checks every six or nine months are a good idea for your cat anyway, but if you notice a fairly sudden increase in drinking or a severe loss of weight, you should have your cat checked without delay. It is a good idea to weigh elderly cats every two or three months and keep a note of their weight so that you will know if they are losing or gaining – it can be very difficult to detect changes by sight alone if you are seeing the cat every day. There are four common causes of weight loss and increased thirst in older cats.

Overactive Thyroid

In recent years, hyperthyroidism has been discovered to be a fairly common cause of increase thirst and loss of weight in elderly cats. The disease is due to a growth in the thyroid gland in the neck. This growth is usually not cancerous, but it produces an excessive quantity of thyroid hormone. Affected cats usually have a voracious appetite, often with diarrhea, and may be hyperactive and nervous. It may be possible to feel a lump in the neck region; a blood test will confirm the diagnosis. While drugs can be used to control the problem, surgery provides the only cure, and although surgery on the thyroid glands is not without problems, many cats have now been successfully cured of this problem.

Diabetes

Diabetes mellitus, or sugar diabetes, is a less common cause of increased thirst. Cats with this disease are often overweight at first but then lose weight as the condition progresses. Sometimes it is possible to detect a smell of ketones, a smell like nail polish remover, on the breath of a diabetic cat. The condition can be diagnosed either by a urine or a

---

THE THYROID GLAND

The thyroid gland is positioned in the neck, as indicated in this diagram. The gland is just below the angle of the jaw, and when it is over-active an enlargement can usually be felt in this region.

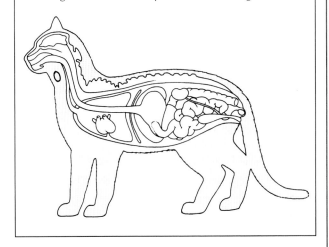

Over-activity of the thyroid speeds up the metabolism, so that affected cats become very hungry and very thirsty, but lose weight and may develop chronic diarrhea. This cat had a very obvious enlargement in the neck region and a blood test demonstrated markedly elevated thyroid hormone levels.

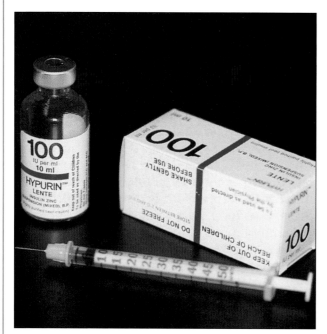

Diabetic cats may show some similar symptoms to hyperthyroid cats. They have to be trained to perform in a litter tray with only a little paper in it, so that the urine can be tested regularly.

A small dose of insulin (above) has to be injected by the owner each day. Insulin that has been produced for human diabetics is also used to treat cats with the disease.

blood test, a test that should not be carried out following a large meal. Treatment may involve a change of diet together with regular injections of insulin. The owner will probably have to collect a urine sample to test regularly. While most owners learn to cope with giving regular injections, they will also need to give a diabetic cat very regular care and attention for the rest of its life. Although the treatment of a cat with diabetes is not simple, many owners have enabled their diabetic cats to live out the final year or two of their lives in a reasonably normal and contented manner.

Kidney Disease

Probably the most common form of kidney disease in a cat is chronic interstitial nephritis. If your vet suspects this disease, he or she may take a blood test to measure your cat's blood urea levels. This is the best test for measuring whether a cat is suffering from some degree of kidney failure. Cats with kidney disease will also tend not to eat, have bad breath, and may suffer from vomiting and/or diarrhea. It is important to realize that by the time signs of this disease develop in an elderly cat with kidney failure, a large part of both kidneys will have been irreversibly damaged and replaced with scar tissue. Therefore, any treatment that your vet gives can only prevent further deterioration – kidney transplants are still a long way off for cats! Treatment for kidney disease may include an attempt to increase the amount of starchy foods the cat eats, but this may not be

successful with a cat that is not eating well anyway. It is better for the cat to eat anything rather than nothing at all. Your vet may well prescribe drugs to try to support your cat. These often include anabolic steroids, which help to build up body weight and slow down muscle wasting. Under the guidance of your vet, you should also administer a suitable vitamin supplement, since cats tend to lose certain vitamins through the kidneys when they are not functioning normally. While some cats do not respond well to treatment for kidney disease, there are many cats that do seem to respond and, with treatment, have been able to live out a year or two of happy lives.

Cancer

Neoplasia, or cancer, is unfortunately fairly common in cats of all ages. It may affect any part of the body, and may lend itself well to surgical removal. The most common form in cats is lymphosarcoma, a cancer of the white blood cells, which may develop as a result of exposure to feline leukemia virus. It is mentioned here as it is a common cause of weight loss in older cats, often despite a voracious appetite. In older cats it usually settles in the lymph nodes of the intestines or along the wall of the bowel, interfering with the absorption of food. If it affects the liver or kidneys, it may also cause increased thirst. Definitive diagnosis may be possible from the clinical signs or from a blood test, but it may be necessary to carry out an exploratory operation to remove a small piece of tissue for examination under the microscope. Anti-cancer drugs may be used to treat some mild cases of lymphosarcoma, but they will only prolong life and not cure the underlying problem. Other forms of cancer may affect the skin or any of the internal organs. Cancer is not one disease, but many different diseases that all result in excessive and uncontrolled growth of certain body tissues. Treatment will depend upon the type of tumor involved – it can include surgery, chemotherapy (drugs), or even radiotherapy.

What other problems can affect an older cat?

Heart Problems

While cats do not get thickening of the arteries and coronary heart diseases as humans do, elderly cats are prone to cardiomyopathy, a degeneration of the heart muscle. This causes a build-up of fluid on the chest leading to labored breathing; it can also cause blood clots to form in the arteries. The most likely place for such clots to form is in the arteries supplying the legs. This causes iliac thrombosis and results in severe cramps in the hind leg muscles. The outlook for cats with such symptoms is poor, since the underlying heart problem will remain even if the blood clot is removed surgically. Some cats with cardiomyopathy are treated with aspirin to discourage blood clotting, but since the drug can be very poisonous to cats, it must be given in very low doses under close veterinary supervision. Drugs may also be given to assist the heart and remove fluid from the chest, but unfortunately few cats survive a weak heart.

Constipation

Occasionally, elderly cats develop a "lazy bowel," resulting in bouts of constipation. Some owners become very concerned if their cat does not have a bowel movement every day, but there is generally no need to worry unless your cat is straining and unable to move its bowels or has not moved them for several days. Do not confuse straining due to constipation with straining due to a urinary obstruction – the latter is a serious problem and requires immediate veterinary attention. If your cat does suffer from constipation, give a teaspoonful of mineral oil daily for a few days – if the cat does not have a bowel movement within 24 hours or if it becomes distressed, contact your vet. Frequent dosing with mineral oil may affect the absorption of certain vitamins, and a balanced vitamin supplement should be given to compensate. Constipation can be aggravated if the cat swallows a lot of hair. Regular grooming will help to prevent this. Long-haired cats especially will benefit from your assistance. You should examine the cat's coat for signs of any problems that might be causing excessive molting, particularly the presence of fleas – which should be dealt with promptly.

Incontinence

Some cats that have been housetrained throughout their lives may become incontinent when they grow older. This may simply be due to laziness, and the cat may respond to more litter boxes around the house for it to use. Unfortunately, some cats will still soil indoors. They should be checked by a vet to see whether there is any physical problem, such as a urinary or kidney infection. If the cause is simply senility, the cat has either to be confined to an area where the soiling does not matter, or put to sleep.

Cataracts

Cloudiness of the lens within the eye is very common in the eyes of elderly cats. They usually progress gradually and do not cause blindness until they are well advanced. Elderly cats seem to adapt to a gradual loss of vision reasonably well, and although surgery to remove the cataracts is theoretically possible, it is not usually considered wise for an old cat.

Bad Teeth

Due to an accumulation of tartar on the teeth over the years bad teeth are common in older cats. Tartar causes the gums to become inflamed (gingivitis) and to recede. This allows infection to attack the roots of the teeth (periodontitis), causing them to loosen and eventually drop out. Having tartar removed before the gums become too inflamed will save a lot of pain later on. Once the teeth have been cleaned, a diet that exercises the teeth may help to slow down the rate at which tartar builds up again. A small amount of dry cat food will exercise the teeth. Or your cat may like to chew on some meat gristle.

INFLAMMATION OF THE GUMS

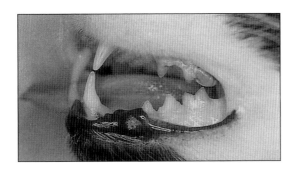 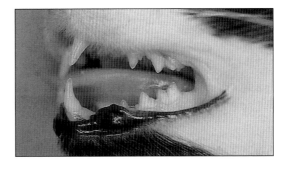

Tartar is formed on the teeth from an accumulation of food, bacteria, and substances in the saliva (above left). Small amounts only discolor the teeth and possibly cause bad breath, but as it builds up it pushes on the gums and causes them to become inflamed, a condition known as gingivitis. If left untreated, the roots become infected, and the teeth become loose and painful. Removing the tartar by scaling the teeth under anesthetic "stops the rot" and allows the gums to heal (above right).

However, this does not prevent the further build up of tartar with time, and regular scaling may be necessary. Even given identical diets, some cats seem to build up tartar more quickly than others, and there is probably a hereditary factor involved, associated with the composition of saliva.

EUTHANASIA

Since the cat may well have been a much-loved member of the family, it is not surprising that many owners go through a very real period of mourning when the cat dies. The decision to have a cat put to sleep may be inevitable.

How do I know if the time has come for my cat to be put to sleep?

Most vets and cat owners would agree that it is not the length of a cat's life that is of prime concern, but the quality of its life. There is obviously no necessity to put down all cats at a certain age because they are old – different cats will age at different rates. There are plenty of sixteen-year-old cats around that still behave like kittens. Similarly, there is no need to put a cat to sleep simply because a terminal condition such as cancer has been diagnosed – the cat may well be able to live several more happy months before life becomes a misery. If your cat is very old or unwell, you must decide whether he or she is still getting any enjoyment out of life or whether you are just prolonging life to avoid having to make a difficult decision or because you cannot bear to parted with your pet. Do not be afraid to discuss the matter with your vet. He or she will be happy to offer advice – but

If a terminal disease is proved to be painful and the need for medication becomes a constant necessity – when happiness turns to misery – it is time to put the cat to sleep.

remember, you are the person living with your cat, you are in the best position to judge the quality of life your cat is having, and only you can make the final decision when the time comes.

It may be necessary to put a cat to sleep that has a severe behavioral problem, such as severe incontinence, that makes it unsuitable as a pet. There is a limit to the inconvenience that any owner can be expected to tolerate, particularly if the cat is posing a health hazard. It is not wise to re-home a cat with behavioral problems unless the new owner is fully aware of the nature of the problem and is confident of being able to cope.

An even more difficult decision may have to be made if the owner of a cat is no longer able to keep a pet, perhaps due to a change of accommodation or moving overseas. It can be very difficult to re-home an adult cat, and many older cats do not adapt at all well to a change of home. Euthanasia may be the only alternative, but it is always unpleasant to have to put a healthy animal to sleep.

How can I tell if my cat is in pain?

It is impossible to measure what pain any animal is feeling when unwell – we can only look at the nature of its disease and the way the animal is behaving and make a subjective judgment of what it must be feeling. A cat may make obvious signs, such as growling or screaming when certain parts of its body are touched, to show that it is in pain. Or it may display symptoms that must be unpleasant for it, such as repeated vomiting. In fact, cats generally seem to be more tolerant to what we would consider to be painful stimuli by producing natural painkillers known as endorphins in the brain. Many owners do not realize that their cats are ill until the disease is very advanced because cats are so good at masking their illnesses and coping with life as best as possible. As an owner, you will be familiar with the normal behavior pattern of your cat and will soon notice if there is a change. If you cat is eating normally, seems alert, and is going about life as usual, you can reasonably assume that it is not in any great degree of pain. If you are in doubt, do not hesitate to discuss the matter with your vet.

Is it kinder to let my cat die naturally or to have him put to sleep?

Many owners dread having to make a decision to put their pet to sleep, and when that pet is very old or terminally ill, they naturally hope that the cat will die peacefully in its sleep. This would be fine if one

Deciding that it is kinder to put a pet to sleep is always a heartbreaking time for the cat owner.

could be sure that the end would be painless and peaceful, but unfortunately that is often not the case. In that sense, our pets are lucky – it is not necessary for them to suffer when the time comes for them to end their days. Euthanasia is quick and painless and need cause the cat no more pain or distress than having an anesthetic. It is usually kinder to find the courage to make a decision and insure that your cat is put quickly and painlessly to sleep than to risk the possibility of a drawn out and painful death.

Is it a good idea to have my cat put to sleep at home in familiar surroundings?

Since a visit to the vet's office can be a frightening experience for cats, many owners want their cat to end its days in its environment at home. However, many vets feel that the procedure can be carried out more quickly and painlessly in their offices. Since a house visit will take up very much more of your vet's time, it will also be considerably more expensive than taking the cat to the office. Discuss the matter with your vet; he or she will advice you depending on the nature of your cat and maybe his or her personal opinion on the issue.

How does a vet put a cat to sleep?

Pet cats are normally put to sleep with an injection of a large dose of a barbiturate, either into a vein of a leg or directly into an organ such as a kidney. The drug usually works very quickly, with the cat becoming unconscious within seconds and its breathing and heartbeat stopping soon afterward. The drug used is very similar to that used for anesthesia and causes no pain other than the pinprick caused by the needle itself. If the cat is very difficult to handle, it may be necessary for the vet to administer a sedative first, or to put the cat into a chamber into which an anesthetic gas can be administered. While this is not as quick as a barbiturate injection, it may be kinder for a cat that is very frightened of being handled.

What arrangements should I make for my cat afterward?

Most owners leave the arrangements to the vet who has put the cat to sleep. Pet animals are usually collected from the office and cremated, or buried at a landfill site. If you wish your cat to be buried in an established pet cemetery or individually cremated, your vet should be able to arrange it on your behalf. Some owners prefer to bury their pets near to their homes – that is fine if you have a suitable site, but be sure that you bury the cat at least three feet deep, preferably placing a paving stone over the site afterward to prevent the grave being dug up by scavengers such as foxes.

How Intelligent Is My Cat?

MEASURING INTELLIGENCE

Cats are highly intelligent animals, but that intelligence must be measured in cat terms rather than with our human definitions. In this measure, survival and level of comfort and security are the true gauges of cat intelligence.

Treating your cat to some special attention is fine. The cat will respond in kind. However, expecting human responses can lead to disappointment. The cat can respond only in cat terms and in related ways that it has been conditioned to use.

WE'VE COUNTED THE NUMBER of words that we are certain beyond a doubt that our cocker spaniel Timber knows and reacts predictably to, and the number is somewhere in the neighborhood of 85.

We've never done a similar count for any of the cats we've lived with. There never seemed to be any reason to undertake such an exercise. The concept of commands, or more exactly commands being given by a human who must be obeyed, is vague at best to the cat. This is not to say that some cats haven't been taught a healthy array of commands, but we've never seen the cat that can be counted on 100 per cent of the time to do what is expected when a certain command is given.

Some commands and non-command words will be conditioned into even the most untrained house cat's "vocabulary" through constant exposure to them and/or a system of rewards. But, with cats, obeying commands seems to rest at their whim. If the command fits in with the current wants and needs of the cat, it probably will be obeyed. Otherwise, it will probably not.

So a cat's obedience to commands is in no way a measure of the animal's intelligence. As with every living animal species on the face of this earth, it is a safe assumption that there are smart cats and there are stupid cats.

Some of the smartest cats we've known have not been the most consistent in following our commands. When they did choose to obey, and as long as their attention span held out, they were very expert and precise in their execution of the orders. However, as soon as they tired of the activity or something else caught their highly active attention, that was the end of the exercise.

Cats gain much of their understanding about what we're saying through the tones we use when we're talking to them.

Obedience to commands and the ability to perform tricks are reflections more of the cat's socialization into the household than of the animal's overall intelligence.

CURIOSITY

Curiosity may have killed the cat, but it's also what leads it to learn about its environment and get what it wants. Show your cat what is in a full milk bottle. Then, after tightly sealing the bottle, leave the cat alone in the room with it. There will be lots of looking, then some sniffing, followed by some clawing and pawing, which will probably result in the bottle falling onto its side and the cat jumping back in surprise. Once it has recovered, the cat will again approach the bottle, this time more cautiously. Although the cat is interested in the entire bottle, it will likely focus its actions on the lid because it learned when you showed it the milk that that's how you get to it.

Cats are highly inquisitive creatures. The exploratory nature of our cats is one indication that there is some fairly powerful intelligence at work in those little heads.

Just as obedience to commands cannot be taken as the ultimate measure of a cat's intelligence, neither can any of the animal-IQ tests that have been developed. The same trigger- or color-matching paraphernalia that can occupy a dog or a chimpanzee for lengthy periods, will just as likely put a cat to sleep.

However, although we can't accurately measure out cats' IQs, we know there is a feline intelligence within their brains. The signs of that intelligence are unmistakable. Cats are relatively cautious animals, often sizing up situations, evaluating alternatives and making choices based on risk-benefit equations. They have an almost unquenchable curiosity about their world, making regular explorations into both known and unknown areas. They are independent-minded creatures, as anyone who has spent long afternoons trying to teach a command can attest.

They are problem-solvers, quick to discover and perfect techniques to satisfy their basic needs. The getting of food is probably the area where most of us have encountered this ability. Cats learn quickly which end of a bottle the milk pours from and how to make that happen, or how to cause that special sound with the electric can opener that always signals mealtime.

Various studies that have been carried out show that cats raised with plenty of stimuli, such as handling, hunting and play, develop greater abilities in all the areas we've just discussed. The importance of any animal's adolescent period of exploration and learning in relation to its later successes in life is another measure of intelligence.

Hunting is the most well-known example of this process. While hunting is an instinct kittens are born with, the techniques of finding prey, stalking it, capturing it, killing it and eating it are learned abilities. They are passed on from one generation to the next by the queen to her kittens.

Cats deprived of this learning experience during kittenhood– perhaps because they and their mother were never allowed outdoors – generally do not acquire the skills needed to become successful hunters. The instinct is still alive within them, as demonstrated by their tail-flicking interest in birds outside the window, but they usually don't have what it takes to follow through on that urge.

For those cats that have been given this ability, remembering productive hunting sites is one of the tasks to which they choose to employ their memory capacity. Watch your cat the next time you let it out

Cats easily assimilate into the life of the household to the extent that they allow themselves to join in the fun. However, some are more inclined to this than others. Just like humans, different cats have different personalities.

to roam the garden. Certain spots will require its immediate attention. Similarly, the warmest, cosiest sunning windows and the actions needed to tell the human that food or play is wanted are all readily recalled.

There we have the crux of this whole question about cat intelligence. Catch them in the act of using their memory or their reasoning to their own ends and on their own terms and you'll be amazed. Try to direct those same powers into behavior considered to be desirable by humans, such as not ripping the new upholstery, and you'll be frustrated as often as not.

Yet another measure of intelligence comes in the form of the many tales we hear of cats being able to find their way home across significant distances. You can rest assured that cats can remember the location of their homes, but don't assume that it is their owners and families that they are seeking. It's the territory that they've claimed and developed that draws them home.

Evidence suggests that cats perform this feat by combining two mechanisms: the first is an internal biological clock that measures time in terms much more elemental than the 24 equal segments we've assigned rather arbitrarily to each day; the second is a sense for the angle of the sun's rays on the cat's home territory, learned over time.

CAT WATCHING

Your cat's daily routine probably coincides with and, in some cases, depends on your schedule. It awakens when you do, goes to bed when you do, eats when you provide food, and goes out when you decide it's time. As it learns your routine, it picks up on preroutine signals, especially when the payoff is food or warmth.

Does your cat jump up on your bed to snuggle in for the night when it sees or hears you get into bed? Or is it already there when you turn in, having heard you turn off the TV or run the water to brush your teeth? Does it come running when it hears the can opener? Or does it anticipate breakfast when you turn on the coffee-maker or emerge from the shower?

Cats begin learning from a very early age. Their mothers are their primary teachers, and hunting skills are among the things they pass on to their kittens. These lessons in being a cat are meant to ensure their survival in the wild.

This ability, also observed in other creatures such as migrating caribou and birds, is termed natural celestial navigation. In human terms – although we've lost much of our ability in this area – it's similar to knowing that you've come toward the sun in leaving your home for a hike and must return with the sun behind you to find your home once again.

Finally, we do have some hard data from science to point toward cat intelligence. This comes in the form of electroencephalogram (EEG) readings of cat brain waves during sleep. Evidence points to the fact that cats experience something similar to our dreams during periods of deep sleep, which is characterized by rapid eye movement and thus labeled REM sleep.

For those of us without the help of these expensive scientific measuring devices in our homes, our cats provide some external evidence of this as well. Watch your cat the next time you notice it in deep sleep, which seems to be about 30 per cent of the 16 to 18 hours most cats spend sleeping every day. You'll see the movement of the paws, the changing positions of the body, the tail flicking, and the ears and whiskers twitching. Most cats will also utter calls, meows, purrs, and even shrieks during these periods of dreaming.

While the things they choose to remember are sometimes less than impressive to us humans, such as the choice sunning spots around the home, cats nevertheless display good memories.

The attention span of many cats is rather short, while the desire for rest and sleep is very strong. This doesn't indicate lesser intelligence, just different needs from our own.

THE IMPORTANCE OF RITUAL

No accurate IQ tests have yet been devised to measure the intelligence behind those eyes. The language barrier will probably always stand in the way of such experiments.

Ritual is an important aspect in any pet's life, and because they share their homes and lives with us our daily comings and goings will become essential parts of their rituals.

All animals, including our domestic cats, survive in part through the application of a standard set of rituals to their everyday lives. The rituals will vary from one animal to the next, but they all have some.

To the wild ancestors of our cats, the most important rituals involved mating, hunting down and killing prey, and maintaining the secrecy of the den location. Sub-rituals that were part of the primary rites included such activities as encountering competing cats and avoiding conflict or besting those competitors, and teaching the young to become successful at the business of being cats.

These rituals are still very much alive in the cats with whom we share our homes. You can see some of them in practice nearly every day.

Life in a human-made environment has resulted in new rituals being developed. The most obvious of these, at least with those cats that are fed on a regular schedule, can be observed at mealtime. There is no standard form here – the particular aspects vary from one cat to the next in their different situations. However, for every cat, you can be certain that there is a noticeable ritual associated with food.

Your arrival home each day is probably the source of another. Do you often find your cat in the same location when you open the front door in the evening? If you have a day off, but spend it mostly away from the cat in some other part of the house, will you find it in the same spot about the time you normally come through the door? What about if you come in through another entrance? Such questions will be similarly revealing about other major times of the day that involve the cat. If it is allowed to sleep on your bed, it probably has its just-before-bed rituals that must be observed.

A friend of ours got into the habit of ambushing her Maine Coon Cat, Tibsy, each evening as the cat came to investigate her absence when she took the dinner dishes from the dining room to the kitchen. She would hide on the far side of the doorway between the two rooms and jump out at Tibsy when he entered the kitchen.

This continued for several weeks, with the cat gaining enthusiasm for the game all the while. But when our friend was entertaining guests, she forgot all about the ritual. She and her husband removed the dinner dishes to the kitchen and returned with dessert. She then returned to the kitchen for a tray bearing a pot of coffee, eight cups, cream, and sugar.

You've probably guessed by now what happened when the hostess started from the kitchen into the dining room this time. Luckily, no-one was burned by the flying pot of hot coffee. Unfortunately, the crockery didn't fare as well.

While these behaviors are often the source of amusement for us humans, they are just as deeply serious for our cats as the rituals of the wild were to their ancestors. Rituals bring much-needed order, comfort, security, and a definite sense of a cat's place within its world. Once established, these rituals must be observed.

Some rituals are more eagerly awaited than others. Regular feeding times help to enforce the comfort that our cats find in ritualistic behavior.

Once a cat has learnt to expect certain things at certain times of the day, it can become very persistent in demanding that the schedule be followed.

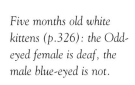

Five months old white kittens (p.326): the Odd-eyed female is deaf, the male blue-eyed is not.

325

IS TRAINING WORTH ATTEMPTING?

Patience, persistence and repetition are the prerequisites for developing any new forms of behavior, or tricks, in your cat. As under wild conditions, the cat must come to recognize the benefits that the new behavior holds for it.

THERE IS A GAG in current use among many cartoonists that depicts a man and his cat in conversation. The man, very agitated, is saying something like "Fluffy, I'm really upset with you. That was a perfectly good plant. But look at what you did to it. It looks like some of your left-over food that's been sitting around for days." The cat, smiling

and content, is actually hearing: "Fluffy, blah-blah-blah. Blah-blah-blah good blah. Blah. Blah-blah-blah food blah-blah-blah."

In other words, Fluffy is understanding only three words: "Fluffy," his name; "good," which the man usually uses to mean he is pleased with something that Fluffy has done; and "food," which Fluffy has

Cats are unlike dogs in their behavior because of millions of years of evolution into separate and distinct lifestyles. Somewhere, in pre-history, the canines and felines did share a common ancestor, however.

learned means something good to eat. So the message that the cat is actually putting together from all this is, "Fluffy, good, food" – something quite different to what the man intended him to hear.

As exaggerated as this cartoon example may be, none of us who has lived with cats can deny the reality underlying it. This is not to say that cats cannot be trained, even to the point of performing tricks, just like dogs. Somewhere in the distant past, the idea arose of cats being totally different from dogs, and, we were told, because of this difference, we must expect them to respond less – if at all – to training. Perhaps both the cats and we humans would be better off if we didn't try to train them. The same false image of cats has led us to expect less affection, dependency and the like from them.

As with most myths about our domestic cats, this one begins with a certain amount of truth. Cats do not respond in the same way to training. Our approach must be entirely different from that we take in training other animals.

Dogs strive to learn your commands for little more than the security of having pleased their master – or, more correctly from the dog's perspective, the leader of their pack. Cats' motives are a bit more inner-directed (some might say downright self-centered).

The positive motivators in a cat's life are food, comfort (most often translated as warmth) and play/company. Negative motivators to a cat are wetness, discomfort (most often translated as anything but warmth) and loud noises.

Food is one of the strongest motivators for our cats. Special treats can bring them to heights of performance.

You are probably destined to disappointment if you are nurturing dreams of turning your cat into a professional performer.

PUNISHMENT AND REWARD

Physical punishment, restraint or force should never be contemplated when attempting to train a cat. This is because the reaction of most cats to such direct, purposeful contact is simple avoidance. "If you want to be that rough," the cat is telling you as it slinks quickly from the room, "I'll see you later." Perhaps the cat will respond in kind with claws and teeth to the first few physical efforts at discipline, but even this will soon be abandoned for retreat. Too many such encounters can leave a psychological imprint in the cat's mind against the "offending" human that can be nearly impossible to mend.

Even sharp verbal commands can have this effect. While a quick "No!" or "Stop!" will probably stop the cat from scratching at the furniture leg, too many of these will leave you with a nervous, retiring and shy animal.

When you yell at your cat, you are making a mental connection between your harsh command and whatever it is that you don't want the cat to be doing. But the cat forgets what it was doing immediately on hearing your sharp tone and instead identifies the discomfort with its source – you. For some reason which the animal cannot fathom, you are causing it discomfort.

This is the reason that so many animal behaviorists today recommend indirect deterrents to stop unwanted behavior. A ball of paper or a short, gentle squirt from a water pistol have power equal to a harsh command in stopping the cat doing wrong, but the animal generally won't trace the source of its discomfort back to you. Consequently, you'll be able to repeat the deterrent as many times as necessary until the cat learns to cease the offending activity without you being identified as the bad guy.

A word of caution: even balls of paper and squirts of water can be carried too far, from the cat's perspective. In a sense, they are being delivered by some unseen enemy and constant, unexpected "attacks" can lead to a very nervous cat. Moderation is crucial. Take corrective measures only when absolutely necessary.

On the other hand, use the positive reinforcements as much as possible. Nothing perks up a cat's attention span and memory capacity like a morsel of its favorite food, even more so if it's something that's not available every day.

For example, to teach the cat its name, hold a bit of the food out toward it and call it by name. If it comes, give it the food, speak in low, soothing tones of praise and pet or stroke it in whatever manner it most likes. Repeat this exercise only a few times at a sitting to avoid losing the cat's attention and your patience, but try to do it at least once a day for a couple of weeks.

Many cat owners have followed this process using food at mealtime instead of the snack morsel. Each time they dished out the cat's meal, they called its name and made a fuss of the cat when it came. At mealtime it's important that the training and praise

Cats will develop their own special behavior and tricks to achieve their own ends. These actions seem to develop more quickly when food is involved.

Cats have cat emotions, cat thoughts and cat behaviors. Living with humans can cause some alterations in all of these, but the perspective remains very much that of the cat.

do not interfere with the cat's eating or the opposite effect from that intended might be achieved.

Whatever training you choose to attempt with your cat and whatever successes you achieve with it, don't fool yourself that you've taught the cat the concepts of right and wrong. These are human words, without any true meaning for any other living creatures on earth.

Cats never feel remorse for any of their actions. They never feel accomplished because of what they have learned and performed. What they feel is their own current level of comfort and security. "Yeah, sure, I learned to do a triple somersault from the top of the shelves, catching my catnip mouse on the way down," they might say, if they could talk. "But how about dinner? Isn't it about that time?"

They will begin doing something and continue to do it only as long as they realize a direct benefit through the action. Conversely, they will cease doing something and not do it again only as long as they realize a negative effect on themselves because of it.

Nevertheless, training your cat is a worthwhile pursuit, requiring extreme patience and understanding on your part. You must be willing to go back to the drawing board time and time again. But it will add a great deal to both your lives. The benefits that you might draw from a well-trained cat are obvious, but cats too gain from the training. They are highly inquisitive animals that will thrive on the stimulation that your efforts will provide for their minds. After all, sleeping for 18 hours per day doesn't provide much in the way of mind-bending challenges.

LAYING DOWN RULES OF BEHAVIOR

Like his comic namesake, Garfield was a terror. Whether the effort to bring his behavior into check had never been mounted or had simply been given up as of no use we never really knew. By the time we came across him, his furniture shredding, drapery tearing and antagonistic attitude toward all visitors was pretty much taken for granted. His humans shared his home, and even provided his food and water, but otherwise Garfield lived mostly independently of them.

To their great credit, we never heard Garfield's humans mention that getting rid of him might be a solution to their mounting problem. It probably never even occurred to them. They are basically gentle souls, who honestly believe that animals have rights equal to humans and live their lives according to such principles.

On the other hand, they had done something of a disservice to Garfield by never enforcing any sense of what was acceptable and what was not. For the lack of a few strong words and perhaps a squirt or two of water in the early development of their cat-human relationship, they had allowed the black Persian to grow into a cat that few people wanted to be around.

Cats need to be shown what is and what is not acceptable behavior. Don't think for a moment that cats in the wild are not taught these valuable lessons by their mother, other cats and other animals. Survival depends upon the passing on and enforcement of certain "rules" from one generation to the next.

But when the cat is in a human-made environment, the situation changes in two very important ways. First, there are additional aspects that need to be incorporated into its behavior so that it is an acceptable member of the household. Second, while nature generally relies much more heavily on negative teaching aids, the human teacher will be more successful when using positive reinforcement.

Cats are very skilled and versatile at solving problems. Given enough time, this cat would have discovered a way to get that mouse from under that glass cheese cover.

REASSURING A NERVOUS CAT

A cat should never be hit, not even the tiniest swat on the rump. Rather than taking this as an incentive to please you the next time, as the pack-loving dog might do, the cat only acknowledges and remembers the fact that you inflicted pain, no matter how minor.

If a cat backs off, probably either with its back arched in defensive posture or crouched in submission, it's likely that it has been abused by the hand of someone at some time in its past. It's also possible that the cat has other reasons, learned and innate, for not liking the feel of a human hand on it, but abuse is always a first consideration.

With such a cat, you must earn its confidence before it will be comfortable with you stroking it. You must assure it, with your tone and with your motions, that it is in no danger from you. Don't expect instant acknowledgment.

To initiate touching with such a cat, very slowly and smoothly extend your flat hand along the floor in its direction. Don't make first contact. Stop your forward motion under the cat's nose and wait for it to sniff your hand. Nothing about your movement should suggest to the cat that you intend to touch it, and make sure you don't betray that pledge by suddenly reaching for it. If the cat runs away, don't follow. Allow it some time alone, at least a half-hour or so, before trying once again.

This may be all the response that a "come" command draws from your cat, not because it doesn't understand the command but because it isn't choosing to obey just now.

Punishment of your cat should never include striking with the hand, or even the threat of striking. This can only cause the cat to view hands as a source of pain and discomfort.

One negative enforcement that you will want to use is a loud, harsh "No!" Consistency in the use of this command whenever the cat is committing the unwanted behavior is essential, although too much use of the word can lead to a nervous cat. Most cats will get the idea long before you've shouted too often.

Reprimand must always come while the cat is engaged in the activity you want to curb. Telling the cat "no" after it has left the scene of the scratched furniture and is eating from its bowl, even if you first carry it back to the furniture, sends some confusing signals. The scratching is in the past. It's already gone from the cat's mind. Why are you shouting at it for eating?

Beyond all forms of punishment, positive reinforcement will bring a cat over to your way of thinking much faster. Feline motivations are these: comfort, security, food and water. Pleasing you with its performance appears nowhere on that list, except as far as it is a means to accomplish one of these.

Food, comfort and security are the most useful tools in trying to train a cat. A morsel of some favorite snack is always welcome but gentle, soothing words and soft stroking are equally effective, because of their direct relationship in the mind of the cat to its comfort and security.

A typical cat response to chastisement is simply to hide from its source, unlike a dog which would attempt to seek forgiveness for whatever it had done wrong.

However cute and cuddly a kitten may look, you're setting up your relationship with the cat for failure if you expect that there won't be some trying moments in your life together.

Your praise for everything the cat does correctly, even the smallest things, should be extreme and exaggerated. Punishment for those actions that you consider undesirable should move in the other direction. It should be reserved and restrained. You might even overlook some of the small problems.

Every breed of domestic cat and nearly every species of wild cat has been trained with these principles. Of course, different individuals have different capacities: some adapt much better to training than others.

When a new problem surfaces in your cat, look for the underlying causes before you begin any corrective measures. Perhaps the inadvertent removal of the scratching post during housecleaning is the real reason for the recent attacks on the furniture. Replace the scratching post and the chances are good that the furniture-scratching will cease. Maybe you're not cleaning the litter box regularly enough and that's the cat's justification for turning elsewhere. Perhaps your cat is experiencing some new emotional stress or physical illness.

Your reaction to this situation (left) could determine relations between you and your cat for the next several days. You want to dissuade such behavior but not to the extent that the cat doesn't want to be near you.

Rarely will cats be caught in the act of doing something that their owner has made clear is undesirable (below). This doesn't mean they won't continue the activity. They just won't get caught.

GRUDGES AND RESENTMENTS

Kaybee is fat by anyone's stretch of the imagination. Her belly drags on the floor when she walks to such a degree that she actually rubs fur from her underside. Her legs are bowed. Picking her up is no easy chore.

But in her mind, she's simply well-fed and maintained in the comfort to which she has become accustomed. Is it any wonder that she resents the efforts that our friend Pauline has employed to enforce a bit of dieting?

That's right, she resents her reduced rations. Resents, as human as that emotion might sound, is the only word that's appropriate here. Kaybee has exchanged her previous greetings at the front door each evening with as purposeful a walk as she can manage in the opposite direction when Pauline gets home from work. She no longer "talks" to her in those little chats the two of them used to share.

As we write this, the diet's been under way for only a few weeks, so there's no way of knowing how far Kaybee will continue her grudge. She may very well come up with new ways to send her message to Pauline. Just as likely, she may call a halt to her protest over time.

Cats definitely hold grudges and feel resentment, although generally for much more basic and understandable reasons than we humans. Whenever they perceive a deprivation of some of the basic necessities that they've come to expect us to provide, they will register their complaints. They're just not as happy and contented as they were before, and it shows in their behavior. That can mean anything from a simple lessening of enthusiasm to acts that might best be described as spiteful.

However, what at first appears to be an act of spite by a cat is more often than not motivated by anxiety or boredom. This is probably the underlying cause of Felix attacking the leg of the couch while you're out, even though he is normally happy to use the scratching post in the kitchen. He has no way of knowing how soon you intend to return. Maybe over the previous seven days you've been out for the same amount of time and Felix hasn't reacted to it. But, for whatever cat reason he may have, today he needed you close. When you weren't there his comfort and security levels dropped and anxiety built up within him, eventually finding this outlet.

Comfort and security are prime motivators in a cat's life. Your cat may try to avoid contact with you if it has reason to perceive you as a disrupting force.

Our homes are a very strange world to our cats, filled with interesting things that we try to prevent them from touching. Such restrictions are quite artificial and foreign to the natural world.

WHO, ME?

You've probably noticed that whenever any indiscretions take place, catching the guilty party in the act (or even in the appearance of guilt) is just about impossible. For example, consider the shelf filled with favorite and fragile collectables that has also attracted the attentions of a cat for whatever reason – perhaps warm air collects there, perhaps there's a special feeling of security, perhaps there is some other reason that you can't fathom. You've made it clear to the cat that the shelf is off-limits, and you never see the cat on it. However, as you approach that room you hear the "thud, thud" of a cat making its way down to the floor from some elevated position. As you enter the room, you see the cat seated on the floor, well away from the shelf, grooming. Sleepily he looks up at you, as if to say, "Oh, hello there. Fancy meeting you. I've just been sitting here on the floor for the past hour or so, grooming myself."

At times like these it's easy to believe in the concept of cat lies. Anyone who has spent much time at all around cats has at least one or two tales that seem to prove beyond a shadow of a doubt that cats do in fact tell lies, and quite often.

However, lying may be too human a concept for what the cats really are doing. You'll recall that comfort and security are among the chief motivators in the life of the cat. What better way for the animal to maintain some control over these areas than with secrecy about what it's been up to and where it's been

An action such as swiping food off a plate gives the cat a measure of reward. This kind of behavior can become difficult to curb if you don't react immediately and consistently.

doing. The cat's philosophy here is this: "Nobody saw me, I didn't do it." The portrayal of innocence on your entry into the room may seem like plain dishonesty, but is in fact another natural mechanism to avoid loss of comfort and security. If you didn't see the cat doing the forbidden action, there won't be any yelling or other punishments.

Our houseplants are a particular source of interest to our cats. They have a natural attraction to plants and will be tempted to claw and chew them.

THE PLEASURES OF PLAY

THE PLEASURES OF PLAY

Play is basically a preparation for the realities of life, but how can we tell when a cat is playing? First, it does not seem to have any purpose and, second, it expends just that bit more energy than is really necessary. Simply, play is almost always characterized by exuberance, if not joy.

ADULT VISITORS TO Gramma's home would smile in disbelief at stories of the antics of Quincy – at least those who visited without children in tow. There was simply no way that they could accept such tales about the pleasingly plump Calico. The only Quincy they had ever seen was a placid cat that did little beyond lie on Gramma's lap and stretch and yawn occasionally. To them that was the only personality that Quincy ever exhibited. Even the basketful of cat toys that Gramma had collected for him never seemed to attract more than a passing glance.

But in the presence of children a completely different cat emerged. Whenever young playmates were available, a roughhousing, fleet-footed, lovingly aggressive fool of a cat occupied Quincy's mind and body. Every conceivable game seemed to come immediately to mind, from ankle-attack tag to all-out wrestling, the rougher the better.

The one trait that Quincy seemed able to carry into either of his personalities was that of gentleness. No matter how rough the play might become, Quincy never used his claws or teeth.

One of the most important criteria in playing with a cats is near-constant motion. Expensive toys are not necessary in providing this – a simple finger will do.

While such a completely split personality is not at all common in cats – at least not when it comes to play – there was much else in the behavior that Quincy exhibited that can be generalized across domestic cats as a whole.

Cats love to play. They even show much originality in the play they invent, such as stalking a spot of light on the wall, and in persuading us to join in with them. But cats also have some pretty strong rules about their play.

All but the most malfunctioning kittens need play. It's the primary means of learning the early lessons

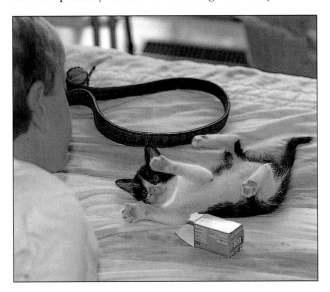

about how to survive as a cat. Even kittens of wild cats, from the bobcat to the African lion, spend much of their early weeks in play. Those kittens that are too weak, or sick, or otherwise unable to engage in the full extent of play with their siblings will have a much tougher time of it throughout their lives.

Most cats carry some of the playful instinct with them into adulthood. They even continue to need the activity, particularly those that are cooped up all day by themselves in small apartments – or even large houses. For these "home alone" cats, the play period that follows the arrival of the humans in the late afternoon and evening is a special time. The activity contributes not only some vital exercise, but also an opportunity for bonding and growing closer. Even roughhouse play, if your cat has demonstrated a liking for it, will serve this purpose.

Laid out like this in print, such set-aside-playtime may sound like an overly taxing drain on your crucial time after a hectic day at the office, but just 10 or 15 minutes is a long time for your cat. Wouldn't such a brief respite be a pleasant way for you to wind down as well?

Everything about this kitten is saying "Please, play with me." How could anyone resist?

New places to explore, regardless of how simple and commonplace, are like amusement park rides to our cats. Don't miss the opportunity to give a box or bag to your cat. These things will provide it with hours of fun.

Some play is more welcome than others, as this kitten is about to find out when it jumps on the sleeping adult.

Providing Play

Movement is the critical aspect in cat play. If something is moving, the cat is suddenly interested. This explains why toys scattered about the house just don't seem to provide an adequate substitute for your hand or foot. Those toys do nothing on their own. They just lie there. You're the energy that brings the toys to life and renews the cat's interest in them.

Think like a mouse. The little rodent scurries as fast as it can from one bit of cover to the next, stopping at each to peer out nervously before starting again on its fleeting way. This is the type of movement that cats most enjoy.

They also enjoy the pounce and capture, which is the ultimate goal of any hunt (now replaced with play). If the cat manages to catch and chew on the mouse (toy) every so often during the play period, its interest will be maintained for considerably longer.

The mother cat encourages play, and she supervises every minute of it. The kittens observe her carefully, and learn her signals and attitudes. Expressions of threat are "taught" by the mother, and then the kittens try them on her.

In the wild state, much of the play behavior of a cat will disappear with maturity. The regular pursuit of enough prey to survive and continue the species brings a much more serious aspect to the whole affair, not to mention the constant attention needed to avoid dangerous enemies.

However, in your house most of these worries have been eliminated, which influences your cat's continued interest in play for two reasons. First, by providing nearly all of your cat's food, you are assuming the role of a parent cat and allowing your feline to retain much of its kitten-ness into and through adulthood. Secondly, it is as well to accept that the hunting instinct never dies and that the well-adjusted cat must find some new routes into which it can channel all the energy that would normally be directed in this manner. Active play is the perfect substitute.

There are some common cat games that will

Sometimes it seems that cats hate to be caught in the midst of some ridiculous action. The truth is that they are generally waiting to see what your response will be to their latest antics.

interest almost any feline. The clichéd activities such as batting at a suspended ball of yarn have become clichéd because so many million cats have perpetuated them down through the generations. Hide and seek, with either you or your cat hiding and then ambushing the other, is also a standard.

Every cat and owner will also invent their own special play. Remain open to each new opportunity that presents itself during play period, and you'll find yourself and your cat doing just that. It's likely that whatever little games the cat comes up with will be clues to what it enjoys most.

Blanket chase, where the owner's hand is attacked while moving beneath a blanket, rug, towel, or some similarly soft covering, will entice even sedentary felines. Hide the toy, in which some of the cat's favorite possessions are hidden about the house, will play upon the natural feline curiosity. This is a particularly good game for you to set up for the cat before leaving for work each morning.

These are some of the games that have proven most enjoyable with the majority of cats we've owned or known, but they are only a starting point and not an all-inclusive list. The important aspect of cat play is not what you play but how much energy and imagination you put into it.

Play is as natural as breathing for kittens and should be encouraged throughout their lives. Play keeps their minds active and their bodies in shape.

345

A playful British Shorthair Silver Spotted tabby kitten.

A Cat's View of Sickness and Stress

A CAT'S VIEW OF
SICKNESS AND STRESS

Cat's are creatures of habit. Comfort and security are high on their list of priorities. They do not have a human understanding of change. When something happens that disrupts a cat's normal routine, its life can be turned upside down.

Cats find their own ways of telling us what they want us to do and what they don't want us to do. They quickly come to recognize certain signals. The sudden appearance of a suitcase can only mean the impending departure of its human.

MOST OF US HAVE HEARD of the elephants' graveyard, that mythical place where all elephants go to die. The legend could just as easily have been developed about a cats' graveyard. There would be as much truth to the latter notion as the former.

The animal response to pain and illness is different to the human one. Animals' first instinct is not to seek out help, comfort and relief from others of their kind, or from human housemates in the case of our cats. They don't have our scientific understanding of what's really amiss under these circumstances.

Instead, they are left to their own analysis of the situation. And what they perceive the pain or discomfort to be is the result of a sudden attack by some enemy, invisible though that enemy might be.

In the face of such an attack, the reasonable animal behavior is to escape and hide. The most secure hiding place in the cat's territory is generally selected as a refuge. Cats that are allowed to roam freely outdoors and are familiar with a much larger territory often just seem to vanish, never to return. Rather than running away, as is commonly assumed, many of these cats have simply curled up and died in some vacant building or stack of rubbish. During episodes of illness, compassion from a human is rather meaningless while the pain or discomfort goes right on attacking. The one exception may be the cat that has been conditioned to view a human's lap or arms as packed with security and comfort. The sudden absence of a cat from its normal "rounds" about the house may be among the very first symptoms of injury or illness. There can be other reasons for a reclusive cat, but if the change in routine comes on suddenly a trip to the vet may be in order.

SOURCES OF STRESS

Injury and illness are just two of the many things that we take for granted in our everyday lives that pose great mysteries to our cats. However, technological gadgets, such as television and refrigerators, that are part of the human environment, will be accepted by cats – and even used to their own advantage. Other aspects of this strange human world will continue to baffle the cat throughout its life. The sudden change in attitude toward the cat's use of furniture when a new living-room suite is brought into the house is beyond Kitty's comprehension. It's not difficult to understand her reaction of avoiding the living room and possibly her humans, who seem to have gone insane and are suddenly scolding her for activities that yesterday were perfectly acceptable. The new furniture represents nothing more than the loss of much beloved, familiar territory to Kitty. She just doesn't have the capacity to understand or share your excitement about this acquisition.

Similar reactions can arise to nearly anything new that we bring into the cat's territory, which coincidentally is also our home. New babies, new pets, rearranged furniture all represent change, and often change accompanied by new attitudes on our part.

Cats also do not understand our attempts to heal them. They will see splints and bandages, such as those on this kitten's leg, as something restrictive and an invasion of their bodies.

The sudden loss of some member of the household, whether through death or simply because they moved away from home, can send some cats into a deep depression.

Another source of cat stress is being forced to spend excessive time alone. This is not widely recognized because of the independent nature of our cats in comparison to other companion animals. It's true that cats are not pack animals, but they do need social contact – with other cats where possible or with their human housemates as a substitute.

Any absence longer than a normal workday, if repeated regularly, is probably enough to cause some degree of loneliness in most cats. Those cat owners who find themselves out of the house for such extended periods may want to bring a second cat into the home, being careful that the two felines are compatible with one another.

Many aspects of the man-made world into which

we bring out cats can cause them stress, although the amount of stress and the reaction to it will vary from one cat to the next. Just like humans, cats are individuals. Just like humans, cats vary in their capacity to deal with stressful situations. And, just as in humans, stress can lead to illness in our cats.

Early symptoms of stress can include drastic changes in normal daily activity, increased amounts of time spent in self-grooming, loss of or increase in appetite, change in the condition of the coat and dullness in the eyes. These, of course, are the early symptoms for a great many cat ailments, so home diagnosis is not practical. If a few such symptoms show up and cannot be explained through your observations on your cat, a visit to the vet is in order.

Cats will often slink away and hide when they feel their security is threatened.

Repeated searches may be conducted for any member of the family who is gone for a longer than normal period.

Many of these same symptoms will be noticed in a depressed cat. Sensitive animals like cats will feel a sense of loss when someone leaves their lives, and they experience a form of depression over the loss. In other words, cats mourn.

They also have many more occasions to mourn than humans do. We've never seen any evidence to point to the fact that cats understand the concept of death, but loss is another thing entirely. The cat feels loss whenever someone from its familiar world is no longer there. This interferes with its feelings of comfort and security, and the cat is therefore anxious about the change.

Death of a family member – and this description includes other pets that share the home – is one reason for loss, but to the cat it is the same when a teenager goes off to college or when the family is broken by divorce. Even something as temporary as a member of the family away for vacation or on an extended business trip has been known to trigger this mourning response in some cats. The fact that the missing individual will be resurfacing from time to time just isn't in the cat's frame of reference.

Kitty's first reaction will be several thorough searches of the home for the missing individual over the first few days of separation. Often, these

Sometimes the addition of a new family member can snap a mourning cat outs of its depression over the loss of a previous member.

investigations are accompanied with regular series of questioning meows.

The next step will usually be a period of sulky, sluggish behavior. The cat will have lost just about all of her normal appetite for play, quite possibly for food as well. She'll spend much more time than normal just lying about, not in sleep but in apparent boredom. At this point, intervention is suggested to prevent the more severe symptoms. Perhaps the cat's focus on the lost companion can be broken with the introduction of a new member to the family. If your conditions permit, this can be a good time to bring a second cat into the home. Having more people over to the house can also help to fill the void.

Also, you might try to "jump-start" Kitty out of her malaise. Add some variety to her life by introducing some new games, particularly exciting games of the ambush variety. Try some new toys, or think up something new to add to her dinner menu. Do anything you can think of to divert the cat's attention from her feeling of loss. Make certain that other things that relate to her levels of comfort and security are maintained, and, if possible, enhanced.

Animals have relatively short attention spans, so you should be able to fill her life so full that she can't help but snap out of it before too long.

ON THE MOVE

A cat will take time to explore and settle in to its new home.

Moving to a new house is probably the change with maximum impact on the cat, who sees only the loss of familiar territory and a massive need for readjustment.

If you move house, keep your cat strictly confined until you and the cat have settled into the new home. When you allow your pet outdoors for its first exploratory wander, make sure it is hungry. Let it out about fifteen minutes before dinner time. It will go through a cursory reconnaissance, but its empty stomach will ensure that it responds to you when you call it in for dinner.

Neighboring cats and dogs have to be gradually lulled into acceptance of the new resident. To ease

There is only one safe way to move a cat. Place it in a secure basket. Neither conversation nor tranquilizers are effective substitutes. Some cats actually enjoy traveling, and owners sometimes risk having a cat loose in a car during the journey. This is not advisable.

the transition for your cat, some experts suggest that, instead of disposing of the contents of the litter tray in the usual way, while the cat is settling into its new home distribute it around the edges of the property. After a couple of weeks of this "marking", the neighborhood animals may have come to accept that a stranger has moved in and intends to stay.

Despite all your care and love there are some cats that will set off to find their old and familiar homes. Those who succeed make news. The orientation mechanism that they use is still not perfectly understood. Sadly, however, most of the cats that set off to find their old homes are never seen again.

There are many other reasons for moving your cat from one place to another. But there is no way to explain to a cat that the move is unavoidable or beneficial. A sick cat will find even the shortest journey to the vet doubly upsetting.

Boarded cats (left) should not come into contact with other cats at the boarding home. If the chalets have outside runs, they should either have solid partitions, or should have a space of at least three feet between them. All the surfaces should be easily cleanable, and the cat should have some sort of ledge that it can jump up onto. Heating is essential in areas where the temperature may drop, and a cleanable bed should be available, with suitable bedding. It is a good idea to take along any familiar personal bedding and toys for your pet.

One of the most common causes of disruption to pets is the annual vacation. If you are able to get someone to live in your home while you are away or can arrange for someone to stop by to check and feed your cat two or three times each day, your cat will probably be less upset than it would be if you moved it to strange surroundings. Your cat may not even notice that you've gone! An arrangement like this, however, may only be less stressful for the cat if you are away for a short period only. Otherwise boarding is preferable because the cat may receive more attention.

When choosing a boarding home, personal recommendation is always the best. Speak to friends who have boarded their cats and find out which they would recommend. Do not be afraid to telephone the boarding home and ask to be shown around. Be sure that the facilities look clean and well-maintained and that boarded cats are not allowed to come into contact with each other and spread disease. If the cat is being boarded for any length of time, it is best for each pen to have its own indoor or outdoor run, which should be separated by a solid divide from other runs, or have a space of at least three feet between each one.

Any boarding home worth its salt will insist that all cats are up to date with infectious enteritis and cat 'flu vaccinations – you should be warned of this when you make your reservation. If your cat is going to be almost due for its booster when it goes in, it is wise to have it boosted before it goes, in order to give maximum protection. Be sure your cat's "Record of Vaccination" has been brought fully up to date by your vet. Most homes will oblige and administer medicines prescribed by your vet if arranged in advance. Of course, it may be necessary for them to call in their own vet at your expense to examine your cat if complications develop while you are away.

The ideal boarding home owner will take great pride in the running of the home and caring for each cat individually. He or she will be eager to discover the likes and dislikes of each boarder and will always be on the look-out for signs of trouble. Each pen must be escape-proof. Also, the entrance to each pen should not be open to the outdoors – in other words, there should be at least two doors between the cat and the big wide world. Pens should be large enough for the cat to move around comfortably and ideally

A cat that travels with its owners will often accept restraint with a harness and leash. These should be made of soft leather or nylon.

Cats from one household can be boarded together. An outdoor cattery has a wired enclosure that allows cats the freedom of the fresh air, without the risk of injury or escape. Ideally, the enclosure should be connected to a shelter with the cats' beds and food.

should have access to an outdoor run. It is essential that each cat be kept completely isolated from other cats at all times (except when more than one cat from the same household are boarded together). All surfaces should be easily cleanable and should be kept clean and in good order. Supplementary heating is necessary in winter. Bring any toys that your cat is fond of and any blanket or similar bedding that is familiar to your cat. Don't forget to take along any necessary medications.

Cats that have been used to traveling regularly since they were young generally travel well and settle into new surroundings quickly. It is important that the cat not be allowed to escape, for if your cat runs off in unknown territory, it will possibly be lost for good. Whether or not a cat is used to traveling, it is important to carry it in a large, sturdy carrying box with plenty of clean newspaper in it. Various types of containers are available for transporting cats.

Do not feed the cat before you set out, but be sure that fresh water is available from time to time. You should certainly never leave a cat locked inside a car parked in the sun.

Some owners insist that, before a long journey, their vet should prescribe tranquilizers. Cats seem to react strangely to many drugs, and some sedatives seem to have the opposite effect in a few cats. Therefore, many vets are reluctant to give sedatives to cats. If they are prescribed, it is probably best to try them out on a "dummy run" before you set out on a long day's journey with an hysterical cat in the rear.

CAT CONTAINERS

There are a number of different types of carriers and baskets on the market designed for moving cats from place to place. For long-term durability, wicker (1) and fibre-glass (2) baskets are preferable. Metal carriers with mesh fronts (3) are the easiest to keep clean and disinfected. A wire basket (4), open on all sides, provides good ventilation. All baskets for carrying cats must provide adequate space and air. Before setting off on a journey, it is advisable to line the base of the carrier with newspaper or bedding for comfort and easy cleaning.

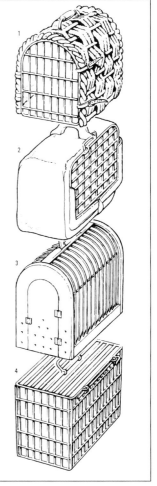

NATURAL HEALTH CARE

THE NATURAL WAY

Interest in natural health care for pets is on the increase. The information given here about illness and its treatments is not a guide to supplanting veterinary involvement in the care of your pet. The diagnosis of ailments and their treatment is strictly the responsibility of a qualified vet. However, if you prefer this approach, you can register your cat with a vet who uses these methods.

THE USE OF THE TERM "alternative medicine" is rather misleading, because these different types of treatment are not mutually exclusive. This is why the description "complementary medicine" is more accurate. A combination of treatments may been be consider preferable in some cases.

Although acupuncture, chiropractic, and osteopathy have all been used successfully in the treatment of cats, the biggest impact complementary medicine has made on veterinary care has been on medication itself. Some confusion does exist, particularly between homoeopathy and herbalism, which represent two quite different approaches to dealing with illness. Both homoeopathy and herbalism are ancient forms of treatment.

Homoeopathy

Homoeopathy dates back to the days of ancient Greece. Its name reflects this link, being derived from *homoios*, a Greek word meaning "like". The rationale behind homoeopathy is that symptoms displayed as the result of an illness are, in reality, the attempts of the body to overcome the disease process. In contrast, conventional veterinary thinking proposes that symptoms are the direct result of the disease rather than the body's reaction to it.

Herbalism

Herbalism may appear to have more in common with current therapy, especially since a number of drugs used in veterinary practice today were originally derived from plants. But herbalists consider disease to be the result of imbalances within the body. Although a cat may be suffering from a particular

illness, the cause may be addressed by different means, rather than a standard therapeutic approach. Each case is individual and is treated accordingly.

Herbal treatments do not rely on seeking out an active ingredient from a plant, but value the entire plant, which contains not only the active medical ingredient but also vitamins and trace elements, which are believed to aid recovery from illness.

In contrast to conventional therapeutic treatment, those used by herbalists are unlikely to result in allergic reactions. They can be valuable in combating minor ailments that may be linked to dietary deficiencies. Not surprisingly, herbs are widely used by cat owners as food supplements.

Distinguishing Medicines and Supplements

It is important to be able to distinguish among the various kinds of herbal products on offer. Only those sold as medicines are licensed and tested for efficiency, as well as for purity of ingredients and safety. They may be in tablet form, and even coated with sugar, to disguise the ingredients. Herbal supplements, in contrast, are not subject to such controls, and are typically used alongside the cat's regular diet.

Animals sometimes appear to have instincts about the benefits of plants when they are sick. Cats troubled with fur balls often resort to eating grass.

USING COMPLEMENTARY REMEDIES

Obviously, if your cat is ill, you should consult your vet without delay, so that the problem can be diagnosed and the appropriate treatment prescribed. In the case of homoeopathic or herbal medicines, these are likely to look just like other prescribed medicines. They may be supplied in the form of tablets, liquids, or even granules.

Dosage Instructions

These should be followed carefully. It is best to give the medication directly to your cat rather than try to disguise it in food. Many such remedies should be given on their own, without food, a fact that will be noted on the label or accompanying instructions.

How Long to Give Medication

Depending on the condition, medication may need to be given over a period that can last up to several weeks or more. You will find the times for specific treatment in the next chapter. Although incorrect dosing is obviously to be avoided, this is less likely to have serious side-effects than with modern drugs.

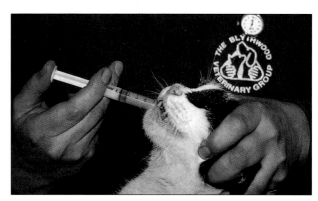

Care is needed to ensure that a cat cannot wriggle free when being dosed with liquid medicine. A helping hand is recommended.

Giving Liquid Medicines

These are often harder to administer than tablets, because there is no easy way of ensuring that the cat swallows the fluid. The most practical method is to run the fluid in from the side of the mouth using a small plastic syringe (without needle). Do not use a glass dropper of any kind as it could break in the cat's mouth. The relative gap behind the long canine teeth at the front of the jaw is the best position for giving liquid medicines. With a syringe, there is less risk of spillage. Allow the medication to flow out steadily in the mouth, pausing if your cat starts coughing and allowing it to lower its head.

Supplements in Food and Drink

Since cats drink relatively little, it is almost impossible to dispense any medicine successfully via drinking water, although granules can be mixed in with food, as can most supplements. These tend to be quite palatable; yeast, for example, which is a valuable source of B vitamins, is taken readily by cats, in powdered form, sprinkled over food or simply as a tablet.

Storing Medicines and Supplements

Homoeopathic and herbal remedies should be stored under similar conditions to drugs, in dry containers, preferably out of the light in a medical cabinet. As a general rule, they should remain suitable for use for at least five years when kept in the right conditions.

HOW TO GIVE A TABLET

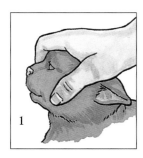

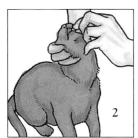

This is not especially difficult, although with difficult cats you may require the assistance of someone else. Gently tilt the cat's head upwards and, placing your left hand around the sides of the cat's mouth, hold the upper jaw (1). Push down on the lower jaw with your right hand (2), and then slip the tablet as far back on the cat's tongue as possible (3). Then close the jaws immediately, keeping the head tilted and tickle the cat on its throat. This will encourage it to swallow the tablet. The tablet may go down more easily if it is lubricated first with a bit of butter.

The nutritional needs of kittens differ from those of adult cats. Special diets or supplements can be used. These should be discussed with your vet.

HOMOEOPATHIC REMEDIES

While a number of treatments can be purchased without prescription, some homoeopathic medicines must be prescribed, as must homoeopathic alternatives to conventional inoculations against the serious viral diseases that can afflict cats. These products are known as nosodes and oral vaccines, and they can be used to prevent disease, in a prophylactic manner, and therapeutically, if the need arises.

Nosodes and Oral Vaccines

The term "nosode" is derived from the Greek word for disease, nosos. Such products are obtained from an animal afflicted with the disease for which the inoculation is required. The disease-causing micro-organism may not be present, but this is not considered significant, because it is the products produced by the body in combating the illness that underline the efficiency of the nosode rather than the virus itself. In some cases, typically those which have proved refractory to treatment, autonosodes are prepared. These are based on material obtained from the sick cat itself.

There is a degree of overlap between nosodes and oral vaccines, although the latter are derived specifically from the harmful micro-organism responsible for the disease or from their toxins. In the case of bacteria, an oral vaccine may be made from an emulsion, comprising both bacterial and toxins, or a filtrate that contains just toxins. The appropriate oral vaccine can not only act to guard against a disease but can also have a curative role, giving rise to rapid recovery in cases where there is no long-term problem.

Bowel Nosodes

The so-called group of bowel nosodes are more accurately described as oral vaccines, because they are manufactured directly from micro-organisms cultured for this purpose. These are used primarily in chronic cases, where previous sustained treatment

has not been successful and several different treatments appear to be indicated.

There are five main bowel nosodes, each of which has specific functions and may be used in conjunction with other appropriate remedies and have far-reaching effects on the body. They may be given daily over a short period of time, and then used again several months later if required.

"Potency" Explained

The potency of a homoeopathic remedy is a reference to the strength of the medication being used. This may typically vary from 3c to 200c, with the letter "c" simply indicating a pharmacological code, based on the centesimal scale, whereas "x" refers to the decimal scale. The number in this instance refers to the dilution factor that has been used. The so-called mother tincture, sometimes indicated simply as "0" is the starting point made from the substance to be used. This is then typically diluted with alcohol (although with some homoeopathic substances a different diluent is used), with one drop being added to 99 parts of alcohol in the first instance. This gives a dilution factor of 1:100, written in code as 1c. If diluted again, there will be one unite of mother tincture in 10,000 parts alcohol, to create a 2c preparation. A 200c description confirms that the solution has been successively diluted through 200 stages. The higher the number preceding the letter, the more dilute is the solution, but the more potent is the remedy. The concept that a little may be of some benefit, so a more concentrated solution will be of greater value is never more misplaced that in homoeopathy.

A number of the products used for homoeopathic treatment would be deadly if not correctly prepared. This is not an area for experimentation. Only correctly potentized formulations obtained from vets should be used.

Where Homoeopathic Medicines Come From

More than 60 per cent of the 2,500 or so treatments are of plant origin. Careful preparation of remedies involving potentially lethal plants, such as Deadly Nightshade (*Belladonna*) ensure that only their beneficial properties become apparent during treatment. The stage at which the plant is gathered can be critical. In the case of *Belladonna*, this should be after flowering.

Minerals, including precious metals such as gold and silver are also used in homoeopathic preparations. So too are a very diverse range of animal products. These include bee venom, formic acid from ants, eel serum and the shell of oysters.

The venom of the deadly Bushmaster snake from South Africa is now used in homoeopathic treatments for various conditions.

HERBALISM AND ITS APPLICATIONS

In the broadest sense, herbs are plants that are of value to people and animals for a wide variety of purposes. Three different herb types have long been recognized as foods: sweet herbs, now referred to as culinary herbs, such as sage; salad herbs, which have long been valued for the table; and pot herbs such as onions, which have become better known as vegetables. Although there are obvious botanical differences between them, fungi may also be considered as herbal plants.

Interest in herbs as a basis for treatment dates back to 2700 BC in China. The tradition spread to Europe, where it was developed by the Greeks and Romans.

Herbalism Today

There have been significant changes over the centuries, with few of today's herbalists using the potentially poisonous plants that were used in medieval times. Indeed, one of the characteristics of herbalism today is that the remedies are safe and are not associated with adverse side-effects.

Herbs are often used alone for treatment purposes, being described as "simples". Occasionally, several different herbs may be used together. With herbs, as with homoeopathy, or indeed conventional medicine, it is vital first to obtain an accurate diagnosis of an animal's illness from a vet. The appropriate herbal treatment can then be commenced.

Care with the Correct Treatment

There are some contra-indications, even with herbal medicines. For example, it would be sensible not to dose a pregnant cat with pennyroyal, because this may cause it to abort. While cats that have a history of calculi (stones) in the urinary tract should not be provided with rhubarb if they become constipated.

Aside from being of value in illnesses, some herbs are also valuable in combating parasitic problems. Again, veterinary advice is vital. For example, the male fern (*Dryopteris felix-mas*) has long been known as a means of combating tapeworm infestations. However, if used in too high a dose, it can cause blindness and even death. Herbal treatments that have been produced for people may not always be suitable for cats.

Making Herbal Treatments

Herbal treatments are available in a range of forms, which may relate to the way in which the active ingredient has been extracted, as well as the way in which it is going to be used. The different parts of the plant may also contain active ingredients in varying proportions. Extraction methods mean that in most cases making herbal treatments cannot be carried out

satisfactorily at home, though there are certain processes that are possible at home with a variety of herbs. A relatively simple one is infusion, which enables water soluble substances to be extracted from the softer parts of the plants, such as their leaves, stems or flowers. Ideally, you should collect only herbs that you have grown yourself, because you can then be certain that they will be uncontaminated. Most herbs can be grown quite easily from seed.

Making Infusions

To make an infusion, you will need to gather 30 g (1 oz) of plant material, which should first be washed under running water and shaken dry. It must then be chopped up finely and placed in a suitable lidded container. This can be made of glass, stone or porcelain, but it is important that the lid is tight-fitting, otherwise volatile substances released during the infusion process will be lost into the surrounding atmosphere. The plant material should then be covered with 500 ml (20 fl oz) of boiling water, and the lid put in place. It should be left to stand for about 15 minutes, before the liquid is strained off into a separate container and allowed to cool. This can be given to the cat to drink, although it is generally better to pour the infusion over the cat's food, allowing it to be absorbed, since cats will nor normally drink a large volume of liquid on its own.

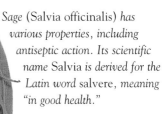

Onion (Allium cepa) is a valuable source of vitamins, as well as being helpful in dealing with respiratory infections and gastro-enteritis.

Sage (Salvia officinalis) has various properties, including antiseptic action. Its scientific name Salvia is derived for the Latin word salvere, meaning "in good health."

Apart from tablets, it is also possible to administer the benefits of herbs in the form on an infusion (right), which can be poured over the cat's food.

HEALTH CARE

While you will obviously need some veterinary assistance if your cat falls ill, there is much you can do yourself, in terms of nursing care, to help your pet through illness and speed up its recovery.

THE SIGNS OF ILLNESS are often clear-cut, with loss of appetite, lethargy, vomiting, diarrhea and discharges, coughing and physical weakness or disability all likely indicators of a potential problem.

To find a vet who uses complementary medicine, try homoeopathic associations, which have lists of vets who provide this service. Alternatively, contact local practices and ask if they can treat your cat with homoeopathic remedies. When consulting your vet, you should provide as detailed a history as possible, and follow the treatment instructions carefully. Details about dosage of tablets and other medications will be given on their labeling. There may be accompanying instructions concerning withholding food for a period after administering the tablet; this is quite usual practice with many homoeopathic treatments.

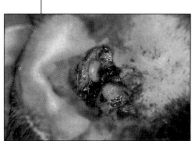

An accumulation of ear wax may contain bacteria, mites and fungi, all of which can cause ear infections. A cat with an ear infection may scratch repeatedly at the ear and resent this area of the body being touched.

Wax in the Ears

Olive oil is very useful for cleaning a cat's ears, breaking down any accumulation of wax. Warm the oil first, so that it flows more freely, by standing a small glass jar of the oil in a container of hot water. Then carefully run about a teaspoonful into each ear in turn. Start by gently tilting the cat's head on one side, so that you have a clear view of the ear canal. Using a spoon, the sides of which have been bent upward to form a funnel, makes applying the oil easier. Allow it to trickle slowly down into the ear. Do not rush the procedure, because the oil will simply run down the sides of the cat's face, rather than into the ear.

Gently massage the cat's ear from behind and below, and after a short time you should be able to detect a change in consistency, indicating that the wax has been broken down.

A cotton-wool bud can be used very carefully to absorb the waxy debris, taking care not to poke the bud into the ear canal, which could be painful. If the ear appears very sore, calendulated oil – made up by stirring a couple of drops of calendula tincture into 25 ml/1 fl oz of olive oil – may be used for its soothing properties.

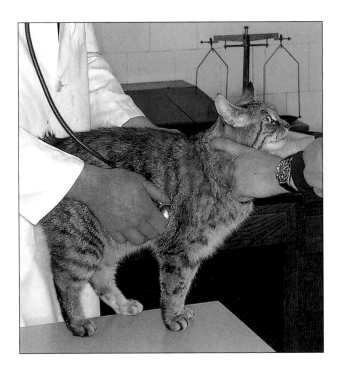

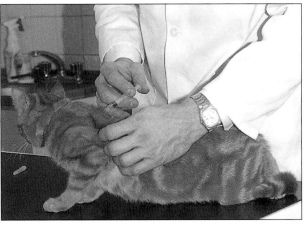

The vet should be a cat's best friend, diagnosing and treating any problems and providing preventive care.

Help for Respiratory Infections

Although cats are generally very healthy, they can be prone to respiratory infections. In such situations, bathing a cat's nose to remove any secretions will not only assist the cat's recovery, it will also encourage its appetite. There are various soothing agents that you can apply to prevent soreness and assist the healing process. Almond oil, gently rubbed on the nose two or three times a day, is one such, another is calendulated oil.

Soothing Sore Eyes

The cat's eyes may also be affected in a case of respiratory disease. They are often also injured in fights with other cats. A mild solution of salt, made by dissolving half a teaspoonful of sea salt in 600 ml (1 pt) of distilled water, can be used initially to bathe the eyes, applying the solution on cotton-wool.

ELIZABETHAN COLLAR

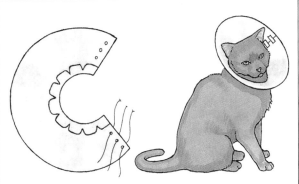

This serves to stop a cat from scratching itself on the head, or biting stitches after surgery. In most cases cats soon adapt to wearing this type of collar without becoming distressed.

Infected eyes should be bathed carefully, with particular attention being paid to the corners close to the nose, where the majority of debris is likely to accumulate. This treatment may need to be repeated several times daily.

Both male and female cats are prone to fighting, a small bite can easily become infected.

Alternatively, the salt solution can be boiled and then used to form a herbal infusion, by adding a heaped teaspoonful of eyebright (*Euphrasia rostkoviana*) to a cup of the solution. Allow it to cool before applying it to the cat's eyes, up to three times a day. Provided that it is covered and small quantities tipped into a separate container, this infusion will remain fresh for a day.

Eye drops should be given carefully with a special dropper, to ensure that the medication is not lost from the eyes.

SKIN PROBLEMS

Abscesses

Male cats, in particular, are prone to fight, and may continue to do so even after they are neutered. They are often bitten in fights, while females can also be bitten. The result of a bite is often an abscess forming at the site of the bite. The sudden appearance of an abscess can be very alarming, especially as the puncture wounds in the first instance are often inconspicuous enough to go unnoticed.

The cat's owner will probably first see a swelling, often on the side of the face The swelling usually increases rapidly in size. This is a result of bacteria being effectively injected into the cat's body by the opponent's bite. The skin then heals quite rapidly, and the abscess, which will be full of pus, starts to develop.

An abscess cannot be cured quickly. It should be allowed to come to a head and then burst. At first, the cat may lose its appetite, particularly if the bite is on the head, while the abscess itself will feel hot to the touch.

Vitamin C, in the form of 250 mg tablets, given three times a day over the course of three days, can help to boost the cat's immune system. The use of *Ledum*, especially with *Hypericum*, and given three times daily over the course of two days, starting out with one tablet every two hours on the first day, is typically recommended in such cases. The potency used varies from 6c to 200c.

As the abscess becomes ready to burst, *Hepar sulphuris* can speed the process, initially given at a potency of 6c, which can be increased to 200c for healing purposes. In addition, tincture of calendula, prepared using one quarter of a teaspoonful to a cup of hot distilled water, and sponged on to the abscess twice daily, will also bring relief.

While many abscesses will heal uneventfully, there can be complications, giving rise to a more chronic infection. This may be prevented by the use of *Silicea*, at a potency of 200c, being used three times a week over a month. It is advisable to prevent the drainage holes from healing prematurely, before all the pus has been drained out; bathing helps prevent the holes from healing. Wiping the skin area with hydrogen peroxide should help to ensure successful healing.

The abscess on this cat's head developed as a result of a bite from another cat.

Rodent ulcers used to be thought to be the result of a cat's hunting activities, being caused by a harmful micro-organism spread by rodents, such as rats and mice. The exact cause of these ulcers is still not known.

Treatment of rodent ulcers may require cryosurgery, which entails freezing the diseased area with liquid nitrogen, in the hope that it will be replaced by healthy tissue. Successful healing can be achieved in some cases, as here.

Rodent Ulcer

It used to be thought that this condition was somehow caught by cats from rodents, but the precise cause has not yet been established. Rodent ulcers typically occur on the upper lip and may extend toward the nose, although they can occur elsewhere in the mouth. The affected area is brownish and tends to create an irregular profile along the lip, with the edge rolling over where it is affected.

Treatment is invariably difficult, though *Kali bichromicum*, at a potency of 200c, has been known to give good results. The lesion itself appears to cause the cat relatively little discomfort. A single dose given three times a week for a period of six weeks may be required to cure the ulcer.

Military Eczema

A skin problem that can arise from neutering, especially in female cats, is military eczema. Hormonal treatment will be required. *Folliculinum* is the favored hormone for female cats. The usual recommendation is a 6c dose twice a day for three weeks; after an interval of a week, recommence with a 30c potency, given three times a week for a

Skin disorders can often be traced back to a cat's diet. The vet may need to take a skin scraping from the cat for analysis.

month. Relapses may occur and the characteristic pimply rashes may return, most notably along the back. The treatment should then be repeated.

Testosterone is the chosen remedy for male cats suffering from the condition, with similar potencies being used, although results are sometimes less encouraging than remedies for female cats.

The cause of other skin ailments in cats may be less clear-cut, but your vet will be able to carry out tests, following a skin scraping of the affected area, to try to ascertain the cause. Sometimes, skin disorders can be linked to the cat's diet. Again, sulphur may prove a valuable remedy, with calendula ointment helping to relieve any irritation.

Ringworm

In spite of its name, this is a fungal, rather than a parasitic, ailment and is of particular concern in that it is a zoonosis – that is, a disease transmissible to people. Ringworm lesions are often very inconspicuous in cats, in contrast to cattle, for example, on which the circular patches caused by the fungus are very evident, being paler than the rest of the coat.

It is at the proximity of the lesion that there is the greatest concentration of fungal spores. Two different forms of fungus may be implicated in cases of feline ringworm, of which *Microsporum* is far more common than *Trichophyton*. In some cases it is possible to confirm ringworm by examining the cat's coat in a darkened room using a Wood's lamp. This special lamp shone on the cat will cause the affected areas to fluoresce apple-green.

People can pick up ringworm without realizing it, because of a lack of clinical signs of the infection in their pet. (Red, circular patches on the arms are typically seen in cases of human ringworm.) Close examination of the cat may then reveal slight hair loss, often on the head. Should this not fluoresce, your vet will be able to arrange for cultures to be made, to detect any fungus.

Care needs to be taken because the fungal spores survive well in the environment. Thorough cleaning of the cat's quarters is essential, bedding should be disposed of and, ideally, the cat should be kept confined until treatment is completed. This will take at least a month, and possibly longer.

A suitable homoeopathic treatment is *Trichophyton* and *Microsporum* nosodes in a combined form, at a 30c potency. The dose needs to be given weekly, for a period of six weeks, while the affected areas should be treated each day as advised with a solution of *Hypericum* and *Calendula* (Hypercal).

Oil of lavender painted onto the bald areas each day is recommended as a herbal treatment and is easily applied using a brush. Wear disposable gloves when handling a cat with ringworm, and always wash your hands thoroughly, using cold rather than hot water, as it is less likely to open up your skin pores, making it harder for the fungal spores to become established and infect you.

A classic case of human ringworm (right), acquired from a cat. Circular lesions of this type should always receive medical attention. They are often on the forearm, because as the person picks the cat up, so its hair rubs against this part of the arm.

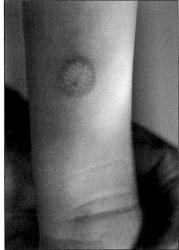

Ringworm is clearly visible on this cat's head (below). The most infective part is around the perimeter, where healthy and diseased hair meet.

A Wood's lamp (left) is being used to examine a cat for evidence of ringworm. Most types of ringworm will fluoresce under this light, assisting the diagnostic process. In contrast, it can take several weeks for the fungus to grow on special media in the laboratory.

SKIN PARASITES

Ticks are especially common in sheep-farming areas, with the cats acquiring the ticks as they move through grass. This photograph shows a tick on a cat's ear.

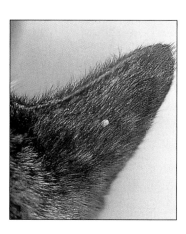

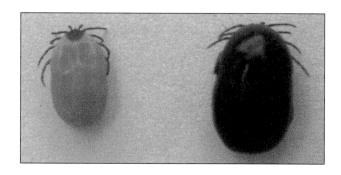

Ticks will swell in size as they feed on blood (above). However, it is possible to eliminate them quite easily.

Cats can get a variety of mites, lice, ticks, and fleas on their bodies, although the susceptibility of individual cats varies. Cats that are well fed and generally healthy are far less likely to suffer from a heavy infestation of lice, although the cat's nutritional state does not appear to affect the incidence of fleas. Ticks are most common in agricultural areas and feed on the cat's blood.

The herbal powders recommended for the treatment of fleas will control these other parasites as well. In the case of ticks, the simplest method of control is not to resort to chemicals or attempt to pull off the tick, because you will inevitably leave its headparts lodged in the cat's skin, where they are likely to cause a localized infection.

Instead, simply smear the tick with petroleum jelly, especially over its rear where it has a respiratory pore. Unable to breathe, the tick will eventually let go and fall off. Control of ticks is important, because they can be responsible for spreading blood-borne diseases in some parts of the world.

Lice can be killed quite easily using pennyroyal shampoo. They are much easier than fleas to control, because they lay their eggs on the cat's hairs, and so do not occur elsewhere in the home. It is worthwhile repeating the shampoo treatment, because the eggs, sometimes called nits, can be more resistant to treatment. An interval of two weeks between applications should be adequate to kill all lice.

You should also look carefully at the cat's diet, and try to give it a boost, using brewer's yeast and other supplements, because a heavy infestation of lice is often indicative of poor feeding.

Mange is, thankfully, not common in cats, but it can cause serious problems when it does arise, with two distinct forms being recognized. Notoedric mange, caused by a parasite known as *Notoedres cati*, causes severe irritation, with the mites themselves burrowing into the skin. It is very contagious among cats. The other form of mange, called demodectic, is less likely to spread to other cats, but can prove difficult to treat, whatever remedy is used. Even so, in some cases, it may resolve spontaneously.

Demodectic mange is most likely to occur on the head, with the cat pawing repeatedly at these areas. The hair becomes thinner, and if the mange is left untreated, the mites may spread down toward the body. *Sulphur* is often recommended as a homoeopathic remedy for mange, and needs to be given for about a month. Topical treatment of the lesions with lemon juice is also to be recommended, in conjunction with the sulphur treatment.

Thallium acetas has been used to stimulate hair regrowth after mange, at a potency of 30c. It is recommended that it is given daily for a period of three weeks.

These diagrams show some common external cat parasites.
1. Fur mite (Cheyletiella). 2. Harvest mite (Trombicula).
3. Cat louse (Felicola). These are uncommon in cats, although sickly kittens can be affected by them. 4. Sheep tick (Ixodes).

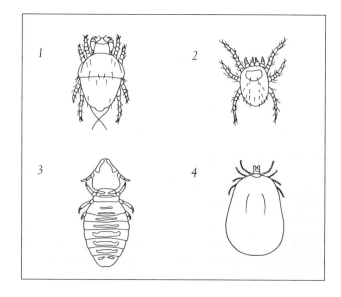

DEALING WITH FLEAS

Careful grooming will enable you to detect some troublesome parasites, such as fleas. Grooming is best carried out outdoors if you suspect that your cat has fleas. A fine-toothed flea comb will confirm their presence, even if you do not see these troublesome parasites, and will even catch a few of them. Look for tiny blackish-red specks among the fur on the comb, these are likely to be flea dirt, containing traces of undigested blood. You can confirm this by moistening them on a white sheet of paper: a red deposit will develop if it is flea dirt.

Fleas are usually found towards the base of the tail and over the hindquarters, although they may occur anywhere in the fur. They are very agile, and the easiest means of destroying any found is to drop them into a container of water.

It is very important to kill fleas, because not only will their biting distress your cat, but there is also a real risk that the cat could become sensitized to their saliva, giving rise to a condition sometimes described as "flea bite allergy." Fleas can also be the intermediate host for tapeworm, with the cat becoming infected when it consumes the flea when grooming itself. Treatment for tapeworm is often recommended after a severe flea infestation.

The aim should be to prevent the cat suffering from fleas as far as possible. Partly as a result of concerns over the chemicals contained within traditional flea collars, there has been a move towards incorporating more natural remedies into them. Since cats often spend much of their time climbing around, it is vital that a flea collar should be elasticated. Then, if it becomes caught on a branch, the cat can wriggle free and not strangle itself inadvertently.

A variety of herbs known to act as flea repellents have been incorporated into collars. It is possible to re-use some of these collars by immersing them in the recommended herbal solution.

Certain aromatic herbal powders can also be applied to the cat's coat. As always, read the accompanying instructions carefully. Cats are especially vulnerable to anything applied to their coats, because they spend long periods licking their fur and can ingest the active ingredients.

Pennyroyal *(Mentha pulegium)*, a form of mint, has a long history of combating fleas on people as well as animals. The plant grows quite easily in most parts of the world, with the American pennyroyal *(Hedeoma pulegioides)* having identical properties. Eucalyptus *(Eucalyptus globulus)* is another aromatic plant that is often incorporated in herbal flea remedies. Wormwood *(Artemisia absinthium)*, rosemary *(Rosmarinus officinalis)* and rue *(Ruta graveolens)* are other herbs considered of value in fighting fleas.

It is also important to treat the cat's environment, because flea eggs accumulate here, rather than on the cat. Bedding must be washed regularly, and vacuuming the cat's sleeping areas will also help to remove microscopic flea eggs before they can hatch.

A chalk-like substance, produced from fossilized algae and marketed as diatomaceous earth, also offers a means of fighting fleas in the home. Harmless to animals, it destroys fleas by damaging their boding casing. While fleas tend to be a particular problem in late summer, plagues can arise at other times of the year, especially in centrally heated houses.

It is important to soothe the skin of a cat suffering from flea bites. Lemon juice, suitably diluted, can be soothing. Slice up a lemon and add it to 600 ml (1 pt) of warm water, leaving the solution to stand for about 12 hours. Then bathe the affected area with the solution, applied on cotton-wool.

LIFE CYCLE OF A FLEA

1. Adult fleas are about one-twelfth of an inch in length and flattened from side to side. They feed by sucking blood from their victim, and then jump off in order to lay eggs. One flea may lay up to 500 eggs in its lifetime.

2. Eggs are laid anywhere that the cat lies. These hatch into larvae between 2–16 days.

3. Larvae are about one-eighth of an inch long and actively burrow down into bedding and carpets away from the light, feeding on dust and debris. They may also pick up tapeworm eggs. After about a week, the larva forms a cocoon.

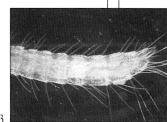

4. The larva normally develops for 2 weeks within the cocoon before emerging as an adult flea. As larvae hatch in response to vibrations, they may lie dormant for months, or even years.

INJURIES AND TRAVELING DIFFICULTIES

Unfortunately, fractures among the feline population appear to be on the increase. As the roads become busier and busier, many of the fractures suffered by cats are a direct result of collisions with vehicles. While it is vital to get an injured cat to the vet as quickly as possible for specialist treatment, homoeopathy can help the healing process and relieve pain. Comfrey (*Symphytum officinale*) is invaluable as it helps speed up the formation of a callus at the fracture site. This particular remedy also acts as a mild analgesic.

Arnica, derived from the plant popularly known as mountain tobacco, is another helpful homoeopathic remedy. *Arnica* can relieve the severe bruising that

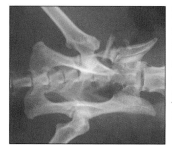

X-rays are valuable in determining the extent of an individual injury, and guiding a vet on the best options for treatment. This cat has a fractured pelvis – a common result of a collision with a car.

usually follows accidents. Four doses, given at hourly intervals, are recommended for initial treatment, with further tablets being used as necessary, on the following days, when the interval is increased to eight hours.

BLEEDING

Bleeding should be stopped by applying pressure to stem the blood flow in the first instance, and then a bandage can be applied.

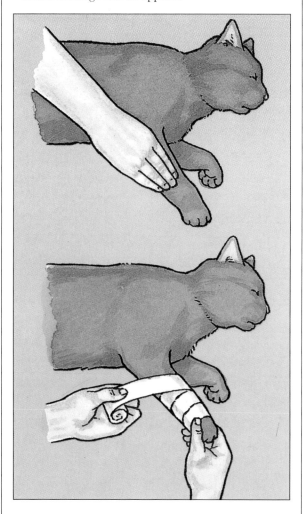

INJURED CAT

A cat that has been injured should be carried on its side, without being tipped, in case its diaphragm has been torn. Otherwise, the body organs may shift position through this gap between the chest and the abdomen. Alternatively, if the cat is restless, gently pick it up by the scruff of the neck and, supporting the rump, place it into a cardboard box or suitable carrier (2). If the cat struggles violently, then it is a good idea to wrap it up in a towel (3), prior to placing it in the cat carrier.

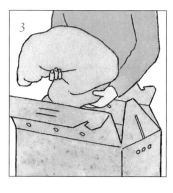

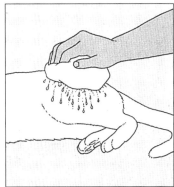

Cats not used to traveling, or nervous when in a car, may be given sedation before the journey and should always be transported in a carrier (left).

Apply cold water to a burn, holding the injured area under a running tap if necessary (above). This can be critical in reducing the extent of the injury. Only then should you seek veterinary assistance.

Arnica is also useful in cases of haemorrhage, although the most satisfactory way of stemming blood flow is usually to exert pressure on the area concerned, and apply calendula lotion, adding two drops to a tablespoonful of water. Where the blood flow is severe, bandaging to maintain the pressure may be helpful. *Ferrum phosphoricum* tablets can be of help, if *Arnica* is not available, while *Aconite* will assist in overcoming the symptoms of shock.

Similar remedies may also help heal bites inflicted in a cat fight. A bite wound should be cleaned thoroughly before using the herbal remedies.

Cats can also be quite badly hurt at home. They may burn themselves badly on a hot hob, for instance, or scald themselves, should they knock over a saucepan or kettle. There are suitable homoeopathic ointments to treat burns available for emergencies, especially one made with *Urtica*, which soothes, and *Hypericum*, which has an analgesic action. *Cantharis* tablets are also helpful. If the injury or burn is anything other than minor, you should seek veterinary advice.

Most cats are not used to traveling and often become so distressed that they may remain difficult to handle once they arrive at their destination. Homoeopathic treatment with *Cocculus* can be helpful to prevent travel sickness, while a combination of skullcap and valerian herbs in tablet form is a herbal option to counter the problem of sickness and help soothe a distressed cat. Tablets should be given to the cat before a journey, if it is known that it is likely to become distressed.

Traveling is often a source of distress for a cat.

DIGESTIVE PROBLEMS

Cats fed on a wet diet, particularly as they get older, may suffer from a build-up of plaque on their teeth and inflamed gums, which often results in halitosis (bad breath). Problems with teeth can also affect a cat's appetite.

It may help if you can persuade your cat to allow you to brush its teeth regularly. Encouraging a routine of toothbrushing from kittenhood is most likely to be successful. Toothpastes intended for pets are pleasantly flavored, and do not foam to the same extent as products intended for humans.

Herbal toothpaste for pets typically contains sage oil, which helps teeth to maintain their white coloration and keeps a cat's breath smelling fresh. Bad breath does not result exclusively from a problem affecting the teeth and gums, however, since it can also be linked to kidney problems.

Should the cat's gums appear badly inflamed, you should consult the vet, as it may be necessary to remove some teeth as well as clean off the tartar. The cat is likely to indicate its discomfort by eating reluctantly, and often salivating profusely.

Mercurius iodatus remedies are often favored to reduce inflammation, with the yellow or red form being used, depending on whether the right or left side of the mouth is worse affected. A potency of 30c, given three times daily for a week, is usually recommended in either case. When there are clear signs of ulceration, *Borax* may be the correct remedy, at a potency of 6c, given twice daily over a fortnight.

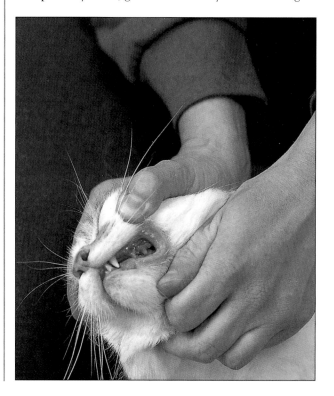

GUM INFLAMMATION

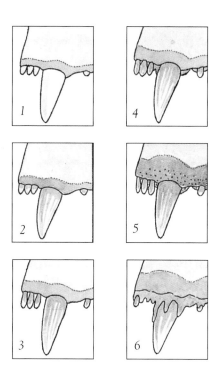

An inflammation of the gums is called gingivitis and often first shows where teeth and gums meet (1). It can be caused by a build-up of a hard coating of tartar on the teeth (2), which causes the gums to be pushed back (3), showing the base of the teeth and exposing pockets of space where food can collect (4). This is an ideal site for a secondary infection (5) and may lead to a more serious inflammation of the gums and a discharge (6). To remedy the situation, antibiotics, cleaning or even removal of the teeth and saline washes are needed.

Difficulty in Swallowing
When the cat has clear difficulty in swallowing, as distinct from chewing, an examination must be carried out to ensure this is not because of some physical obstruction at the back of the mouth. If the problem is an infection, the glands in the area are likely to be sore and swollen. *Aconitum* is often recommended for treatment at the outset, although

Tartar is formed on the teeth from an accumulation of food, bacteria, and substances in the salvia. If left untreated, the roots become infected, and the teeth become loose and painful.

Bowel nosodes are often a favored remedy in the treatment of diarrhea. Homoeopathy utilizes specially prepared nosodes to give protection against the main killer viral diseases of cats. Young cats, in particular, can benefit from nosodes.

a number of other remedies, including *Lachesis*, can be of value. A fur ball in the stomach can also have an adverse effect on a cat's appetite, as mentioned previously. Aside from mineral oil/liquid paraffin, *Nux vomica* is sometimes used for this condition.

Diarrhea and Its Aftermath

Occasional bouts of diarrhea may occur, especially in young kittens. Withholding rich foods and offering plain foods, such as a little chicken and rice, for example, will usually overcome the problem, but if your cat's condition shows signs of deterioration, veterinary advice should be sought. Again, a range of homoeopathic remedies can be used to treat diarrhea, with bowel nosodes often being favored.

Constipation can either precede or follow diarrhea, until the normal rhythm of the gut is restored. Dehydration can predispose a cat toward constipation, though it may also be a symptom of a systematic illness. A simple solution is to give olive oil on the cat's food as a laxative; homoeopathic remedies for the problem include *Bryonia*.

URINARY TRACT PROBLEMS

Spraying

One of the most widespread problems encountered with cats is their desire to spray urine indoors. This is usually a behavioral problem, rather than a medical one, being linked, in male cats, to territorial marking. Neutering may help to resolve the problem, but if this is not desired in the case of a breeding tom, then *Ustillago maydis* may be helpful. This homoeopathic remedy needs to be given three times a week, for a month, using a potency of 200c.

Spraying may continue for a period after neutering has been carried out, and *Staphisagria* can be useful at this stage, a dose of 7c being administered three times a day, for a week initially, although it can be continued at a higher potency less frequently for up to a month. It is also important to clean up thoroughly where the cat has been spraying so it will not be encouraged to reinforce the scent marking by spraying again in the same place.

Choose the disinfectant for the purpose carefully, because some simply reinforce the scent. White vinegar is suitable, in contrast to ammonia, which should be avoided. Bleach is also effective, depending on the surface concerned. Blot away as much of the urine as possible and wash the area several times, to remove all traces of urine. Should the condition persist, it may be necessary to resort to potentized hormones, such as *Folliculinum* and *Testosterone*, for a month.

The spraying of urine around the home and garden serves to mark a cat's territory.

375

THE URINARY SYSTEM

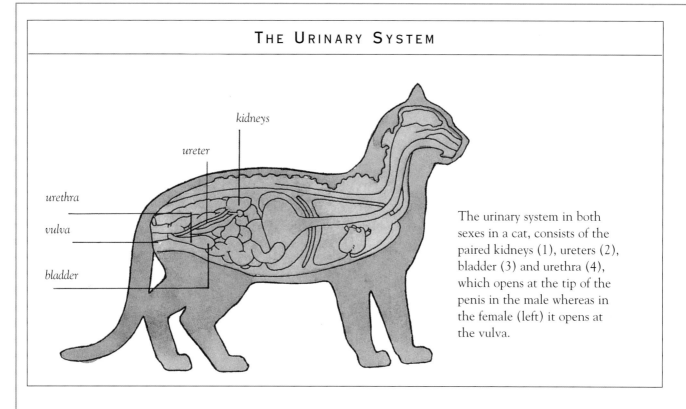

kidneys

ureter

urethra

vulva

bladder

The urinary system in both sexes in a cat, consists of the paired kidneys (1), ureters (2), bladder (3) and urethra (4), which opens at the tip of the penis in the male whereas in the female (left) it opens at the vulva.

A cat will crouch down with its back straight when urinating under normal circumstances.

Urinary Tract Blockage/FUS

Although it can be difficult with a cat that spends much of its time outside, you should try to check that it urinates without any apparent difficulty. A cat that attempts to urinate repeatedly, passes very little and cries out in pain is likely to be suffering from a blockage in the urinary tract. Rapid veterinary attention is essential, because the bladder could rupture, spilling urine into the abdominal cavity.

To help a cat recover from treatment for urinary stones, called calculi, and hopefully prevent any recurrence, *Hydrangea* can be useful at a potency of 30c. It should be given daily over a period of three weeks. A number of other homoeopathic remedies are also considered helpful to counter urolithiasis, as this problem is known. They include *Urtica urens* and *Calcarea phosphorica*, which may be used as a preventative in young cats.

Inflammation of the Bladder

Inflammation of the bladder, or cystitis, is another very painful condition, particularly in acute cases, and may produce similar symptoms to urolithiasis. *Aconitum* helps to overcome the pain when used at a potency of 10m. Five doses need to be given, at half hourly intervals, if there is a sign of any purulent material discoloring the urine.

Catching Urine Samples

In any problem involving the urinary tract, it is helpful to provide a urine sample for your vet, in order to establish the most satisfactory course of treatment. This will require forward planning on your part because cats rarely cooperate, particularly if they are in pain. Have ready a shallow container, such as a small disposable plate, covered with kitchen foil. When the cat squats in its litter tray to urinate, place the plate under its rear end and try to catch any urine.

You will also need a clean, screw-topped glass or plastic container, ideally one with a fairly narrow diameter – your vet will be able to provide you with a suitable receptacle if necessary. By carefully creating a funnel from the foil on the plate, you can channel the urine safely into the container.

On occasions, blood may be apparent in the urine. This is likely to be linked to a problem such as acute cystitis. Diagnosis of the urine will establish the cause and the treatment required and prevent the problem becoming chronic. If this occurs, the bladder walls become thickened, and the cat will urinate more frequently than usual, passing smaller volumes. You should always be on the alert for such signs if your cat has previously suffered from cystitis, because it is a condition that can recur.

Treating Kidney Infections

While kidney function invariably deteriorates as a cat becomes older, there is also a risk of kidney infections at any age. The cat will adopt a characteristically hunched posture, be reluctant to walk, and its back will be tender when touched.

While *Aconitum* is again potentially helpful to counter this discomfort, *Apis mellifica*, given at a potency of 10m, in four doses at hourly intervals, may bring more direct relief.

Eel serum can encourage urinary output, which makes it useful in cases of acute nephritis. A potency of 30c, given three times daily over a period of three days, is usually recommended in such cases.

Kidney Failure in Older Cats

In older cats, impairment of kidney function will be inevitable, and the typical symptoms associated with chronic nephritis will then become apparent. Weight loss may be most apparent, with the cat also suffering from halitosis (bad breath). By this stage, it is likely that at least 70 per cent of the kidney tissue is not working effectively, so that instead of being excreted from the body in urine, waste products of protein metabolism build up in the blood.

In addition, because the kidneys are no longer able to concentrate urine effectively, water is lost from the body, with the urine being dilute and of greater volume than normal. This makes the cat thirsty, and its fluid intake may well increase markedly, if it is not to suffer from dehydration. It may be sick, and appear rather dull, with its coat condition also deteriorating.

While there is no cure for kidney failure in old cats, you can help to alleviate the symptoms, by adjusting the cat's diet. You should reduce the amount of protein, so as to decrease the burden on the kidneys. Offer foods that have a higher carbohydrate content, if possible, although not all cats are keen to adapt their feeding habits. You should also supplement their vitamin intake, because water soluble vitamins are often lost through the kidneys.

Where there is ulceration in the mouth, and as a general treatment, *Natrum muriaticum* is often recommended as an effective relief from the symptoms. This needs to be given over a relatively long period, at progressively higher potencies, starting at 200c for a month, with the treatment being administered three times a week. Then the potency should be increased to 10m, for a similar duration, and finally Cm. Even so, it is important to bear in mind that, although there is no curative treatment available, it may be possible to stabilize the cat's condition, perhaps for a year or two, before there is a final, terminal decline.

Elderly cats are prone to kidney failure and, while there is no known cure for this condition, there are a number of things you can do to alleviate the symptoms.

Glomerulonephritis

Cats can sometimes suffer from another kidney complaint, known as glomerulonephritis. This condition results in the swelling of the lower parts of the limbs and the abdomen. This is an immune system disease and, although it can ultimately progress to chronic renal failure, treatment in the initial stages is very different from that for kidney failure. This is because glomerulonephritis causes a loss of protein from the body via the kidneys. As a result, a high-protein diet is indicated, to prevent the cat's condition deteriorating.

CARDIOVASCULAR COMPLAINTS

Actual heart disease is not especially common in cats, with the most common condition being cardiomyopathy, which is a failure of the heart muscle to pump effectively. This can give rise to blood clots forming within the circulatory system, because of the stasis of blood in the chambers of the heart. The clot may then be passed out into the arteries, causing a blockage, called a thrombosis.

Thrombosis

The most common site for a thrombosis in cats is where the aorta divides to supply the hind legs, giving rise to the condition known as iliac thrombosis. The loss of blood supply causes the limb to feel cold, and there is also no pulse.

Homoeopathic vets rely on a range of treatments derived from snake venom to deal with this condition and to break down the clot. These treatments often achieve excellent results. *Crotalus horridus* is widely used, being given at a high potency of 10m, twice daily over five days. *Secale* is then favored to ensure healthy blood flow continues, once the condition has been cured. A potency of 200c, given three times a week for a month, is usually advised in such cases.

Where pain and paralysis are highly evident, *Vipera* is a frequently used homoeopathic remedy. A dose with a potency of 1m should be given with the same frequency as recommended for *Secale*. If the left leg is more severely affected, with accompanying signs of cyanosis, reflected by a bluish discoloration of the skin, then *Lachesis* may be preferred. Treatment in this case is shorter, with a 30c potency being used twice daily for 10 days.

THE CAT'S CIRCULATORY SYSTEM

Blood clots in the terminal branches of the aorta, where it divides into the rear legs, are responsible for the condition known as iliac thrombosis. The aorta is part of the arterial system, shown in red, whereas the venous system is shown in blue.

Congenital heart disease covers a range of defects in the heart that are present at birth. These defects are very rare in cats – about 1 in 1000 kittens – and when they do occur may be mild and not cause any symptoms or illness, allowing the cat to lead a normal life.

A healthy appearance is no guarantee that a cat is not suffering from anaemia. A look at the mouth membranes will give some indication.

Valvular Problems

Valvular problems affecting the heart are decidedly uncommon in cats, but have been known. Again, veterinary diagnosis and treatment will be required. There are a number of homoeopathic treatments that may be of value in such cases. Where the cat may be suffering from breathlessness as well as an irregular pulse, then *Lycoplus* may be given. The potency in this case is 3x, being administered twice daily for 30 days. In contrast, if the pulse is weak and rapid, *Lilium tigrinum* is favored, using a potency of 3c. Two separate doses need to be given to the cat each day for 30 days.

Anaemia

A shortage of red blood cells in the circulatory system, known as anaemia, can result from a variety of causes. It may arise from blood loss as a result of injury, in which case it is called haemorrhagic anaemia. Provided that the blood flow can be stemmed, then the cat should recover uneventfully.

The use of a coagulant will help to stem the loss of blood before it becomes life-threatening. The lack of oxygen in the circulatory system, resulting from the shortage of red blood cells, causes weakness. This can also arise from warfarin poisoning, in which the poison interferes with the blood clotting mechanisms and results in spontaneous haemorrhages. The lack of red blood cells in the circulation can result also in the inside of the mouth being very pale, although because the mucous membranes and gums of most cats are often pale, this need not be a sign of anaemia.

The red blood cells themselves are produced in bone marrow, and any disease affecting this tissue can result in a depressed output of red blood cells and lead to what is known as hypoplastic anaemia. This can result either from dietary deficiencies of the key

NEVER USE ASPIRIN!

Cats cannot break down a number of drugs very effectively in the liver, thereby detoxifying them. These may then accumulate, and exert a harmful effect on the bone marrow. Aspirin is among the most dangerous of these drugs and is toxic to cats. Not only is it likely to cause haemorrhaging, especially in the gastrointestinal tract, but it also depresses bone marrow activity, to the extent that red blood cells cannot be replaced. Aspirin should therefore never be given to cats. The antibiotic chloramphenicol also has a depressant effect on a cat's bone marrow.

ingredients needed for the manufacture of red blood cells, such as iron, or because of the toxic effects of some drugs. The effects are unlikely to be evident in the short term, because red blood cells have a life-span of just under 12 weeks.

If a cat is suspected to be suffering from anaemia, a blood test to establish the type of anaemia is an essential first step. In some cases, the red blood cells may actually be destroyed directly in the circulation, as the result of a parasitic infection, for example, or as the result of poisoning, giving rise to the condition known as haemolytic anaemia. Treatment must then be directed to resolving the individual cause, although the use of vitamin supplements, particularly vitamin E and the B group vitamins, can be of help in all cases.

Anaemia can also be a complication associated with Feline Leukemia Virus. This is because the virus can damage both the haemapoetic tissue in the bones, and may also destroy red blood cells directly. The prognosis in such cases is very poor.

RESPIRATORY PROBLEMS

Viral Infections

The most serious respiratory disorders in cats are the result of viral infections, such as Feline Viral Rhinotracheitis (FVR). All cats should receive protection against such infections, which can be serious and result in long-term complications.

It has become increasingly clear in recent years that aside from viruses, chlamydia can be an important component of respiratory disease in cats. The resulting infection, known as chlamydiosis, typically affects the upper respiratory tract, causing an often severe conjunctivitis and an unpleasant rhinitis as well, with young kittens often displaying the most severe symptoms. There is a risk that this infection could also be transmissible to people, so care should be taken when dealing with a sick cat. Always wash your hands thoroughly immediately after handling the cat.

Bathing the eyes is important, so that the cat can continue to see without too much difficulty. *Argentum nitricum*, administered at a potency of 30c, can be of use under such circumstances. A daily dose for 10 days will be required.

Bacterial contamination will almost inevitably result in the rhinitis becoming muco-purulent; again, bathing of the nostrils will be important in assisting the cat's recovery. *Kali bichromicum* is valuable in cases of nasal congestion, with a potency of 200c. The dose needs to be given twice a week for a month to assist recovery. Where chlamydiosis is confirmed, there is a nosode available, which needs to be given daily for 10 days. The potency normally recommended is 30c, and it can be administered alongside specific remedies.

Protection against the killer viral diseases will be essential if your cat is to go into a cattery for any period of time. You will need to provide veterinary certification to this effect.

23323431411

Respiratory infections may give rise to longer term complications such as sinusitis, as in the case of this cat above. Ensuring that your cat maintains its appetite is important through this type of illness.

Sinusitis

It is not uncommon for some breeds, especially the Oriental ones, including the Siamese, which have encountered a respiratory infection early in life, to be left with chronic sinusitis. This condition flares up from time to time, resulting in an unpleasant discharge from the nostrils.

It can be a difficult problem to overcome, whatever method of treatment is used. When a bout does occur, *Lemna minor*, at a potency of 6c, given three times daily over five days may lead to a speedy resolution, and can stop any accompanying sneezing. Another remedy that may be advised for sinusitis is *Silicea*, which can help to overcome stubborn cases. A dose of 200c potency needs to be given three times a week for a month.

Pharyngitis

Other upper respiratory tract problems that may arise include pharyngitis, in which the pharyngeal region becomes swollen, usually as the result of infection, making it difficult for the cat to swallow easily. This condition may well be accompanied by a temperature raised above the cat's normal figure of about 38.6°C (101.5°F).

Mercurius cyanatus, at a potency of 30c, can relieve pharyngitis. The dose is given twice daily over a three-day period. If symptoms are noticeable elsewhere, affecting the eyes for example, then *Rhus toxicodendron* may be indicated. A potency of 1m will need to be given in a daily dose for two weeks. In chronic or refractory cases, a *Streptococcus* nosode can be used as well, in the form of a 30c dose administered each day for five days.

Laryngitis, resulting in the cat losing its voice, may also occur, sometimes being so severe that the cat has difficulty in swallowing. There are several treatments that can be applied, depending on the degree of infection. *Apis mellifica* may be administered in cases where the area is badly swollen. If the cat is coughing, but not producing mucus, then *Spongia tosta* may be the preferred remedy, while in more extreme cases, *Drosera rotundifolia* might be recommended. *Calcarea fluorica* is recommended to assist the healing process, being given at a potency of 30c, three times a week for a month. Garlic tablets are also considered beneficial to assist recovery from upper respiratory tract ailments, either alone or in combination with fenugreek.

Lung Disease

Cats that show symptoms of labored breathing or dyspnoea are very likely to be suffering from lung disease. This calls for detailed veterinary investigation, and if there is fluid involved, a sample may be required for examination. The symptoms may result from an accident, an infection or even a tumor or heart disease.

The remedy must clearly address the cause, but where there is an accumulation of fluid in the lung, described as oedema, then *Apis mellifica* is recommended to aid resorption and make it easier for the cat to breathe normally. A potency of 6x, given four times daily for a 10-day period, should be adequate. More specific remedies may be required, if heart disease, for example, is found to be the cause.

Should the lung be inflamed, then *Antimonium tartaricum* can bring relief, especially where there is mucus. A 30c potency administered twice a day for a week is often recommended. Should there be accompanying pleurisy, as well as pneumonia, treatments such as *Bryonia* may be required.

The temperature of a cat is usually taken rectally with a well-lubricated thermometer. However, it is not a procedure that is taken to kindly by most cats, and it is probably best left to the vet.

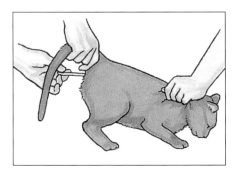

REPRODUCTIVE PROBLEMS

Cats can breed for most of the year, although there is a quiescent period extending from late autumn to mid-winter, when queens are most unlikely to conceive. The age at which reproductive maturity is attained may be as early as four months in the case of precocious breeds such as Siamese, while in larger breeds, such as Persian Longhairs, breeding may not begin until they are 18 months old. Cats tend to have smaller litters as they grow older.

If cats appear to be infertile, it is important to find the cause, and whether the problem rests with the male or female. Obviously, introducing them at the wrong time of year is unlikely to result in pregnancy. However, when a queen repeatedly fails to conceive successfully, a number of remedies can be used.

Sepia officinalis, given at a 200c potency once a week for three weeks, should help to improve hormonal activity and so allow mating to proceed successfully. In the case of Siamese, *Platina* is considered the most suitable homoeopathic remedy, because the breed exhibits qualities associated with this treatment. A 30c potency given three times a week for two weeks is recommended. In the case of male infertility, a herbal combination of damiana (*Turnera diffusa*) and Kola tablets are useful tonics.

If the cat has a history of previous spontaneous abortions during pregnancy, *Viburnum opulis* will be of value in the first month. It should be a potency of 30c, given twice weekly through this stage. Subsequently, *Caulophyllum* should be given, and can also be used in the case of a difficult birth, with one dose being given every 30 minutes for two hours.

Arnica montana is valued for helping to ensure a rapid recovery after birth, and is given at a potency of 30c, in three doses each day for two days before the birth is due. A queen's pregnancy typically lasts about 64 days, but it can vary slightly, lasting for either a slightly longer or shorter period.

Herbalists favor the use of raspberry leaf, usually in tablet form, as a means of ensuring an easy birth and assisting the queen's recovery. This is typically administered from the third week following mating until a week after the kittens are born.

If the queen appears to have difficulty in producing sufficient milk for her litter, *Urtica urens*, in the form of a 30c potency given three times daily for five days is often helpful. Other remedies that can be used on a similar basis include *Ustilago maydis* and *Agnus castus*.

Should the cause of the problem be mastitis, with the mammary glands being inflamed and swollen, then *Phytolacca decandra*, administered in 30c potency, initially three times a day for three days and then on alternate days, should help to give relief.

Belladonna (6c) may help if the gland is badly inflamed, with five doses being given at two-hourly intervals. In long-standing cases, a better resolution may be a 200c potency *Silicea* preparation, administered twice weekly over a six-week period.

Cats remain fertile throughout their lives. However, they tend to have smaller litters as they grow older.

A young ginger cat, washing on the bedspread

HEALTH CARE AND NUTRITIONAL REFERENCE GUIDE

This section of the book summarizes the main homoeopathic treatments and the various bowel nosodes, as well as giving information about key ingredients of a cat's diet, in terms of vitamins, minerals and trace elements. In all cases of treatment, however, you should be guided by a homoeopathic vet. In terms of diet, if you are using fresh foods, variety is generally the key to ensuring that your cat remains healthy and should not develop any nutritional deficiencies. Again, your vet will be able to advise you if you have any particular concerns about feeding your cat, or in terms of using vitamin and mineral supplements. Overdosing with such products can be harmful.

Many cats today are benefiting because their owners favor a natural approach to health care.

VITAMINS, MINERALS AND TRACE ELEMENTS

The following tables summarize the key ingredients required in a cat's diet, how these can be obtained from different foods, and their functions in the body.

VITAMIN	DIETARY SOURCES FOR CATS	TYPICAL FUNCTIONS
FAT SOLUBLE GROUP	STORED IN THE LIVER WITH ANY EXCESS LIKELY TO BE HARMFUL	
PRE-FORMED A	BUTTER, CHEESE, EGG YOLK, LIVER, COD LIVER OIL, WHOLE MILK	Improves resistance to infection. Healthy vision. Assists protein synthesis. Important also for healthy skin, coat, and respiratory system.
VITAMIN D	DAIRY PRODUCTS, EGG YOLK, COD LIVER OIL	Absorption of calcium and phosphorus from the intestinal tract and metabolism in the body. Healthy bones and teeth. Growth and production of thyroid hormones.
VITAMIN E	EGG YOLK, WHEATGERM AND OTHER VARIOUS OILS SUCH AS SUNFLOWER, SAFFLOWER AND SESAME OILS, DARK GREEN VEGETABLES	Protects vital components of the body against oxidation. Helps to assist normal functioning of the reproductive system. Assists pancreatic function. Helps to prevent blood clots in the circulatory system.
VITAMIN K	WHOLE MILK, EGGS, FISH LIVER OILS, KELP, MEAT, POLYUNSATURATED OILS	Assists liver function, and the health of the body's blood clotting mechanism.
WATER-SOLUBLE GROUP	NOT GENERALLY STORED IN THE BODY TO ANY SIGNIFICANT EXTENT	
B GROUP COMPRISING: **B1 (THIAMINE)** **B2 (RIBOFLAVIN)** **B3 (NICOTINIC ACID)** **B5 (PANTOTHENIC ACID)** **B6 (PYRIDOXINE)** **B12 (CYANOCOBALAMIN)** **BIOTIN, INOSITOL,** **CHLOLINE,** **PABA FOLIC ACID**	BREWER'S YEAST AND EXTRACTS, EGG YOLK, DAIRY PRODUCTS, WHEATGERM, FISH, OFFAL (Supplements contain all members of the group, with brewer's yeast and extract being most valuable for this purpose)	Important in many metabolic processes in the body. Significant for healthy red blood cells.
VITAMIN C (ASCORBIC ACID)	FRUIT AND VEGETABLES INCLUDING PARSLEY, WATERCRESS, AND ROSEHIPS	Helps the body's resistance to disease. Also leads to healthy teeth and bones, and of value to the circulatory system.

VITAMIN	DIETARY SOURCES FOR CATS	TYPICAL FUNCTIONS
CALCIUM	MILK, WHEATGERM, CHEESE, BREWER'S YEAST	Healthy skeletal structure and blood clotting, as well as muscular contractions.
CHROMIUM (TRACE ELEMENT)	LIVER, CHEESE, BREWER'S YEAST	Immune system. Brain and nervous functions.
COPPER (TRACE ELEMENT)	MEAT, BREWER'S YEAST, CEREALS	Blood, healthy pigmentation absorption of iron and various metabolic processes.
IODINE (TRACE ELEMENT)	KELP, GARLIC, MILK, SEAFOODS, EGGS	Production of thyroid hormones, which have a key role in the body's metabolism.
IRON	BREWER'S YEAST, EGG YOLK, LIVER, LEAN MEAT, WATERCRESS	Vital for haemoglobin – the oxygen-carrying component of red blood cells, with a deficiency causing anaemia.
MAGNESIUM	FISH, SEAFOODS, WHEATGERM, BREWER'S YEAST	Helps to protect against stress. Important for synthesis of hormones, and assists healing.
MANGANESE (TRACE ELEMENT)	OFFAL, WATERCRESS, SEAWEED, WHEATGERM	Vital for the correct functioning of the brain and nervous system. Also has metabolic functions.
PHOSPHORUS	EGGS, DAIRY PRODUCTS, OFFAL, WHEATGERM, BREWER'S YEAST	Present in every living cell forming phosphotipid membranes, and occurs in association with calcium in the musculo-skeletal system. Vital for various metabolic processes as well.
POTASSIUM	KELP, GREEN, LEAFY VEGETABLES, WHEATGERM	Essential for muscle contraction and cell metabolism, also for the transmission of nerve impulses.
SELENIUM (TRACE ELEMENT)	FISH, BROWN RICE, EGGS, GARLIC, BREWER'S YEAST	Important especially for male reproductive tract and protecting against oxidative processes, which could destroy fat soluble vitamins, for example, in conjunction with Vitamin E.
SODIUM	SALE, YEAST EXTRACTS, BACON, KELP, SMOKED FISH AND MANY PROCESSED FOODS	Regulates acidity level of the blood, ensures muscle contractility and transmission of nerve impulses. Maintains body's osmotic pressure.
ZINC	BROWN RICE, HERRING, BREWER'S YEAST, EGGS, SEAFOOD AND DAIRY PRODUCTS	Correct functioning of the reproductive system. Assists the healing process, glandular activity and metabolic processes.

A–Z OF HOMOEOPATHIC REMEDIES

This table sets out a range of homoeopathic treatments, their origins and the likely ailments that they can be used to treat. Homoeopathy tends to be used more widely in veterinary medicine than herbalism, because treatments are often easier to administer, and dosing is less arduous.

SOURCE	COMPONENT	APPLICATIONS
ABIES CANADENSIS (HEMLOCK SPRUCE)	BARK AND BUDS	Digestive ailments
ABROTANUM (SOUTHERNWOOD)	FRESH LEAVES	Joint ailments Intestinal parasites
ABSINTHUM (WORMWOOD)	–	Epilepsy and disorders of the central nervous system
ACHILLEA MILLEFOLIUM (YARROW)	WHOLE PLANT	Haemorrhaging
ACIDUM SALICYLICUM (SALICYLIC ACID)	POWDER	Joint ailments Gastric haemorrhage
ACONITUM NAPELLUS (MONKSHOOD)	WHOLE PLANT	Shock
ACTAEA RACEMOSA (BLACK SNAKE ROOT)	RESIN	Muscular ailments
ADONIS VERNALIS (FALSE HELLEBORE)	WHOLE PLANT	Cardiac and respiratory disorders
AESCULUS HIPPOCASTANUM (HORSE CHESTNUT)	ENTIRE SEED CAPSULE	Liver ailments and cardiac disease
AGARICUS MUSCARIUS (FLY AGARIC)	WHOLE FUNGUS	Joint ailments Muscular cramp
AGNUS CASTUS (CHASTE TREE)	RIPE BERRIES	Sexual problems
ALETRIS FARINOSA (STAR GRASS)	ROOT SYSTEM	Female reproductive disorders
ALLIUM CEPA (ONION)	ENTIRE PLANT	Upper respiratory tract infections
ALUMEN (POTASH ALUM)	CRYSTALS	Central nervous system disorders
AMMONIUM CARBONICUM (AMMONIUM CARBONATE)	SALT	Respiratory conditions
AMMONIUM CAUSTICUM (HYDRATE OF AMMONIA)	SALT	Respiratory and cardiac complaints
ANGUSTURA VERA	BARK	Musculo-skeletal problems
ANTIMONIUM ARSENICOSUM (ARSENATE OF ANTIMONY)	SALT	Pneumonia and other respiratory complaints such as emphysema

SOURCE	COMPONENT	APPLICATIONS
ANTIMONIUM CRUDUM (SULPHIDE OF ANTIMONY)	SALT	Skin swellings
ANTIMONIUM TARTARICUM (TARTAR EMETIC)	SALT	Respiratory system ailments
APIS MELLIFICA (BEE VENOM)	WHOLE INSECT OR VENOM	Swellings
APOCYNUM CANNABINUM (INDIAN HEMP)	WHOLE PLANT	Respiratory and cardiac problems Uro-gentical system disorders
ARGENTUM NITRICUM (SILVER NITRATE)	SALT	Ophthalmic ailments and blood disorders
ARNICA MONTANA (LEOPARD'S BANE)	WHOLE PLANT	Injuries, bruising and haemorrhages
ARSENICUM ALBUM (ARSENIC TRIOXIDE)	SALT	Coccidiosis and skin ailments
ARSENICUM IODATUM (IODIDE OF ARSENIC)	SALT	Respiratory problems refractory to other remedies
ATROPINUM (BELLADONNA ALKALOID)		Ophthalmic conditions
BAPTISIA TINCTORIA (WILD INDISO)	BARK AND ROOT	Septicaemic conditions
BARYTA CARBONICA (BARIUM CARBONATE)	SALT	Respiratory system ailments
BARYTA MURIATICA (BARIUM CHLORIDE)	SALT	Ear infections Glandular swellings
BELLADONNA (DEADLY NIGHTSHADE)	WHOLE PLANT WHEN IN FLOWER	Fever
BELLIS PERENNIS (DAISY)	WHOLE PLANT	Muscular ailments including sprains and bruises
BENZOICUM ACIDUM (BENZOIC ACID)	GUM	Urinary tract problems
BERBERRIES VULGARIS (BARBERRY)	ROOT BARK	Liver and kidney ailments, especially where there is jaundice
BERYLLIUM	METAL	Viral pneumonia
BOTHROPS LANCEOLATUS (YELLOW VIPER)	VENOM	Haemorrhages of septic causation Prevention of gangrene
BROMIUM (BROMINE)	SOLUTION	Laryngeal and mucous membrane ailments of the respiratory tract
BRYONIA ALBA (WHITE BRYONY)	ROOTS, BEFORE FLOWERING OCCURS	Respiratory diseases
BUFO BUFO (COMMON TOAD)	SKIN VENOM	Epilepsy and hyper-sexuality

SOURCE	COMPONENT	APPLICATIONS
CACTUS GRANDIFLORUS (NIGHT-BLOOMING CEREUS)	STEMS AND FLOWERS	Cardio-vascular disease
CALCAREA CARBONICA (CALCIUM CARBONATE)	SALT	Skeletal problems
CALCAREA FLUORICA (FLUORSPAR)	SALT	Bone diseases such as actinobacillosis
CALCAREA IODATA (CALCIUM IODIDE)	SALT	Glandular disease
CALCAREA PHOSPHORICA (CALCIUM PHOSPHATE)	SALT	Musculo-skeletal disorders, especially of kittens
CALC, RENALIS PHOSPH CALC, RENALIS URIC	SALTS	Stones in the urinary tract, often in conjunction with other remedies
CALENDULA OFFICINALIS (MARIGOLD)	LEAVES AND FLOWERS	Wounds, ulcers, eye ailments
CAMPHORA (CAMPHOR)	GUM	Enteritis, especially caused by Salmonella bacteria
CANNABIS SATIVA (AMERICAN HEMP)	FLOWERING TOPS	Cardiac and urinary problems
CANTHARIS (SPANISH FLY)	WHOLE INSECT	Kidney and bladder inflammation
CAPSELLA BURSA-PASTORIS (SHEPHERD'S PURSE)	WHOLE PLANT	Cystitis
CARBO VEGETABILIS (VEGETABLE CHARCOAL)	BURNT PLANT MATERIAL	Venous circulatory disorders
CARDUUS MARIANUS (ST MARY'S THISTLE)	SEEDS	Liver ailments, especially cirrhosis
CAULOPHYLLUM (BLUE COHOSH)	ROOT	Female reproductive tract problems
CAUSTICUM (POTASSIUM HYDROXIDE)	SALT	Neuro-muscular system disorders
CEANOTHUS AMERICANUS (NEW JERSEY TEA)	FRESH LEAVES	Splenic conditions
CHELIDONIUM (GREATER CELANDINE)	WHOLE PLANT AT FLOWERING STAGE	Jaundice and other liver ailments
CHIMAPHILLA UMBELLATA (GROUND HOLLY)	WHOLE PLANT	Uro-genital tract problems
CHININUM SULPHURICUM (SULPHATE OF QUININE)	SALT	Ear and other recurrent infections
CHIONANTHUS VIRGINICA (FRINGE TREE)	SALT	Liver ailments cirrhosis
CICUTA VIROSA (WATER HEMLOCK)	ROOT DURING FLOWERING PERIOD	Nervous diseases

SOURCE	COMPONENT	APPLICATIONS
CINCHONA OFFICINALIS (PERUVIAN BARK)	BARK	Debility and fluid loss
CINERARIA MARITIMA (DUSTY MILLER)	WHOLE PLANT	Ophthalmic conditions
CINNABARIS (MERCURIC SULPHIDE)	SALT	Ophthalmic conditions Superficial uro-genital complaints
COCCULUS (INDIAN COCKLE)	SEEDS	Travel sickness
COCCUS CACTI (COCHINEAL)	BODIES OF FEMALE INSECTS	Respiratory and urinary tract ailments
COLCHICUM AUTUMNALE (MEADOW SAFFRON)	BULB	Allergies and anti-inflammatory treatment
COLOCYNTHIS (BITTER CUCUMBER)	FRUIT	Digestive disturbances, especially diarrhea
CONDURANGO (CONDOR PLANT)	BARK	Internal malignancies
CONVALLARIA MAJORIS (LILY OF THE VALLEY)	WHOLE PLANT	Valvular heart disease
COPAIVA (BALSAM OF PERU)	BALSAM	Pyelonephritis, cystitis and urethritis
CORNIUM MACULATUM (HEMLOCK)	WHOLE PLANT	Paralysis
CRATAEGUS (HAWTHORN)	RIPE FRUIT	Arrhythmic heart conditions
CROTALUS HORRIDUS (RATTLESNAKE)	VENOM	Septicaemia and snake-bite
CROTON TIGLIUM	SEEDS	Digestive disturbances especially diarrhea
CUBEBA OFFICINALIS (CUBEBS)	UNRIPE FRUIT	Uro-genital problems
CUPRUM ACETICIUM (COPPER ACETATE)	SALT	Muscle weakness
CUPRUM METALLICIUM (COPPER)	METAL	Central nervous system disorders especially epilepsy
CURARE (ARROW POISON)	FROG'S SKIN	Muscular paralysis
DATURA STRAMONIUM (THORN APPLE)	WHOLE FRESH PLANT AND ITS FRUIT	Central nervous system disorders, where sense of balance is affected
DIGITALIS PURPUREA (FOXGLOVE)	LEAVES	Cardiac failure resulting from valvular disorders
DROSERA ROTUNDIFOLIA (SUNDEW)	WHOLE PLANT	Lymphatic conditions Inflammation of the larynx

SOURCE	COMPONENT	APPLICATIONS
ECHINACEA ANGUSTIFOLIA (RUDBECKIA)	WHOLE PLANT	Septicaemia and toxaemia
EEL SERUM	SERUM	Toxaemia and kidney disorders
EPIGEA REPENS (TRAILING ARBUTUS)	FRESH LEAVES	Urethral and bladder stones
EUPHRASIA OFFICINALIS (EYEBRIGHT)	WHOLE PLANT	Conjunctivitis, corneal ulceration
FERRUM IODATUM (IODIDE OF IRON)	SALT	Iron deficiency
FERRUM PHOSPHORICUM (FERRIC PHOSPHATE)	SALT	Febrile illnesses Pulmonary congestion
FICUS RELIGIOSA (RUBBER PLANT)	LEAVES	Haemorrhages. Also sometimes coccidiosis
FLUORICUM ACIDUM (HYDROFLUORIC ACID)	SALT	Ulcers; necrotic bone disease
FORMICA (FORMIC ACID)	LIVE ANTS	Joint ailments
GELSEMIUM SEMPERVIRENS (YELLOW JASMINE)	ROOT BARK	Muscle tremors and resulting weakness
GLONOINUM (NITROGLYCERINE)	CHEMICAL	Heat stroke
GRAPHITES (BLACK LEAD)	CHEMICAL	Eczema
HAMAMELIS VIRGINICA (WITCH HAZEL)	FRESH BARK OF TWIGS AND ROOTS	Bruising Venous system disorders
HECLA LAVA (HECLA)	VOLCANIC ASH	Bone tumors; dental disease
HELLEBORUS NIGER (CHRISTMAS ROSE)	ROOT JUICE	Cardiac rhythm disorders
HEPAR SULPHURIS CALCAREUM (IMPURE CALCIUM SULPHIDE)	CALCIUM CARBONATE BURNT WITH FLOWERS OF SULPHUR	Purulent conditions
HYDRANGEA ARBORESCENS (HYDRANGEA)	FRESH YOUNG SHOOTS AND LEAVES	Urolithasis
HYDRASTIS CANADENSIS (GOLDEN SEAL)	ROOT	Catarrhal and other mucopurulent discharges
HYDROCOTYLE ASIATICA (INDIAN PENNYWORT)	WHOLE PLANT	Skin ailments Female genital disorders
HYOSCYAMUS NIGER (HENBANE)	WHOLE PLANT	Hyperexcitability
HYPERICUM PERFORATUM (ST JOHN'S WORT)	WHOLE PLANT	Nerve damage linked to lacerated wounds. Spinal injury in the coccygeal area

SOURCE	COMPONENT	APPLICATIONS
IODIUM **(IODINE)**	TINCTURE	Ovarian problems. Glandular treatments, especially for the thyroid
IPECACUANHA	DRIED ROOT	Haemorrhages and use post-partum
IRIS VERSICOLOR **(BLUE FLAG)**	FRESH ROOT	Glandular disorders, especially those affecting the pancreas
KALI ARSENICUM **(POTASSIUM ARSENITE)**	SALT	Eczema and other skin conditions
KALI BICHROMICUM **(POTASSIUM DICHROMATE)**	SALT	Sinusitis, broncho-pneumonia and pyelonephritis
KALI CARBONICUM **(POTASSIUM CARBONATE)**	SALT	Weakness
KALI CHLORICUM **(POTASSIUM CHLORATE)**	SALT	Urinary tract problems
KALI HYDRIODICUM **(POTASSIUM IODIDE)**	SALT	Ophthalmic and respiratory disorders
KREOSOTUM **(BEECHWOOD CREOSOTE)**	SOLUTION	Ulceration and likely gangrenous states
LACHESIS **(BUSHMASTER)**	VENOM	Haemorrhage and sepsis
LATHYRUS SATIVUS **(CHICK PEA)**	FLOWER AND SEED PODS	Local paralysis and possible mineral deficiencies
LEDIUM PALUSTRE **(MARSH TEA)**	WHOLE PLANT	Eye injuries and puncture wounds
LEMNA MINOR **(DUCKWEED)**	WHOLE PLANT	Catarrhal complications and flatulence
LILIUM TIGRINUM **(TIGER LILY)**	LEAVES AND FLOWERS	Pyometra
LITHIUM CARBONICUM **(LITHIUM CARBONATE)**	SALT	Arthritis and some urinary ailments
LOBELIA INFLATA **(INDIAN TOBACCO)**	DRIED LEAVES	Emphysema and as a recovery stimulant
LYCOPLUS VIRGINICUS **(BUGLE WEED)**	WHOLE PLANT	Cardiac problems and raised blood pressure
LYCOPODIUM CLAVATUM **(CLUB MOSS)**	SPORES	Pneumonia, alopecia and loss of appetite resulting from liver problems
MAGNESIA PHOSPHIRICA **(PHOSPHATE OF MAGNESIUM)**	SALT	Muscular spasms
MELILOTUS **(SWEET CLOVER)**	WHOLE PLANT	Haemorrhaging
MERCURIUS **(MERCURIUS SOLUBILIS)**	METAL	Anaemia and diarrhea

Cats are often involved in cat fights. Marsh tea (Ledum palustre) is a homoeopathic remedy for eye injuries and puncture wounds.

SOURCE	COMPONENT	APPLICATIONS
MERCURIUS CORROSIVUS **(MERCURIC CHLORIDE)**	SALT	More potent than mercurius; possibly useful for coccidiosis
MERCURIUS CYANATUS **(CYANATE OF MERCURY)**	SALT	Toxic conditions, arising from bacterial infections
MERCURIUS DULCIS **(CALOMEL)**	SALT	Ear and liver ailments; including mild cirrhosis
MERCURIUS IODATUS FLAVUS **(YELLOW IODIDE OF MERCURY)**	SALT	Salivary gland swellings and similar glandular disorder
MERCURIUS IODATUS RUBER **(RED IODIDE OF MERCURY)**	SALT	Muscular stiffness in the neck and glandular swellings
MUREX PURPUREA **(CUTTLEFISH)**	INK SAC	Regulates female reproductive cycle and counters cystic ovaries
MURIATIC ACID **(HYDROCHLORIC ACID)**	SOLUTION	Septicaemia and ulceration
NAJA TRIPUDIANS **(COBRA)**	VENOM	Cardiac problems resulting in oedema
NATRUM MURIATICUM **(SODIUM CHLORIDE)**	SALT	Chronic nephritis and anaemia
NATRUM SULPHORICUM **(NITRIC ACID)**	SALT	Liver ailments; head injuries
NUX VOMICA **(POISON NUT)**	SEEDS	Digestive problems
OCIMUM CANUM	LEAVES	Urinary complaints
OPIUM **(POPPY)**	POWDER	Nervous system disorders
PALLADIUM	METAL	Female reproductive system especially for inflamed ovaries
PANCREAS	GLANDULAR EXTRACT	Pancreatic disorders
PAREIRA **(VELVET LEAF)**	FRESH ROOT	Bladder stones
PETROLEUM **(ROCK SPIRIT)**	OIL	Dry skin and eczema
PHOSPHORICUM ACIDUM **(PHOSPHORIC ACID)**	SOLUTION	Combats diarrhea and flatulence
PHOSPHORUS	ELEMENT	Wide-ranging
PHYTOLACCA DECANDRA **(PORE ROOT)**	WHOLE PLANT	Glandular swellings, especially mastitis
PLATINA **(PLATINUM)**	METAL	Female genital tract; inflamed ovaries
PLUMBUM METALLICUM **(LEAD)**	METAL	Renal deterioration with hepatic involvement. Central nervous system disorders

SOURCE	COMPONENT	APPLICATIONS
PODOPHYLLUM PELTATUM (MAY APPLE)	WHOLE PLANT	Gastro-intestinal conditions affecting kittens
PTELEA (WATER ASH)	ROOT OR BARK	Stomach and liver ailments
PULSATILLA (ANEMONE)	WHOLE FLOWERING PLANT	Catarrh and some female reproductive disorders
RANUNCULUS BULBOSUS (BUTTERCUP)	WHOLE PLANT	Muscular ailments and skin conditions
RHODODENDRON (SNOW ROSE)	FRESH LEAVES	Stiffness and orchitis
RHUS TOXICODENDRON (POISON OAK)	FRESH LEAVES	Muscle and joint ailments and some skin conditions
RUMEX CRISPUS (YELLOW DOCK)	FRESH ROOT	Respiratory and digestive ailments, reducing the discharge from mucous membranes
RUTA GRAVEOLENS (RUE)	WHOLE FRESH PLANT	May facilitate labor, also used to assist rectal prolapses
SABINA (SAVINE)	OIL	Uterine conditions
SANGUINARIA (BLOOD ROOT)	FRESH ROOT	Circulatory congestive conditions and female reproductive tract disorders
SECALE CORNUTUM (ERGOT OF RYE)	FRESH FUNGUS	Smooth muscle conditions affecting the uterus, including post-partum haemorrhage
SEPIA OFFICINALIS (CUTTLEFISH)	DRIED LIQUID FROM INK SAC	Ringworm Encouraging maternal instincts
SILICEA (PURE FLINT)	ELEMENT	Bone disorders
SODIUM BIBORATE (BORAX)	SALT	Stomatitis and gastro-intestinal tract irritations
SOLANUM DULCAMARA (WOODY NIGHTSHADE)	FRESH STEMS AND LEAVES BEFORE FLOWERING	Ringworm and kidney ailments
SOLIDAGO VIRGA (GOLDEN ROD)	WHOLE FRESH PLANT	Renal problems
SPIGELIA (PINK ROOT)	DRIED HERB	Ophthalmic conditions
SPONGIA TOSTA (ROASTED SPONGE)	WHOLE ANIMAL	Disorders of lymphatic system and cardiac treatment
SQUILLA MARITIMA (SEA ONION)	DRIED BULB	Heart and kidney ailments with signs of dropsy
STAPHIS AGRIA	SEEDS	Hormonal eczema; cystitis
STROPHANTHUS (ONAGE)	SEEDS	Diuretic; improves heart action

Source	Component	Applications
STRYCHINUM	Solution	Disorders of the central nervous system
SULFONAL (COAL TAR DERIVATIVE)	Solution	Central nervous system conditions affecting the state of balance
SULPHUR	Element	Skin conditions including eczema and mange
SYMPHYTUM OFFICINALE (COMFREY)	Whole plant	Fractures and for ophthalmic conditions
SYZYGIUM (JUMBUL)	Seeds	Pancreatic disorders, especially diabetes mellitus
TABACUM (TOBACCO)	Plant	Travel sickness
TARANTULA HISPANICA (SPANISH SPIDER)	Whole arthropod	Excitement and excessive libido in tom cats
TELLURIUM	Metal	Conjunctivitis and ear ailments
TEREBINTHINAE (OIL OF TURPENTINE)	Solution	Haemorrhaging and nephritis
THALLIUM ACETAS	Salt	Alopecia and other skin conditions
THUJA OCCIDENTALIS (ARBOR VITAE)	Fresh twigs	Warty growths and related skin conditions
TURNERA DIFFUSA (DAMIANA)		Encourages libido
URANIUM NITRICUM (URANIUM NITRATE)	Solution	Pancreatitis; often in combination with *Iris versicolor*
URTICA URENS (STINGING NETTLE)	Fresh plant	Urinary tract problems
USTILLAGO MAYDIS (CORN SMUT)	Fungi	Uterine conditions; alopecia
UVA URSI (BEARBERRY)	Dried leaves and fruit	Disorders of the urinary tract, notably cystitis and pyelonephritis
VERATRUM ALBUM (WHITE HELLEBORE)	Roots	Cases of collapse
VIBURNUM OPULIS (WATER ELDER)	Fresh bark	Smooth muscle problems; for countering repeated spontaneous abortions
VIPERA (COMMON VIPER)	Venom	Oedema with venous congestion, making it useful in some liver conditions as well
ZINCUM METALLICUM (ZINC)	Metal	Fever and anaemia

Bowel Nosodes

Nosodes are obtained from an animal afflicted with the disease for which the remedy is needed. As a group they can be used both to prevent and to treat diseases. Bowel nosodes tend to be used in long-standing cases of illness, affecting particular body systems, where several other remedies could be indicated, because of the range of symptoms. High potencies are less favored for bowel nosodes than with many homoeopathic remedies. Also, after a course of treatment, there is usually an interval of several months before the nosode is given again.

NOSODE	INDICATION	ASSOCIATED REMEDIES
GAERTNER-BACH	EMACIATION AND MALNUTRITION	Phosphorus; Silicea; Mercurius
PROTEUS-BACH	CENTRAL AND PERIPHERAL NERVOUS SYSTEM	Natrium muriaticum; Cuprum metallicum
MORGAN-BACH	DIGESTIVE AND RESPIRATORY SYSTEMS, PLUS SKIN AILMENTS, EG, ECZEMA	Graphites; Petroleum; Psorinium; Sulphur
DYS CO-BACH	DIGESTIVE AND CARDIAC SYSTEMS	Argentum nitricum; Arsenicum album
SYCOTIC CO-PATERSON	ULCERS ON MUCOUS MEMBRANES AND SKIN	Mercurius corrosivus; Natrum sulphorium; Nitricum acidum; Hydrastis canadensis

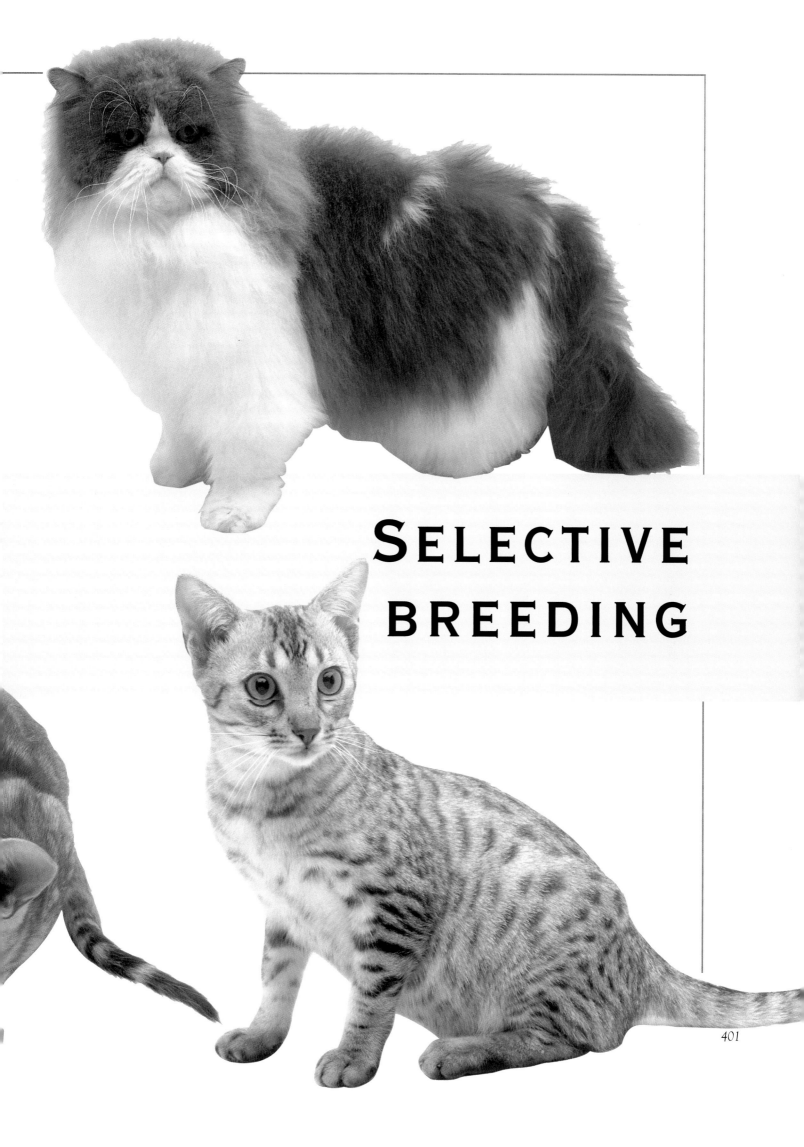

SELECTIVE BREEDING

A QUESTION OF GENETICS

A little time spent figuring out the theoretical basis of genetics will be rewarded with a much greater understanding of the factors that control the varying external characteristics of cats.

HOW IT POSSIBLE THAT two cats with short-haired coats can mate and produce some kittens with long-haired coats?

In order to learn how characteristics are passed on from generation to generation it is necessary to understand a little about the principles of inheritance. In the latter half of the nineteenth century, an Austrian monk by the name of Gregor Mendel studied the inheritance of characteristics of garden pea plants. This led to the branch of biology known as genetics – the study of heredity. He found that the basic unit of heredity was the gene. Genes match in pairs, and each pair of genes determines a different trait such as eye color, hair length and so on – although some traits such as body shape may be controlled by several different genes. The cells responsible for reproduction, the sperm in the male and the ova in the female, each carry only one of the pair of genes for each trait so that when the two reproductive cells unite at the time of fertilization, the new cell formed has inherited half its genes from its male parent and half from its female parent. This cell then multiplies many times to form all the cells of the new kitten. Each cell contains the identical genetic code passed on from the parents to that first cell. The genetic code controls the shape and function of all the various tissues in the body.

SPHYNX
Those who love the apparently hairless Sphynx work tirelessly for its recognition. Others consider that a breed that might not be viable in the wild should not be encouraged.

Hair Length

A cat can be either long-haired or short-haired. There are therefore genes that we call "L" for short hair and "*l*" for long hair. A capital letter is used to denote the short-hair gene, L, because it is dominant over the long-hair gene, *l*, which is therefore called a recessive gene. This means that if the pair of genes in the genetic material of a cat are both L, or short-hair genes, then the cat will have short hair. If both genes are *l*, or long-hair genes, then the cat will have long hair. However, if the cat has one short-hair gene, L, and one long-hair gene, *l*, it will have short hair because the short-hair gene is dominant and suppresses the long-hair gene.

However, that short-haired cat will be heterozygous for that particular trait, and can pass on the long-hair gene to future generations. If it mates with another heterozygous short-haired cat, it can produce a long-haired kitten – quite a surprise for the owner! If,

SYMBOLIZING GENES

L L   L *l*   *l l*

For convenience when discussing genetics, the genes are abbreviated to a single letter, written in the upper case if dominant (L), and lower case for recessive (*l*). For example, since short hair (L) is dominant over long hair (*l*), a cat has to possess two recessive long-hair genes (*ll*) to have long hair. The genes interact at random, and the expected ratios of genotypes will only be seen if the average of a large number of matings is taken. For example, it is unlikely, but possible, that two heterozygote short-haired cats could produce a litter of three long-haired kittens. It is much more likely that they would produce three short-haired or two short-haired and one long-haired kitten.

INHERITANCE

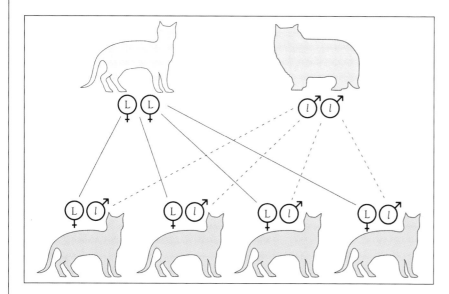

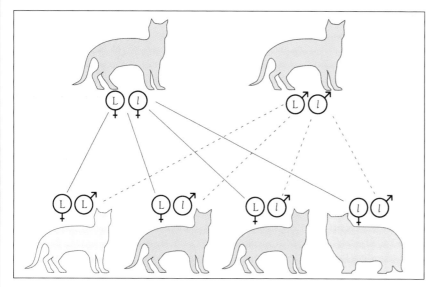

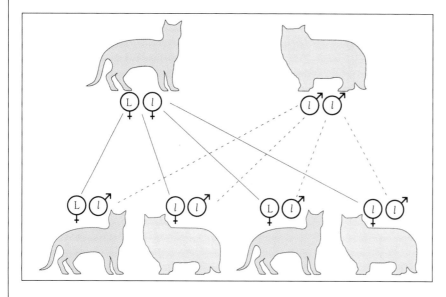

If a homozygous long-haired cat (*ll*) is crossed with a homozygous short-haired cat (LL), the resultant kittens will be dominantly short-haired, but will be heterozygous carriers of the long-haired gene (top diagram).

If two heterozygote cats (L*l*) are crossed, they will produce kittens in the ratio of three short-haired to one long-haired kind (middle diagram). But, if a heterozygote short-haired cat (L*l*) is crossed with a homozygote short-haired cat (LL), only short-haired kittens are produced. However, one in four of the kittens will be heterozygous and carry the long-hair gene.

If a heterozygote short-haired cat (L*l*) is crossed with a homozygote long-haired cat (*ll*), the cross will produce homozygote long-haired kittens and heterozygote short-haired kittens in equal proportions (bottom diagram). If homozygotes are crossed (either LL plus LL or *ll* plus *ll*), they will "breed true" and produce offspring with the same trait.

In reality, if two short-haired cats are mated and produce a long-haired kitten, it becomes apparent that they must both be carriers of the long-haired recessive gene *l* – a long answer to a short question. However, understanding the theory does answer the question of how traits are passed on from generation to generation.

KEY

(*l*)♂ = gene from male

(L)♀ = gene from female

L = long-haired   *l* = short-haired

however, both genes are the same – LL or *ll* – then the cat is homozygous for that trait. Therefore, it follows that if a cat is long-haired, it must have homozygous long-hair genes, *ll* but if a cat is short-haired it may be heterozygous, L*l*, or homozygous short-hair LL.

There is no way to tell by looking at a short-haired cat, or in genetic terms a cat with a short-haired phenotype, whether the cat is homozygous or heterozygous for that trait – only an analysis of the offspring of that cat will reveal its hidden genetic make-up, or genotype.

How can a breeder tell if a cat is carrying a particular recessive trait?

By crossing the cat with a known homozygote, that is, a cat demonstrating the recessive trait in its phenotype. It is generally accepted that if at least seven and preferably ten offspring are produced without showing the recessive trait, then that cat is a homozygote and is not carrying the recessive trait. Even if only one kitten shows the recessive trait, it is immediately known that that cat must be a heterozygote and is carrying the recessive gene.

How is the sex of the kittens determined?

The genetic material that determines the genes is present in strands called chromosomes. The cells of the cat have have 38 chromosomes arranged in 19 matching pairs. However, one pair of chromosomes, known as the sex chromosomes, may consist either of a matching pair of large X chromosomes if the cat is female, or a large X chromosome and a smaller Y chromosome if the cat

SCOTTISH FOLD
The Scottish Fold was refused recognition by some associations on the premise that the tightly folded ears are impossible to keep clean and healthy, and because some skeletal anomalies were apparent in some early kittens of the breed.

SEX DETERMINATION

XX	XY
XX	XY

The female ova all carry X sex chromosomes, whereas the sperm may either carry an X or a Y chromosome. If, at random, the female ova unites with a sperm that is carrying a Y chromosome, a male cat will be formed (XY). If the female ova unites with a sperm that is carrying an X chromosome, a female cat will be formed (XX).

---

is male. Ova from the mother always contain one X chromosome, whereas semen contains an equal number of sperm with one X and with one Y chromosome, so there is an even chance of the new offspring being either XX, and thus female, or XY, and thus male. The chance is completely random.

Are tortoiseshell cats always female?

Yes – or at least they are never normal males! The most common tortoiseshell coloring is a mixture of black, yellow, and orange, with the addition of orange controlled by the dominant O gene. This gene is found only on the X chromosome and is therefore sex-linked.

The tortoiseshell color is an expression of a combination of a dominant O gene for orange coloration and a recessive o gene for normal coloration (the precise color depending on other genes present). Therefore, an OO female cat will be orange (normally called red by breeders), an oo female will not have any red coloration, and an Oo female will be tortoiseshell color. Since a male cat has only one X chromosome, he can only be O – in which case he will have a red coat coloring, or o, in which case he will not have a red coat.

There are a few reported cases of tortoiseshell cats that are apparently male. These cats actually have a disorder of the sex chromosomes. For example, they may have two X chromosomes and one Y chromosome. Such a cat may appear to be a male tortoiseshell but is, in fact, sterile.

TORTOISESHELL GENETICS

The black and orange patterning on a "tortie" typically occurs in female cats with one orange (O) and one non-orange (o) gene. It is linked to sex because the genetic message associated with this trait is normally only found on the female, X, chromosome.

YX

XY

Males normally only possess either the orange (O) gene or the non-orange (o) gene. But, very rarely a genetic mistake occurs and a male with two X and one Y chromosome crops up (XXY). If one of these X chromosomes carries the orange (O) gene and the extra X chromosome carries the non-orange (o) gene, a tortoiseshell male is produced.

XXY

XXY

The recessive, dilute gene d, has a dramatic effect upon coat color. Chocolate, or champagne, is a brown coat color found in Burmese cats (top right) But if a cat that carries the same genes as a chocolate Burmese also carries two of the recessive dilute genes, the coat color will be transformed to lilac, also known as platinum (below).

Are ginger or orange cats always male?

No. This is a common fallacy. These cats, more correctly called red tabbies, may be male or female.

How do new varieties of characteristics such as coat color come about?

The nature of a gene may suddenly change in an individual cat by mutation, a random mistake in the order of the chemical code within the genes. These mutations occur very infrequently when embryos are developing and sometimes cause harmful disorders in the development of the animal – sometimes so harmful that the affected embryo dies or is born with congenital defects.

However, on occasions, these mutations are not harmful and may result in the production of a new characteristic, such as the recessive "dilute" mutation, d, of the normal gene, D, that controls the density of hair pigmentation. For example a cat with two of these recessive genes will have a blue coat color as opposed to a black coat color for a cat with either two D genes or one of each. The dilute gene will also lighten the coat of a cat, that would otherwise be brown, to a lilac color. Therefore, the color and characteristics of a new-born kitten depend on its genetic background.

BLUE CREAM COLORPOINT
Although the standard of points requires eye color in the Colorpoint to be a clear definite blue, this has proved difficult to achieve in most varieties.

The silver tabby was specially bred for its beauty and is just one variation of the original brown tabby coat pattern and color, which provides an excellent camouflage.

My kitten has extra toes – is this likely to cause problems?

Having extra toes, or being polydactyl, is not uncommon in cats and is due to a dominant mutant gene. It does not usually cause any problems at all.

Why are the points of a Siamese cat darker than the rest of the body?

The striking Siamese coloring is produced by a recessive form of the dominant C full color genes known as c^s. These genes produce the light-colored coat with dark points and blue eyes. The darker pigmentation on a Siamese cat – at the points of the ears, legs, face, and tail – are due to the fact that the skin temperature is slightly lower in those places. Siamese kittens that are reared in a cool environment will often grow a darker coat than those kittens reared in a warmer environment. In the same way, any bandaging on a Siamese cat will retain body heat and make the covered area grow lighter,. On the other hand, if the hair is clipped for surgery, this will cool the skin by removing the insulative effect of the hair and cause the new hair growth to be darker. This is a clear demonstration of how the environment can alter inherited characteristics.

White cats usually have orange eyes, blue eyes, or one of each – like this "odd-eyed white". Congenital deafness is most commonly seen in white cats with blue eyes.

What is the original coat color of the domestic cat?

The basic or "wild" type of coat color for a cat is the tabby. Every domestic cat is a tabby at heart, but often the tabby markings are masked with another color and are not visible. The wild or striped type of tabby marking provided the cat with excellent camouflage in its natural wooded environment. Variations on this include blotched, spotted, mackerel and Abyssinian tabbies. In the latter case, the lighter agouti color covers most of the body, and stripes are usually only visible on the face and sometimes faintly on the legs and tail. This coloring can be combined with a distinctive body type to produce the breed of cat known as the Abyssinian, but Abyssinian coloring may be found on any feline body shape. The normal agouti and black color of a tabby cat can be altered to produce variations such as blue, cream, red (ginger), or silver tabbies.

Why do solid-color cats often have tabby markings when kittens?

This is known as epistasis, or masking. For example, tabby coloring is determined by the agouti gene, A, which is dominant over the non-agouti gene, a. The agouti gene produces the hairs in the lighter bands of a tabby cat. These have a black tip, a yellow band in the middle and a light-colored base. When the hairs lie against each other they produce the speckled agouti coat color – which combines with the dark bands of coat color produced by the dominant T gene and results in a tabby cat. Cats with only one coat color genetically still have the stripes of a tabby, but the recessive non-agouti genes they carry make the pale agouti areas of the coat black. However, the striped pattern can often be seen when the cats are

still kittens. There are a wide range of solid colors, including black, blue, chocolate, lilac, red and cream. Of course, many pedigreed breeds are normally solid-colored including the blue-coated British Blue, Korat, and Russian Blue cats, as well as the popular Burmese cat, which can have a wide range of coat colors.

Is it true that white cats are often deaf?

Yes. White cats usually have orange eyes, blue eyes, or one of each – "odd-eyed whites." Deafness is most common in blue-eyed whites due to a degeneration of the hearing apparatus deep within the ear that develops between four and six days after birth and can affect one or both ears. The white coat color is usually due to the dominant white gene W, which will mask any other colors the cat may carry in its genes, although a colored spotting can often be detected in the coat of young kittens.

RED BURMESE
Tangerine rather than red in color, this variety is bright and very attractive, particularly when it has the desired golden eyes.

Chinchilla coats are classically long-haired, but, the same silver hairs with black tips can be found in short-haired cats, such as in this British Tipped Shorthair.

The Scottish Fold is a controversial breed, due to congenital problems, consisting of deformities of the limbs as well as the ears. It is no longer recognized in its native country.

What is a Chinchilla cat?

Chinchilla refers specifically to a coat color produced by white hairs with black tips. The coloring is due to the effect of a dominant inhibitor gene, I, which suppresses the development of pigment in certain areas of the cat's coat. In fact, this gene can produce differing degrees of inhibition of pigment resulting in a range of coat colors, from the almost white chinchilla coloration with only a touch of black on the tips of the hairs, through pewter, which has more black on the ends of the hairs, to the smokes with heavy coloration along most of the length of the hair but with white at the base. Cameos are red versions of this range of tipped chinchilla coat colors, and Golden Chinchillas have yellow hairs with black tips.

What are Rex cats?

Rex cats have very short and curly coats due to recessive Rex genes. There are two main types of Rex gene, producing the Cornish and Devon Rex breeds, with different characteristics and hair types. The Cornish Rex was first noticed as a mutation in a kitten by the name of Kallibunker, born to a farm cat in 1951, whereas the first Devon Rex was born in 1960 to a feral curly-coated cat by the name of Kirlee. Each of these two kittens went on to found their respective breeds with the future generations of Devon Rexes bearing the characteristic "pixie-shaped" face that Kirlee possessed. The Rex genes can be crossed with other breeds and coat colors to produce interesting varieties such as the Si-Rex, a Red cat with Siamese markings. Rex cats make good pets with a lively and inquisitive nature. They require very little grooming, do not shed hair about

the house and may be ideal for someone who is allergic to cat hair but still wishes to keep a cat as a pet. Some breeders advise adding a little extra fat, such as shredded suet, to the diet since it is rich in calories and helps to produce the extra body heat needed to compensate for the extra heat loss due to the poor insulative qualities of their coat.

Do some breeds have particular genetic problems?

Yes, the Scottish Fold cat is the centre of quite a bit of controversy. The Scottish Fold has very distinctive ears that start to fold over from about four weeks of age. This is due to a dominant folded-ear gene, Fd. This gene may also cause a thickening of the tail and the legs. Due to concern about the shape of the ears causing ear problems and the thickening

The Cornish Rex has a long thin tail, long legs, a straight nose and dense wavy coat.

The squint, sometimes seen in Siamese cats develops to compensate for a defect in visual signals to the brain. It is considered to be a fault in the breed.

of the legs making movement difficult for affected cats, the Governing council of the Cat Fancy of Great Britain decided to stop registration of the breed in the 1970s. This decision was hotly opposed by breeders of Scottish Folds. The American and Australian cat societies, however, give the Scottish Fold full recognition.

Another well-known example is the Manx, a very old breed. The lack of tail is due to a dominant Manx gene, M. All Manx cats are heterozygous for this gene because homozygous MM cats invariably die in the womb due to severe spinal deformities. Even heterozygous cats are often born with serious congenital abnormalities such as spina bifida.

Are Siamese cats supposed to have a squint?

No. The Siamese gene may cause a fault in the nervous pathways that carry messages from the eyes to the brain, and the cat may squint to try to compensate for it. It is considered a fault, as are other hereditary problems such as a "kink" in the tail and an absence of canine teeth – both of which can occur in the breed but do not seriously affect their health.

Can selective breeding cause health problems as it does in some breeds of dog?

The pedigreed cat remains much closer to the original wild cat than that of many breeds of dog. One would like to think that this is due to sensible restraint on the part of cat breeders, but it must also be said that pedigreed cats have been selectively bred for a much shorter time than dogs and there has been less time to produce the more extreme variations. Certainly, any highly inbred animal is likely to be less resistant to disease than one with a very wide mix of genes, and some of the effects of selective breeding may mean that the pedigreed cat will need closer attention than a mixed breed cat. For example, the coat of longhairs will often cause severe problems if the cat is left to groom itself. Similarly, the "pushed-in" face of many Persian cats tends to make the eyes run due to interference with the mechanism that drain tears away from the eyes.

Some Manx cats are completely tail-less (known as rumpies), others have a small dimple of a tail (rumpy-risers, like the cat on the left). There are also short-tailed Manxes (stumpies) and those with a fairly long tail (longies).

The Peke-faced Persian has such a flat-shaped face that eye and respiratory problems are more likely. For this reason it is not recognized as a breed in many countries.

CREDITS

Quarto would like to acknowledge and thank the following
for pictures reproduced in this book

Creszentia Allen, Animals Unlimited, Ardea London (photos:
Ian Beames, Arthus-Bertrand, Jane Burton, Jean-Paul Ferrero,
Kenneth W. Fink, Clem Haagner, Dr Charles McdDougal, W.
Weisser), Norvia Behling, Ed birch, Myer S. Bornstein, Arthur
J. Boufford/Visuals Unlimited, Mike Brucelle, Mike Busselle,
Diane Calkins/Click The Photo Connection, Cleo freelance
photography, Tom Corner, W. Cortesi, Anne Cumbers, Joel
Dexter, Michael Freeman, Glaxo, Jim Hays, Marc Henrie,
Tamara Liller, Joe McDonald/Visuals Unlimited,

Robert Marien, D. Newman/Visuals Unlimited, Duane Patten,
Paul A. Pavlik, Photri Inc., Mae Scalan, GregoryK. Scott,
John Solden/Visuals Unlimited, Solitaire Photographic, C.
Strock, Sally Anne Thompson, Dave Underwood/Click The
Photo Connection, Bradley Viner, Sally Weigand, Gerald L.
Wicklund.

All other photographs are the copyright of Quarto Publishing Plc.